TO SERVE THE ☆DEVIL☆

TO SERVE

THE DEVIL

VOLUME II:

COLONIALS AND SOJOURNERS

BY Paul Jacobs
AND Saul Landau
WITH Eve Pell

VINTAGE BOOKS
A Division of Random House
New York

Acknowledgment is gratefully extended to the following for permission to reprint from their works:

Guardian, independent radical newsweekly: "Student Revolt in Puerto Rico," *Guardian,* September 28, 1968.

University of North Carolina Press: From "Racial Myth and Family Tradition—Worship Among the Part-Hawaiians," by Margaret M. Lam, *Social Forces,* Vol. 14, No. 3, March, 1936.

Charles E. Tuttle Company of Rutland, Vermont, and Tokyo, Japan: From "Hawaiian Autonomy," by Queen Liliuokalani in *Hawaii's Queen,* 1964.

Stanford University Press: As excerpted and translated from *El Mundo,* November 3, 1950, pp. 1 & 6, in *Party Politics in Puerto Rico,* by Robert William Anderson.

Fleming H. Revell Company: "Letter by A. Bishop, a missionary, written in 1838," from *Pilgrims of Hawaii,* by Orramel Hinckley Gulick.

The Macmillan Company: From *Shoal of Time,* by Gavan Daws.

FIRST VINTAGE BOOKS EDITION, February 1971

Library of Congress Catalog Card Number: 76–85616
Standard Book Number: 394–714160–1

Manufactured in the United States of America by H. Wolff Book Mfg. Co., New York

To Dr. W. E. B. Du Bois, a man who not only participated in the life of his own time, but studied the past in order to understand the future

ACKNOWLEDGMENTS

We acknowledge, gratefully, the help we received in writing this book. Joan Bowman and Karen Shillington assisted us in the early stages of research. Barbara Madison was our copyeditor and Jane Clark Seitz assumed the difficult task of general editor. We thank both of them. Donna Dowsky worked on the final steps of the manuscript. We thank especially Frances Strauss, who sometimes criticized, sometimes goaded, but always encouraged us. The Center for the Study of Democratic Institutions subsidized much of the research for the book.

"The nature of men is identical; what divides them is their customs."

Confucius, 551–478 B.C.

"Tribe follows tribe, and nation follows nation, like the waves of the sea. It is the order of nature, and regret is useless. Your time of decay may be distant, but it will surely come, for even the white man whose God walked and talked with him as friend with friend, cannot be exempt from the common destiny. We may be brothers after all. We will see."

Chief Sealth, 1855

CONTENTS

INTRODUCTION

". . . in those days, the public both in the South and the whole of the West, together with a considerable portion of the public elsewhere, was hoodwinked by such methods as were used and actually supposed our acquisition of the new territory to be a God-fearing act, the result of the aggression and of the sinful impotence of our Spanish neighbors, together with our own justifiable energy and our devotion to the cause of freedom. It is to be hoped that this lesson, showing us as it does how much of conscience and even of personal sincerity can co-exist with a minimum of effective morality in international undertakings, will some day be once more remembered; so that when our nation is another time about to serve the devil, it will do so with more frankness and will deceive itself less by half-conscious cant. For the rest, our mission in the cause of liberty is to be accomplished through a steadfast devotion to the cause of our own inner life, and not by going abroad as missionaries, as conquerors or as marauders, among weaker peoples."

Josiah Royce, *California, a Study of American Character, 1886*

THE UNKNOWN HISTORY

In the year A.D. 73, a group of Jewish zealots in the cliff fortress of Masada were besieged by the Romans for months. Finally they realized they could no longer hold out against the superior forces of the enemy. They faced a choice of being captured alive and forced into slavery or dying as free people.

They chose to die. And the account of their unique suicide pact has become one of the classic documents of history. The description of their deliberations and the manner in which they carried out their death pact was written by Flavius Josephus, the apostate Jew who was a recorder of the Roman conquests. Josephus used two women who had hidden themselves rather than die as his sources for the story. If they had not remained alive, and if Josephus had not been with the Romans at that time, the incredible story of Masada would probably have gone untold.

Documentary material such as Josephus' account provides historians with some sense of the past and its connections to the present and future. But because some societies have no written language nor a tradition of maintaining a written history, the outsider's knowledge of them is limited.

American history certainly does not suffer from a shortage of written documents. In fact, anyone undertaking the task of relating the past to the present may be overwhelmed by the amount of material available, some of it dating back to the first day a white man ever set foot on this continent.

In the usual presentation of American history through documents, a special kind of selectivity has prevailed: only those documents that have interpreted American history as a gradual unfolding of progress and democracy have been used. As a result, few Americans know that such ideas as "Black Power" and self-determination, which today are considered new, have historical antecedents. Today's ghetto and *barrio* politics were *not* born with "Black Power" or *La Raza,* but date back to the formation of the first segregated—or self-segregated—communities in America. The ancestors of Malcolm X and Eldridge Cleaver are Nat Turner and Toussaint L'Ouverture. Reies Tijerina, in New Mexico, comes from a long line of Hispano-Indian leaders who organized resistance against the Anglos.

From the start, nonwhite people in this country have had to make decisions forced upon them by the white Europeans' insatiable need to increase their land holdings: should they, the natives, give up the earth on which they have lived and the civilizations associated with it, and accommodate to the conquerors; should they resist, at the cost of physical annihilation; or should they try to remain as a separate community? The Word plus the Gun forced each nonwhite group to examine its collective sense of self-preservation and explore all the options open to it.

One such option—a racial state—made familiar in the 1960s by the black separatists, is an integral part of early American Indian history, although it is rarely discussed in that context. For example, the earliest published Indian treaty signed by the newly formed United States was with the Delaware Indian tribe in September, 1778. It gave an opportunity to the Delawares and "any other tribes who have been friends to the interests of the United States to join the present confederation, and to form a state, whereof the Delaware nation shall be the head and have a representative in Congress. . . ." Not until early in the twentieth century, and the dissolution of the Cherokee nation, did Indians formally give up the notion of exercising "Red Power" by forming a separate Indian state with its own representative in Congress.

As far back as 1812, Tecumseh, the Shawnee leader, and Pushmataha, the Choctaw orator, debated fiercely at a Choctaw and Chickasaw council over the issue of how best to deal with the white man. "Are we not being stripped, day by day, of the little that remains of our ancient liberty?" Tecumseh asked the council. "Do they not even now kick and strike us as they do their blackfaces? How long will it be before they tie us to a post and whip us and make us work for them in corn fields as they do them? Shall we wait for that moment or shall we die fighting before submitting to such ignominy?"

Pushmataha opposed Tecumseh's plea for armed resistance and implored the tribes to accept the white man's good intentions. He urged them "to submit their grievances, whatever they may be, to the Congress of the United States according to the articles of the treaty existing between us and the American people. . . ."

Such bitter debates among the Indians were paralleled by similar disputes among the Spanish-speaking people. Should we let the white man come in and take our land, they asked, or should we take up arms to fight for our land and our culture? But the records of those quarrels remain buried, untranslated, in the columns of old newspapers and in *corridos,* or folk ballads.

Only recently have some young *chicanos,* the militant Mexican-Americans, rediscovered their folk heroes in reviving the tradition of *La Raza.* They have discovered that men like Juan Cortina, Gregorio Cortez, Joaquin Murieta, and Tiburcio Vasquez were not bandits, as they are described in most American history books, if they are described at all. They were champions of *La Raza,* who fought with pistols against the white conquerors, and killed any of their own who accepted the role of a conquered people.

A stanza of a Texas *corrido* begins: "Long live our country, although suffering setback . . . the mother country is home, that loves son and daughter, for Mexico has fame, military discipline."

But no folk ballad tells the story of how some of the proud Polynesian people who lived in the Hawaiian Islands tried to resist the white political and cultural invasion of their shores. "The Hawaiian people will be trodden underfoot by the foreigners," said the people of Lahaina on the island of Maui in 1845. "The laws of those governments will not do for us. These are good laws for them, our laws are for us and are good laws for us which we have made for ourselves. We are not slaves to serve them. When they talk in their clever way we know what is right and what is wrong. . . ."

It did no good for the Hawaiians to know what was right and what was wrong. Their country was taken over by the *haoles* (whites), in the course of only a few decades. The *haoles* did it with guns and religion. And the native Hawaiians began the slow descent to what they are today—a pitifully small remnant of their race, occupying the lowest rungs on the social and economic ladder of the Islands.

Few *haoles* know that the Chinese in Hawaii, like the Japanese, argued among themselves about whether to accommodate to the white man's brutal treatment or engage in active resistance to it. Resistance included helping Chinese workers to escape from the slave conditions under which they lived on the white-owned plantations. At one point, in the late nineteenth century, hundreds of Chinese gathered at a mass meeting in Honolulu to

> solemnly protest against the injustices, degradation and insult threatened to be imposed upon us and our race. . . . While we ask for nothing more than equality with other residents of equally good behavior, we shall be satisfied with and shall support and respect nothing that accords to our race a lesser degree of consideration and justice than residents of other nationalities enjoy.

The white community's response to this protest was made clear by a leading Island newspaper. The Chinese, it said,

> assume an attitude plainly defiant and closely bordering on the dominant and dictatorial. From the weak and lowly field hand of the time of 1851 and the wage scale of $3 a month, they have, by an unparalleled and alarming evolution, reached the station of an assertive element in the policy of the nation.

Shortly after that arrogant statement was published, the Chinese Hawaiians organized a protective group and purchased rifles to defend themselves and their homes from the whites.

The Japanese immigrant community in Hawaii was torn

apart by similar conflicts. Some Japanese, at the turn of the century, sought to resist the brutalities of white plantation owners by organizing for better conditions. These organizers were jailed for their efforts; they were also attacked from within the Japanese community by accommodationists who believed that "certain things" existed in the Japanese that caused them to be "disliked by American people."

In the years before World War II, the argument within the Japanese community in Hawaii had its counterpart on the mainland. Many Nisei, or second-generation Japanese-Americans, who lived there insisted that the only way to demonstrate their Americanism was to become more American than whites; others insisted on retaining ties with Japan; a third group resisted being treated as second-class citizens.

Pearl Harbor, however, decided the fate of the American Japanese. *All* Japanese, citizens and aliens, no matter what their attitudes, were taken to relocation camps—"for the sake of internal quiet," said President Franklin Roosevelt. But the debates went on in the camps. They were now accompanied by violence. The "Blood Brothers," a group of Nisei determined to fight against the treatment they were receiving, physically and verbally attacked those who were willing to accommodate to relocation. The "Blood Brothers" called such Japanese *inu* (dogs). When the Nisei were asked to sign a loyalty oath to the United States, nearly 50 percent of them refused to do so out of resentment at the treatment they had received. After the war, some 8,000 of them emigrated to Japan. Ten years later, one congressman admitted that he had been wrong in his attitude toward the Japanese-Americans. But, while making that concession, he retained the concept of color as a gauge of loyalty. "The Japanese-Americans," he said, "were just as loyal as those whose skin was white."

The direct relationship between skin color and loyalty to America, voiced so openly by that congressman, is an important element in the American character.

Some historians have now begun to examine American

racism as a product of capitalism and imperialism. The colonizers came to the New World believing that colored people were inferior, and used that ideology to justify the enslavement of blacks, the killing of Indians and Mexicans, and the importation of Oriental labor for work considered unfit for whites. The identification of colored skin with evil, with the devil, with inferiority, infused the entire culture of the Anglo-Saxons during the first centuries of colonization.

In each case, the racism coincided with economic need for slave labor and for land. At the same time, racist attitudes were institutionalized in laws, religion, and everyday practice. Each school child learned, along with the principles of republicanism and democracy, about the inferiority of colored people. Ministers explained to their flocks that slavery was God's will.

Racist law and racist behavior became an integral part of American culture, as much a part of it as democracy. Racist attitudes not only made whites feel superior by virtue of their skin color, it also made all colored, colonized people feel inferior because of their skin color. Writings on American history are filled with racist axioms. It is sometimes conceded that the colored peoples have suffered injustices. But their attempts to resist, their politics and debates, were not considered important enough to merit inclusion.

Thus the history that has been and is being written, by its nature, is a racist history, which excludes minorities and women from its pages. And so written American history, along with American culture, law, religion, and philosophy, has skewed the attitudes of the American people. To blacks, Indians, Mexicans, and Orientals, George Washington was not the father of the country, but a slaveholder and a racist —as was Jefferson. If the great heroes of the history books were judged by the character of their behavior to the colored peoples, Jackson would be called a bitter racist; Lincoln's belief that blacks were innately inferior would be decried; and Woodrow Wilson would be criticized for writing history that apologized for slavery and favored segregation.

But these men remain heroes for most Americans, white and colored, because for more than three centuries the values, the criteria for judging good and bad, superior and inferior, what is worthy of record and what is not, have not taken racism into account.

The history and struggles of the colored peoples, the losers, have rarely been recorded. Only now are they becoming subjects deemed worthy of investigation. The documents on the colonized peoples' resistance, and their anguish, are an indictment not only of America's past but of all those writers who have excluded the colored peoples' struggle for freedom from their work. Too much of American history has been a celebration of a past that merits severe criticism. But the celebration of America was brought to an end for many people in the 1960s. The task of rewriting American history, with a new perspective on racism as well as democracy and progress, is just beginning.

Nonwhites have permanent alien status in the white society of America. The documents in this book demonstrate the nonwhites' belief that they are never completely trusted by most whites, and that they are always considered inferior no matter how superior they may be either within their own community or even in the larger world outside it.

TO SERVE THE DEVIL

"We shall be as a city upon a hill," John Winthrop told the Puritan settlers in 1630. Winthrop assured the men and women who had risked the Atlantic crossing that they had been sent from the Old World to the New at the Lord's bidding, to build a Zion in the Wilderness, a place from where the light could shine. The Puritans were convinced that only in the New World, unspoiled by centuries of European warfare and sin, could they build a new society.

It would be fit for the return of Christ, a society so pious that He would reward His children by ushering in the Kingdom of the Millennium.

But as pious as the Puritans were, they could not ignore the vast wealth of the new continent that lay before them. So they incorporated these riches into their theology, made the great wealth a central part of their religious mission. The need to expand the frontier, so essential to the early economy of the North and the South, came to be interpreted as the Lord's will. The massacre of Indians and the profits from the slave trade were also justified in the name of the Lord's will. Developing American Protestantism combined the teachings of the Church of England, Calvin, and John Locke with the values of British mercantilism. It damned the Indians, reduced the blacks to soulless animals, and made a virtue of expanding capitalism.

The men in the New World kept pushing onward. They expressed but a twinge of anxiety over the fact that they were abandoning the Lord's mission along the way. And a handful of moralists felt that some day there would be a terrible atonement and begged the settlers and pioneers: "stop and reflect upon what you are doing." Dr. Increase Mather, for one, gave a thundering address to the students at Harvard in 1696:

> It is the Judgment of very learned Men, that, in the glorious Times promised to the Church on Earth, *America* will be *Hell.* And, although there is a Number of the Elect of *God* to be born here, I am very afraid that, in Process of Time, New England will be the wofullest place in all *America;* as some other parts of the World once famous for Religion, are now the dolefullest on Earth, perfect pictures and emblems of *Hell,* when you see this Academy fallen to the Ground, then know it is a terrible Thing, which God is about to bring upon this land.

Most of the young men at Harvard paid no heed to Mather; expansionism made his Puritan piety seem anachronistic. Eccentrics and radicals like Mather were either ignored or put in jail. If the Lord had not wished us to conquer the West, the colonists rationalized, why would He have sent us to the New World and laid before us such a challenge?

The American expansion proceeded, spurred on by economic needs and sanctioned by a pious but pragmatic religion. That religion damned adultery, but ignored the Ten Commandments when Indians were killed and their land stolen, and Negroes enslaved. (The word "Negro" has been used historically by both races until recently. Many blacks now resent the word, linking it, correctly, with centuries of white domination in culture, language, and thought. In the succeeding chapters "Negro" is used only in a historical context, so that the separation between the usage of the past and our contemporary language does not get lost in our attempt to present some of our history as it was thought of by previous generations of Americans.) The original missionary fervor remained, but it became more and more secular. By the 1760s the British had taken the place of the Devil as the enemy of progress and justice. One of the things the British did was to limit westward expansion with the Proclamation of 1763. The British refusal to support expansion became one of the most important grievances uniting the colonies against the mother country.

Each of the thirteen colonies had its own distinct culture and economy. But some of the more visionary colonists realized that conquest of the West would be impossible for thirteen separate nations. Among other factors, the lure of western land helped the colonies to submerge their differences and unite as one nation in a war for independence and the right to own and exploit the rich western lands.

The newly formed nation called on its God to justify the expansion. By the time of the heated political debates preceding the writing of the Constitution, God had been converted into an active advocate of white expansionism.

"Providence has been pleased," wrote John Jay in one of the Federalist Papers, "to give this one connected country to one united people—a people descended from the same ancestors, speaking the same language, professing the same religion, attached to the same principles of government, very similar in their manners and customs. . . ." Providence, then, was handily available to justify white lust for the land and wealth owned by Indians, Mexicans, Spaniards, Hawaiians, and Eskimos. Providence supported the plantation owners in the use of Negro slaves, Providence vindicated the indenturing of Orientals and the importation of Filipinos and Puerto Ricans as cheap laborers. All these groups were nonwhites, and by nature inferior to those whom Providence had marked as virtuous because of the color of their skin and their ability to conquer. Might became Divine Right, and Providence justified the acceptance of slavery in the Constitution, which said a slave was only 3/5 of a man (for voting purposes only).

The function of Negroes, described in the Federalist Papers as "this unfortunate race," was to work for the white man. The Indian, who proved to be poor slave material, got in the white man's way, so the Puritans theologized that the Red Man was predestined to damnation even though he heard the revealed Word. The Mexican, although not exactly colored like Indians and Negroes, was another cultural enemy who occupied territory the white man needed. The Hawaiians were also to be civilized by having their lands taken from them.

Justifying the need for missionary work among the Indians, a minister of the gospel wrote, typically, "One thing is very certain, that the influence of the gospel will have the tendency to make them more submissive to the rule of the whites. . . ."[1] The same missionary spirit moved the Christian missionaries in Hawaii in the middle of the nineteenth century. "Christianity civilizes in the broadest sense. Commerce, science and industry all accompany her majestic march to universal dominion. Thus while it denies the sufficiency of commerce alone to transform the savages, it

[1] "The Oregon Missions as Shown in the Walker Letters, 1839–1851," edited by Paul C. Phillips, in *Frontier Omnibus,* pp. 105–111. Cited by Alvin Josephy, *The Nez Percé Indians and the Opening of the Northwest,* New Haven, 1955, pp. 222–23, footnote 31.

encourages a legitimate commerce and even courts its alliance as one of its most important instrumentalities."[2]

Yet there were always some Americans who recognized that Mephistopheles had agents in the pulpit as well as in business circles and government. These Americans resisted being recruited to serve the Devil. Their roster is a long one, and includes both famous and obscure names.

Among the first colonists were dissenters who protested against the manner in which their fellow settlers acted toward the Indians. Later, their counterparts voiced indignation at American behavior during the Mexican War and the way the United States acquired the West and Southwest. From the day the first slaves were brought to the colonies, there were some white Americans who attacked the practice and sought to abolish it. Some white Americans objected to the manner in which the lands of the Mexicans and Hawaiians were taken. And others resisted national policies based on fear of "The Yellow Peril," policies which ultimately forced thousands of Japanese-Americans into detention camps during World War II.

But moralists who called upon the nation to stop and think about its policies, who pointed to slavery and racism as a deep, internal sore that could not be healed by constantly pushing outward, were always an isolated minority; often they were castigated as traitors. Perhaps the proudest and most righteous voice of morality was John Quincy Adams. Despite the misgivings of his family, he "stepped down" to run for Congress after he had been defeated for his second term as President. He soon became hated and feared by the slavocracy for his attacks on slavery and the values that supported it. Adams described John C. Calhoun as "the high priest of Moloch," and called Daniel Webster "a heartless traitor to the cause of human freedom" because of his "traffic with slavemongers."

But the more Adams pointed to the moral sickness he felt

[2] Statement of Professor W. D. Alexander in an article on "Science and Missions," in 1857, in *Pilgrims of Hawaii* by Rev. and Mrs. Oramel Hinckley Gulick. Fleming H. Revell Co., 1918, p. 299.

would destroy the nation, the more isolated he became. He was considered an obstacle in the path of progress, a hindrance to the dynamics of American economics. The country's economic and political leaders had built an expanding system for an ambitious people and could not afford to hear the pleas and cries of such moralists. Intellectuals had molded a pragmatic God and a convenient Clio to reassure Americans that what they were doing—no matter how bloody—was right, necessary, and even pious. The dissenters stood alone against the forces of expansion and the racism that accompanied it. Even in history books written years later, these lonely figures are portrayed as brave but overanxious prophets who did not have faith in the American system and character.

The emerging American system was based on the increase of land holdings. Land was the great stake, and the whites always won any fight for it. They won not only because they had more deadly arms, but because Indians, Mexicans, and Hawaiians did not understand the white Europeans' view of the land or the depths of their desire for it. Individual possession and use of land was not a concept people like the Indians understood. They believed in a mystical relationship between Earth and the Sun, and thought that the land was for everyone. Sitting Bull once said his people were willing "to yield to our neighbors, even our animal neighbors, the same right as ourselves, to inhabit this land."

Such concepts, forged from a sense of collective identity, were unknown in the Old World, and so were foreign to most white Americans. There were exceptions, of course. The Quakers understood the meaning of what one Indian chief said to the Governor of Pennsylvania in 1796:

> We love quiet; we suffer the mouse to play; when the woods are rustled by the wind, we fear not; when the leaves are disturbed in ambush, we are uneasy; when a cloud obscures our brilliant sun, our eyes feel dim; but when the rays appear, they give great heat to the body and joy to the heart. Treachery darkens

the chain of friendship; but truth makes it brighter than ever. This is the peace we desire.

But the majority of the Indians were not to have the peace they desired, any more than were the Negroes, the Mexicans, the *Californios,* the Hawaiians, the Maroons, or any other group who were seen as obstacles to expansion.

"If human progress follows a law of development, if 'Time's noblest offspring is the last,' our civilization should be the noblest; for we are 'The heirs of all the ages in the foremost files of time' and not only do we occupy the latitude of power, but *our land is the last to be occupied in that latitude,"* wrote Frederick Jackson Turner in 1898. "There is no other virgin soil in the North Temperate Zone. If the consummation of human progress is not to be looked for here, if there is yet to flower a higher civilization, where is the soil that is to produce it?"

Foreign observers have found the American Experience puzzling. Gunnar Myrdal, for one, has described it as a dilemma. America is the birthplace of modern democracy, yet the new nation created an institutional racism. The ideals of equality and freedom were born on the same soil where slavery and racism already existed. A frontier democracy restricted to whites was shaped in the wars against the Indians and Mexicans, for only through collective agreement and political unanimity could the white settlers protect the lands they had taken. The voting franchise was extended to all whites. By the 1830s each white man, but not woman, was entitled to one vote. Assimilation of European immigrants, combined with the westward movement, shaped new, democratic institutions on the frontiers. But these new institutions, it turned out, functioned within the context of the old racial hates that pervaded urban centers and southern slave culture. This linking together of racism and democracy made for the bigotry that has been transmitted down through every generation of Americans. Yet in the face of reality, American history has been distorted into a glorious example of freedom and democracy for all peoples. Until recently the history of the colored peoples got short shrift or was relegated to small paragraphs in obscure texts. That is beginning to change.

AMERICA THE MYTH

Today most Americans who live outside the ghettos still know so little of what is happening inside them that they are surprised and shocked when racial conflicts rip cities apart, when anti-Semitism affects an election in New Jersey, when Mexican-Americans become mountain guerrillas in New Mexico, when Indians in the Pacific Northwest go to jail rather than give up their rights to fish.

They are shocked because they live in a mythical country "discovered" by Columbus. As far as they are concerned, the Indians did not exist until a white European found them. In this mythical America, the conditions of Negroes, Indians, and Spanish-speaking Americans are assumed to be gradually but inevitably improving, as court decisions, government efforts, and education break down the barriers of discrimination and prejudice. The injustices and crimes committed by frontier Americans against the Indians are described as regrettable but necessary. The reservation system, for example, in which the government actually made wards of the Indians, is explained as a genuine effort to redress those wrongs. The wholesale theft of land from Mexico through the expedient device of the Mexican War and the degradation of Spanish-speaking people are claimed as further regrettable but necessary episodes in the country's expansion.

Modern Americans tend to feel that the dark-skinned people, some of whom lived on the land long before English was ever heard, are now becoming part of the larger society after all; a few colored people are even in Congress. Many assume that a gradual movement toward equality has been occurring. Slavery is acknowledged as a moral wrong, although some unreconstructed historians and novelists still mourn the passing of an aristocratic way of life based on slavery. Overt discrimination is also considered wrong. The grade school textbooks say so, and every recent President has put the country on record. "We shall overcome," President Johnson said in his speech proposing the new Civil Rights Bill for 1965.

In mythical America, the first stop of the white immigrants who came to the country during the period of unlimited immigration was the cities along the Eastern Seaboard. There, in the legendary America, they lived together in slum areas, maintaining their Old World cultures, eating their own kinds of foods, practicing their own religions, and still speaking the language of their homelands.

Then, goes the myth, the children and grandchildren of the immigrants become assimilated into the American mainstream. The acculturation process is accompanied by the development of tension between the first generation of immigrants and the second, which is not familiar with old ways, cannot speak the language of their parents, and rejects the old customs. The second generation is in turn succeeded by another, for whom the past is not so disturbing; they have become so sure of their American identity that they are able to find a source of pride in their foreign heritage. In the meantime, the original ghetto changes, as the descendants of the original immigrants move out. It becomes a harbor for a new wave of immigrants who prepare, in their turn, to be melted down into homogeneous Americans.

This social process has a mythical economic parallel in which the immigrant groups begin at the bottom of the work ladder, performing the most difficult, least desirable and lowest-paid jobs. In the acculturation process, they move up the economic scale, and the newer immigrant groups take their place on the lower rungs.

Like all myths, the one about America as the melting pot of the world does have some basis in fact. It is true that a great many white immigrants and descendants of white immigrants have achieved political power, financial success, and considerable social status. The walls that once separated these groups from the white Americans who preceded them have been broken down. But a great many Americans still live in enclaves, separated from each other and from the mainstream by their colors, countries of origin, ethnic backgrounds, and religions.

In Milwaukee, Wisconsin, Gary, Indiana, and other cities, the sense of Slavic identity is still so strong that the cry of "Black Power" was met with the cry of "Polish Power." Whole wards of Slavs voted against black candidates and fiercely resisted attempts to break segregated housing patterns.

On Long Island, in New York, the "Golden Ghettos" are towns where virtually no one but middle-class Jews live, isolated in their social and cultural life from the gentiles who surround them. In Los Angeles, crowds of Jews, young ones as well as those from older generations, throng Fairfax Avenue, which has become a Jewish street with Jewish restaurants, kosher meat markets, fish stores, and bookstores featuring Hebrew books and Hebrew records.

In every American city, the ghettos are almost totally black. In the *barrios,* from metropolitan New York to rural California, Spanish is the spoken language, even in the third and fourth generations. In fact, one of the demands being made by the younger Spanish-speaking groups is that the schools of the South and Far West use Spanish along with English as a teaching language.

New Little Tokyos are growing up in the cities where most of the Japanese-Americans live, while in San Francisco those Chinese-Americans who cannot afford the fantastically high rents of Chinatown move out to the edges of the city, where they clump together in what will soon be Little Chinatowns. On weekends, though, they return to the older and larger Chinatown, anxious to visit with their families, eat in familiar restaurants, do their shopping, and see their friends. Here, too, in the streets of Chinatown, the young have taken a new interest in things Chinese; they identify themselves, openly and proudly, as Asians.

What America is witnessing is a new kind of clustering together of ethnic groups. They are perhaps afraid of being isolated from the familiar and reassuring. In a country that seems to be spinning apart in a centrifugal storm of politics and social upheaval, one's own special identity becomes increasingly essential for survival.

When a black leaves New York's Harlem for Los Angeles, he goes quickly to that city's Central District, leaving behind him the potentially hostile white world for the reassurance of black faces like his own, the "soul" food he has always eaten, and customs he has been familiar with since he was born. To the Jewish stranger in a city, the synagogue or temple is much more than a place of worship; it is a place to meet other Jews with whom to visit and socialize, a place where no one need worry about what the Christians might say if they overheard the conversation.

The real life of the Chinese in San Francisco's Chinatown, the life that goes on in the homes behind the shops and restaurants, is just as unknown to the Caucasians who walk the districts' streets today as it was when the Chinese were first brought to America to supply the cheap labor that was needed to expand the country's frontiers. Few Caucasians notice the irony of children in San Francisco speaking Chinese as they walk to public schools while carrying Dick and Jane readers under their arms.

What is true for the Chinese has also been true for some white groups. Only recently have Catholic priests and nuns been seen inside synagogues and Protestant churches; the Irish wake in Boston is as queer a ceremony to the New England Unitarians as is the burial rite of a tribe in New Guinea. Few "strangers" ever venture into the store-front card rooms where Italian men sit for hours. Anyone who is not an Italian from that neighborhood is a "stranger."

While more than twenty million blacks continue to live in ghettos; while Orientals, Mexicans, Filipinos, and other colored people remain in their racial enclaves; while millions of white Europeans cling to their neighborhoods and their old languages—other white Americans cling tenaciously to the idea that America is truly a great melting pot. They are not aware of the fact that in 1960 at least nineteen million Americans still had a mother tongue, a primary language other than English,[3] and that approximately half of these people were born in America, and that 15 percent of them are third generation.[4]

Society was willing to absorb only those white immigrants who assimilated most easily, accepted racism most readily. Poles in Milwaukee, Italians in New York, Jews in Los Angeles, to mention just a few examples, practice open racism toward one or more minority groups; to do otherwise would be un-American, they think, and might reveal their uneasy feelings about their true status in the United States.

The assimilated immigrant is the one who has blended into the kind of America seen in TV commercials which glorify the middle-class way of life, so attractive to the truck driver who hates niggers and curses them in Polish or Italian. To be truly assimilated is to have only memories of the Old World culture, romanticized myths about the "good old days." By the third and fourth generation there is a truly assimilated progeny whose grandfathers are as foreign a cultural type to them as a Georgia slave is to a black auto worker in Detroit. To be sure, a cultural heritage remains —food, religion, certain family behavior patterns.

But if the third-generation European immigrant tries to merge successfully into the middle class, he must join the American of the TV screen. And if he remains in the working class and continues to live in an Old World enclave, he will affirm his Americanism through racist attitudes toward blacks and newly arrived immigrants. In both cases, a blending of cultures *does* occur. In one, a bland, homogenized representative of suburban America emerges; his

[3] Joshua A. Fishman, *Language Loyalty in the United States,* The Hague, The Netherlands, 1966, p. 392.
[4] *Ibid.*, p. 42.

origins are distinguished only by a "sky" or "itz" at the end of his name. In the other, a bitter acceptance of the worst of both cultures occurs; primitive and reactionary Old World attitudes are combined with notions of white supremacy and worship of gaudy consumer goods.

Immigrants from Europe encountered white America's racism, and a new outlet was provided for the ancient hostilities which had permeated their lives in the old countries. There, Norwegians and Danes hated Swedes, northern Italians despised Sicilians, Poles persecuted Jews, Serbs killed Croatians, the Irish fought the English, the Germans made war on the French, and the French felt nothing but disdain for the Spanish.

But now, in the New World, the old hatreds and feuds were put aside as the Europeans tried to become Americans. And to become an American meant accepting the white stereotype of the black, brown, red, and yellow-skinned peoples. Religious, national, and regional prejudices of Europe were converted to the color prejudices of America. The American culture was so thoroughly suffused with racism that the immigrants found it comparatively easy to adjust to the new society. That aspect of America was familiar to them; only the objects of the hatred were different. So the newcomers quickly and passionately adopted precisely that part of the American heritage which was destined to keep democracy from ever functioning properly. Descendants of the first Virginia slaveholders have little in common with the sons and grandsons of midwestern Polish steelworkers. Virginians have accepted very few Polish Old World patterns, but second- and third-generation Poles have assimilated the racist heritage of the first Americans. Ironically, the melting pot did work—but only in one direction.

D. H. Lawrence once expressed his judgment of this country. It was harsh, but fitting.

> The American landscape has never been at one with the white man. Never. And white men have probably never felt so bitter anywhere, as here in America, where the very landscape in its very beauty, seems a bit devilish and grinning, opposed to us.

The desire to extirpate the Indian. And the contradictory desire to glorify him. Both are rampant still, today. . . .

But you have there the myth of the essential white America. All the other stuff, the love, the democracy . . . is a sort of by-play. The essential American soul is hard, isolated, stoic, and a killer. It has never yet melted.

TO SERVE THE ☆DEVIL☆

THE HAWAIIANS

The evening air is warm and soft. In the outdoor night club, the sound of the sea is close enough to mute the noise of traffic on Kalakaua Avenue, the main street of Honolulu's Waikiki district which is jammed with tall, concrete hotels and apartment houses. On the stage, five Polynesian men from all over the South Pacific bring out their drums and get ready to play for the dancing Polynesian girls, who are the club's main attraction.

"We used to dance these dances for our kings," a young Polynesian drummer says sourly, as he opens the program, "but our old kings are dead and so now we dance for you, the tourists, our new kings."

But the tourists don't catch his sarcasm. They are busy talking about their bus trip to the Polynesian Cultural Center on the windward side of the island and the luau they are going to attend on the grounds of the hotel where they are staying.

At twilight the next evening, part-Hawaiian girls in grass hula skirts give plastic leis to the tourists gathering for the luau. The visitors—many of them wearing matching clothes, the men in Aloha shirts and their wives in muu muus*—stand holding paper cups filled with Mai Tais, the rum drink much favored in the Islands. They watch other "natives," young men in lava-lava skirts, prepare to lift the pig out of the oven in which it has been roasting. Almost all the tourists have cameras.*

When they hear a voice boom out over the public address system, they turn to a rock where another "native" stands, a part-Hawaiian, who is speaking into a microphone. He explains the purpose of the luau, describes how the pigs have been roasted for many hours, wrapped in leaves from the ti plant. Then he shouts, "When I count to three, the pig will be lifted out and I want all you tourists to take lots of pictures. You tourists are rich and if you take lots of pictures, we Hawaiians will get rich, too, and be able to send our children to college.

"Ready now? Get your cameras ready, then. All right. One, two, three!"

The young men hoist the roast pig high in the air and, everywhere over the open grassy area, cameras click and lights flash, capturing the photos to be treasured for years to come. The master of ceremonies ends with "This is how we Hawaiians make our covenant with our past." Then with the microphone lowered, he adds in a voice heard only by those standing next to him, "Three nights a week."

(*Actually, most Hawaiians and part-Hawaiians act out their special roles not just three nights a week for tourists, but 365 days a year, for everybody—including themselves.*)

John Dominis Holt, an educated, part-Hawaiian descendant of a Polynesian chief, lives in the middle of a sugar plantation in his family's old home, surrounded by portraits of his ancestors. He writes:

> Always, here in the land of our ancestors, we are psychologically captive to the spirit of the past. The harsh legacy of early observers, who endlessly shouted the myth of superiority of their beliefs over those of Hawaiians, we must constantly live down. . . .

The weight of classic mores and beliefs (not as potent, nor as functional anymore, as they were in the time of the *kapu* system, the chiefs, the *kahuna* and the *heiau*) is nonetheless a burden that Hawaiians must still bear. We are inescapably the heirs to this welter of tradition, whether we like it or not. Some of us try to understand it—to accept and keep those aspects of tradition which we like and discard the rest. Many of us are confused. We do not know how to think of the past, even if we have some glint of knowledge of what happened then.[1]

The effects "of what happened then" can be seen not only in the dispirited confusion of people like John Dominis Holt, but in the behavior of many "local boys," as the uneducated Hawaiians and part-Hawaiians are called. In Waimanaloe, a semirural area not far from Honolulu, gangs of tough Hawaiian kids war with each other and with any *haole,* as a white person is called in Hawaii, or Oriental foolish enough to be out in the streets at night. Little girls now peddle plastic leis on the streets of Waikiki and beg from tourists. Homesteads, parcels of land set aside by the state for Hawaiians, are becoming slums with palm trees. But these aspects of island life are rarely seen by the hundreds of thousands of tourists who flock to Hawaii from the mainland United States and the rest of the world.

To many mainland Americans, shivering in winter storms, Hawaii appears to be a warm and fragrant paradise of palm trees and blue water, where happy brown-skinned people strum ukuleles, sing melodic songs and dance graceful, charming hulas. So they flock to Hawaii to live out their fantasies. Dozens of hotels have been built solely for the tourist trade, and dozens more are in construction or being planned. Tourism has become one of the most important industries in the Islands and a special school of travel industry management has been heavily endowed at the university. The former president of the university is now director of the Hawaiian Visitors Bureau.

In past years, thousands of tourists crowded into an outdoor stadium on the beach near Waikiki to watch and photograph a troupe of hula dancers whose free perfor-

[1] John Dominis Holt, *On Being Hawaiian.* Hawaii: Star-Bulletin Publishing Co., 1964, pp. 21–22.

mance was sponsored by the Eastman Kodak Company. Following each performance, white-skinned middle-aged men and women painfully tried to follow the dancers in a few steps of the hula. No one bothered to tell them the history of the hula: that the original hulas were sexual in origin. One, for example, was danced to celebrate the size of the kings' genitals.

Phallic worship is hardly a respectable religion in America and one not likely to bring many church groups into the tour agency offices. So the true history of the hula is left untold.

Even a *haole* newspaper had this comment to make on the hula in 1893:

> . . . we stand face to face, with that which reminds us of . . . the monstrous incarnation of brutishness, the benighted *phallic* worship, whose leprous visage was so horrid that even the Senate of pagan Rome found it necessary to interdict it as an intolerable nuisance. No "cleanly wantonness" this but a deliberate attempt to exalt and glorify that which every pure mind must hold as the type of what is to be kept out of sight, and out of mind as the representative of all that which is animal and gross, the very apotheosis of grossness.[2]

TIME OF TROUBLE

O, honest Americans, as Christians hear me for my downtrodden people! Their form of government was as dear to them as yours is precious to you. Quite as warmly as you love your country, so they love theirs. With all your goodly possessions, covering a territory so immense that there yet remains parts unexplored, possessing islands, although near at hand had to be neutral ground in time of war, do not covet the little vineyard [of Naboth's] so far from your shores lest the punishment of Ahab fall upon you if not in your day in that of your children, for "be not deceived, God

[2] From the *Hawaiian Gazette,* February 28, 1883, as cited in Gavan Daws, *The Shoal of Time*. New York: The Macmillan Co., 1968, p. 219.

is not mocked." The people to whom your fathers told of the living God and taught to call "Father" and whom the sons now seek to despoil and destroy, are crying aloud to Him in their time of trouble and He will keep his Promise and will listen to the voices of His Hawaiian children lamenting for their homes.[3]

That sad plea for help was made in 1898 when Queen Liliuokalani, the last monarch of Hawaii, appealed to America to halt its annexation of Hawaii and its Polynesian people.

"It is for them," she cried out, "that I would give the last drop of my blood; it is for them that I would spend, nay am spending everything belonging to me. Will it be in vain?"[4]

It was. Americans did annex the Islands. This proved to be simply the formal legalization of the semicolonial status which the islanders had enjoyed almost from the time the British arrived at the Sandwich Islands, as Hawaii was first called by the English in 1778.

The process by which the Polynesian inhabitants of the Islands became "Americanized" is familiar. They died of newly introduced western maladies, of venereal disease, leprosy, and alcoholism; their lands were taken from them; their ancient religion and culture were destroyed by Christianity and commerce; and most of their leaders became puppets manipulated by their white conquerors. In Hawaii, as in few other places, the native inhabitants participated in their own destruction, either by adopting the white man's ways or by committing suicide, literally, on a mass scale, so deeply affected were they by the white man's contempt for their way of life.

Some Hawaiians resisted the whites from the beginning. But the Islanders were not equipped to deal with the use of guns, concepts of private property and commerce, and militant, American missionary Christianity.

[3] Queen Liliuokalani, *Hawaii Story by Hawaii's Queen.* Rutland, Vt. and Tokyo, Japan: Charles E. Tuttle Co., 1964, Ch. LVII.

[4] *Ibid.*

Before the white man came, the people had been dependent upon their chiefs for leadership, but after the whites arrived, the chiefs "stopped caring for the people," said David Malo in 1839. Because of the whites, the attention of the chiefs, said Malo, "has been turned more to themselves and their own aggrandizement and they do not seek the welfare of the people as a nation and therefore they are more oppressed at the present time than ever they were in ancient times. . . ."[5]

Today, little more than hard-to-pronounce street names, like Kalanianaole Boulevard or Kieaumoku Street, remain from Hawaii's ancient times. Many Hawaiians eke out their existences on the poor land set aside for them. Occasionally plaintive voices still call for a Hawaiian renaissance. But these voices are drowned out by the din of construction of new hotels being built on every beach, by the noise of traffic on the crowded streets of Waikiki, and by the sounds of television commercials brought across thousands of miles of ocean by satellite.

B.C.—BEFORE COOK

The eight Hawaiian Islands lie 2,100 miles southwest of California. Only two of the Islands are separated from each other by more than eighty miles; almost all of the others are no more than twenty-five miles apart, making it possible for the early inhabitants to move easily from island to island by boat and canoe.

Evidence suggests that the first inhabitants arrived in the Islands from Polynesia sometime in the ninth or tenth century, in large double canoes. Those first voyagers were able to establish a new, Polynesian-type society in the uninhabited islands. This society worshiped gods and goddesses of

[5] David Malo (as translated by L. Andrews), "On the Decrease of Population in the Hawaiian Islands," *The Hawaiian Spectator,* April, 1839, Vol. II, No. 2, p. 126.

the sea and erupting volcanoes. It remained intact for seven or eight hundred years, until Captain Cook, a British explorer, sighted the Islands in 1778.

Until that time, the Islanders' survival depended upon communal effort and sharing of the scarce resources. (Even today, with modern agricultural methods in use, less than 8 percent of the total land is arable.) Before the white man came probably less than 1 percent was used for agriculture. Fresh water was in short supply in some areas of the Islands, while in other places, especially in the mountainous forests, the rainfall was superabundant. Fishing was done in fleets of ten or twenty large canoes holding three to eight men each. The crews used large nets and the catch was shared by all those who participated.

This need to cooperate created a social structure in which some individual acts were considered antisocial. Nature forced the islanders to live and work together, and share the products of their efforts.

The social structure of the Islands in the prewhite days had powerful chiefs, the *ali'i,* who were reinforced by the *kahuna,* the priests who interpreted the *kapu,* the complicated systems of religious tabus which were accepted by all Hawaiians as being commands of the gods. The *maka'ainana,* the common people, had to allocate a certain portion of what they produced to the *ali'i,* who in turn dispensed what they had been given to their subchiefs, advisors and priests. In exchange, the chiefs were expected to provide leadership and expert technical advice, and protection for the *maka'ainana*. Below the common people were the *kauwa,* a despised class of social outcasts.

The land was in the hands of the chiefs, who allocated it to their subchiefs. These men, in turn, divided the land so that eventually the common people had their own plots of ground to work. Intermittently the chiefs declared war against each other.

Despite the power exerted by the chiefs on those below them, the *maka'ainana* were not the chattels of the *ali'i.* They were not tied to any specific piece of land, but were free to move about at will. Families were not located in just one area, but were connected by marriage and other relationships to people throughout the Islands. Visits of long duration were made by families or individuals who, even as guests, participated in cooperative work efforts.

The society was basically primitive, but many islanders possessed high degrees of skill. Agriculture was diversified and an ingenious system of irrigation had been developed. The lack of iron ore in the Islands was a great handicap since without iron few durable tools could be made. However, fish ponds flourished; the islanders also produced the best and most attractive tapa cloth in the Pacific. Navigation was well developed among the islanders, who understood and passed on an uncanny knowledge of tides, winds, and ocean currents. Astronomy and botany were well developed, also, and at a time when New Englanders were burning "witches," the islanders understood the concept of mental illness so well that they recognized more than twenty categories of such disturbances. Even more impressive, perhaps, is the fact those who were ill were not treated as if they had been possessed by evil spirits or the Christians' Devil, but with an understanding of the complex problems of identity. Modern psychiatrists might learn a great deal from the ways in which the Hawaiians combined visits to the *kahuna* with hypnosis, physical therapy, herbs, and intensive family support.[6]

Several aspects of pre-European life in the Islands are not known: the extent of infanticide and the killing of common people who either violated certain tabus or were sacrificed to the gods, are among the questions debated today. But whether these practices did occur on a wide scale, and whether they still existed when Cook arrived, the whites believed they did, thus providing one of their justifications for "civilizing" the Islands. Although the Island culture had no written language, skilled genealogists and oral historians could recite in minute detail the history of the Islands.

[6] Lorin Gill, "Basic Community Maladjustments," in Andrew W. Lind, *Modern Hawaii*. Honolulu: University of Hawaii Press, 1967, p. 62.

Prewhite Hawaiian society functioned on the basis of sharing, but a great contrast existed between the living conditions of the chiefs and the common people. Early travelers to the Islands noted how the common people were crowded into small huts while the chiefs and priests occupied larger, luxurious quarters. Even so, life in the Islands was essentially homogeneous and based on common religious beliefs. Kinship groups were large and their relationships extremely complicated. Among the families of chiefs brother-sister relationships were acceptable because it was thought they would produce offspring of the highest quality. Only a few *kapu* existed for sexual relationships and the concept of sexual constancy in marriage was nonexistent; Hawaiians enjoyed sexual relationships without shame or guilt.

The notion of buying and selling for profit was virtually unknown in the Islands. Instead, a kind of barter system prevailed in which the special products of one island were exchanged for those better produced on another. The islanders freely gave and took certain kinds of possessions from one another.

CIVILIZATION ARRIVES— GONORRHEA AND SYPHILIS

British sailors were the first white men the Hawaiians ever saw. No one knows, with any degree of certainty, whether or not they thought the men with white skins were gods; but gods or humans, the whites were treated generously by the Hawaiians. "Aloha, aloha," shouted the brown-skinned Islanders from their small boats, as they paddled around the British ships offering food, water, garlands of flowers, and sexual joy.

The British did not understand such generosity but accepted it. An incident involving property, however, led to the first killing. Cook wrote of how he had sent boats from his ships to seek out water on the Islands and how one of his officers had attempted to land,

> but was prevented by the natives, who, coming down to the boats in great numbers, attempted to take away the oars, muskets, and, in short, every thing that they could lay hold of; and pressed so thick upon him, that he was obliged to fire, by which one man was killed. . . . It did not appear to Mr. Williamson, that the natives had any design to kill, or even to hurt, any of his party; but they seemed excited by mere curiosity, to get from them what they had, being, at the same time, ready to give, in return, any thing of their own. . . .[7]

Cook was ambivalent about the Hawaiians. He wrote in his *Journals:* "These people, merited our best commendations, in this commercial intercourse, never once attempting to cheat us, either ashore or alongside the ships." But Cook followed this high praise with the statement that "Some of them, indeed, as already mentioned, at first, betrayed a thievish disposition; or rather, they thought, that they had a right to everything they could lay their hands upon, but they soon laid aside a conduct, which, we convinced them, they could not persevere in with impunity."[8] Then he added, "They seem to be blest with a frank, cheerful disposition. . . . They seem to live very sociably in their intercourse with one another; and except the propensity to thieving, which seems innate in most of the people we have visited in this ocean, they were exceedingly friendly to us. . . ."[9]

He also observed, "with how much affection the women managed their infants, and how readily the men lent their assistance to such a tender office; thus sufficiently distinguishing themselves from those savages, who esteem a wife and child as things rather necessary, than desirable, or worthy of their notice. . . ."[10]

[7] James Cook and James King, *A Voyage to the Pacific Ocean.* London: G. Nichol and T. Cadell, 1785, Vol. II, pp. 197–98.
[8] *Ibid.,* p. 205.
[9] *Ibid.,* pp. 229–30.
[10] *Ibid.,* p. 230.

Cook's *Journals* also reveal a degree of genuine concern over the impact his expedition was making on the Islands. He attempted, unsuccessfully, to prohibit his crews from going ashore, lest the men infect the islanders with venereal disease:

. . . which, unfortunately, had already been communicated by us to other islands in these seas. With the same view I ordered all female visitors to be excluded from the ships. . . . They would as readily have forced us with their company on board as the men; but I wished to prevent all connection which might, too probably, convey an irreparable injury to themselves, and through their means to the whole nation. Another necessary precaution was taken by strictly enjoining that no persons known to be capable of propagating the infection should be sent upon duty out of the ships. Whether these regulations, dictated by humanity, had the desired effect or not, time can only discover.[11]

Cook's precautions did not have "the desired effect." The "fatal disease" was imported into the Islands.

Cook returned to Hawaii in late November of 1778 for a longer visit. Then, in February, 1779, he set off on his explorations again, but had to return to the Islands after a storm damaged one of his ships. In the middle of February, Cook and a small group of his marines battled with Hawaiians on the Kona Coast of the island of Hawaii and Cook was killed. The Hawaiians had taken a boat away from Cook's crew and he was determined to recover it. Cook's men, in attempting to get it back, fired their muskets into a crowd of Hawaiians and killed them. The angry Hawaiians bludgeoned Cook to death. The British were simply defending their private property.

Cook's death was a direct result of the conflict between European values concerning possessions and those of the Hawaiians. Cook felt he had been engaging in fair exchanges with the Hawaiians when he gave them nails, which they wanted very much, in return for food and water. But the Hawaiians' insatiable desire for iron pushed them into

[11] James Cook, as quoted in *A Hawaiian Reader,* edited by A. Grove Day and Carl Stroven. New York: Popular Library, 1961, pp. 22–23.

taking anything made of it whenever they could. Gavan Daws, a Pacific historian, suggests that perhaps "stealing" from Cook's expedition was a kind of game in which the Hawaiians tried to demonstrate their superiority over the white men.

The initial contact between the British and the islanders, short as it was, disrupted forever the old way of life in the Islands. During the brief time Cook and his men were there, they precipitated the breakdown of the *kapu,* the internal system of tabus which had always governed the lives of the islanders. They introduced the notion of selling goods and services for profits and introduced firearms. They persuaded the chiefs to use their positions and authority over the people for the benefit of the white men. The British, with the help of many chiefs, used their technology, especially in weapons, to trample Hawaiian culture.

Initially, the British saw the Hawaiians as savages. Later, they learned something about the Hawaiians' true nature. Thomas Manby, who sailed with Captain George Vancouver on an exploratory voyage to the Pacific in 1791, wrote:

> Before we became acquainted with these people we considered them as a ferocious and turbulent set of savages. This character they are by no means entitled to, as they are mild and tractable; uncivilized, unpolished, and in a true state of nature, they possess great courage and will not tamely bear an insult or an injury. Their few laws are strictly adhered to, and was their code more numerous, I conceive they would abide by them with equal promptitude. To each other they are free, easy and cheerful, and show more real good nature than I have seen in your better regulated societies. During the whole of my stay I was never witness to a quarrel: they delight in jokes, which were never known to produce an angry brow or uplifted arm.[12]

In the twenty years that followed Cook's first visits to the Islands, extraordinary changes in society, politics, and economics began to occur. The hitherto sporadic warfare among the chiefs grew more intense, and one chief more

[12] Day and Stroven, *op. cit.*, p. 47.

powerful than all the others emerged. He was Kamehameha, a tall, powerfully built man and a descendant of a long line of high-ranking *ali'i* who possessed keen political and military skills. He used both to consolidate his power. An important key to his success, however, was his use of British muskets.

Kamehameha's efforts to unify the Islands and establish his undisputed right to rule them were assisted by the British, who were anxious to gain possession of them. But the British realized that the Islands had to be stabilized before this could happen. Captain Vancouver reported that the island of Hawaii was ceded to the British, but Kamehameha refused to give them possession. Kamehameha, however, took advantage of the military equipment he had received from the British to wage a series of bloody wars against other island chiefs. He emerged victorious and became king of all the Islands.

While Kamehameha was struggling for power, commerce was rapidly developing. Cook's crew had traded with American Indians in the Northwest, receiving furs which they discovered could be sold for high profits in China. Within a few years, fur trading was being carried on by the English, French, Russians, and especially the Americans. In the long voyage from America to China, the Hawaiian Islands became the most important port for picking up fresh supplies of food and water, for repairing and refitting ships, as well as a place where crews could relieve the tedium of their long, lonely voyages with women and liquor. Supplying these services became the Islands' first business.

Along with the fur trade with China came commerce in sandalwood, then in great demand in China. It grew in abundance in the Islands, and as soon as the whites, especially the Americans, discovered the huge potential market for the fragrant wood and Hawaii's enormous supply of it, they began to buy it from the chiefs. The chiefs forced the common people to collect the wood from all over the Islands and carry it, often for long distances, to the ports where it was sold to the white traders. This new enterprise was accompanied by a profound change in the old relationship of the chiefs to the people. The chiefs began to exploit their own people in order to acquire the costly goods shown them by the foreign traders who were flocking to the Islands.

One traveler described this new trade:

> Commerce has attracted to this place some Americans, who, in the hope of speedily making their fortunes, established themselves here several years ago. I cannot say that they carry on any regular trade here, but rather contraband: they can obtain whatever they want at so cheap a rate. In the morning they take half a dozen bottles of wine to the Governor, and the good soul is soon stretched at their feet; they make presents of a few hatchets and muskets to the principal chiefs; all the rest of the population are then quite at the disposal of these gentlemen. Some strong and active men are sent to the mountains; the forests are examined, and some sandalwood trees are cut down: these are conveyed to the water's edge at night by about twenty women, who are paid for either carrying or dragging them along with a few ells of European cloth or linen; thence to be embarked on board a vessel that is always stationed in the harbour. On the arrival of spring, their correspondents on the North-west coast of America come here with a cargo of furs, to obtain provisions, and increase their rich ventures with the acquisitions of their partners; and, sure of an immense profit, they push on to Macao, or Canton, to sell their cargoes to the lazy Chinese for dollars, sugars, or silks, which they know how to transmit speedily to Europe.[13]

The abrupt transition from the old relationships between the chiefs and the common people brought about a new life style for the Hawaiians. The chiefs succumbed to the lure of the goods and finery white traders offered them and began to ape the whites in clothing and behavior. But to do this, the chiefs had to exploit the labor of the common people and deplete much of the Islands' natural resources for trade with the whites.

The rise of Kamehameha to undisputed power during this same period also contributed to the breakdown of the old order. Kamehameha used the traditional *kapus* as

[13] From a description by Jacques Arago, 1823, in *Changes in Land Tenure in Hawaii, 1778–1850,* by Marion Kelly. Unpublished M.A. Thesis, University of Hawaii, 1956.

weapons to consolidate his authority and the *kahuna* were pressed into service to justify, on religious grounds, Kamehameha's military and political wars.

Certain *kapus* began to lose their power. For example, the prohibitions against women participating in certain activities and those defining their roles with men were openly flouted in the wake of active sexual relations between the native women and sailors. Initially the women simply gave themselves to the whites, but soon they and their men discovered it was possible to receive rewards for spending nights on shipboard. Husbands and fathers would bring their women to the ships at night because, as John Li, a Hawaiian, put it years later, "of a desire for clothing, mirrors, scissors, knives, iron hoops from which to fashion fishhooks, and nails."[14] In the morning, a ship's cannon would go off and the sleepy females would get up from the decks where they had been lying with the sailors to return to shore. The equally sleepy sailors left behind would lazily work through the warm tropical day, anticipating the night to come. These easy and casual sexual relationships brought a rapid, deadly spread of venereal disease among both the Islanders and the sailors.

The whites also introduced alcohol to the Islanders, who had never known it before. Its effects were physically and psychologically catastrophic. But some of the whites were thrown off balance by the languorous and sensual atmosphere of the Islands. The stories of the white beachcomber, the sailor who jumps ship in the South Pacific and becomes a tropical bum, had their origins in the adventures of those British crews who first tasted the joys of life in the tropics.

Not all the whites who decided to stay in the Islands became beachcombers. Some of them were hard-working, ambitious craftsmen and skilled artisans who were willing to serve the Hawaiian chiefs and the king for high wages or land or both. More and more white men began to take part in the government, as advisors to Kamehameha.

The system of land ownership changed. Since Kamehameha had conquered the local chiefs his claims to their

[14] Daws, *op. cit.*, p. 45.

land went undisputed. After he died in 1819, his son and heir, Liholiho, continued the new system of land tenure. Instead of reverting to the chiefs for redistribution, the land continued to be held by the king, and was often given to *haole* advisors and supporters as a reward for their services.

After the sandalwood was exhausted in the Islands, another equally disruptive form of commerce arrived with the coming of the whaling ships. Hundreds of whalers thronged the Islands while their ships anchored off shore, waiting for goods and supplies. Many of the whaling ships remained in the Islands during the off-season, making greater demands on the Islands' resources. Honolulu on the Island of Oahu, and Lahaina, a port on Maui, became typical sailor towns —rough and bawdy, filled with bars and bordellos. Once again the chiefs became brokers, exchanging the labor of their people and the natural resources of the Islands for the money and goods of the foreigners.

Soon the Islands' natural resources proved insufficient to meet the demands of so many ships. European and American traders met these demands by bringing supplies to the Islands from their own ships. With the profits made from these transactions, they started building businesses and buying property from the chiefs. More and more foreigners began to play key roles in the Islands, while young Hawaiian men became part of the ships' crews, replacing the foreign seamen who had deserted. Each month, more of the old Polynesian culture vanished under the impact of the aggressive white commercial system.

GOD ARRIVES TO HELP TRADE

During the period of the breakdown of Hawaiian culture, with its disastrous effects upon the Island population, the first American missionaries arrived. The whites who had come to the Islands before the missionaries had come for the profits to be gained; the missionaries came, at least initially, to make Christians out of the Hawaiians. They created an Hawaiian alphabet, opened schools, set up printing presses, built churches—and introduced the idea of sin. They also insisted that the Hawaiians dress themselves in all-enveloping clothing, which evolved into the *muu muus* sold today in every shop in the Islands.

The missionaries helped stabilize Hawaiian society by filling the vacuum created by the collapse of the old customs and relationships with the religious beliefs of Protestantism. Since Protestantism incorporated into its theology a belief in the business ethic, the missionaries saw nothing wrong in encouraging American commerce in the Islands. The missionary model for the ideal relationship between Christianity and commerce was expressed by Professor W. D. Alexander, writing in 1857 of the missionary work in Hawaii: "Christianity civilizes in the broadest sense. Commerce, industry, science and literature all accompany her majestic march to universal dominion. Thus, while it denies the sufficiency of commerce alone to transform the savage, it encourages a legitimate commerce and even courts its alliance as one of the most important instrumentalities."[15]

Not all commerce was considered "legitimate." Missionaries fought the sale of alcohol to Hawaiians and opposed the brothels that had been established for the ships' crews. This opposition led the missionaries into bitter conflicts with the ships' captains and the merchants who served them.

In place of distilleries and brothels, the missionaries, using their prestige and influence with the kings, encouraged other kinds of commercial activities. In 1835 King Kamehameha III gave the first long-term land lease for a sugar plantation to an American firm. This had the support of the missionaries. The three Americans in the firm were described as "Men of high character and purpose; much

[15] Professor W. D. Alexander, "Science and Missions." Originally published in 1857, reprinted in *Pilgrims of Hawaii*, by Rev. and Mrs. Orramel Hinckley Gulick. Fleming H. Revell Co., 1918.

above that of most of the traders who had preceded them in the islands."[16]

With the help of the missionaries, these "pious traders," as the new merchants were scornfully described by the less scrupulous ones "who had preceded them," increasingly gained control over the Islands' economy. A mission letter sent out in 1838 reported that: "Incipient measures have been taken for two establishments for the manufacture of raw silk; and one of sugar is now in successful operation at the islands. These are conducted by foreigners, men of Christian and moral principles who are giving encouragement to labor in their immediate vicinity and are, therefore, hailed as auxiliaries in the work of civilizing the people."[17]

Two years later, Rev. William Richards wrote from Lahaina, Maui,

> I think that the merchants generally are beginning to feel that they are indebted in no small degree to the influence of the mission, procuring for them that perfect security and patronage, and their facilities for doing business which have with very few exceptions commanded for the government the respect of visitors from all nations. It is a common saying among the businessmen here, "We shall regret the day that the influence of the American missionaries is destroyed or materially diminished."[18]

The businessmen had no need to worry; the influence of the American missionaries continued to increase. The missionaries established a relationship with the chiefs and the royal family, just as the traders had done. One important measure of their new relationship was the control they exercised in the education of the kings' and chiefs' children. Another area in which the missionaries used their growing influence was to gain control and ownership of the land for themselves.[19]

Getting "legal" possession of the land was the key issue

[16] Arthur C. Alexander, *Koloa Plantation, 1835–1935*. Honolulu: 1937, p. 3.

[17] Rev. and Mrs. Orramel Hinckley Gulick, *op. cit.*, p. 162. The quotation is from a letter dated June 4, 1838.

[18] *Ibid.*, from a letter dated July 27, 1840.

[19] A common saying among Hawaiians is that "the missionaries came to do good for the natives and instead did very well for themselves."

in the *haoles'* effort to gain control of the Islands. The men who traded in furs and sandalwood and supplied the whaling fleets sought the right to invest in land to back up their business enterprises and insure their political influence in the Islands.

Quarrels over land rights were a continual source of tension between the Hawaiians and the foreign population of Americans, British, and French. In almost every case, the white foreigners ended the disputes by the threat of military force. The pattern of foreign domination was described by one American businessman who wrote a former associate about the state of his affairs:

> Our business and profits have increased greatly the last eighteen months. By continuing our business for a few years, I anticipate a large fortune for each of us. We have capital and credit, and are firmly established. Property is much safer here now than formerly—the visits of the American, English and French men-of-war during these sixteen months have established inviolability of property and persons and the natives taught and made to fear the "Laws of Nations"; and that a sovereign and a government come under the ban of laws as well as subjects or individuals.[20]

Such "visits" of warships to the Islands continued throughout the 1830s and 1840s. The purpose of each "visit" was to force the Hawaiians into a treaty giving foreigners more controls over their island enterprises and more permanent rights in land ownership—especially the rights to sell, lease, and transfer land. Under the threat of the warships' guns trained on their villages, Hawaiian rulers signed the treaties. The treaties then became another source of tension because interpretations of them were disputed.

Deeply troubled by the increasing power of the foreigners, David Malo wrote to Kineau, Premier under King Kamehameha III, in 1837:

> I have been thinking that you ought to hold frequent meetings with all the chiefs . . . to seek for that which will be of the

[20] Henry A. Pierce, writing in 1837, as quoted in *A History of C. Brewer & Co., Ltd.: One Hundred Years in the Hawaiian Islands, 1826–1926,* by Josephine Sullivan. Boston: 1926, p. 62.

greatest benefit to this country; you must not think that this is anything like olden times, that you are the only chiefs and can leave things as they are. . . . This is the reason. If a big wave comes in, large fishes will come from the dark Ocean that you never saw before, and when they see the small fishes they will eat them up. . . . The ships of the white man have come, and smart people have arrived from the great countries . . . they know our people are few in number and living in a small country; they will eat us up. . . . God has made known to us through the mouths of the men of the man-of-war things that will lead us to prepare ourselves. . . . Therefore get your servant ready who will help you when you need him.[21]

But neither the king nor the chiefs heeded Malo's advice. Two years later, Malo pointed out:

In former times, before Kamehameha, the chiefs took great care of their people. That was their appropriate business, to seek the comfort and welfare of their people, for a chief was called great in proportion to the number of his people, for he was a high chief or low chief, according as his people were many or few; wherefore it behooved the chiefs to look well to their people against the time of war.

But from Liholiho's time to the present, the chiefs seem to have left caring for the people. Their attention has turned more to themselves and their own aggrandisement, and they do not seek the welfare of the people as a nation, and therefore they are more oppressed at the present time than ever they were in ancient times. . . .

Another cause of the diminution of the people of the islands is the licentiousness existing between Hawaiian females and certain foreigners that come here without wives. Because of the licentious habits of such foreigners, contracted perhaps in other countries, they came here polluted with a filthy disease, and they have thus polluted with a filthy disease the females of Hawaii. This disease has, moreover, become prevalent among the people, and even children, and all the people of the islands, are miserably diseased; and it is clear, that from the arrival of Captain Cook to the present day, the people have been dying with the venereal disorder. Foreigners have lent their whole in-

[21] David Malo, in a letter, dated August 18, 1837. Archives of Hawaii, Foreign Office and Executive File.

fluence (*hookaika loa*) to make the Hawaiian islands one great brothel. For this cause, God is angry and he is diminishing the people and they are nigh unto desolation.

Through the great evils that have not usually existed until the present time, and the great evils that have been brought here from foreign countries, the chiefs and the people have been beguiled (*houwalewaleia*) and led astray. They [the evils] have also been increased by intoxicating liquors and all their increasing train of evils.[22]

But Malo's warnings were again ignored. He died in 1853, embittered toward both the whites and the Hawaiians who followed their example. He was buried, at his own request, high on a mountainside, so that in death he would be as far away as possible from those who had destroyed or permitted the destruction of his beloved land.

Because of the enormous pressures of dealing with foreign nations, the Hawaiian rulers turned to the American missionaries for help. From teaching the chiefs' children, the missionaries moved to lecturing the king and chiefs on political economy and land reforms. They developed the concept of constitutional government, helped establish a hereditary kingdom, managed financial affairs, and negotiated treaties of recognition for the kingdom. Some of the missionaries even became Hawaiian citizens.

The missionaries justified their influence over the Hawaiians in the following terms:

. . . the government has been going more and more into the hands of naturalized foreigners . . . the more important affairs, indeed I may say *all* the important affairs of the government are now administered by these *adopted* foreigners. It must necessarily be so seeing this nation is now shoved in among the great family of civilized nations and its foreign relations a good deal involved. The native chiefs are far from being competent to manage these complicated affairs and hence the aid of foreigners is called in. . . .[23]

[22] David Malo, "On the Decrease of Population in the Hawaiian Islands," *op. cit.*, pp. 125–29.

[23] Rev. Richard Armstrong, quoted in Ralph S. Kuykendall, *The Hawaiian Kingdom, 1778–1854*. Honolulu: University of Hawaii Press, 1st ed., 1938; reprinted in 1947, p. 238.

The common people of the Islands paid a heavy price for the increasing dependence of their rulers on the missionaries. As the missionary influence increased, the Americans imposed their standards of morality and behavior. The missionaries were Protestant, so they drove out the Catholics, thus producing antagonism among the French population. The missionaries were committed to monogamy and strict observance of the Protestant sexual ethic, so they succeeded in making the Polynesian sexual practices illegal. The missionaries were convinced that the accumulation of private property, especially of land, was God's way, so they disrupted the native concept of land tenure—managing, incidentally, to accumulate a great deal of land for themselves and their families in the process. The missionaries believed in the virtues of labor, so they imposed work discipline on the Islanders. Since the missionaries were Americans, they used their influence to bring the Island kingdom under U.S. hegemony.

Thus the first step in the destruction of Hawaii's Polynesian culture took place when the British explorers tried to take over the Islands for England in the 1790s; the second step took place when the American missionaries, convinced they were doing God's work, began to destroy the immoral and heathen Hawaiian society and build a new one based on the American Christian model.

Some Hawaiians, like Malo, understood and resented what was happening to their society as the influence of the missionaries flourished, and attempted to persuade King Kamehameha III to cut himself loose from their influence. In 1845 a petition was directed to the king from the people of Lahaina, on the Island of Maui, pointing out that

> The Hawaiian people will be trodden underfoot by the foreigners. Perhaps not now or perhaps it will not be long before we shall see it. . . . Another thing, the dollar has become the government for the commoner and for the destitute. It will become a dish of relish and the foreign agents will suck it up. With so many foreign agents the dollar will be lost to the government through the cleverness of foreigners and their cunning

and instead of good coming to the Hawaiian people, strangers will get the benefit from the wealth of the government.[24]

The Lahaina petitioners decried the attempt of the king to duplicate the laws of other governments in Hawaii: "The laws of those governments will not do for us. Those are good laws for them, our laws are for us and are good laws for us, which we have made for ourselves. We are not slaves to serve them. When they talk in their clever way we know very well what is right and what is wrong. . . ."[25]

The king defended his actions, telling the Hawaiians he desired "all the good things of the past to remain . . . and to unite them with what is good under these new conditions in which we live. That is why I have appointed foreign officials, not out of contempt for the ancient wisdom of the land but because my native helpers do not understand the laws of the great countries who are working with us." The king did not seem to realize that, inevitably, the "laws of the great countries" would bring about the destruction of traditional Hawaiian culture.

The missionaries, for their part, attributed the decline of the Hawaiian population almost completely to "ALCOHOL and DISEASE propagated through licentious intercourse with white men," as described by the Rev. Artemas Bishop in 1838. The Rev. Bishop wrote:

I think it will appear . . . that these two destroying angels of the pit have done, and they are now doing, more mischief in the Pacific Ocean, nay in the world, than all other evils combined. . . . If Englishmen and Americans have entailed upon them a mortal disease, let help also come from the same quarter to heal their malady. We appeal to foreign residents and visitors from civilized lands and ask them to lend a helping hand with those already engaged in the work of doing good. We do not ask them to renounce their appropriate business and sacrifice their prospects of emolument, to become teachers and physicians for these people. But let each do what he can in this benevolent work, without turning aside from his own appropriate sphere.

[24] S. M. Kamakau, *The Ruling Chiefs of Hawaii.* Honolulu: Kamehameha Schools Press, 1961, p. 399.
[25] *Ibid.*

The crisis is now approaching and the question will soon be decided, whether the Hawaiian nation is to remain a distinct people or be annihilated. . . .[26]

At the time of Cook's first landing in 1778, an estimated 400,000 to 500,000 people lived in the Islands; forty years later, nearly half the population had been wiped out and by 1840 the Hawaiian population had dwindled to a little over 100,000.

Disease played a major role in killing off the Hawaiians, especially venereal diseases. Measles and cholera swept through the population and alcoholism weakened the islanders so badly that they often succumbed to the common cold. But more important was the psychological sickness that struck the islanders as their culture and religion disappeared. *"Na kanaka okuu wale aku no I kau uhane"* ("The people dismissed freely their souls and died").

It was only a question of how long it would take the whites to totally dominate the life of the Islands. In their efforts to gain control over the Islands, some missionaries renounced their American citizenship and became Hawaiians; others married into the royal family or into the families of the chiefs. The marriages gave them control over the land.

Beginning in 1836, Kamehameha III was forced to concede the special rights of foreigners to hold the land. Then, under the increased influence of the missionaries of the king, more *haoles* were given the right to lease land for commercial enterprises. But these men did not want to merely lease the land; they wanted to own it outright so they could then sell or lease it to others. There were protests from some Hawaiians who charged that these "pious traders" were becoming subjects of the king only to gain control of the land, but the *haole* encroachment on the land continued unabated—especially after the Great Mahele in 1848, a dividing of the land between the king and 245 chiefs.

[26] Rev. Artemas Bishop, "An Inquiry Into the Causes of Decrease in the Population of the Sandwich Islands," *The Hawaiian Spectator,* January, 1838, pp. 52ff.

The division was extremely complicated and caused legal disputes which are still going on today. The king and the chiefs made an initial division, each giving up his rights to the others' lands; then the king divided his land into crown land, over which he retained control, and government land, which was given to the legislature.

But the ultimate effects of the Great Mahele were disastrous for the common Hawaiians, like the Indians, had little understanding of land values. The king kept a little less than a third of the land; the chiefs "owned" a little more than a third; and the government approximately the same amount. Theoretically the common people were given the right to claim lands which they or their ancestors had been cultivating for many years. But they ended up with less than 30,000 of the 4,000,000 acres in the Islands. Within another forty years, two-thirds of the government land was in the hands of the *haoles;* land owned by the chiefs and the common people was sold or leased to the Americans for very little money. Even the crown lands started to drift into the possession of the *haoles,* first through leases and then through purchases. The *haole* cultural, religious, and political takeover was now almost complete. Soon thereafter the land was in *haole* hands and with it economic control.

"TO ANNEX OR NOT TO ANNEX . . ."

By the middle of the nineteenth century, the stakes in the economic future of Hawaii were enormous. The discovery that sugar could be grown there made the Islands of even greater importance than they had been to the American business community on the mainland. In the next few decades, American businessmen took an active interest in convincing the United States Government to annex the Islands. In 1856 American interests in the Islands established the *Pacific Commercial Advertiser,* a newspaper representing the United States businessmen. The paper criticized any opposition to American expansion in the Islands.

Resistance to American influence, nevertheless, developed in the royal family; Kamehameha IV was anti-American and inclined to favor the British and Europeans. One reason for his attitude was that he had traveled through Europe, where he was treated royally, and through America, where he had been badly treated because of his dark skin.

But the pressure for American annexation continued, and a series of complicated intrigues and political alliances developed in the struggle for control of the Islands. One group of Americans living in the Islands favored annexation; other groups opposed it, visualizing greater benefits for themselves through connections with the royal family. Also, by this time some *haoles* had intermarried with high-ranking members of the monarchical group, so their part-Hawaiian children had a stake in resisting annexation.

Those opposed to annexation were inadvertently aided by the arrogance whites exhibited toward the nonwhite Hawaiians. Throughout the South Pacific most whites thought of "natives" as either *kanakas,* ferocious savages, or "niggers"—people to be despised and enslaved. Even those whites who opposed slavery were convinced Hawaiians were like children, unable to govern themselves or make sensible judgments. Every Hawaiian, including the royal family, felt the effects of these attitudes. When young Prince Alexander Liholiho traveled in the United States, he was mistaken for a black by a train conductor and told to move to another carriage. Indignantly he refused and was finally allowed to remain in his seat only after the conductor had been informed of the prince's rank. The incident made a marked impression on the young Hawaiian who wrote in his journal that because "[I] had a darker skin . . . I must be treated like a dog to go and come at an Americans [sic] bidding."

But to some extent the youthful prince's reaction to the callous treatment given him came from his conception of himself as being of royal blood. The models Hawaiian rulers emulated were not their own dark-skinned ancestors, the Polynesian chiefs, but the European kings and queens. In their clothing, forms of recreation, political institutions, and general deportment, the Hawaiian rulers followed white patterns—they had become imitation whites.

The effect of the royal behavior on common Hawaiians was to reinforce the notion of white American and European superiority. The Europeans and Americans, helped, of course, by assiduously spreading the notion of their superiority through the benevolent paternalism of the missionaries and the malevolent greediness of the businessmen. The Hawaiians found themselves living in a world in which they were surrounded by so much evidence of white superiority, attested to even by their own rulers, that they, too, began to see themselves as innately inferior to the whites.

The interests of ordinary Hawaiians were never considered; they were considered unimportant to businessmen since they were unwilling to work on the sugar plantations. Meanwhile the royal family busied itself in duplicating European court life in the Islands.

The strength and influence of the pro-annexation Americans grew in Hawaii, and on the mainland where the concept of expansion and "manifest destiny" was attracting a growing number of adherents. To the expansionists, Hawaii had military as well as political and economic importance; Pearl Harbor, for instance, is one of the best natural harbors in the world and the military saw it as a potentially important installation.

Hard-core resistance to American annexation developed during the reign of King Kalakaua, who came to power in 1874; he shifted from cooperation with the Americans to fierce opposition. Kalakaua's jaundiced view of the Americans was fostered, at least partially, by the way pro-annexation Americans mocked him and his sister, Liliuokalani, for being the bastard children, allegedly, of a Negro bootblack who had, supposedly, been their mother's secret lover. The Americans, in their efforts to diminish Kalakaua's influence, would hold up an effigy of the bootblack whenever Kalakaua was speaking.[27]

Encouraged by anti-American part-Hawaiians, and even by some Americans, and aided by the financial help of Claus Spreckels who sought a sugar monopoly in the Islands, Kalakaua began to develop the idea of a Polynesian empire with Hawaii as its ruling center. To counter this threat, pro-annexation *haoles* tried to use political influence, and when that failed they used guns. By the middle of the 1880s, they had formed five rifle companies to oppose the Polynesian empire supporters, thus representing a serious threat to King Kalakaua.

Under the threat of *haole* guns, Kalakaua gave in to the demands of the pro-annexation group and established a new constitution that gave the *haoles* more power than he had.

The king's capitulation created tremendous resentment and stirred some Hawaiians to active resistance. They tried to replace Kalakaua with his younger sister, Princess Liliuokalani, who was committed to protecting the Hawaiians. To meet this threat, the *haoles* asked the American minister to Hawaii to send a warship and land American marines in Honolulu. The marines were landed and the revolt was squashed.

United States-oriented *haoles* remained in effective control of the government until the death of Kalakaua and the crowning of his sister, Liliuokalani. The new queen was determined to get back control of the Islands from the *haoles*. She was convinced that they had wrested it away from the Hawaiians only by the threat of force.

Queen Liliuokalani posed so serious a menace to the Americans that they began a conspiracy, under the leadership of a group called "The Committee of Safety," to take over the Islands. The Committee's leading spirit, Lorrin Thurston, a Honolulu publisher, kept the American State Department informed of the group's plans to overthrow the

[27] Daws, *op. cit.*, p. 284.

queen's government and maintained close contact with the American Minister to Hawaii, John L. Stevens.

Stevens supported the Committee. Furthermore, he wrote the State Department that the choice was either annexation by the U.S. or loss of the Islands to the Asian world, especially to the growing influence of Japan. The pro-Americans, Stevens reported, had economic power over the Islands but if left "unaided by outside support" would be "too few in numbers to control in political affairs. . . ." President Benjamin Harrison's administration responded with assurances that the United States would be happy to annex Hawaii and that military force would support such a move if necessary.

While all this was going on, the color issue flared up again, this time in a more vicious and brutal way than before. The old scandal about the queen mother's black lover was revived and one of the busiest tale-bearers was the influential Reverend Sereno Bishop, an eminent missionary who served as Hawaiian correspondent for the United Press and wrote for mainland magazines. He portrayed her daughter, the queen, as a black, heathen, libertine woman who indulged in pagan rites and devil worship and encouraged her people to further drunkenness and shiftlessness.[28]

"The Committee of Safety," encouraged by the American Government's position, overthrew the queen in 1893 with the threat of force and set up a provisional government. Minister Stevens recognized the coup government, established an American protectorate over it, and sent word to Washington: "The Hawaiian pear is now fully ripe and this is the golden hour for the United States to pluck it." The leaders of the provisional government joined in urging the United States to annex the Islands. President Harrison, then a lame-duck president, tried, unsuccessfully, to get an annexation treaty passed by the Senate. When Grover Cleveland was elected President he opposed the pro-annexation actions of his predecessor and refused to support the overthrow of the queen.

[28] *Ibid.*, p. 284.

Cleveland dispatched his own representative, John L. Blount of Georgia, to the Islands to investigate. Thurston was convinced that Blount would support the provisional government because, "As a Southerner, he is thoroughly familiar with the difficulties of the situation . . . attendant upon government with an ignorant majority in the electorate. . . ."

On the contrary, Blount's report to the President horrified the annexationists. He made it clear to Cleveland that the mass of native Hawaiians opposed the new government, which had been established through the use of force (with the help of the American Government). As a result of Blount's report, Cleveland demanded that the queen's power be restored to her; his demand was rejected by the annexationist leaders and he later withdrew it.

Thwarted in their efforts to achieve immediate annexation of Hawaii the provisional government established the Republic of Hawaii. The basis of the Republic was, as one *haole* leader described it, "an uncommonly strong government with very large powers in the hands of a few." The Republic's constitution made certain that few, if any, Hawaiians took part in government or even voted. The justification for this policy was expressed by Reverend Bishop when he wrote, "The common people were not entrusted with rule because in their childishness and general incapacity, they were totally unfit for such rule. . . . The masses of the native people are destitute of such qualifications. They are babes in character and intellect. . . ."[29]

The new Republic continued to meet with opposition and even the possibility of armed resistance from a few Hawaiian leaders who were supported by many commoners. The resistance was quickly scattered by the threat of massive military power. In retaliation, the opposition drew up a plan to restore the queen and establish constitutional rule—at gunpoint. But the plot was discovered on January 6, 1895, one day before it was to go into action, and the leaders captured. The country was placed under martial

[29] Rev. Sereno E. Bishop in *The Friend,* a missionary magazine.

law; the queen's supporters, labeled as revolutionaries by the Americans, were arrested, and the queen imprisoned in her Honolulu palace. Eight days later she was released in exchange for her promise to support the Republic. She then pleaded for the release of her supporters and within a year most of them were freed and the death sentences given to others were commuted to jail terms. (To this day, however, there are Hawaiians who are convinced that their ancestors were tortured to death in the Republic's prison.)

With the opposition smashed, the way was clear again for the annexationists, who were beginning to meet with increased support within the United States. But there was now a new factor pushing the *haoles* to achieve annexation. The sugar planters had imported thousands of Japanese to work on the plantations, and many *haoles* feared the Islands would be taken over by the Orientals unless the United States beat them to it.

Fear of the "Yellow Peril" struck a sympathetic note in the United States where a vicious anti-Oriental prejudice was quite open, especially on the West Coast. It fitted, too, into the pattern of American imperialism whose captains were casting covetous eyes on the Pacific territories. Grover Cleveland was replaced by William McKinley, whose Under Secretary of the Navy, Theodore Roosevelt, gave secret orders to his commanders to take over the Islands at the first sign of Japanese aggression. The truth was, however, that the only country with aggressive interests in Hawaii was the United States itself.

Finally, in 1898, annexation took place. In character with most of the previous American actions in the Islands, the annexation procedures bordered on the illegal. An annexation treaty failed to get the necessary two-thirds vote required in the Senate, so a joint resolution of annexation, which needed only a simple majority in the House and Senate, was passed. Hawaii became a U.S. territory.

Formal governance over the new territory was now in the hands of the *haoles*. They controlled the way of life of the Islands, living much like feudal lords.

A TERRIBLE BURDEN

"Hawaiians in Hawaii are inescapably a part of the living tissue of Island history. In some respects, it is a terrible burden. We are, to some extent, the walking repositories of island antiquity: living symbols of a way of life long dead, but which strangely persists in shaping the character of life in the fiftieth state."[30]

Remnants of the Hawaiian common people lived scattered over the Islands in isolated places, where they tried to live as their ancestors had, growing taro for poi, fishing, and making tapa cloth. But they were not successful, for the old way of living was of no use to them in the new *haole*-controlled Hawaii. They were little more than reminders of an earlier age. Those who left rural isolation for Honolulu lived there in squalid tenements or makeshift shacks, victims of an aggressive culture with which they had little in common and whose values they did not comprehend.

In the years following annexation, the native Hawaiian population decreased. The Hawaiian infant death-rate was nearly ten times that of the *haoles,* and their crime rate was much higher than that of any other group. Their employment was marginal at best, and their children dropped out of school early. The Hawaiians had become strangers in their own land and very self-conscious of the fact. They were constantly judged by the *haoles* and Orientals who considered them incapable of adjusting to the new culture based on commerce and private property. Many of the Hawaiians accepted this image of themselves as a valid one and so their lives became self-fulfilling prophecies. A few part-Hawaiians, *hapa-haoles,* mainly from the families of the old kings and chiefs, escaped degradation; they were

[30] John Dominis Holt, *On Being Hawaiian.* Honolulu, Hawaii: Star-Bulletin Printing Co., 1964, p. 23.

tolerated by the *haole* ruling class and even encouraged to seek political careers. They became policemen, some even became judges, others started to teach. But they were never able to exercise economic and political power; that was reserved for the *haole* oligarchy.

The Hawaiians' greatest asset was their past which was fast becoming only a romantic legend. But their past held them back, kept them from becoming even part-American. In politics, for example, they still looked to their chiefs to tell them how to vote and what political party to join.

The descendants of the monarchs and chiefs were in an uncomfortable position also. They were tolerated by *haoles,* but were never permitted to enter *haole* society. Yet they were also cut off from the *maka'ainana,* whose behavior often embarrassed them. So they turned to the past and embellished it with qualities it never had. Meanwhile, underneath their surface politeness to *haoles* lurked a real hostility to whites, one of the few things they shared with common Hawaiians.

"*Nana I Ka Ili*" ("Look for the skin"), the old Hawaiians would admonish their young, warning them not to trust the *haoles*. The upper strata of Hawaiians, descendants of the kings and chiefs, were given good reason to heed that warning. Two leaders of the Hawaiians, Prince Jonah Kuhio and John Wise, were able to get the legislature to set aside public lands on which Hawaiians could work and live. But the lands turned out to be useless for agriculture—or anything else. The result was that in some homestead areas so little could be done with the land the Hawaiians fell into idleness; in other places, Hawaiians still unable to cope with the concept of private property leased out their lands to the more aggressive Orientals and *haoles*.

Hawaiians today occupy the bottom rung of the Islands' social ladder. The *haoles* make up the largest group, the Hawaiians the lowest. Five-sixths of the total Island population lives on Oahu, but not a single full-blooded Hawaiian male can be found there in a professional or managerial position. To this day Hawaiians remain a source of cheap labor, working as menials in the hotels and tourist trades.

Recently, a few native Hawaiians, joined by some of Japanese and Chinese ancestry, have begun to think of themselves as members of the Third World and have organized a Third World Liberation Front at the University of Hawaii. These young Hawaiians are seeking to know their past and they openly express their resentment of *haoles*. "I hate all *haoles,*" said a half-Oriental Hawaiian of seventeen. "I resent everything the *haoles* have done since Captain Cook arrived," said a full-blooded Hawaiian co-ed at the University of Hawaii. "They have ruined everything we had."

Other Hawaiians, less educated and less concerned with the past, amuse themselves by watching fat midwestern insurance salesmen trying to wiggle their hips in the hula. Their remarks to tourists are increasingly bitter, but they are still far from being arrogant or truly proud.

Many years ago old Hawaiians prayed that Madam Pele, the powerful goddess of fire who lives in the volcano on Big Island (the island of Hawaii), would come alive again and destroy the *haoles* in her molten lava.

When Pele finally spoke, her eruption wiped out the native Hawaiians who lived below her volcano. Since that day, *haoles* have done to Pele's volcano what they succeeded in doing to the Hawaiians—made it, like them, into a successful tourist attraction.

Introduction to Hawaiian Documents

"No big ting" is how most Hawaiians see their own past; for like the Indians, the Hawaiians had no written language when the white man came.

Most Hawaiians are unaware of their national heritage. Earlier Hawaiians learned history through legends and accounts passed from generation to generation by oral historians. But these men vanished along with the culture they had described.

Only a few documents of the past remain, a few word-shards which suggest the bitterness and resentment felt by some of the Hawaiians toward the civilization that replaced their own.

(1)

Captain Cook Encounters the Hawaiians*

Captain Cook noted the kindness and generosity of the Hawaiians, as well as the fact that their notion of private property differed from that of the "civilized" West.

They [the Hawaiians] seem to be blest with a frank, cheerful disposition; and, were I to draw any comparisons, should say, that they are equally free from the fickle levity which distinguishes the natives of Otaheite, and the sedate cast observable amongst many of those of Tongataboo. They seem to live very sociably in their intercourse with one another; and, except for the propensity to thieving, which seems innate in most of the people we have visited in this ocean, they were exceedingly friendly to us. And it does their sensibility no little credit, without flattering ourselves, that when they saw the various articles of our European manufacture, they could not help expressing their surprise, by a mixture of joy and concern, that seemed to apply the case, as a lesson of humility to themselves; and, on all occasions, they appeared deeply impressed with a consciousness of their own inferiority; a behavior which equally exempts their national character from the preposterous pride of the more polished Japanese, and of the ruder Greenlander. It was a pleasure to observe with how much affection the women managed their infants, and how readily the men lent their assistance to such a tender office; thus sufficiently distinguishing themselves from those savages, who esteem a wife and child as things rather necessary, than desirable, or worthy of their notice. . . . In the afternoon, I landed

* James Cook and James King, *A Voyage to the Pacific Ocean,* Vol. II (London: G. Nichol and T. Cadell Publishers, 1785).

again, accompanied by Captain Clerke, with a view to make another excursion up the country. But, before this could be put in execution, the day was too far spent; so that I laid aside my intention for the present; and it so happened, that I had not another opportunity. At sun-set, I brought every body on board; having procured, in the course of the day, nine tons of water; and, by exchanges, chiefly for nails and pieces of iron, about seventy or eighty pigs, a few fowls, a quantity of potatoes, and a few plantains, and *taro* roots. These people merited our best commendations, in this commercial intercourse, never once attempting to cheat us, either ashore, or along-side the ships. Some of them, indeed, as already mentioned, at first, betrayed a thievish disposition; or rather, they thought, that they had a right to every thing they could lay their hands upon; but they soon laid aside a conduct, which, we convinced them, they could not persevere in with impunity. . . .

The civilities of this society were not, however, confined to mere ceremony and parade. Our party on shore received from them, every day, a constant supply of hogs and vegetables, more than sufficient for our subsistance; and several canoes loaded with provisions were sent to the ships with the same punctuality. No return was ever demanded, or even hinted at in the most distant manner. Their presents were made with a regularity, more like the discharge of a religious duty, than the effect of mere liberality; and when we enquired at whose charge all this munificence was displayed, we were told, it was at the expence of a great man called Kaoo, the chief of the priests, and grandfather to Kaireckeca, who was at that time absent attending the king of the island. . . .

While the boats were occupied in examining the coast, we stood on and off with the ships, waiting for their return. About noon, Mr. Williamson came back, and reported, that he had seen a large pond behind a beach near one of the villages, which the natives told him contained fresh water;

and that there was anchoring-ground before it. He also reported, that he had attempted to land in another place, but was prevented by the natives, who, coming down to the boats in great numbers, attempted to take away the oars, muskets, and, in short, every thing that they could lay hold of; and pressed so thick upon him, that he was obliged to fire, by which one man was killed. But this unhappy circumstance I did not know till after we had left the island; so that all my measures were directed as if nothing of the kind had happened. Mr. Williamson told me, that, after the man fell, his countrymen took him up, carried him off, and then retired from the boat; but still they made signals for our people to land, which he declined. It did not appear to Mr. Williamson, that the natives had any design to kill, or even to hurt, any of his party; but they seemed excited by mere curiosity, to get from them what they had, being, at the same time, ready to give, in return, any thing of their own.

(2)

Captain King's Observations*

After many Hawaiians had been murdered by the sailors, Captain Cook himself was killed on shore. His replacement in command of the expedition, Captain James King, described a subsequent incident. Natives had been showering stones upon the ships as the sailors attempted to take on water. After being dispersed once by the ships' guns, the natives resumed their attack.

However, the natives soon after made their appearance again, in their usual mode of attack; and it was now found absolutely necessary to burn down some straggling houses, near the wall, behind which they had taken shelter. In executing these orders, I am sorry to add, that our people were

* James Cook and James King, *A Voyage to the Pacific Ocean,* London: G. Nichol and T. Cadell, 1785, Vol. II.

hurried into acts of unnecessary cruelty and devastation. Something ought certainly to be allowed to their resentment of the repeated insults, and contemptuous behavior, of the islanders, and to the natural desire of revenging the loss of their Commander. But, at the same time, their conduct served strongly to convince me that the utmost precaution is necessary in trusting, though but for a moment, the discretionary use of arms, in the hands of private seamen, or soldiers, on such occasions. The rigor of discipline, and the habits of obedience, by which their force is kept directed to its proper objects, lead them naturally enough to conceive, that whatever they have the power, they have also the right to do.

I have already mentioned, that orders had been given to burn only a few straggling huts, which afforded shelter to the natives. We were therefore a good deal surprized to see the whole village on fire; and before a boat, that was sent to stop the progress of the mischief, could reach the shore, the houses of our old and constant friends, the priests, were all in flames. I cannot enough lament the illness, that confined me on board this day. The priests had always been under my protection; and, unluckily, the officers who were then on duty, having been seldom on shore at the *Morai,* were not much acquainted with the circumstances of the place. Had I been present myself, I might probably have been the means of saving their little society from destruction.

Several of the natives were shot, in making their escape from the flames; and our people cut off the heads of two of them, and brought them on board. The fate of one poor islander was much lamented by us all. As he was coming to the well for water, he was shot at by one of the marines. The ball struck his calibash, which he immediately threw from him and fled. He was pursued into one of the caves I have before described, and no lion could have defended his den with greater courage and fierceness; till at last, after having kept two of our people at bay for a considerable time, he expired, covered with wounds. . . .

On coming on board, [a friendly priest] had seen the heads of his countrymen lying on the deck, at which he was exceedingly shocked, and desired, with great earnestness, that they might be thrown overboard. This request Captain Clerke instantly ordered to be complied with.

In the evening, the watering party returned on board, having met with no farther interruption. We passed a gloomy night, the cries and lamentations we heard on shore being far more dreadful than ever. Our only consolation was the hope that we should have no occasion, in future, for a repetition of such severities.

It is very extraordinary, that, amidst all these disturbances, the women of the island, who were on board, never offered to leave us, nor discovered the smallest apprehensions either for themselves or their friends ashore. So entirely unconcerned did they appear, that some of them, who were on deck when the town was in flames, seemed to admire the fight, and frequently cried out, that it was *maitai,* or very fine.

(3)

A Missionary Describes His Task, 1838*

The missionary influence upon Hawaiian life was deep, but the missionaries worried, continually, about how effectively they were carrying on their work. In this letter, a missionary explains the kind of problems they were encountering among the natives.

. . . The religious aspect of things, not only here but throughout the islands, has been much improved during the year past. Some of those for whom we had hoped better things have already gone back to their former sins and are excluded from Christian fellowship. Such, I believe, has

* "Letter by A. Bishop, a missionary, written in 1838," in Rev. Gulick and Mrs. Orramel Hinckley, *Pilgrims of Hawaii,* p. 161 (Fleming H. Revell Co., 1918).

been more or less the case in all parts of the islands, but we are not taken by surprise. It is no more than what we had expected from the first, and no human foresight or sagacity could have anticipated the persons who should be of the number. This people have much idle time on their hands, which we feel anxious to have employed to some valuable end. It is a most difficult task to teach industry to an idle people. But it is necessary to the promotion of their Christian character. An idle, improvident Christian is a contradiction in terms. And such have ever been the lazy habits of this people that they cannot improve on themselves without the influence and example of those who are willing to persevere in teaching and encouraging them to work. A little labor will suffice to provide a supply of food for their own consumption and, besides this, the wants of nature's children are few. Our Hawaiian Christians find themselves in consequence in possession of much idle time, and their previous habits make it sit easily upon them. They would be glad to hire out at day's work, but there are none to employ them. Their time must therefore be spent in indolence or, what is worse, in exposure to corrupting influences to which their fondness for each other's society peculiarly leads them. To this influence our churches will continue to be exposed until some means of employment can be devised which shall tend to raise them from their poverty and degradation.

(4)

On the Decrease of Population on the Hawaiian Islands, 1839*

David Malo was one of the outstanding native political figures among the people of Hawaii. His analysis of the reasons for the decline of his people was published

* "On the Decrease of Population on the Hawaiian Islands," by David Malo, as translated by L. Andrews in *The Hawaiian Spectator,* Vol. II, No. 2 (April, 1839).

in *The Hawaiian Spectator,* April, 1839. Malo died in 1853 and was buried, at his own request, high up on a mountainside, as far away from the *haoles* as possible.

It is not now certain what were the causes of the increase and diminution of the people in ancient times, for sometimes there were few, and sometimes there were many; but at the present time it is certain that the people are on the decrease.

One reason perhaps why the people ever were diminished in ancient times may be found in the ignorance of the people and the barbarity of the times; for they were not able to manage the affairs of the kingdom, the cultivation of the land, and the comforts of life. The bare subsistence of life was all that occupied their thoughts. They knew nothing of doing kind offices for each other, there were no laws published for the general good or that tended to secure peace and safety among themselves. They yielded, however, implicit obedience to their chiefs; insomuch that if the chiefs sent to have a man killed, he was sure to be killed; if the chiefs did that which was wrong, it was right in the estimation of the people; and if the chiefs did that which was right, it was also right in their opinion; and if the chiefs were disposed to appropriate to themselves the property of others, it was right also.

As a consequence of this, all the people that could, attached themselves to the persons of the chiefs for the sake of getting a living, and became flatterers of the chiefs, and even urged them to possess themselves without reward of all the property of the people; the chiefs freely assented to the proposition, without, however, expressing any thanks to the people. From that time numberless were the people that came into the train of the chiefs; the company of the shiftless and those given to petty mischief, and the lazy, and those given to folly, were the persons that lived with the chiefs, and the chiefs followed their counsel.

When the chiefs saw that they had many people at their

control, they were lifted up with pride and one chief desired to be greater than another. The people also under the chiefs followed in their steps and there arose a strong desire . . . in the minds of the people and the chiefs to take the property of others without their consent, and the desire of fraudulent gain increased greatly in the chiefs and the people. As a consequence of these things, evils innumerable sprang up; among others, war; and that may be considered one cause of the decrease of population; for multitudes were wantonly destroyed in war from ancient times even to the time of Kauikeaouli. . . .

The love of gain was also a great evil, and tended to diminish the number of people, inasmuch as the desire of one toward the property of another leads to robbery; and a vast many were killed by robbers who sought to gain property.

Theft also was a means of destroying them, and many died through stealing. Even the unborn child did not escape, but was put to death; for mothers thinking they should prematurely become old women without having gained property, pierced their unborn children, and thus many a child was destroyed before it was born. Others, from the time of conception to the birth of the child made it their business to extinguish its life. The child was frequently destroyed either because the father had no property, or because the mother feared the father would leave her and seek another wife, or because neither sustained such a relation to the chief as to be supported by him, and in that case the relatives of the parents destroyed the child. On this account, but few women had any desire for children, and many had the contrary desire of not having them, and therefore drank such medicines as would prevent conception, and some absolutely denied themselves the consequences of the marriage state. . . .

Another cause of the diminution of the people was the number of human sacrifices the chiefs made to their false gods. . . .

Another thing that tended to diminish the population was

indolence. Neither men nor women had any desire to work, therefore some lived a lazy, wandering life or attached themselves to those who had property for the sake of sustenance. . . .

But at the present time, it is evident the people are diminishing, if we merely look at the scattered condition of the houses and the solitary state of the lands. The following are some of the causes from my own personal observation.

In the reign of Kamehameha, from the time I was born until I was nine years old, the pestilence visited the Hawaiian islands, and the majority of the people from Hawaii to Niihau, died. From my knowledge and reflection on the subject, the great mortality that prevailed arose from the ignorance of the people at that time, their manner of living, the want of care and nursing when sick; and their ignorance of the proper use of medicine. Therefore multitudes died, who, nevertheless took medicine; many died with famine, many with cold, and more still from the unavoidable evil condition they were in. . . . But from that time to this it is clear that there has been a steady decrease of the people.

The following are some of the things that tended to diminish the people of the islands. The want of skill perhaps in the chiefs to manage the affairs of the kingdom, and seeking the comfort and convenience of the people. In former times, before Kamehameha, the chiefs took great care of their people. That was their appropriate business, to seek the comfort and welfare of the people, for a chief was called great in proportion to the number of his people, for he was a high chief or low chief, according as his people were many or few; wherefore it behooved the chiefs to look well to their people against the time of war.

But from Liholiho's time to the present, the chiefs seem to have left caring for the people. Their attention has been turned more to themselves and their own aggrandisement, and they do not seek the welfare of the people as a nation, and therefore they are more oppressed at the present time than ever they were in ancient times. In ancient times war was an oppressive thing; but the oppression from debt at the present time far exceeds it. The people have been burdened in seeking sandalwood to pay the debts of the chiefs—many have died in the mountains; this continued until the sandalwood was exhausted, but the debts remain unpaid. Even at this present time the chiefs are in debt, and the people are generally seeking for money to pay the chief's debts. In doing so, some perish on the ocean, some are driven from their lands for the want of money, and some give a pile of wood for the want of dollars; thus the property of the people is sold at a sacrifice that they may gain their tax-money and save their lands. Some of the people are now in search of their tax-money, some are collecting fire-wood, some in one way and some in another are seeking to pay the debts of government, but it will not be paid, the greater part will probably remain.

There are also some hardships upon the people of recent occurrence; the frequent punishment of crimes by the sequestration of lands, which are not thus punishable; this is hard upon the people; the frequency of tax gathering—the frequency of fines and other things of a similar nature in vogue at the present day and by which the people are oppressed.

On account of this want of care on the part of the chiefs for the people, some of the people are losing their attachment to the land of their birth; they forsake their places of residence, their kindred, and live here and there where they can find a place. Some, however, follow after the chiefs, or after the people near to the chiefs, but many stand aloof without seeking any land near the residence of the chiefs; and living without land, they are without food, and of these, some are induced to go to foreign countries to obtain a subsistence. This, therefore, becomes a means of decrease in the population; of the many that sail to foreign countries, some become sailors by profession and do not return as inhabitants of the islands, being satisfied with the wages for their labor and the food they receive. Some dwell permanently in the countries to which they go, and some upon other islands.

Some, however, return and are married to young girls who become attached to them, and in this state quickly spend without economy . . . the property they may have acquired, and when it is gone, they go to seek another ship and sail again and leave behind the women they have married. Thus the wives live without their husbands for many years, and when some of them return, it appears that in some foreign port they have become acquainted with other women and are diseased, and returning, infect their own wives with the contagion, and when they perceive their own wives diseased they forsake them again and go to foreign countries. On this account their wives find themselves in straitened circumstances, on account of poverty, and hunger and disease, without any husband to take care of them. Perceiving themselves deserted of their husbands, some become confirmed in licentiousness, and others indulged in other vices and thus are childless.

Another cause of the diminution of the people of the islands is the licentiousness existing between Hawaiian females and certain foreigners who come there without wives. Because of the licentious habits of such foreigners, contracted perhaps in other countries, they came here polluted with a filthy disease, and they have thus polluted with a filthy disease the females of Hawaii. This disease has, moreover, become prevalent among the people, and even children, and all the people of the islands, are miserably diseased; and it is clear, that from the arrival of Captain Cook to the present day, the people have been dying with the venereal disorder. . . .

On account of the magnitude of these evils which have come upon the kingdom, the kingdom is sick—it is reduced to a skeleton, and is near to death; yea, the whole Hawaiian nation is near to a close. . . .

(5)

A Hawaiian Historian's Petition to Kamehameha III, 1845*

This passage is from a book called *The Ruling Chiefs of Hawaii,* by S. M. Kamakau. Kamakau was born in 1815 and died in 1876. He was very active in politics, served in the Legislature, and was also among the outstanding Hawaiian historians. It was said of him that, "Kamakau wrote for Hawaiians and lived at a time still close enough to the old life to have access to firsthand information on the ancient culture, and yet far enough away so that he felt it necessary to explain the disappearing customs to his changing people."

Kamakau has been discussing the reign of the governor of Maui in 1845. This was when King Kamehameha III was ruling the Islands.

There was then a change made in the office of Premier. More *Koai'e* wood panels were cut on Puukapele [the place on Kauai where this wood was found] in order to give the government more oarsmen to paddle. A learned man had arrived with knowledge of the law and the foreigners who were holding office in the government hastened to put him forward by saying how clever and learned he was and what good laws he would make for the Hawaiian people. The truth was, they were laws to change the old laws of the natives of the land and caused them to lick leaves like the dogs, and gnaw bones thrown at the feet of strangers while the strangers became their lords, and the hands and voices of strangers were raised over those of the entire race. The commoners knew this and one and all expressed their

* "Letter from S. M. Kamakau to King Kamehameha III," in S. M. Kamakau, *The Ruling Chiefs of Hawaii* (Honolulu: 1961).

disapproval and asked the king not to place foreigners in the offices of government lest the native race become a footstool for foreigners. Here is one of the letters they sent:

[Addressed to]
King Kamehameha, III
[Sent from]
Lahainaluna, July 22, 1845

A point for discussion: sometime ago your servant [Kauwa] sent for some of [the] old people who had lived in the time of Ka-hekili and of Kamehameha I, and we talked about how the government was administered in their day. The old men said, "In the time of Kamehameha the orators were the only ones who spoke before the ruling chief, those who were learned in the ways spoken by the chiefs who had lived before his day. When the chief asked 'What chief has done evil to the land and what chief good?' then the orators alone were able to relate the deeds of the chiefs of old, those who did good deeds and those who did evil deeds. And the king would try to act as the chiefs acted who did good deeds in the past." Then I said, "Dependence upon those things which were done in the past is at an end; the good which is greatest at this time is that which is good for the foreigner. At the time when the government was taken we were in trouble, and from foreign lands life has been restored to the government." . . . The old men said, "We love devotedly the King, Kamehameha III; but perhaps the kingdom would not have been taken away if we had not lost the good old ways of our ancestors and depended upon the new good ways. That is why a struggle for supremacy has arisen and plots of evil. Perhaps it is not Great Britain alone which has these treacherous thoughts. There may be men living right among us who will devastate the land like the hordes of caterpillars in the fields; they hide themselves among us until the time comes, then they will be on the side of their own land where their ancestors were born. Here is another thing: the king has chosen foreign ministers, foreign agents (*luna*). This is wrong. The Hawaiian people will be debased and foreign exhalted. The Hawaiian people will be trodden underfoot by the foreigners. Perhaps not now, or perhaps it will not be long before we shall see it. . . . Another thing, the dollar has become the government for the commoner and the destitute. It will become a dish of relish and the foreign agents will suck it up. With so many foreign agents the dollar will be lost to the government through the cleverness of foreigners and their cunning, and instead of good coming to the Hawaiian people, strangers will get the benefit from the wealth of the government.

"And therefore we believe that we ought to all stand together against the foreigners holding office in Hawaii. Let chiefs be placed in the vacancies and do not let all of the government positions go to foreigners." "What chiefs are there who will be able to fill the vacancies?" I asked. "There are Lele-io-hoku, Paki, and John Young." I said to them, "Perhaps these men are already at work, or perhaps they are not able to handle the work of the posts given to foreigners. They are puzzling positions for the ignorant. Perhaps the people of Lahaina and Wailuku were mistaken in thinking that the powerful nations agreed to the independence of our government; perhaps they agreed only if we governed intelligently. Who of us knows enough to translate the laws of Great Britain into the language of Hawaii and take the right of the country for the right of this? That is what America did and France and all the independent governments of Europe and the good laws of those governments will become beneficial to Hawaii. Therefore I disapprove of the people's protest against foreign officials since it is the desire of the rulers of Great Britain, France, and the United States of America to educate our government in their way of governing, as I have heard. I understand this to be the command of Her Majesty Queen Victoria who rules the Empire of Great Britain and Ireland, and of King Louis Phillippe who rules France. These rulers believe that the Hawaiian group has a government prepared to administer laws like other governments and that they allow Hawaii to remain independent. We ought therefore not to object to foreign officials if we cannot find chiefs of Hawaii learned enough for the office."

The old people spoke again: "This is an amazing thing! Let us see it with our eyes! The laws of those governments will not do for our government. Those are good laws for them, our laws are for us and are good laws for us, which we have made for ourselves. We are not slaves to serve them. When they talk in their clever way we know very well what is right and what is wrong. Kamehameha was not taught in this school, but his name was famous for good government. We do not believe that Kamehameha would put faith in the skill and cunning of strangers. He depended upon his own skill and judgment and upon that which he found within his own kingdom; he never accepted without question the advice of others or of foreigners. He had some foreigners like the foreign doctor Naea and the captains Barber, George Beckley, and Winship, and there were a great many other honored and clever foreigners living with Kamehameha, but it was never heard that he followed completely the advice of the foreigners and he never made them members of his secret council to discuss good government. It was a British foreigner who advised Kamehameha, 'do not shelter foreigners for they are graspers of land.' Entertaining foreigners therefore is the beginning which will lead to the government's coming into the hands of the foreigner and the Hawaiian people becoming their servants to work for them. And by and by you will see the truth of it. We shall see that the strangers will complain of the natives of Hawaii as stupid, ignorant, good-for-nothing, and say all such evil things of us, and this will embitter the race and degrade it and cause the chiefs to go after the stranger and cast off their own race.

"You are greeting to the King and the chiefs, but we say what we think and what is our opinion."

I place our words before the King and his minister. I am one of the least of his servants who is seeking wisdom.

[signed] S. M. Kamakau

(6)

The Common People Petition Kamehameha III, 1845*

In 1845, a controversy developed between some of the common people of Hawaii and King Kamehameha III, supported by his chiefs. The following documents are the common people's petition, the King's reply, and a second petition sent to the King from another group of citizens on the island of Maui.

A Petition to your gracious Majesty, Kamehameha III, and to all your Chiefs in Council assembled.

To His Majesty Kamehameha III, and the Premier Kekauluohi, and all the Hawaiian chiefs in council assembled; on account of our anxiety, we petition you, the father of the Hawaiian kingdom, and the following is our petition.

1) Concerning the independence of your kingdom.

2) That you dismiss the foreign officers whom you have appointed to be Hawaiian officers.

3) We do not wish foreigners to take the oath of allegiance and become Hawaiian subjects.

4) We do not wish you to sell any more land pertaining to your kingdom to foreigners.

5) We do not wish taxes in a confused obscure manner to be imposed in your kingdom.

6) This is the cause of our wishing to dismiss these foreign officers. On account of difficulties and apprehensions of burdens that will come upon us. There are your chiefs, who may be officers under you, like as their fathers were under your father, Kamehameha I, and good and

* "Petition to King Kamehameha III, June 12, 1845," in *The Friend* (Honolulu: August, 1845).

intelligent men, in whom you have confidence; let these be officers.

Therefore we make known unto your most gracious Majesty, and to the Premier Kekauluohi, and to all the chiefs of the Hawaiian kingdom, some of our thoughts relative to the above named articles.

1) Concerning the independence of the Hawaiian kingdom.

We assure your Majesty, and the Premier Kekauluohi, and the chiefs and all your common people that we understand your kingdom to be independent. You and your chiefs perceived the perilous situation of the Hawaiian kingdom in reference to foreigners. Therefore you sent one of your own men and a foreigner, viz: T. Haalilio and Mr. Richards, respectfully to beseech large independent nations that your nation might be independent. These large nations, viz: the United States, Great Britain, France, and Belgium, have declared your kingdom to be independent. By this distinct expression, that these large nations have declared the independence of the Hawaiian kingdom, therefore it is very clear to us, that it is not proper that any foreigner should come in and be promoted in your kingdom, among your chiefs, and your people. But that it be according to the petition of the ministers, whom you sent to these large nations, praying that the Hawaiian kingdom might be independent by itself.

This is independence; that your gracious Majesty, Kamehameha III be King, and the chiefs of your kingdom be your assistants, and also your own people.

Thus may you and your chiefs act, that your kingdom and all your people may be blessed.

On account of these our thoughts, we petition and beseech you and your chiefs.

We the common people of your kingdom hereby subscribe our names.

[It is said that over 1,600 names were subscribed to this petition.]

Reply of the Council Assembled to the Petition.

July 3, 1845.

To His Majesty and to the Nobles of the Council assembled, and to the delegates of the common people.

This is our reply to the petition of the common people of Lahaina, and Wailuku and Kailua, and it is submitted for your approbation or disapprobation.

1) "Concerning the independence of your kingdom."

This is the meaning of independence—that Kamehameha III be King of the Hawaiian Islands, and there be no other king over him. This is the reason of the independence; Great Britain and France, America and Belgium say that "the Hawaiian government are qualified to transact business with foreigners."

How can they transact business with foreigners? In this way only; let His Majesty select persons skilful like those from other lands to transact business with them.

2) "That you dismiss the foreign officers whom you have chosen to be Hawaiian officers."

If these shall be dismissed, where is there a man who is qualified to transact business with foreigners? There is no one to be found at the present time; hereafter perhaps the young chiefs will be qualified, when they have grown up to manhood, and shall have completed their education.

3) "We do not wish foreigners to take the oath of allegiance and become Hawaiian subjects."

Shall foreigners who become officers take the oath? If not, then they have a chief in another land, and Kamehameha III is not their proper sovereign, and they will not act righteously between the King and their own countrymen. But if they take the oath of allegiance to Kamehameha III, will they not be faithful to him? And will they not cease to have regard for the chief they have forsaken?

Shall other foreigners take the oath of allegiance? This is a land which lies where ships in the Pacific ocean often come. Shall not foreigners come on shore? They do come on shore. Can they not be permitted to live on shore? According to the treaties they can. Who shall be their proper sovereign? Will not difficulties arise between some of them and the Hawaiians? Difficulties will arise, for formerly there were many difficulties, and the land was taken; it was not taken because the government was really in the wrong, but because evil was sought. Here is the difficulty which ruins the government, viz: the complaint of foreign governments followed by the infliction of punishment. Foreigners who take the oath of allegiance can apply to only one sovereign, viz: Kamehameha III; he will adjust their difficulties in a proper manner, and they will render important services to Hawaii, their land.

Some say, let none but good foreigners take the oath of allegiance. How then shall it be with those who are not good? Shall they not live on shore? How can they be driven off? Shall they be put on board another man's ship? If so, the owners will forsake the ship, and the government must pay the damages. Messrs. Bachelot and Short were thus treated, and the result was a fine of $20,000.

Let no one have apprehensions concerning those who take the oath of allegiance. If they conduct properly, then the land is blessed by them. If they transgress, here are laws to punish them, and there is no other nation which will interfere in behalf of wicked foreigners, when we punish them. Here is wherein other nations will favor us; they will not take the part of their people, who transgress our laws, neither will they punish us without a cause, as they did formerly.

4) "We do not wish you to sell any more land pertaining to your kingdom to foreigners."

This is our opinion; it is by no means proper to sell land to aliens, nor is it proper to give them land, for the land belongs to Kamehameha III; there is no chief over him. But we think it is proper to sell land to his Majesty's people, that they may have a home. But if these persons wish to sell their lands again, they cannot sell to aliens, for there is only one sovereign over those who hold lands; but if the people wish to sell to those who have taken the oath of allegiance, they can do so, for Kamehameha III is king over them. If his

Majesty thinks it expedient to sell lands to his own people, is it proper for him to refuse another, who has forsaken the land of his birth, and his first chief, and become a Hawaiian subject? By no means, for this would be using partiality. There has not been much land sold, but foreigners have heretofore occupied lands through favor, without purchasing. It is better to sell. The people have not thought much about purchasing lands; but those who have been to the Columbia River, see the advantage of purchasing land, and they will hereafter wish to purchase lands.

If the common people had petitioned that land should not be sold to sailors, would not the petition be unjust? It is proper to sell small farms to natives and also to foreign subjects, and let them cultivate alike, that the skilful may instruct the ignorant in the work.

5) "We do not wish taxes in a confused obscure manner to be imposed in your kingdom."

That is right, they are not thus imposed. They were so indeed, formerly, to the injury of the common people; but now this matter is regulated by law, and so it will be hereafter should new laws be enacted.

This is our reply to the petition laid before you, with due reverence.

John Young
John II

This reply was corrected and approved by the assembly of chiefs and delegates of the common people in the hall of legislation, on the eighth of July, 1845, with no dissenting voice.

Kamehameha

Concerning Foreigners Taking the Oath of Allegiance. Is it proper for foreigners to take the oath of allegiance? There is perhaps a difference of opinion among foreigners on this subject; but among us, the common people, there is no difference of opinion. If it is proper for foreigners to become chiefs, and the greater part of the wealth of the nation is to become theirs; it is proper for foreigners to take the oath of allegiance under them (i.e., under foreigners) and let the nation become a nation of foreigners. But, if the nation is ours, what good can result from filling the land with foreigners? Let us consider, lest the land pass entirely into the hands of foreigners.

The following are our thoughts:

1) *Good foreigners will become no better by taking the oath of allegiance under our chiefs.* Good people are not opposed to us; they do not evade the laws of the chiefs; they do not wish this kingdom to be sold to others. What good can result from their taking the oath? We do not see any good reason why they should take the oath of allegiance.

2) *Taking the oath of allegiance to this government will be the cause of greatly increasing wicked men in this land.* Foreigners will come in who are covetous, lovers of pleasure and skilful in deeds of wickedness, they will at once take the oath for their own personal benefit. If any one wishes a good piece of land, or a wife, then he will at once take the oath, that he may immediately obtain his wishes. On account of this taking the oath, many foreigners stop on shore, and many also marry Hawaiian women.

3) *Foreigners taking the oath of allegiance will be the cause of wicked men waxing worse and worse.* Formerly, foreigners could not marry till they had lived on shore two years. Now, they take the oath and marry immediately the women whom they entice. Some foreigners, who have wives in America or England, marry immediately here, not having heard that they have wives in another land. Instances of this kind have occurred here at Lahaina. It is our opinion that wicked men taking the oath of allegiance with no delay, will be immediately detrimental to this kingdom.

4) *It is not to benefit his people, but for their own personal interests that foreigners suddenly take the oath of allegiance to this government.* Who are they who take the oath suddenly? These are the persons. Those who want a building spot, or a large piece of land for themselves; those who wish to become chiefs, or head men upon the lands,

and those who wish to marry wives immediately. These are the persons who are quick to take the oath of allegiance under this government. Do they desire this people to become enlightened? It is not clear to us that they do. If any one of us become assistants of the chiefs, his pay for the most part is in goods; the most of the dollars are for the foreign chiefs. The following is what schoolteachers get for their services, property which cannot be sold for cash, that which it is very difficult to dispose of; but property which can be converted into cash is forbidden unto us. From whence this regulation? From the foreign chiefs, not from Kauikeauli, for he desires us to be properly remunerated.

5) *What is to be the result of so many foreigners taking the oath of allegiance?* This is it, in our opinion; this kingdom will pass into their hands, and that too very soon.

Foreigners come on shore with cash, ready to purchase land; but we have not the means to purchase lands; the native is disabled like one who has long been afflicted with a disease upon his back. We have lived under the chiefs, thinking to do whatever they desired, but not according as we thought; hence we are not prepared to compete with foreigners. If you, the chiefs, decide immediately to sell land to foreigners, we shall immediately be overcome. If a large number of foreigners dwell in this kingdom, some kingdom will increase in strength upon these islands; but our happiness will not increase; we, to whom the land has belonged from the beginning, shall all dwindle away. If we had not been loitering around after the chiefs, thinking to accustom ourselves to that mode of life, then perhaps we should be prepared to compete with foreigners. But now, where are our oxen and carts, plows and shovels, and other tools for cultivating the soil? In years which have past, we desired to pasture cattle, that we might have some property, but the most of us were forbidden to pasture cattle; therefore we have no cattle, nor any thing with which to purchase cattle. And now the chiefs are admitting foreigners into the country to possess the good lands of Hawaii, and to deprive us of the same, with the exception perhaps of our small cultivated patches.

Foreigners will say to us perhaps, purchase according to your ability to purchase and husband well.

Very well; but why are we poor at this time? Because we have been subject to the ancient laws, till within these few years. Is it proper at this crisis that we should be turned in with wealthy foreigners to purchase ourselves lands? That is equivalent to the land with the life of the kingdom passing into the possession of foreigners.

If this kingdom had passed into the possession of the British, then we should have mourned with regret and love for the chiefs, who had been made destitute. But if the kingdom is now given to foreigners on account of their intrigue, who will pity us? The former would have been our guiltless misfortune; the latter is our mistaken policy.

Our King and Sovereign Kamehameha, have compassion upon us, and deliver your people from this approaching perilous condition, if many foreigners shall be introduced into this kingdom. If the introduction of foreigners into this kingdom could be deferred for ten years perhaps, and we could have places given us suitable for cultivation and pasturing cattle, by that time some of our embarrassments might be removed, and it might be proper to introduce foreigners into the kingdom.

But if many foreigners are introduced into the kingdom at this time, this will be our end; we shall become the servants of foreigners.

Love to you our Sovereign; our concluding remarks are recorded in Esther, IV: 13, 14. "Think not with thyself that thou shalt escape in the king's house more than all the Jews. For if thou altogether holdest thy peace at this time, then shall these enlargements and deliverance arise to the Jews from another place, but thou and thy father's house shall be destroyed; and who knoweth whether thou art come to the kingdom for such a time as this?"

From us whose names are here subscribed;—Mt Kenui,

Tiona, Nawaakoa, Kilipina, Paele, Hare, Kaialiilii, Nehhmia, Kiha, Bai, Kaia, Kl, Kuaha, Es. Kaua, Nahimalau, Kuameo, Kaheonioniolo, Laukua.

Lahaina, Maui, June 12, 1845.

(7)

The Journal of Prince Alexander Liholiho

Prince Alexander Liholiho, who was scheduled to become king, took a trip to the United States and Europe in 1850. These excerpts from his journal give the young prince's reactions to his treatment by the Americans.

NEW YORK, JUNE 5, 1850

We arrived in this city yesterday afternoon about ten o'clock from Philadelphia. We left Washington on Tuesday morning at nine o'clock. The train was some time getting in to the station.

We bade adieu to our friends in Washington the day before. . . . The next morning, while at the station waiting for the baggage to be checked, Mr. Judd told me to get in and secure seats. While I was sitting looking out of the window, a man came to me and told me to get out of the carriage rather unceremoniously, saying that I was in the wrong carriage. I immediately asked him what he meant. He continued his request, finally he came around by the door and I went out to meet him. Just as he was coming in, somebody whispered a word into his ears—by this time I came up to him, and asked him his reasons for telling me to get out of that carriage. He then told me to keep my seat.

I took hold of his arm, and asked him his reasons, and what right he had in turning me out and talking to me in the way that he did. He replied that he had some reasons, but requested me to keep my seat. And I followed him out, but he took care to be out of my way after that. I found he was the conductor, and probably [had] taken me for somebody's servant, just because I had a darker skin than he had. Confounded fool.

The first time that I ever received such treatment, not in England or France, or anywhere else. But in this country I must be treated like a dog to go and come at an American's bidding. . . .

In England, an African can pay his fare for the cars, and he can sit alongside of Queen Victoria. The Americans talk and they think a great deal of their liberty, and strangers often find that too many liberties are taken of their comfort, just because his hosts are a free people. . . .

(8)

Queen Liliuokalani Pleads Against Annexation, 1898*

Queen Liliuokalani was the last monarch of Hawaii. In 1898, she wrote a book about her native land. In the following excerpts from *Hawaii Story,* she speaks out vigorously against Hawaii's annexation by the United States and attacks the manner in which the annexation policy had been carried out.

. . . will it be thought strange that education and knowledge of the world have enabled us to perceive that as a race we have some special mental and physical requirements not shared by the other races which have come among us? That certain habits and modes of living are better for our health and happiness than others? And that a separate nationality, and a particular form of government, as well as special laws, are at least for the present, best for us? And these things remained to us, until the pitiless and tireless "annexation policy" was effectively backed by the naval power of the United States.

* Queen Liliuokalani, *Hawaii Story by Hawaii's Queen* (Rutland, Vermont & Tokyo, Japan: Charles E. Tuttle Co., 1964).

To other usurpations of authority on the part of those whose love for the institutions of their native land we could understand and forgive we had submitted. We had allowed them virtually to give us a constitution, and control the offices of state. Not without protest, indeed; for the usurpation was unrighteous and caused us much humiliation and distress. But we did not resist it by force. It had not entered into our hearts to believe that these friends and allies from the United States, even with all their foreign affinities, would ever go so far as to absolutely overthrow our form of government, seize our nation by the throat, and pass it over to an alien power . . .

Perhaps there is a kind of right, depending upon the precedents of all ages, and known as the "Right of Conquest," under which robbers and marauders may establish themselves in possession of whatsoever they are strong enough to ravish from their fellows. I will not pretend to decide how far civilization and Christian enlightenment have outlawed it. But we have known for many years that our Island monarchy has relied upon the protection always extended to us by the policy and the assured friendship of the great American republic.

If we have nourished in our bosom those who have sought our ruin, it has been because they were of the people whom we believed to be our dearest friends and allies. If we did not by force resist their final outrage, it was because we could not do so without striking at the military force of the United States. . . .

The conspirators, having actually gained possession of the machinery of government, and the recognition of foreign ministers, refused to surrender their conquest. So it happens that, overawed by the power of the United States to the extent that they can neither themselves throw off the usurpers, nor obtain assistance from other friendly states, the people of the Islands have no voice in determining their future, but are virtually relegated to the condition of the aborigines of the American continent.

Is the American republic of states to degenerate and become a colonizer and a land grabber?

And is this prospect satisfactory to a people who rely upon self-government for their liberties, and whose guarantee of liberty and autonomy to the whole Western Hemisphere, the grand Monroe Doctrine, appealing to the respect and the sense of justice of the masses of every nation on earth, has made any attack upon it practically impossible to the statesmen and rulers of armed empires? There is little question but that the United States could become a successful rival of the European nations in the race for conquest, and could create a vast military and naval power, if such is its ambition. But is such an ambition laudable? Is such a departure from its established principles patriotic or politic . . . ?

(9)

I Regret I Have Hawaiian Blood*

Contrary to the myth that racial harmony prevails in Hawaii, attitudes of racial superiority and inferiority are painfully real and deep-seated. Here, an Islander of mixed Chinese and Hawaiian ancestry expresses his contempt for Hawaiians and his regret that he has Hawaiian blood.

A Hawaiian is always a Hawaiian—no matter how educated he is, he is always a Hawaiian. He never succeeds in business. I don't like Hawaiians. I don't care to have anything to do with them. In business they are just the same. From a business standpoint they are failures. I have no credit for Hawaiians in my book. In business with them I always lose out. They never pay their bills. It's funny, but the Hawaiians never look ahead. It is always just for today

* "Racial Myth and Family Tradition-Worship Among Part-Hawaiians," by Margaret M. Lam, *Social Forces,* Vol. 14, No. 3 (March, 1936).

and that's all they care. If they get a job they do something wrong—embezzle money and things like that and then they go down. You never see a Hawaiian in business. There's only one Hawaiian in this territory who owns a store—he is in Kona, but you don't see any other. If they see another Hawaiian climbing they get jealous and they want to pull him down. I don't know why they are like that. I have wondered myself why they are that way.

I think I waste a lot of my time on my own kind, I mean the Hawaiians. They are not enlightening, not developing, not progressive people. . . . The natives are really not progressive people. All they do is to eat and sleep and play the guitar.

I'm a Hawaiian myself and I hate to say this, but I don't care much for them . . . they are not ambitious people. Their only ambition is to play music. They don't care for anything else. Then you see a Hawaiian does not come to work after a pay-day. Pay-day today and the next day no work. I don't know what they do with their money, but I think they drink a lot. Sometimes he gets drunk on his job or does something wrong and he gets kicked out. . . . It's hard for a Hawaiian to get a job.

I don't like their ways. They are funny. I think they are silly. They don't behave decently on the street. They misbehave. I know when I go out with them I feel funny when they don't behave decently.

I don't care to mingle with them because most of them are not educated. They don't do anything; most of them are loafers and I don't care to go with loafers.

They are so dirty. They eat just like pigs with their hands. Gee, there's one Hawaiian boy who sits right next to me . . . and his feet are full of dirt and mud. Gee! dirty, can't stand it! And over here [pointing to his neck] full of dirt. When I see him like that I turn my back to him.

I hate Hawaiians, oh, I hate Hawaiians! If you treat 'em good they come back and treat you bad. If you do good to them, they do bad to you. They talk about you and tell all kinds of things about you. That's true, I feel this way. If you say something they tell people something you never said. That's how they make trouble. . . . They are jealous people.

I hate Hawaiian! Oh, Hawaiian kind of low. I wish I didn't have any Hawaiian blood. I regret I have Hawaiian blood.

THE CHINESE

"Take away your opium and your missionaries and you will be welcome."

Prince Kung to the Americans
in the late nineteenth century

"Now, why is it that when our people come to your country, instead of being welcomed with respect and kindness, they are, on the contrary, treated with contempt and evil? It happens that many lose their lives at the hands of lawless wretches. Yet, although there are Chinese witnesses of the crime, their testimony is rejected. The result is our abandonment to be murdered and our business to be ruined. . . . Thus we are plunged into numberless uncommiserated wrongs. But the first root of them all is that degradation and contempt of the Chinese as a race . . . which begins with your nation and which you communicate to people of other countries, who carry it to greater lengths. Now, what injury have we Chinese done to your honorable

people that they should thus turn upon us and make us drink the cup of wrong even to its last poisonous dregs?"

Letter sent from a Chinese man
to a Caucasian friend in the 1850s,
San Francisco

Millions of tourists from all over the world would not consider their visit to San Francisco complete without a tour of Chinatown. There they peer into shop windows at the strange foods and herbs on display, buy souvenirs manufactured in Japan, Taiwan, and Hong Kong, and eat at least one meal in a real Chinese restaurant. They stand outside the restaurant, looking in and saying, "Let's go into this one. Lots of Chinamen are eating there, so it must be authentic." Inside the cheaper restaurants, the Chinese waiters are surly and spit out commands while pushing tourists about. In the more expensive restaurants, the waiters are humble and overindulgent. The visitor thinks either place has "real" Chinese flavor.

Amid the din of exploding firecrackers and the cheers of thousands of people, the mayor of San Francisco annually inaugurates the Chinese New Year. City officials stand next to the "mayor" of Chinatown, chosen by the Chinese residents to speak for them to the outside world. Together the Caucasian and Chinese mayors review the colorful, noisy parade as it winds through the jammed narrow streets of Chinatown and downtown San Francisco. After the parade celebrating the Year of the Snake or perhaps the Year of the Horse has ended, the crowds shout "Gun Heh Fat Choy!" (*Happy New Year!*) *and mill about the streets.*

Beginning in the middle of the 1960s, however, new sounds and ugly notes have been creeping into the New Year celebration. Gangs of teenage Chinese boys and girls have been roaming the streets of Chinatown, snatching purses from women tourists and jostling Caucasian men. In 1969 a near riot took place. Seventy Chinese youths were arrested after cherry bombs had been thrown into the crowds and injured several people. The image of the Chi-

nese New Year as a celebration by a peaceful, hardworking people was badly shaken. This image is fostered by those Chinese and Caucasians who have an important economic and emotional stake in the continued existence of Chinatown.

Behind the lure of Chinatown lies a double myth: it is an exotic place conjuring up visions of Dr. Fu Manchu, opium dens, and white slavers; it is also a demonstration of how one group of immigrants has made it in America by being self-sufficient, refusing help from the outside, and bringing up their children properly. "Aren't they adorable?" sigh the tourists, as they look at the little Chinese children who never seem to make the kind of trouble associated with other minority groups. "We no like hippies here," says a Chinese tourist guide in heavily accented English. "Hippies, they live in the Haight and Ashbelly district, not here in Chinatown. We all good boys here." The guides speak perfect English among themselves. But if they had done so with the tourists, the out-of-towners would have been disappointed. After their tours are completed, the guides sit around drinking beer and laughing at the tourists' questions.

The Chinese Six Companies describes itself "as the voice of the entire Chinese community" and is the dominant "establishment" of the Chinatowns all over the country. It clings to the clichés that sustain the tourists' image of the Chinatowns. "The Chinese are known to be an industrious and thrifty people," says a Six Companies bulletin. "Most Chinese use their funds to educate their children, purchase real estate and invest in securities . . . the young Chinese American . . . still is a 'good boy' . . . the reputation of the Chinese community as being law-abiding citizens is a long and honorable one. . . . The Chinese people are not Communists and will never accept Communism. . . . Chinatown is a believer in strict enforcement of fire, safety, building and health laws."[1]

[1] Chinese Consolidated Benevolent Association Fact Finding Committee, "Chinatown, U.S.A. In Transition." October 2, 1967.

Actually, the official views of the Six Companies reflect the attitudes of the Chinese-American elite in the United States. This group has, until recently, dominated life in the Chinatowns all over the country. Its views are reflected in the words of the sixty-five-year-old, American-born, college-educated widow of a prominent San Francisco Chinese businessman:

People do not understand the way we are. They see people living in a small three-room apartment and they think that's awful. They don't understand that many people can afford to move to a larger apartment but it would be considered ostentatious. The life here represents upward mobility for people coming from China—now they have running water and they don't have to go outside to—you know. . . . The life is much better here. They're not unhappy in those apartments.

She pauses a moment. Then glancing down at her expensive jewelry, she continues:

We only spend our money on things which have lasting value, we only place value on what a person is—if he supports the community, if he brings his children up to bring honor to the family. . . . If the child is bad, the parent considers it his own fault for not raising him right. You see, what we do can bring honor to the family or can disgrace the family and we do not want to bring disgrace on the family. . . . We respect people for what they are and for what they can do—if a man is an artist, and he is lazy that's no good, but if he is an artist and he develops this talent, then it is very good—our value system has nothing to do with money and people cannot understand that.

Statistics about Chinatown, however, belie the statements of the Six Companies, and those of the businessman's widow. San Francisco's Chinese have the highest tuberculosis rate in the city and a death rate three times higher than that of whites and Negroes. Their suicide rate is three times higher than the national rate. Unemployment and underemployment rates in Chinatown are among the highest, ranging from one-and-a-half to nearly three times that of the rest of the city. Forty percent of the families in Chinatown have incomes below $4,000 per year.

Recent statistics on juvenile delinquency in the Chinatowns of America explode the myth that the "young Chinese American . . . is a 'good boy.'" In 1960, for example, there were 32 juvenile arrests per 1000 juveniles in the San Francisco Chinatown area, compared to 55 per 1000 for the city as a whole. In 1961 the number had increased to 84 per 1000. By 1965 it had shot up to 282 per 1000, an increase of more than 300 percent. And what is true for San Francisco is true for every other large Chinatown in the country.

The recent influx into the United States of refugee families from Hong Kong accounts, in part, for the sharp increase in delinquency. Teenage refugees do not speak English, have enormous difficulty in finding employment, and are intensely disliked by the native-born Chinese, who consider them ignorant and backward. As a result the newcomers cluster into gangs of their own kind, thus reinforcing their isolation from the American Chinese. However, a significant number of delinquents have turned out to be Chinese-American youths. According to Dr. Sanford Tom, a Chinese-American psychiatrist who was the first to practice in San Francisco's Chinatown, these youths are suffering from "an identity crisis that besets Chinese of all ages but youth in particular." A young Chinese-American describes his dilemma:

> As the young Oriental faces life in America he stands with a strong background of Oriental heritage. He has grown up in surroundings that give him a yellow character and with this background he must adopt the American way. He must take on a completely American character, often moving away from his Oriental heritage. He becomes a white man's yellow man. He may resent the idea of being Oriental. But then he may go in a different direction . . . represented by the immigrants who are so foreign in ideas, they do not change, group together and remain separated from the rest of the community. In the middle of both these groups are those who work and live within the American community, go to church and because of strong Oriental ties look down on inter-racial dating. The major problem here is deciding which way to go.[2]

[2] Statement submitted by David Wayne Louis to the Council of Oriental Organizations, Los Angeles, 1968.

Americans have tended to see and speak of the China-towns as homogeneous entities divorced from American ways of thought and life. But on the contrary, from the very first migration of Chinese to America, a complicated inter-action between the two cultures has led the Chinese-Ameri-cans to assume roles that would best help them survive and prosper in a hostile environment. Fear affected Chinese behavior and attitudes toward whites—fear of the physical violence directed toward all Orientals, fear of exposure of the illegal immigrant status forced on many of them, and fear of racial discrimination. So, until recently, the Six Companies maintained a cloak of secrecy about the com-munity's relationship to whites in an attempt to perpetuate the stereotype of Chinese inscrutability. As long as the Chi-nese were considered inscrutable, it was futile for whites to try to understand their exotic institutions and behavior patterns.

MIGRATION TO GOLD MOUNTAIN

"The Chinese of the present day are grossly superstitious . . . most depraved and vicious: gambling is universal . . . they use pernicious drugs . . . are gross gluttons. . . . The most horrid tortures are used to force confession and the judges are noted for being grossly corrupt; the variety and ingenuity displayed in prolonging the tortures of miserable animals . . . can only be conceived by a people refined in cruelty, blood thirsty and inhuman."

Edmund Roberts in 1837

"They are a people who destroy their own tender offspring; a nation wherein the most infamous crimes are common . . . where the merchant cozens his fellow-citizen and the

stranger; where a knowledge of the language is the remotest boundary of science; where a language and a literature, scarcely adequate to the common purposes of life, have remained for ages unimproved; where the guardians of morals are people without honor or probity; where justice is venal to an extent unexampled on the face of the earth; where the great legislator Confucius, so much revered, is unworthy [of] *perusal, unless we excuse the poverty of his writings in consideration of the ignorance of the times in which he lived; where a chain of beings, from the emperor to the lowest vassal, live by preying upon one another."*

W. S. W. Ruschenberger in 1838[3]

White attitudes toward the Chinese were stereotyped even before the Chinese migration to the United States began. "The Chinese are considered by most persons who have seen them, as very contemptible, however importantly they think of themselves," Thomas Randall wrote from China to Alexander Hamilton. He was detailing Chinese maltreatment of Americans and Europeans.[4] The early American missionaries to China also helped create an unfavorable image of the Chinese before a single one set foot on American shores. Protestants who tried to convert the Chinese reported in their newspapers and pamphlets how young women in China, the "land of darkness," were "lured" into the "gates of hell" where they performed "abominable acts" ending in a "full unchecked torrent of depravity."[5] The first American traders in the Far East made their contribution by passing on to the Americans at home a picture of the Chinese that was, in many respects, as ugly as that presented by the missionaries.

Some American contractors, nevertheless, hoped to import Chinese to the West as a source of cheap labor. "One

[3] Stuart Miller, "The American Trader's Image of China, *1785–1840," Pacific Historical Review*, Vol. XXXVI, No. 4, 1967, pp. 391–92.

[4] Stuart C. Miller, *The Unwelcome Immigrant: The American Image of the Chinese, 1785–1882*. Berkeley and Los Angeles: The University of California Press, 1969, p. 378.

[5] *Ibid.*

of my favorite subjects or projects is to introduce Chinese emigrants to this country," wrote one Californian early in 1848. ". . . Any number of mechanics, agriculturalists and servants can be obtained. They would be willing to sell their services for a certain period to pay their passage across the Pacific. . . ."[6]

The discovery of gold in 1848 created a demand for cheap labor to service the needs of the Forty-Niners. At the end of that year, only seven Chinese were registered as living in California. One year later, there were more than 700. Over the next few years the numbers jumped into the thousands. Initially the Chinese who immigrated to the United States were accepted—despite preconceived bad feelings—because they supplied a needed pool of laborers. "There is no more peaceable set of men in the country than the China boys, nor more industrious," said a California newspaper in 1850.[7] (No matter what their ages, they were called "China boys.") These first immigrants were not crude laborers—the "coolies"[8] who came later and were viewed with contempt—but small landowners and shopkeepers from the provinces around Canton.

The principal spur to the migration was the collapse of the agricultural economy in China in the mid-nineteenth century. The economic collapse, coupled with a population explosion, a disastrous flood, and increased political and social unrest, forced many southeastern Chinese to seek their livelihood abroad. California was seen as a place where fortunes could be made. The first Chinese pioneers in America wrote letters back to China about the possibilities in the new land; some even became agents to bring in more Chinese.

The first Chinese were sojourners, permanent strangers who intended to make their fortunes from the gold boom and then return to China as wealthy men. The sojourner

6 Thomas W. Chinn, ed., *A History of the Chinese in California: A Syllabus.* Published by the Chinese Historical Society of America, in San Francisco, 1969, p. 15.

7 *Daily Alta California,* San Francisco, October 7, 1850.

8 A Sanskrit word meaning "just a laborer or common laborer."

was expected to send money home to support his family and to repay the family or district association that had underwritten his trip. He clung to his cultural heritage and his ethnic group. Those immigrants who had been merchants in China were willing to play whatever economic role was assigned to them in California, wanting only to maintain, even reinforce, strong relations with their families and district associations back in China. The early Chinese migration was predominantly male. In 1880, 71,000 of the 75,000 Chinese in San Francisco were men,[9] many of whom had left wives and children behind.

The initial welcome extended to the Chinese immigrants was based on their willingness to do the menial jobs in the cities, on the farms, and in the gold fields. "Under our laws and with the treatment they will receive here they will be valuable citizens," proclaimed one California publication. "And we shall be pleased to see large additions during the coming years to this class of our population. We congratulate our farmers on the prospect of obtaining that description of labor of which the country is so much in need."[10]

"These celestials make excellent citizens and we are pleased to note their daily arrival in large numbers," said the *Alta California,* a daily newspaper which only a few years later would be denouncing the same celestials in the most violent and intemperate language.

In 1850, during the honeymoon between the Americans and the celestials, the small Chinese community in San Francisco was brought together by the missionaries to receive religious tracts printed in Chinese. After the presentation, they were asked by the mayor to participate in a mock funeral procession for the recently deceased president, Zachary Taylor.[11] A few days later, a letter was sent to the mayor saying: "The China Boys wish to thank you for the kind mark of attention you bestowed upon them. . . . The

[9] The Census of 1880 as cited by Alan S. Wong, *Behind the Gate.* San Francisco: Economic Opportunity Council, 1967, p. 1.
[10] Charles Caldwell Dobie, *San Francisco's Chinatown.* New York & London: D. Appleton-Century Co., Inc., 1936, p. 39.
[11] Thomas W. Chinn, ed., *op. cit.,* p. 9.

China Boys feel proud of the distinction you have shown them and will always endeavor to merit your good opinion and the good opinion of the citizens of their adopted country. . . . Strangers as they are among you, they kindly appreciate the many kindnesses received at your hands, and again beg leave with grateful hearts to thank you. . . ."[12] One commentator pointed out: "In 1852 the Chinamen were allowed to turn out and celebrate the 4th of July and it was considered a happy time. In 1862 they would have been mobbed. In 1872 they would have been burned at the stake."[13]

By 1851 the number of Chinese in California was 2,700. By the end of 1852, because there were as yet no restrictions on immigration, 20,000 Chinese had entered the United States. However, many Chinese were returning home in those years, having made the fortunes they sought on "Gold Mountain" (the Chinese name for California).

Nevertheless, more Chinese arrived than left, since gold fever was not the only motivation for their migration. The crisis in China caused by the Tai Ping Rebellion contributed to the influx all during the 1850s and 1860s.

The Chinese who disembarked at San Francisco, then as now the main port of entry from the Far East, tended to congregate around a few streets in what is now Chinatown. At first they were not as rigidly segregated as they were later in the century. Some lived and worked in other parts of the city. Even so, they tended to gather along one street still called by the older Chinese, *Tong Yan Gai* (the Chinese Street). That street and the area around it was described by a writer of the time:

> . . . The majority of the houses were of Chinese importation, and were stores, stocked with hams, tea, dried fish, dried ducks, and other . . . Chinese eatables, besides copper pots and kettles, fans, shawls, chessmen, and all sorts of curiosities. Suspended over the doors were brilliantly-colored boards, about the size and shape of a headboard over a grave, covered with Chi-

[12] Dobie, *op. cit.*, p. 37.
[13] Richard H. Dillon, *The Hatchet Men*. New York: Coward, McCann Publishing Co., 1962, p. 99.

nese characters, and with several yards of red ribbon streaming from them; while the streets were thronged with . . . Celestials, chattering vociferously as they rushed about from store to store, or standing in groups studying the Chinese bills posted up in the shop windows, which may have been play-bills—for there was a Chinese theatre—or perhaps advertisements informing the public. . . .[14]

To white American citizens, the Chinese on the western frontier were indeed strange. They were thought to be socialists because of their dedication of purpose, their clannishness, their habit of living and working together. Despite the harsh winters, "John Chinaman," as whites called all Chinese, always wore his black pajamas. His long queue or pigtail hung down his back. Chinese walked single file with their feet turned outward. They looked like ducks to some whites.

There were few women on the frontier and the Chinese were willing to do the women's work—washing clothes, mending and sewing, preparing meals. Nothing seemed to bother the industrious Chinese since they did not intend to remain as laborers. In addition, they loaned money on a weekly basis, and their knowledge of roots and herbs gave them a reputation as healers. One of their skills, allegedly, was the ability to cure venereal disease, very prevalent then in the mining areas.

Many whites began to worry that the living stream of strange-looking Chinese seemed to have no end. One account describes how ". . . a living stream of the blue-coated men of Asia, bearing long bamboo poles across their shoulders, from which depend packages of bedding, matting, clothing and things of which we know neither the names nor the uses, pours down the plank. . . ."[15] The sight of all those Chinese pouring off the boats conjured up nightmares in which white America would be overrun by a yellow horde of poor, diseased, filthy, illiterate "coolies." The "coolies" were the lowest class of Chinese, about whom

[14] Thomas W. Chinn, ed., *op. cit.*, p. 10.
[15] Chinn, *op. cit.*, p. 16.

the Americans had heard from white traders in China. (It must be remembered that the first Chinese immigrants had actually been of the educated and merchant classes.)

The Chinese did not come only to the United States. "Coolies" were shipped, under conditions paralleling the horrors of the black slave trade, from China to Cuba and Peru where they were used as laborers on plantations and in the mines. The "coolies," also called "pigs," were collected in China by recruiters called "crimps." They were recruited from among prisoners taken in clan fights, from among people who had been kidnapped, from among people who had acquired heavy gambling losses and could only pay off their debts by selling themselves.

The "pigs" were forced to sign contracts selling their labor for long periods of time. Their contracts were then sold to employers. In some countries these contracts were strictly held to and the Chinese were kept in virtual slavery. In the United States, however, it was very difficult to enforce such contracts.

Most Chinese immigrants came to the United States under the credit-ticket system. Chinese workers who wanted to emigrate to the United States had their passage money advanced to them and were expected to repay the debt out of earnings made in the United States. Credit-ticket companies sprang up in ports of embarkation, like Hong Kong, and were associated with groups in the United States who found work for the Chinese and then collected the passage money from the immigrant workers. In some cases American steamship lines were associated with the credit-ticket system and therefore had a financial stake in filling their ships with as many Chinese passengers as possible. One credit-ticket agreement, made in 1849, provided that the Chinese

> mechanics and laborers, of their own free will, will put to sea, the ship to proceed to *Ka-la-fo-ne-a* and port of *Fuh-lan-sze-ko,* in search of employment for the said mechanics and laborers. . . . On arrival, it is expected that the foreign merchant will search out and recommend employment for the said laborers,

and the money he advances on their account shall be returned when the employment becomes settled. The one hundred and twenty-five dollars passage money, as agreed by us, are to be paid to the said head of the said Hong, who will make arrangements with the employers of the coolies, that a moiety of their wages shall be deducted monthly until the debt is absorbed: after which they will receive their wages in full every month. . . .[16]

Providing Chinese labor for the United States became a thriving trade in the late 1840s and early 1850s. Brokers set up their operations in Hong Kong and supervised shipments of Chinese to America. In a typical contract, skilled workers, such as tailors or cooks, agreed to work for three years at $15.00 per month for an employer selected by the broker. "Coolies," being unskilled workers, were guaranteed only $12.00 per month for the same period. The brokers were paid for their services by the employers.

Certain aspects of this system antagonized and frightened whites on the West Coast who became overtly hostile to the Chinese as a result. The "coolie" trade touched the raw nerves of the Abolitionists; the credit-ticket system infuriated the emerging working class; and an increasing number of southerners, who were becoming influential in the West, brought with them their special brand of contempt for all nonwhites.

Even those whites who tolerated or actually welcomed the Chinese did so only if the Orientals did not compete with whites in the decisive areas of economic and political power. Even to this group, all nonwhites remained, essentially, foreigners (including the native *Californios* who had lived in the state long before the whites arrived).

"If foreigners come, let them till the soil and make roads or do any other work that may suit them, and they may become prosperous," wrote one American, "but the goldmines were preserved by nature for Americans only, who possess noble hearts and are willing to share with their fel-

[16] Agreement between the English Merchant and Chinamen, in Wells Fargo Bank History Room, San Francisco, California.

low men more than any other race of men on earth, but still they do not wish to give all. . . . We will share our interest in the goldmines with none but American citizens."[17]

To make absolutely certain that the mines were preserved for Americans only, four separate and exorbitant monthly taxes were enacted from 1850 to 1856. They were designed to drive the Chinese and Mexicans out of the mines. Furthermore, whites needed no pretext for robbing, beating, and murdering the Chinese and all other "foreigners," and they did so with impunity.

The *Nevada Journal* said about the tax:

There is a species of semi-legalized robbery perpetrated upon the Chinese. . . . Many of the collectors are gentlemen in every sense of the word but there are others who take advantage of their position to extort the last dollar from the poverty-stricken Chinese. They date licenses back, exact pay in some instances for trouble in hunting up the terrified and flying Chinamen, and, by various devices fatten themselves upon the spoils thus obtained. . . .[18]

Another newspaper pointed out that

A foreign-miners tax collector may be a good man, and be honest and lenient, but his commission does not hinder him from being the opposite; it really tends to make him so. He may exercise fiendish cruelty, and plead the necessity of doing his duty. "I was sorry to have to stab the poor fellow but the law makes it necessary to collect the tax; and that's where I get my profit." "He was running away and I shot to stop him. I didn't think it would hit." "I took all the dust he had. There were seven of them besides and they didn't pay me last month."[19]

If the Chinese miners refused to pay the tax, reported one observer, the collectors

. . . struck, stabbed or shot them; perhaps tied them to a tree and whipped them; perhaps drove them on foot with a horse-

[17] From the *Panama Star,* February 24, 1849, as quoted by Ruth E. McKee, *California and Her Less Favored Minorities.* A mimeographed report of the War Relocation Authority, April, 1944.

[18] George F. Seward, *Chinese Immigration in Its Social and Economic Aspects.* New York: Charles Scribner's Sons, Inc., 1881, p. 39.

[19] *Ibid.*

whip, the collector riding behind them, lashing them as they ran to some other town where they could exercise other compulsory measures. A tax collector once related . . . in great glee, how he had to run so many Chinamen on a dark night when the ground was covered with snow, in which they often fell down, he yelling and lashing them from his horse. . . .[20]

In 1862 a joint committee of the California legislature reported that it had been

. . . furnished with a list of eighty-eight Chinamen who are known to have been murdered by white people, eleven of which number are known to have been murdered by collectors of the foreign-miners tax, sworn officers of the law. But two of the murderers have been convicted and hanged. Generally, they have been allowed to escape without the slightest punishment.

The above number of Chinese who have been robbed and murdered, comprise probably a very small proportion of those who have been murdered; but they are all which the records of the different companies or societies . . . show. It is a well known fact that there has been a wholesale system of wrong and outrage practiced upon the Chinese population of this state, which would disgrace the most barbarous nation upon earth.[21]

The brutal physical attacks on the Chinese miners, followed by a general decline in mining employment, and the anti-Chinese sentiment that prevailed during the 1850s and 1860s, cut Chinese immigration from more than 16,000 in 1854 to only 3,300 the next year. For the next decade, immigration continued at the lower rate, and the Chinese population stabilized at about 50,000 people, almost all of whom lived in California.

Then came a new and unprecedented demand for labor. The transcontinental railroads were desperate for workers willing to endure the terrible hardships, the burning desert sun, freezing mountain snows, landslides, back-breaking hours with pick and shovel, and the isolation from cities, for months at a time. And all this for low wages. Few white workers were willing to take on these jobs, and in despera-

[20] *Ibid.*
[21] *Ibid.*, p. 43.

tion the railroad builders turned to the Chinese. Charles Crocker, one of the western railroad tycoons, said

> . . . we could not get sufficient labor to progress with the road as fast as was necessary and felt driven to the experiment of trying Chinese labor. . . . Our force never went much above 800 white laborers, with the shovel and pick, and after pay day it would run down to 600 or 700; then before the next pay day, it would get up to 800 men again, but we could not increase beyond that amount. Then we were compelled to try Chinese labor. . . . They are equal to the best white men. . . . They are very trusty, they are very intelligent and they live up to their contracts.

The efforts of the railroads to recruit Chinese workers directly or through recruiting agents and brokers, met with no opposition from the Chinese Government. Until the middle of the nineteenth century, the government had not been favorably inclined to any large-scale emigration. But then, in 1859, the authorities of Kwantung Province gave foreigners permission to recruit Chinese for work in other countries. In 1860 this action by a local government was ratified by the central government in the Treaty of Peking, which was signed by England and France, and the United States. Finally, in 1868, in the Burlingame Treaty, the Chinese Government recognized the "inherent and inalienable right of man to change his home and allegiance."

The details of the methods used by the railroads to recruit Chinese workers under the terms of the Burlingame Treaty are obscure. Railroad officials maintained that little or no recruiting on a mass scale had taken place in China, but a good many of their records were deliberately destroyed to avoid governmental scrutiny on this point. The railroad builders had a great stake in the importation of Chinese workers in large numbers because not only were the Chinese equal to whites in skills, but they would work for less pay. As Crocker once explained to a newspaper correspondent, "he [himself] devised the scheme of employing, working, and paying them by the wholesale."

The railroads maintained that they paid equal wages to

Chinese laborers. This was generally true; but they usually neglected, however, to add that Chinese workers were forced to pay for their own food and the whites were not. In effect this meant that Chinese workers earned from $10 to $15 a month less than whites for exactly the same work.

Any attempt the Chinese railroad workers made to better their wages or working conditions was quickly suppressed. In 1867, for example, a group of Chinese went out on strike against Charles Crocker's railroad. A newspaper article of the time tells how Crocker

> went to the Summit [Pass] the other day and made a war speech to the Chinamen. The Chinamen told him, "Eight hours a day good for white man; all the same for Chinamen," but he [Crocker] "couldn't see it." He had finally convinced them that "strikes were no good" and all had gone to work upon the old terms. . . .
>
> Question—"Charlie, in your Summit speech did you speak in the Chinese language?"
>
> Says I—John Chinaman[22] no make laws for me; I make laws for Chinaman. You sell for $35 a month, me buy; you sell for $40 and eight hours a day, me no buy."[23]

Crocker was giving the Chinese workers an ultimatum: either they reported for work or be subjected to heavy fines for each day they stayed off the job. In addition, he cut off their food supplies. They reported back to work.

Isolated physically, without much, if any, knowledge of English, completely dependent upon the Chinese boss who acted as their representative and intermediary with the whites, the Chinese workers were incapable, at the time, of responding independently. If they had done so, they would have been smashed.

By the time the railroads had been completed in 1869, from 10,000 to 12,000 Chinese had worked on them. Without the Chinese, the transcontinental lines would not have been built until much later. The Chinese did almost all the dangerous work, sometimes being lowered in baskets from cliff tops to blast away at the sides of gorges, some-

[22] John Chinaman—name for any Chinaman; like "boy" for a black.

[23] Mariposa *Gazette*, July 13, 1867.

times laboring in the freezing cold and living in snow tunnels, sometimes broiling in the furnacelike heat of the desert. The phrase "He hasn't a Chinaman's chance" was coined in this period; it reflected the untold numbers of Chinese who lost their lives in the building of the railroads.

No one bothered to keep records of the experiences of the Chinese workers. Although essential, they were only considered important as they could be used by a variety of groups in the country. The Chinese Associations used them to build their own prestige and wealth; the industrialists used them as a source of cheap labor and as strikebreakers; the newspapers used them to woo readers with lurid stories; and the politicians used them as scapegoats to gain votes, especially after the unions became the most vociferous and demanding of the anti-Chinese groups.

None of this could have happened, of course, except within the context of an emerging, fluid, industrial society that combined dynamic growth with belief in white supremacy. The threat posed by Chinese immigrants to the purity of the white race was assumed to be great. To combat that threat, science developed genetic theories to justify the exclusion of Orientals, and political theorists demonstrated how Asiatics could not be absorbed into the American political structure.

The response of individual Chinese to the increasing hostility was partly conditioned by their concept of themselves as sojourners in a foreign land; they would endure the affronts while pursuing their original aims of amassing capital and returning to China. In addition, because of the disturbed governmental situation at home, they were distrustful of any established authority, especially in a foreign land. Another important consideration in the Chinese response to hostility, was the attitude of the various regional and family Associations to which each Chinese owed allegiance. Because these Associations dealt in illegal goods and services as well as illicit immigration, they were reluctant to call attention to Chinese problems, preferring to handle all problems within their own community.

In addition to the cultural and legal obstacles to resistance, the Chinese were unable to defend themselves; they were outnumbered and were killed if they offered physical resistance. Furthermore, they had no recourse to the legal system for protection of any kind. In 1854 the Supreme Court of California ruled that the Chinese were legally nonwhites and could not testify against whites in court. California law provided that "No black or mulatto person or Indian shall be allowed to give evidence in favor of or against a white man."

The court stated that the "evident intention" of the law "was to throw around the citizen a protection for life and property, which could only be secured by removing him above the corrupting influences of degraded castes." The court also held that even if any legal issue were in doubt, it would make the same decision on the "grounds of public policy"; if the Chinese were allowed the right to testify in court, that "would admit them to all the equal rights of citizenship and we might soon see them at the polls, in the jurybox, upon the bench and in our legislative halls."[24]

The court's ruling intensified the Chinese fear of whites since it made any attack upon them nearly impossible to prove. To make matters worse, the weak government in China, humiliated by the Opium War losses in 1840, made no effort to protect their people overseas. In fact the Chinese Government did not even have a consulate in the United States until the late 1870s. "When the Emperor rules over so many millions, what does he care for a few waifs that have drifted away to a foreign land?" said a high Chinese official in 1858 to an American representative in China.[25]

[24] People v. George W. Hall, 4 Cal. 399. 1854.
[25] Chinn, ed., *op. cit.*, p. 12.

THE CHINESE ORGANIZE THEIR OWN SOCIETY

"Filial piety is the force that continues the purposes and completes the affairs of our forefathers. . . . To gather in the same place where they before us have gathered; to perform the same ceremonies which they before us have performed; to play the same music which they before us have played; to pay respect to those whom they honored; to love those who were dear to them; in fact, to serve those now dead as if they were living, and those now departed as if they were still with us. This is the highest achievement of filial piety."

Confucius[26]

The educated Chinese, the first to come to this country, were shocked by the treatment they received. A Chinese, who described himself as a "republican and a lover of free institutions," pointed out to the Governor of California in 1855,

. . . that when your nation was a wilderness, and the nation from which you sprung *barbarous,* we exercised most of the arts and virtues of civilized life; that we are possessed of a language and literature, and that men skilled in the sciences and the arts are numerous amongst us . . . and that, for centuries, colleges, schools, charitable institutions, asylums, and hospitals, have been as common as in your own land. . . . As far as regards the color and complexion of our race, we are perfectly aware that our population have been a little more tan than yours. . . . As far as the aristocracy of skin is concerned, ours might compare with many of the European races; nor do we consider . . . that the framers of your declaration of rights

[26] Confucius, as quoted in Ch'u Chai and Winberg Chai, *The Changing Society of China.* New York: Mentor Books, 1962, p. 80.

ever suggested the propriety of establishing an aristocracy of skin. . . .[27]

Asing was wrong about the intentions of the framers of the declaration of rights; they most certainly had intended to establish an aristocracy of white skin in which blacks, browns, and yellows were given only servile or subordinate roles.

Despite their difficulties the Chinese maintained their own culture and values and developed their own internal system of governance, which also dealt with the world outside. In December of 1849, for example, three hundred Chinese in San Francisco met in a Chinese restaurant and discussed their mutual problems. At the meeting's conclusion, they passed a resolution expressing their needs:

WHEREAS, it becomes necessary for us, strangers as we are, in a strange land, unacquainted with the language and customs of this, our adopted country, to have some recognized counselor and adviser, to whom we may all appeal, with confidence, for wholesome instruction and advice, in the event of any unforeseen difficulties arising, wherein we should be at a loss as to what course of action it might be necessary for us to pursue; therefore RESOLVED, that a committee of four be appointed to wait upon Selim E. Woodworth, Esq., and request him, in behalf of the Chinese residents of San Francisco, to act in the capacity of arbitrator and adviser for them.[28]

Dealing with the white world through a Caucasian continued for more than a hundred years. Even today, for example, the Six Companies are frequently represented by a white lawyer.

A natural consequence of the situation in which the Chinese found themselves was the formation of Associations in the United States organized on a geographical basis by the districts in China from which the immigrants had come. The Kong Chow Association in California, for example, the first to be established, was made up of all the Cantonese

[27] In a letter from Noman Asing to the *Daily Alta California,* May 5, 1855.

[28] From the *Daily Alta California,* December 10, 1849 as quoted in Dobie, *op. cit.,* p. 32.

from six districts (roughly comparable to American counties) in Kwangtung Province. In 1851, when Kong Chow was created, nearly 10,000 of the 12,000 Chinese of California were from those six districts.

The establishment of Kong Chow was followed by the organization of Associations for people from other areas. There were also subgroups which split off. By 1854 the more than 40,000 Chinese in California were members of Associations based on six geographical areas in China, hence the Six Companies.

Disputes arose, based on clashes of family or clan interests, both strong in the life of China. As a result of these quarrels, the Chinese in America created another set of organizations based on family and clan membership.

With the informal sanction of white officials, the Chinese district Associations and clans began to govern Chinese immigrants living in small groups scattered around the mining areas and in the cities where Chinatown ghettos were beginning to emerge.

The district Association dominated the politics, laws, and internal judicial systems of the Chinatowns; the clan or family Association took care of the general well-being of individual members. But there were no hard-and-fast rules and frequently the functions of the two types of Associations overlapped. Most Chinese belonged to both.

When the Associations began, they were headed by scholars, who were often brought over from China for just that purpose. As the Chinese were forced first from the mines into the urban areas and then into ghettos within the cities, an emerging class of Chinese merchants began to accumulate wealth and power. Within a few years the wealthy merchants, who sold Chinese food and clothing to their countrymen and engaged in importing labor, became the dominant figures in the Associations and clans. By the end of the nineteenth century, they had taken over the presidencies of the Associations.

The Associations performed many functions and most of Chinatown's activity revolved around them. When immigrants arrived in San Francisco, they were met at the boats by representatives of the Six Companies. Space had been arranged for them in Association dormitories and employment found for them with either Chinese or Caucasian employers.

The same journalist who wrote about the living stream of Chinese reported: ". . . as they come down the wharf . . . being recognized through some to us incomprehensible free-masonry of signs by the agents of the Six Companies they are assigned to places on the long broad shedded wharf (to await inspection by the customs officers). . . ." After the customs inspection, ". . . They are turned out of the gates and hurried away towards the Chinese quarters of the city by the agents of the Six Companies. Some go in wagons, more on foot, and the streets leading up that way are lined with them, running in 'Indian file' and carrying their luggage suspended from the ends of the bamboo poles slung across their shoulders."[29]

The role of the Associations in making the arrangements for Chinese workers to come to the United States is ambiguous. They were often accused by anti-Chinese groups of actually participating in the "coolie" trade. They denied the charge. In 1855 a member of one Association gave his version of his group's activity:

> Our house is built throughout of brick. It is surrounded by a brick wall. . . .
>
> In China it is common to have councils, and in foreign lands ui-kans (company halls). The object is to improve the life of our members and to instruct them in principles of benevolence. The buildings are somewhat like American churches. The company furnishes beds, fuel and water to guests who remain but for a short period; also lodging and medicines for the infirm, aged and sick. Means are bestowed upon the latter to enable them to return to China.
>
> There are three agents employed, also a servant who sweeps the house. . . .
>
> Objects for which money collected is expended are: (1) purchase of our buildings; (2) salaries of agents and servants; (3)

[29] Chinn, ed., *op. cit.*, p. 16.

fuel, water, candles and oil; (4) to assist the sick to return home; (5) for bestowment of medicines; (6) for coffins and funeral expenses of the poor; (7) for repairs of tombs; (8) expenses for lawsuits; (9) taxes on house in Sacramento; (10) drayage and outlays for people landing or departing by ship. . . .

Our company has never employed men to work in the mines for their own profit; nor have they ever purchased any slaves or used them here.[30]

Charges were also made against the Associations accusing them of making certain no Chinese immigrant returned to China without first paying off his contract-ticket debt. These allegations were denied by the Associations. They claimed that they collected only "departure fees . . . to help maintain the Six Companies so that it could continue to work for the general good of those brethren who still had their fortunes to make. . . ."[31] But there is much evidence indicating that the Associations did engage in the profitable importing of "coolie" labor.

As part of their work for the general good, the Associations acted as census takers, charging each immigrant one dollar for the "privilege" of being registered; served as an internal court system since the Chinese were barred from the regular judicial system; and set up medical and hospital services for the Chinese because they were not allowed into the regular hospitals. The Associations established Chinese-language schools for their children. They were also responsible for the shipment back to China of the bones of deceased Chinese, a very important aspect of Chinese culture. They witnessed business contracts and ratified trade agreements in the community and between communities.

The Associations policed their own communities since the city police forces did not or, as was often the case, would not. The city police were generally corrupt and undependable as far as the Chinese were concerned. When guards were required to protect Chinese stores and persons from whites, the Associations hired private policemen. Here

[30] William Hoy, *The Chinese Six Companies.* San Francisco: Chinese Consolidated Benevolent Association, 1942, pp. 3–4.

[31] *Ibid.,* p. 24.

is the report of one such guard: "At 8:20 P.M. put a noisy sailor out of the store at Choy Jee Tong. At 10:15 P.M. compelled a white man to pay the barber at the shop, 853 Clay Street. At 11:20 P.M. ordered two soldiers out of Chinatown. Were annoying Chinese pedestrians. At 1:30 A.M. put out of Chinatown a drunken white man who was sleeping on the sidewalk. . . ."[32] The Associations also posted rewards for information about lawbreakers, both Chinese and white, who used violence or destroyed property. The relationships between the Chinese and the police were always difficult, but became more so after the secret societies or *tongs* were created within the Chinese community.

The *tongs* further complicated and divided the internal structure of Chinatown. The clans and *kongsi* (family associations) considered the *tongs* as rivals for political and economic power. Like the clans, the *kongsi,* and the regional and language Associations, the *tongs* originated in China; but unlike them, the *tongs* were often formed by rebels and outcasts, and served as political units opposing state and government control in China.

The origin of the *tongs* has been traced as far back as the tenth century. The most important one for American Chinese was the Triad Society, or Heaven and Earth or Hung League,[33] formed in the eighteenth century[34] for the purpose of restoring the Ming Dynasty to power. However idealistic its origin, by the nineteenth century the Triad was increasing its wealth and power both by forming alliances, at certain times, with rebellious peasants and, at other times, with feudal landlords. The Triad sometimes fought for both sides and then served as mediator. By the mid-nineteenth century, the Triad's supposed devotion to the

[32] *Ibid.,* p. 20.

[33] Stanford M. Lyman, "The Structure of Chinese Society in 19th Century America," an unpublished Ph.D. dissertation, University of California, Berkeley, 1961, p. 224.

[34] The origin of the Triad is disputed. Some scholars trace it back to the ninth century; others trace it to the seventeenth century and some even connect it with freemasonry. See Lyman, *ibid.,* p. 224 fn.

restoration of the Ming Dynasty was seen by revolutionaries as an anachronistic façade for crime. To the Emperor, they were bandits who shall "immediately after seizure and conviction suffer death by being beheaded."[35]

In general the secret societies in China attracted clansmen ostracized from their family or language groups, disappointed office seekers, poor peasants, and political rebels. Gradually the *tongs* gave up their dynastic reform goal.

In the United States, several *tongs* were linked with the Triad Society in China, but the first secret society to be formed here came into being through the efforts of dissatisfied Chinese-Americans.[36] Members of weak clans and of clans divided into factions during the 1850 depression and rebellions, were gradually recruited into the *tongs*. The secret societies in this country, comparable in many ways to the Sicilian Mafia, moved into the illicit goods and service markets in overseas Chinatowns and became serious rivals of the *kongsi*. Immigrants were serviced by the *tongs,* who organized gambling and other vices, and especially prostitution.[37]

Chinese men immigrating to this country without their wives provided a constant market for prostitution, and dealers in women made their profitable business even more so by bringing young Chinese girls into the country as slaves. By 1885 an estimated seventy brothels existed in Chinatown, and trade in women had reached the proportions of a major business. "Girls were sold from the houses as concubines, and sometimes re-sold. . . . Girls were sold as domestic servants for $100 to $500 each and for prostitution purposes for from $1,500 to $3,000 depending on age and appearance."[38] (Reformers like Donaldina

[35] *Ibid.,* p. 226.

[36] Eng Ying Gong and Bruce Grant, *Tong War!* New York: Nicholas L. Brown, 1930, p. 25.

[37] Stewart Culin, "Chinese Secret Societies in the United States," *Journal of American Folklore,* July, 1890, pp. 39–45; and Lyman, *op. cit.,* p. 241.

[38] Lyman, *op. cit.,* p. 332.

Cameron fought against the female slave trade by establishing refuges for young prostitutes.)

The organization of the Chinese communities in America became so complicated that few scholars have been able to unravel the history of conflicts within the community. These internal conflicts took place as the dominant society continued its persecution of the Chinese. When the news of the torrid struggles inevitably came to the attention of the white public, it tended to confirm existing prejudices against the Chinese. Factions had developed within the secret societies, struggles occurred for control of drugs and gambling, and "hatchetmen" of rival *tongs* attacked each other in the fight for domination of the Chinese underworld. The white press viewed the *tong* wars as further evidence of Chinese immorality and reinforced the stereotype of Chinatown by describing it as a place of dark and fetid alleys, spawning opium smokers, prostitutes, "hatchetmen" who struck down their prey from behind with meat cleavers.

The great mass of Chinese were dependent upon the merchants for leadership and as their only voice to the outside world. The merchants, however, whose formal instrument of power was the Six Companies, were concerned with maintaining control over the community. When their control was threatened, as it was by the *tongs,* the merchants tried to solve their problem with a minimum of help from the outside.

Ultimately the Six Companies managed to suppress the *tongs* and eliminate their internecine wars. At one point they asked for Chinese policemen and detectives to patrol the area because they were convinced that crime in Chinatown would never be eradicated by white policemen, who were often on the payrolls of crime lords. That request was greeted with jeers of derision by whites. An editorial cartoon caricatured Chinese detectives over the caption, "You bet me plenty somebody now!! Plenty money—plenty number un—better job lan highbinder."[39]

[39] San Francisco *Examiner,* March 17, 1900, p. 7.

THE YELLOW PERIL

There was a popular belief among whites that the Chinese were dirty and carried germs and disease. "BE CAUTIOUS!" warned a typical food market advertisement in a San Francisco newspaper in the 1880s. "A due respect for a natural prejudice against using MEATS Handled By Chinese and kept in their Unventilated Dens until sold for market use, has decided us to advertise the fact that we SELL NO MEATS that have been handled by CHINAMEN." The Chinese supposedly ate cats and dogs stolen from their neighborhoods and if they ran out of those animals, they ate rats. White slavery and the kidnapping of young white girls for Chinese men were assumed to exist on a large scale.

Such popular beliefs were not limited to the West Coast, although anti-Chinese sentiment was strongest there since most Chinese in the United States lived there. The Chinese had become objects of national phobia. Stuart Miller, in his book *The Unwelcome Immigrant: The American Image of the Chinese, 1785–1882,* clearly refutes the traditional view that hostility toward the Chinese existed exclusively in the West. He claimed that the rest of the country accepted that view because of their fear of the West's growing political power.

In 1854 Horace Greeley's New York *Tribune* inveighed against permitting the Chinese into the country. According to the *Tribune,* "The Chinese are uncivilized, unclean and filthy beyond all conception without any of the higher domestic or social relations; lustful and sensual in their dispositions; every female is a prostitute of the basest order."[40] Only the "Christian races or any of the white

[40] Stuart Miller, *The Unwelcome Immigrant: The American Image of the Chinese, 1785–1882, op. cit.,* p. 169.

races" could assimilate, said Greeley in thundering tones. He approved, as did many other eastern editors, of California's attempt to stop "this flood of ignorant, filthy idolaters."[41]

In 1862 Congress responded to anti-Chinese sentiment by passing a law forbidding American ships to transport "coolies" and declaring that any other Chinese immigrating to the United States must be certified by an American official as a voluntary passenger who understood the conditions of his work contract.

Anti-Chinese sentiment became linked with the slavery issue, thus skewing much of eastern and northern opinion. In 1865 the *New York Times* said:

Now we are utterly opposed to the permission of any extensive emigration of Chinamen or any other Asiatics to any part of the United States. There are other points of national well-being to be considered beside the sudden development of material wealth. The security of its free institutions is more important than the enlargement of its population. The maintenance of an elevated national character is of higher value than mere growth in physical power . . . with Oriental blood will necessarily come Oriental thoughts and the attempt at Oriental social habits. . . . We have four millions of degraded negroes in the South. . . . And if there were to be a floodtide of Chinese population—a population befouled with all the social vices, with no knowledge or appreciation of free institutions or constitutional liberty, with heathenish habits, and heathenish propensities, whose character, and habits, and modes of thought are firmly fixed by the consolidating influence of ages upon ages— we should be prepared to bid farewell to republicanism and democracy.[42]

However, after the emancipation of the slaves, several attempts were made to bring in Chinese as plantation and mill workers in the South. These efforts provided new ammunition for the anti-Chinese forces in the East and West. "Why Are Not the Laws Prohibiting Coolie Importation Enforced By President Grant?" thundered a headline in the New York *World*.[43] The *New York Times* explained that

[41] *Ibid.*, p. 170.
[42] *Ibid.*, p. 172.
[43] *Ibid.*, p. 175.

although the Chinese "are patient and reliable laborers, they have characteristics deeply imbedded which make them undesirable as a part of our permanent population. . . ." The Chinese religion, said the *Times,* "is wholly unlike ours, and they poison and stab. . . . mixing with them on terms of equality would be out of the question."[44]

When the Chinese began to move eastward after 1870 and establish new Chinatowns, their strange ways and customs evoked reactions as hostile as those they had received in the West. Chinatown in New York was described by the *New York Times* as "an abode of idolatry" where young white girls could be seen in opium dens. The owner of one such den answered a question about a girl "with a horrible leer. 'Oh, hard time in New York. Young girl hungry. Plenty come here. Chinamen always have something to eat and she likes white girl, He! He!' "[45]

ATROCITIES COMMITTED AGAINST THE CHINESE

During the 1870s anti-Chinese hysteria mounted, fostered by depression-induced fears that Chinese labor would take over already scarce jobs, particularly in the West. The depression and the rise of the Workingmen's Party on the West Coast turned much attention away from the job of Reconstruction and memories of the Civil War. The Chinese became scapegoats for the economic and social crises of that period on the West Coast. For example, the Chinese constituted one-fourth of California's wage earners, although they made up only one-twelfth of the population.[46]

[44] *Ibid.,* p. 171.
[45] *Ibid.,* p. 184.
[46] Alexander P. Saxton, "The Indispensable Enemy: A Study of the Anti-Chinese Movement in California." Berkeley, Calif., University of California, Unpublished Ph.D. Thesis, 1967.

The Chinese on the West Coast suffered a new wave of violence; the fierce attacks of the 1850s and 1860s were mild compared to the mob assaults and murders of the 1870s.[47] Beating the Chinese was considered a legitimate form of amusement for whites. A letter to the editor of a San Francisco newspaper during this period reports a typical incident:

. . . A party of young scamps—the oldest not more than eleven years—attacked a peaceable Chinaman, without provocation, and beat him in an unmerciful manner. They pulled him down, beat and kicked him, and pelted him with stones till the blood ran out of the wounds. A large crowd stood around at the time, and none of them offered to interfere. One man—elbowing and pushing himself up to where the poor fellow lay—seeing that it was a Chinaman, exclaimed, "O, it's nothing but a Chinaman! Served him right; been a good thing if they had killed him entirely!" When the policeman arrived the boys had decamped; and when he proceeded to lift the Chinaman it was found that he was not able to stand, the poor fellow groaning the while in terrible agony. . . .

In another newspaper was the following report:

ILL-TREATMENT OF CHINESE—Not long ago, a gentleman passing along Kearny street, interfered to save a little Chinese boy from the attacks of a dog, whom half a dozen white-skinned scoundrels were setting upon him, that they might enjoy the precious sight of the agony of the screaming child. That instance of inhumanity is not an isolated case. The *Alta* of yesterday morning says:

"Last evening, at the fire on Dupont street, a crowd of Waverley Place loafers, and thieves, and roughs, who were being kept back from the fire by the police, amused themselves by throwing a Chinawoman down the muddy street, and dragging her back and forth by the hair for some minutes. The poor female heathen was rescued from their clutches at last by officer Saulsbury, and taken to the calaboose for protection. He also arrested one of her assailants, who was pointed out by the woman, but as she could not testify against him he was dismissed on his arrival at the calaboose. The woman then begged an officer to take her to her

[47] Description of a few of these assaults follow; fuller accounts are printed in the Documents section.

husband's house, saying, in piteous accents, 'Do pleasy with me go! So many white mans killy me! Do with me go!' "[48]

In 1871 a quarrel between two Chinese in Los Angeles grew into a race riot in which fifteen Chinese were hung and two others shot by angry whites. Four days later another mob in Los Angeles broke into Chinese warehouses, destroyed their contents, and beat up all the Chinese in the area. Eighteen months later two white Los Angelenos murdered a Chinese man. Six weeks after that a rancher who lived near Los Angeles, believing his Chinese servant had stolen some money, hung him. For this offense, the rancher was fined $20.00. A month later a gang of boys in the City of Angels stoned and killed a Chinese man who was working in his garden. The boy who did the actual killing went to prison for two years. Eighteen months after that killing, a white man murdered a Chinese and was given a seven-year sentence with a recommendation for mercy.[49]

By 1876, Chinese living and working in California mining areas had been driven out, their homes and businesses burned, and many of them killed. A year later, five Chinese farmers in Chico, California, were murdered. A year after that, the entire Chinese population of Truckee was driven from the town.[50]

San Francisco, where the largest number of Chinese lived, was the center of the anti-Chinese spirit on the West Coast. The San Francisco *Bulletin* reported in a typical news story in 1877 that "Last Thursday, a Chinaman who has a washhouse on 16th St. was attacked by a hoodlum who struck him over the eye with a billiard cue. A severe wound was inflicted. The police, from the description of the assailant given by the Chinaman, arrested a hoodlum named Sullivan. But it could not be shown he was the person wanted and he was released."

[48] Charles Loring Brace, *The New West.* New York: G. P. Putnam & Son, 1869, p. 212.

[49] J. G. Sayre, "More Chinese Atrocities," *The Nation,* August 10, 1927.

[50] B. L. Sung, *The Mountain of Gold, The Story of the Chinese in America.* New York: Macmillan Co., 1967, p. 44.

Even if the police had proved that Sullivan was the offender he would not have been arrested because the police, like many other people in the city, were not particularly concerned with protecting the Chinese. "I think they do their duty," a physician told a Senate committee about the police in 1861, "though it is under their oath of office and as a duty, and not because they are anxious to favor the Chinaman at all. I do not think the police as a body are favorable to the Chinese, but they perform their duty according to their oath of office."

Incidents like the one above occurred so regularly they received only perfunctory coverage in the press or none at all. One San Franciscan, who told a Congressional committee, "I have often seen Chinese boys with their heads cut and their faces bloody," went on to describe how white boys would throw rocks and other objects at newly arrived Chinese immigrants as they came off the boats into the city.

Not even the Chinese going to their own hospital were safe. There was a woman with a hoodlum son and vicious dog who lived close to the hospital. She sent them out to attack people coming into the hospital. The doctors ended up treating their patients for dog bites and bruises in addition to their original ailment. Even after patients were admitted to the hospital, they were menaced from the outside; the hospital windows were broken by people throwing rocks through them. Conditions in the hospital were generally very bad.

ANTI-CHINESE LEGISLATION

"The more laws and edicts are imposed, the more thieves and bandits there will be."

Lao Tzu

Some states passed laws prohibiting Chinese immigration, and head taxes were levied against anyone who brought them into the country. In the middle of the nineteenth century, after the state immigration laws were held unconstitutional, California invented another law prohibiting Chinese from coming into the state except when driven ashore by accident or weather. This law was held unconstitutional, but as always in such cases, a few years elapsed between passage of the law and its final disposition by a higher court.

The mood of the California legislature was reflected in a report made to it by the State Board of Health in 1871:

> Better it would be for our country that the hordes of Genghis Khan should overflow the land, and with armed hostility devastate our valley with the sabre and firebrand than that these more pernicious hosts in the garb of friends, should insidiously poison the wellsprings of life, and spreading far and wide, gradually undermine and corrode the vitals of our strength and prosperity. In the former instance, we might oppose the invasion with sword and rifled cannon, but this destructive intrusion enters by invisible approaches. . . .[51]

At the local level, Chinese children were prohibited from attending public schools. Ordinances were passed regulating the amount of "cubic air" required in sleeping quarters, preventing persons from walking on sidewalks if they carried poles on their shoulders, and allowing jailers to cut short the long hair of any prisoner. Any laundry that did not use horses for making deliveries was heavily taxed.

These local ordinances were specifically directed against the Chinese and although some of them were later voided by higher courts, others were upheld. Even when a court did declare an ordinance illegal, a similar one would quickly be passed. After the United States Supreme Court denied the Chinese the right to become naturalized citizens in 1878, the second California Constitution was adopted in 1879. It prohibited the employment of Chinese by any corporation or state, county, or municipal government. (Al-

[51] Dr. Arthur B. Stout, "Report on Chinese Immigration," First Biennial Report, State Board of Health in California. Sacramento: 1870–71, pp. 54–55.

though this constitutional prohibition against corporations' hiring Chinese was soon invalidated by the courts, as late as 1914 no Chinese were employed in any public works in California.)

Anti-Oriental legislative and judicial activity continued through the 1870s and 1880s. On the national level, in 1876, a joint Senate and House Congressional Committee held extensive hearings on the Chinese question and recommended that legislation be enacted to prevent further immigration. In 1879 Congress passed the 15 Passenger Bill which limited Chinese immigrants to fifteen per vessel. The bill was vetoed by President Hayes because, in his judgment, it violated both the Burlingame Treaty[52] and the Constitution.

Undeterred, the opponents of Chinese immigration continued their efforts and in 1880 were successful in getting the Burlingame Treaty modified to give the United States the right to regulate, limit, or even suspend the Treaty regulations; this did not include the right to prohibit immigration. Encouraged, the anti-Oriental forces marshaled their strength for a final push—total exclusion of the Chinese. In California, Governor George Perkins proclaimed March 4th as a legal holiday for anti-Chinese demonstrations throughout the state. His hope was to build up public support for total exclusion.

Finally, on May 6, 1882, Congress passed the first Chinese Exclusion Act prohibiting further immigration of all Chinese except a very few in certain categories. In the minds of the exclusionists, this would save the white race.

> Whereas, in the opinion of the Government of the United States the coming of Chinese laborers to this country endangers the good order of certain localities within the territory thereof: . . . Therefore the coming of Chinese laborers to the United States be . . . suspended. . . . That hereafter no State court or court of the United States shall admit Chinese to citizenship. . . .
>
> That the words "Chinese laborers," wherever used in this act,

[52] Chinn, ed. *op. cit.*, p. 25.

shall be construed to mean both skilled and unskilled laborers and Chinese employed in mining.

This Act and amendments to it remained in effect for sixty-one years. In 1943 President Roosevelt repealed it because of World War II ideology and because China was then our ally.

The passage of the Exclusion Act did not stop the legislative, judicial, and physical assaults on the Chinese, which continued through the 1880s. Full blown anti-Chinese racism was now a necessary part of American political and social activity. In 1885, in Rock Springs, Wyoming, American miners murdered twenty-eight Chinese and burned hundreds of others out of their homes. For an entire month the state of Wyoming was torn apart by anti-Chinese demonstrations.

The state of Washington was aflame with anti-Chinese riots during that same month. In one town Chinese hop pickers were attacked by a gang that left three Chinese dead and three wounded. Four days later a Chinese worker at a nearby mine was choked to death and forty-nine others had all their clothing burned. Another group of Chinese miners in a different town were driven from their work and nine of them injured. Only the arrival of federal troops halted a mass murder of the Chinese in Seattle in November of 1885.

The Chinese in Tacoma, Washington, were not so fortunate. They were driven from that city in very bad weather, packed into box cars with their goods, and shipped to Portland. After they were gone, the Tacoma Chinatown was burned to the ground. In 1887 a group of Chinese miners in Oregon were attacked and five or six of them murdered.

In Idaho, six Chinese were lynched for allegedly participating in the murder of a white merchant and a year later 100 Chinese living near Juneau, Alaska, were attacked by an armed gang and set adrift at sea. In Denver, Colorado, an anti-Chinese riot in 1880 ended with every Chinese home and business destroyed and one Chinese murdered.

These incidents of organized mass brutality committed against groups of Chinese must be multiplied by the hundreds for the cases of individual Chinese who were beaten and robbed by whites, who had no fear of punishment. In nearly every case, those responsible were never tried. If tried, they were almost always acquitted.

THE CHINESE AS PAWNS

Much of the killing, burning, looting, and humiliating of the Chinese was done by the newly formed unions, especially those on the West Coast, in the late nineteenth and early twentieth centuries. The anti-Chinese (and later anti-Japanese) attitudes of the unions have not been exaggerated. Their source has been historically attributed to the unions' fear that Orientals would lower labor standards and be a source of potential strikebreakers. That fear had a factual basis.

Employers favoring Chinese immigration were interested in cheap and available laborers who would work long hours and not go out on strike. The Chinese often worked as strikebreakers since the unions would not accept them and they felt no bonds of class solidarity with the white workers. The Chinese worker's loyalty was to his family, clan, and district.

Employers emphasized over and over again, in testimony before state and congressional committees, their desire to keep their present Chinese employees working and to hire new ones. "The employers of the Chinese laborers invariably agree that they are excellent workmen," reported one writer. ". . . They are always 'on hand' at the time agreed upon, always sober and industrious. Now and then they have a difficulty with their 'native bosses' (who manage their affairs with the American employers) because there is 'too much workee and too little payee,' but this is soon set right, and they prove most trustworthy laborers."[53]

Another employer said he "never knew" the Chinese to strike. ". . . we had the Chinamen long ago and have them still. They have been a preventative against strikes. . . . We have had two or three strikes and we found we were obliged to employ Chinamen in place of those who did strike."[54]

However, one manufacturer insisted that, even though the Chinese did not strike, they were "a little crotchety. . . . They understand how much work they can do and how little they can do in order to give you satisfaction before you will learn how much they are capable of doing. . . . They have the power of combining. If you do not happen to get along with them and have a difficulty with one, the whole lot will stand up for each other and as a general thing go together. . . ."[55]

From the unions' economic point of view, the Chinese posed a legitimate threat. But the intensity of the unions' fear of and hatred for Orientals and the cruel methods they used against them grew out of the national racial prejudice.

As the Chinese moved to eastern cities during the late nineteenth century and got low-paying jobs, the racial venom spread with them. The cigar makers union label on cigar boxes stated: "The cigars herein contained are made by WHITE MEN." The competition for cheap cigars made by low-paid Chinese workers frightened this union into a racism that corresponded to the anti-Chinese sentiments of the public at large.

Trade union anti-Chinese activity maintained its feverish pitch into the twentieth century. The National Labor Union and its political arm, the Greenback Party, the Knights of Labor, and the American Federation of Labor—whatever their philosophical differences—shared the anti-Oriental

[53] Brace, *op. cit.*, p. 218.

[54] United States Congress, *Report of the Joint Special Committee to Investigate Chinese Immigration.* Washington, D.C., February 27, 1877, p. 613.

[55] *Ibid.*, p. 554.

views of Dennis Kearney and Samuel Gompers, founder of the American Federation of Labor.

Kearney, an Irish sailor, had gone broke in a mining venture and had become a street orator in San Francisco. An effective demagogue, Kearney combined attacks on the monopolies, especially the railroads and the politicians under their control, with equally effective attacks on the Chinese. One San Francisco newspaper built him up as the spokesman for the "downtrodden workingman." He organized the California Workingmen's Party, which was anticapitalistic and exclusionistic. One of its slogans was, "The Chinese Must Go!" Any politician seeking office in California had to woo Kearney and his party since the anti-Chinese vote was frequently large enough to be decisive.

The British-born Gompers combined Social Darwinism and exclusionism. He claimed that the "maintenance of the nation depended upon maintenance of racial purity and strength," which could be maintained by excluding "cheap labor that could not be Americanized and could not be taught to render the same intelligent efficient service as was rendered by American workers."[56] He called those sympathetic to Chinese problems "dilettante sentimentalists," "profit-hungry businessmen," or "degenerate politicians" whose object was "to Chineseize the American people."

Gompers co-authored an AFL pamphlet demanding that Asiatics be excluded from the United States by law or "by force of arms," since, among other faults, the Chinese "found it natural to lie, cheat and murder." The pamphlet also claimed that ninety-nine out of every one hundred Chinese are gamblers.[57] Gompers was convinced that after a Chinese laborer finished work, he "joyfully hastens back to his slum and his burrow to the grateful luxury of his

[56] Herbert Hill, "The Racial Practices of Organized Labor—The Age of Gompers and After," in Arthur M. Ross and Herbert Hill, eds., *Employment, Race and Poverty*. New York: Harcourt, Brace & World, 1967, p. 389.

[57] Samuel Gompers and Herman Gutstadt, *Some Reasons for Chinese Exclusion: Meat vs. Rice, American Manhood against Coolieism—Which Shall Survive?, ibid.*, p. 390.

normal surroundings—vice, filth and an atmosphere of horror."[58] According to an AFL convention resolution in 1901, the Chinese were "people of vice and sexual immorality who were incompatible with our moral concepts."[59]

Gompers' fear of the Chinese overshadowed his recognition of their potential as a source of cheap labor. When a proposal to organize Chinese workers was presented to the AFL, Gompers objected, even though several successful local organizing campaigns had actually been carried out among some Chinese. Gompers said:

> I am inclined to believe that it would be unwise and impractical, to unionize a Chinese restaurant. Of course, I realize the desirability of having every establishment possible unionized, and to organize our fellow workers, but you must take under consideration the further fact that the American labor movement has set its face against the Chinese coming to this country, and upon our demands the law has been passed for the exclusion of Chinese from the United States or from any of the territories or possessions of the United States. . . . In other words, the American labor movement stands committed against the Chinese coming to our country or any possession of our country.
>
> It would be the highest of inconsistency of our movement to unionize the Chinese against whom we have declared.[60]

When a group of Mexican and Japanese sugar-beet workers applied for a charter from the AFL, Gompers showed that he was equally prejudiced toward all Orientals and refused to issue it unless the Mexicans split from the Japanese.[61] The Mexicans refused.

Continued union refusal to organize or admit Orientals meant that Oriental workers remained a threat to the wage scale and working standards of the unionized workers. And as always the Chinese were available as strikebreakers. Consequently the unions terrorized the Chinese.

[58] *Ibid.*, p. 390.

[59] Resolutions Committee of the American Federation of Labor Convention of 1901; *ibid.*, p. 389.

[60] *Ibid.*, p. 391.

[61] *Ibid.*, p. 391.

In 1887, for example, a year especially filled with danger and tension for the Chinese, a mass meeting of the Workingmen's Party ended with "two hundred or more hoodlums," to quote one newspaper account, "yelling like murderous Sioux 'On to Chinatown, boys!'" Once in Chinatown the mob threw bricks and stones at the washhouses, breaking the glass windows and gutting the interiors. More than fifteen Chinese washhouses were destroyed that night. Two buildings were set on fire and after the fire engines came "some of the hoodlums cut the hose of the engines so that only a small portion of the water could be thrown upon the fire." All the windows in the Chinese Methodist Mission were broken and a great deal of other damage done in Chinatown before the crowd dispersed.

The Chinese acquired a reputation for not fighting back. One case, cited by a congressional committee, typified their patient response. A Chinese man in the shoe business was walking down a street carrying a bunch of new shoes strung together. A white man cut part of the string holding the shoes so that one shoe fell to the street. The white man then insulted and abused the Chinese, who kept walking without making an attempt to stop his tormentor. A passerby picked up the shoe, chased after its owner, and returned it to him. "Thank you, thank you," said the Chinese politely and continued on his way.

At one time, the Chinese organized a quick and effective resistance when a San Francisco mob threatened to attack Chinatown. A newspaper reported that "Chinamen purchased a very large number of pistols and a good supply of ammunition. . . . The leading Chinese merchants have advised their countrymen to fight to the death if they are attacked and there will be no doubt that the advice will be carried out to the letter should occasion arise."

A European observer reported on what may have been the same incident. "The Chinese, fortified on their hills and armed with hand grenades, awaited the attack at any moment. Somehow the mob sensed that these people, though generally peaceful and timid, would defend themselves to the bitter end."[62]

Another rare instance of resistance involved two San Francisco shoe companies. The companies reneged on an agreement to pay a certain sum of money to Chinese laborers. The "laborers finally armed themselves and attempted settlement by direct action, which led to a bloody fight on Dupont Street," reported the *Daily Alta California*.

The rarity of this kind of direct resistance on the part of the Chinese was due less to a lack of concern about being maltreated and more to a fear of attracting the attention of the hostile white establishment. They feared that those who were illegal immigrants would be detected and deported. Furthermore, they knew that legally they had little hope for justice. Also, not to be discounted was the fact that their political energies were directed only within Chinatown.

Through their Associations the Chinese sought protection from sympathetic whites. The Associations tried to improve the condition of their people by petitioning the authorities, calling for a boycott of white merchants, taking cases to court, offering rewards for information about assailants of Chinese people, and occasionally hiring whites to guard Chinese property.

Short of arming themselves, the Chinese had few means of self-defense. Without the vote, they had no political strength. They were not able to accumulate any sizable amount of economic power outside their own community. Because of restrictions and widespread prejudice, they were forced to function, economically, either in the white world doing menial or dangerous jobs no one else would do or within their own communities selling goods and services to their countrymen. With the exception of some wealthy employers and merchants, who were encouraged by ministers, the Chinese had few protectors in the white community.

Nevertheless, employers of Chinese had an obvious self-

[62] Charles Morley (trans.), "Sienkiewicz on Chinese in California," *California Historical Society Quarterly*, Vol. 34, 1955.

interest in keeping them alive and well. The benevolence they exhibited toward the "industrious China boys" was shared by merchants and shopkeepers everywhere, who appreciated the apparent stability of their communities and the control exercised over them by the Associations.

The churches, especially the Presbyterian, supported the rights of the Chinese. Ministers sought converts among the heathens and so became more familiar with Chinese life than those who only read the newspapers. "As a body in this country, they are a quiet, inoffensive, docile people," was the opinion of one churchman. "There are none among them like the hoodlum element in our lawless boys and young men. There are none who compare to the low, profane, debauched, drunken crowds that infest portions of most American and European cities."

THE SLOT SYSTEM

The slot system came about because of the 1882 Exclusion Act and the 1906 San Francisco earthquake, and led to large-scale illegal immigration. According to the immigration law, persons born in the United States are automatically citizens, as are their children. Under certain circumstances children born abroad of a father who is an American citizen also become citizens.

The fires that followed the San Francisco earthquake destroyed most of the immigration and birth records on file in the city. No one could verify whether an individual Chinese had entered the country legally or illegally or whether he had been born here. So it was possible for a Chinese living in the United States to claim American citizenship, visit China, and then say he had fathered a son there. The son would then be eligible to enter the United States and apply for naturalization and citizenship papers because his father was a U.S. citizen. The Chinese also discovered another trick. By changing his name and paying a fee, a Chinese in China could pretend to be the son of a Chinese-American in the United States, immigrate as a "paper son," and join his "father."

The possibilities of this racket were quickly grasped by the *tongs* and it became a big business. The *tongs* developed the slot system, which meant finding a "slot" for an immigrant in exchange for a fee and an agreement to work for a fixed number of years. In effect the illegal immigrant was an indentured servant. He was at the mercy of the *tong,* since he could be turned over to the immigration authorities at any time if he sought release from his servitude before the *tong* was willing to let him go. So the Chinese community in the United States continued to grow despite the tiny quota of legal immigrants permitted to enter each year under the Exclusion Act.

Fear of discovery and deportation dominated the lives of illegal immigrants and forced them to remain in the Chinatowns where they would be safe. They had to avoid contact with governmental authorities, even helpful ones, because it might lead to a check on their citizenship status. If they were starving, they could not apply for welfare. They could not take jobs outside of Chinatown and if their Chinese employers cheated them out of wages, they could not turn to a government agency for help. Their children, born in the United States, grew up fearful that if the true status of their parents were discovered, they would be deported. They, too, shied away from any conflict with the white society surrounding them.

In addition, since they were denied access to the legal system, the Chinese saw no reason to observe its rules. No Chinese considered it his duty to turn over to the immigration authorities the names of illegal immigrants. Illegality became a way of life within the Chinese community. (This had also been true in China, where the authorities, from the Emperor to local officials, were weak and corrupt, and the Associations and *tongs* often possessed great local power.)

When the Exclusion Act was finally repealed in 1943,

more than 80 percent of the Chinese in the United States were foreign-born. No one knows, even today, how many Chinese now living in this country were illegal immigrants or are the children or grandchildren of illegal immigrants.[63] Since 1959 more than 8,000 confessions of illegal entry have been made to the Immigration Service which promised immunity from prosecution to all those who confessed. Even so, many illegal immigrants have no faith in the promises of the Service and continue to hide their illegal status.

THE PURITY AND SWEETNESS OF OUR NATIONAL WATERS

"The condition of the Chinese question in the Western States and Territories is . . . far from being satisfactory."
Grover Cleveland, Message to Congress, 1885

"The United States ought not to interfere unnecessarily with immigration," former Secretary of State William Seward wrote in 1881, "because in doing so we would depart from principles well established in our national life and because arbitrary interference with natural processes prove, as a rule, unavailing and injurious." Seward's words were not heeded in the 1880s. The ideal of white supremacy was assumed at almost all levels of American society. The white man's first duty was to maintain American racial purity; therefore offenses committed against inferior Orientals were not considered important.

President Grover Cleveland, however, fearing bad relations with the Chinese Government over the abuse of Chinese nationals in America, warned Congress in 1885:

[63] Chinn, *op. cit.*

The recent outbreak in Wyoming Territory, where numbers of unoffending Chinamen, indisputably within the protection of the treaties and the law, were murdered by a mob, and the still more recent threatened outbreak of the same character in Washington Territory, are fresh in the minds of all, and there is apprehension lest the bitterness of feeling against the Mongolian race on the Pacific Slope may find vent in similar lawless demonstrations. All the power of this Government should be exerted to maintain the amplest good faith toward China in the treatment of these men, and the inflexible sternness of the law in bringing the wrong-doers to justice should be insisted upon. . . .

Race prejudice is the chief factor in originating these disturbances, and it exists in a large part of our domain, jeopardizing our domestic peace and the good relationship we strive to maintain with China.

But the racial prejudice to which Cleveland referred proved more potent than the principles which guided Seward. Senator Charles Felton of California expressed the dominant American attitude in 1892 when he called for a cutoff of even the limited number of Chinese permitted to enter the country under the 1882 Exclusion Act. "We would first take care of ourselves," Felton told his fellow Senators, "recognizing that in so doing we are making our 'greatest contribution to the welfare of humanity'. . . . We would not permit the purity and sweetness of our national waters to be contaminated or polluted by the mingling of its pure streams with the impure from any source whatsoever. . . ."

To make certain that the purity and sweetness of our national waters were not contaminated by the yellow hordes, the Immigration Service rigidly enforced the Exclusion Act. One Sunday, in October of 1902, in a public display of power, federal immigration officials, aided by local police, cordoned off the Chinese quarter of Boston. Without warrants or any legal charges whatsoever, they arrested about 250 Chinese, brutally shoved them into wagons, and carried them off like cattle. Their only offense was that they could not produce, on the spot, their certificates of residence. In some cases they were arrested without even being asked for the certificates. The Chinese were then penned up in two rooms so small they all had to stand crushed together from eight in the evening until late the next afternoon when they were released.

Federal officials justified this raid by saying they had reason to believe some Chinese in the Boston area were there illegally and the raid was their way of flushing out the illegal immigrants. The consequence of the raid was that 121 of the Chinese arrested were released without charges and only a handful deported. Because the raid was so public and the behavior of the federal and local officials observed, it aroused some protest in the white community of Massachusetts. Nevertheless, none of the police or immigration officers involved were reprimanded in any way.

The rights of the Chinese were trampled upon and abrogated in proceedings which were hidden from public view. These Star Chamber proceedings, as they were characterized by a United States Supreme Court justice in 1905, deprived the Chinese of due process of law and representation by counsel, denied them the right to trial by jury, and prohibited them from confronting witnesses against them. Little could be done, unfortunately, to change the legal position of the Chinese in the early 1900s, since the procedures used by whites were legal under the terms of the Exclusion Act and Immigration Service regulations.

Now the Chinese Government began to take a much more active interest in what was happening to the Chinese in the United States, especially since its diplomats, merchants, and students were often treated as brutally as the immigrants. One case involved the Chinese military attaché assigned to the Chinese Legation in Washington. While in San Francisco on a temporary assignment, he was stopped one night by a white patrolman who questioned him, struck him, and, with the help of another policeman, severely beat him. The attaché was handcuffed and tied to a fence by his queue until a patrol wagon arrived. He was arrested for assaulting an officer and held for trial until his diplomatic status was revealed. The police department then claimed that the arresting officer had mistaken the diplomat for another Chinese and refused to apologize for the incident or punish the patrolman. The attaché committed suicide because of the humiliation to which he had been subjected.

The Chinese Minister to the United States gave his government's position on the treatment of Chinese in this country in a speech delivered in Chicago in January of 1906:

> More Chinese subjects have been murdered by mobs in the United States during the last twenty-five years than all the Americans who have been murdered in China by similar riots. . . . In every instance where Americans have suffered from mobs, the authorities have made reparations for the losses and rarely has the punishment of death failed to be inflicted upon the guilty offenders. On the other hand, I am sorry to say that I cannot recall a single instance where the penalty of death has been visited on any member of the mobs in the United States guilty of the deaths of the Chinese and in only two instances of mob violence out of many has indemnity been paid by the authorities for the losses sustained by the Chinese.

The Chinese Government's protestations failed, however, to bring about any significant changes in the conditions of Chinese living in the United States or the treatment of Chinese diplomats, merchants, and travelers.

A movement to boycott all American goods in China began during the early 1900s. It was sparked by the same spirit as the Boxer Rebellion. The boycott proved so effective that in January of 1906 the London *Times* reported a 70 percent decrease in American imports into China. Anti-American feeling grew so strong in China that in February of 1906 the Secretary of War asked Congress to appropriate an emergency fund to send troops to China to protect Americans there. The American Government turned down the request, but formally asked the Chinese Government to end the boycott. The Chinese Government did nothing and the boycott continued.

The boycott became so serious a threat to American commercial interests in China that President Theodore Roosevelt sought ways to ease enforcement of the exclusion laws. Roosevelt spoke out sharply on the subject: "We cannot expect China to do us justice unless we do China justice. The chief cause in bringing about the boycott of our goods in China was undoubtedly our attitude towards the Chinese who came to this country. . . ." But Roosevelt's words did not effect a change in American policies or attitudes. An American missionary who had just returned from China reported to the White House that "Any display of generosity will be construed by the Chinese as fear. . . . The firmer we act with China, the more friendly she will become." The missionary's belligerent attitude reflected the dominant one, both in China and the United States.

The boycott in China ended after about a year, although students attempted to carry it on longer. Its effects in America had only been temporary. Roosevelt's order to the Immigration Service to go easy on its enforcement of the exclusion laws was soon forgotten and officials returned to their old ways.

In America a new spirit sprang up for a short period within the Chinese communities. In San Francisco a small group of people formed the Chinese Defense League, which began a more open and active campaign to defend Chinese rights than had been carried on by the Six Companies. The League also began publishing a magazine in English; it did not receive much support from within the community and eventually disappeared.

Meanwhile, Japan emerged as a major power after the Russo-Japanese War, frightening many people in the United States and causing "The Yellow Peril" crusade to increase in size and activity. Part of the frightened response washed back over the already persecuted Chinese. The labor movement, and even socialists like Jack London, warned of the dire consequences that would follow further Oriental immigration. Some United States–born Chinese had thought of assimilating prior to World War I, but the rampant racism and events in China—especially the 1911 Revolution led by Dr. Sun Yat-sen—only renewed their interest in the homeland and revived their sojourner concept.

But during World War I, in which China and the United States were officially allies, a few changes began. The first small steps toward assimilation were made. The first organized moves were made to insure protection of Chinese rights and liberties. The Native Sons of the Golden West, later known as the Chinese American Citizens Alliance, was formed by educated, English-speaking Chinese after the so-called "War to Make the World Safe for Democracy." The main idea of the group was that the Chinese were really "here to stay" and could wage organized legal battles to insure against recurrences of the kind of maltreatment received during the preceding seventy years. In addition, a Veterans of Foreign Wars and an American Legion Post were established by Chinese war veterans. The YMCA, the Optimists, and other mainstream groups sprang up in the Chinatowns in most large American cities.

Nevertheless, the Americanization of educated Chinese after World War I did not erase racial prejudice, or the old stereotyped images of the Chinese, or ease immigration policies. Restrictions on Chinese immigration continued just as they had in the past. In 1911, 1912, 1913, and 1917 the exclusion laws were amended and made even more restrictive. The 1924 Immigration Act was an even more cruel blow to the Chinese; it denied the right of an American-born Chinese man to marry an alien Chinese woman and bring her into the country. In view of the small number of Chinese women in the United States, the passage of the 1924 Act meant condemning many Chinese men to an unmarried status for the rest of their lives.

The impact of these laws on Orientals in the U.S., together with the Alien Land Laws which prohibited them from buying property, was direct and painful. These laws and the manner in which they were carried out also had an impact on the people of Asia, reinforcing their feeling of distrust for Caucasian America. In 1938, historian A. Whitney Griswold analyzed the foreign policy of the United States in the Far East: ". . . the germs of race prejudice had polluted American relations with both China and Japan and had profoundly influenced the development of the Far Eastern policy of the United States."[64]

American literature in the 1920s and 1930s reflected consistent anti-Chinese attitudes. Whether one reads Earl Derr Biggers' Charlie Chan books and encounters the numerous racial slurs expressed by his white characters or Dashiell Hammett's *Dead Yellow Women* or the cheap thrillers about the *tong* wars, one can only conclude that popular prejudices about the Chinese had not shifted significantly since the nineteenth century.

If the Chinese forgot or tried to ignore the reality of their condition, they were reminded of it whenever another raid was made in a Chinatown by the Immigration Service or the local police. During one month in 1925, for example, federal officials, aided by local police, rampaged through the Chinese areas in Cleveland, Chicago, Boston, Philadelphia, New York, and other cities. Thousands of Chinese were arrested without warrants on the streets; they were fired at if they tried to escape; homes were broken into and businesses destroyed—all in the name of the law.

Out West there were more Chinese, especially in San Francisco, but their situation was no better. In the former mining and railroad towns, such deep hostility still existed for the Chinese that few of them lived or worked in those areas. In some places like Great Falls, Montana, a Chinese could not operate a business until World War II. The first such enterprise, a Chinese restaurant for the servicemen at a nearby air base, was boycotted by the laundries, bakeries, dairies, food supply agencies, and the unions. Only pressure from the soldiers who wanted the restaurant saved it.

A class of university-educated Chinese emerged and expanded. Since most of them could not compete successfully with white professionals, they returned to the Chinatowns

[64] A. Whitney Griswold, *Far Eastern Policy of the United States.* New York: Harcourt, Brace & Co., 1958.

and merged with or began to challenge the rule of the old Six Companies. The old oligarchy that had controlled the San Francisco Chinatown and Chinese ghettos elsewhere was finally confronted, after more than eighty years, with the facts of modern American life. The Six Companies, however, continued to claim that it spoke as the unified voice of Chinatown and struggled to preserve the white stereotyped images of the Chinese.

By the middle of World War II, racial attitudes had finally begun to change. Mme. Chiang Kai-shek appeared next to Eleanor Roosevelt in a *Weekly Reader* photograph. Even *Gung Ho,* a Chinese Communist battle cry, became a slogan for crack American commandos. A new stereotype emerged. The Chinese became fiercely democratic, friendly, the natural allies of the United States. The new attitudes, especially after the war, increased the possibilities for those Chinese who wished to assimilate. Opportunities previously closed to Orientals opened up, and most of the exclusion laws and local restrictions were swept aside. After receiving educations, perhaps even Ph.D.s or M.D.s from major universities, they no longer considered themselves as sojourners.

Nevertheless, most Americans still considered Chinese-Americans "Chinks," "Chinamen," or "China Boys." Some of the educated Chinese remained in Chinatown to practice medicine or dentistry or whatever and avoided the white world. Others braved it in suburbia. The vast majority of Chinese still suffered under the racism of white society and the old rigid class structure within the Chinatowns.

American ardor for the Chinese diminished after the Chinese Communists won power in China in 1949. The American Chinese community hastened to demonstrate its patriotism by committing itself, at least verbally, to Chiang Kai-shek, thus opposing the Chinese Communists. The American Chinese were still not sure they were being accepted as equals with white Americans. During the Korean War, for instance, the Chinese communities feared that if the war was extended to mainland China, the Chinese in

America might be interned as the Japanese-Americans had been during World War II.

THE RED GUARD vs. THE SIX COMPANIES

"*. . . the Chinese people have only family and clan solidarity, but they have no national spirit. Therefore even though there are four hundred million people gathered together in one China, in fact they are just a heap of loose sand. . . .*"[65]

"When the enemy comes forward, we withdraw;
"When the enemy withdraws, we go forward.
"When the enemy settles down, we disturb him;
"When the enemy is exhausted, we fight him."

Mao Tse-tung

The lack of resistance on the part of the Chinese and their refusal, until recently, to deal with consistent racial oppression was based on the old sojourner concept. It was also a survival technique. Like the Jews in the Russian Pale, the people in American Chinatowns were primarily concerned with maintaining their historic values and living by and with their historic culture. In their minds these could not be destroyed by adverse laws, prejudice, or even murder of individuals. The ancient Chinese culture has lived on in American Chinatowns for more than one hundred years. During that time the Chinese have mastered all aspects of American life that pertain to their survival and prosperity. They endured the abuses—to resist would have been to dignify the barbarians with a response. In any event it would have only increased the oppression.

[65] Sun Yat-sen, W. T. DeBarry, et al., eds., *Sources of Chinese Tradition*. New York: Columbia University Press, 1960, p. 769.

The early Chinese immigrants never considered themselves residents of America, even if they knew they would die here. Those who ruled the Chinese communities directed their energies into manipulating American officials for the benefit of the Chinese through intrigue, self-deprecation, and other tactics.

Although Chinese individuals fought back and some occasionally organized, they generally made little effort to achieve the rights and privileges guaranteed them by the Constitution or to assimilate. Their orientation in life was to provide for children, family, and clan, in this world and in the next. The family name and honor could not be erased by the murder of one member, or fifty. And despite almost a century of oppression, they proved they could survive and prosper. The merchants, for example, used the white stereotypes of the Chinese and converted them into sources of profit. The abuses inflicted on them strengthened their sense of being Chinese. For some, the abuses inflicted by whites proved Americans were culturally inferior and, in fact, barbaric.

Whites must have noted that the Chinese could survive and prosper in the most hostile of environments, that they could do any job cheaper and better than any white could, and that despite all efforts to the contrary they grew in number. To whites, the Chinatowns were psychologically impregnable; neither physical violence nor discrimination could destroy or weaken them. Whites noted that the "diseased, sneaky, sly, mysterious people" lived in poverty, yet were able to start their own business or send their children to the universities. It was claimed that no matter how low the wage, the Chinese, like the Puritan Americans, could save money.

Other immigrants wanted to assimilate. For them America was an open society in which an immigrant could pursue life, liberty, and the acquisition of property—and succeed within one generation. But the Chinese, by race, culture, and way of life, were not only unassimilable by

American standards; they did not want to assimilate. They wished to use the opportunity of gaining wealth in America for purposes not easily understood by American whites.

The Chinese were so secure in their own values and culture that they did not need American privileges and rights to get the wealth they came for. To the Chinese it did not matter that it might take more than one generation to acquire the wealth; that was irrelevant in the larger scheme of things. The American response to Chinese immigrants affirmed their old-country values and forced the Chinese to accept the traditional Chinese ways as important to their survival.

Like all first-generation immigrants, the Chinese rebuilt the old country in the new. The numerous Associations devoted themselves to preserving the ancient way of life, the foods, the religion, art, and culture. At the same time they absorbed from American technology and business what was necessary for survival and prosperity. The class stratification of the old culture was transplanted to the Chinatowns. But in place of the emperor, the war lords, and the ancient bureaucracy, were rich merchants, professionals, and leaders of the fraternal and secret societies. Sometimes they were the same people. As in ancient China, the American Chinese class system provided for some fluidity; the son of a waiter or laundryman could go to the university, get his professional degree, accumulate wealth and achieve status, and take his place among the ruling elite within the Chinese community.

The exploitation of immigrants by Chinese bosses appeared cruel and inhumane to white reformers, but was justified to Chinese workers. For example, a Chinese boss, no matter how greedy, still spoke the language and met some cultural needs as white employers could not; women were permitted to keep their children in the Chinese sweat shops; food was provided by Chinese restaurant owners. The Chinese bosses understood the old folk ways and myths, thus giving a small but necessary comfort to the immigrant workers.

During the 1960s a perceptible change began to take place in the Chinese communities under the impact of the Civil Rights Movement, the student revolts, and the "war on poverty." The young Chinese have begun to assert themselves, to seek some deeper level of Oriental identity than that espoused by such organizations as the Cathay Post of the American Legion. One group of youths, the Red Guard, have openly identified with the politics of the Chinese mainland; they support the revolution in China and advocate a similar one in the United States.

The emergence of the Red Guard and the Third World Liberation Front during the student revolts of the late 1960s marks a new phase in Chinese politics in the United States. To the dismay of the elders in the Six Companies and the many prosperous merchants and tradesmen, a growing number of Chinese youth are demanding full equality—now—and some kind of retribution for the past. This is something the Chinese in America have always been afraid to do. The youth groups have earned a tough reputation for flaunting the feared Six Companies and exposing the inequities within the Chinese community. To do this is to destroy the old, carefully maintained, stereotyped images. It means the beginning of a new kind of resistance to both the white American establishment and the old Chinatown aristocracy.

What the reaction of the Chinese communities is to the communist revolution remains a mystery to most whites. Only the Red Guard's attitude is revealing. But in 1963, when a Chinese film showing favorable progress and spirit in the New China was shown throughout the United States, Chinese audiences flocked to see it. In many theaters the film ended to thunderous applause, which stopped abruptly as soon as the lights went on.

In case any Chinese in America has forgotten how the Chinese are still regarded by white America, Secretary of Transportation John Volpe provided a living reminder on May 11, 1969. He was the featured speaker at the 100th Anniversary of the completion of the transcontinental railroad. The celebration was attended by representatives of the railroads, various patriotic societies, the Taiwan Consul General of San Francisco, and representatives of Chinese communities throughout the country. The latter group were descendants of the men without whose work the railroads would never have been completed. "Who else but Americans could drill ten tunnels in mountains 30 feet deep in snow?" said Volpe, speaking in a flat, nasal, Bostonian accent. "Who else but Americans could chisel through miles of solid granite? Who else but Americans could have laid ten miles of track in 12 hours?"[66] The painful truth is that none of those Chinese railroad workers were Americans. In fact they were ineligible for citizenship! The older Chinese dignitaries sat silently as Volpe blatantly ignored the role of the Chinese in American history. Philip P. Choy, chairman of the Chinese Historical Society, was deeply injured; his organization had been trying "to correct various incorrect impressions concerning the Chinese and their role in building the West."

For the young Red Guarders such a task seems futile. Their solution to the oppression of the Chinese in America is a revolution directed against both American society and the ruling elite of the Chinatowns. Their allies, as they see them, are the blacks, the *chicanos,* and all colored people inside and outside America. Their models are the Chinese Communists, the Vietnamese, Cubans, all anti-imperialists, and socialist revolutionaries.

But the hills of San Francisco are not the Sierras of Cuba, and the bicycles used as vehicles of struggle in Vietnam would be smashed to bits by the traffic in New York's Chinatown.

A new, amorphous, and still very uneasy movement of young Chinese is emerging, committed to making basic changes in the structures of their communities, but uncertain about how this can be done. Part of their uncertainty is linked to their own ambiguous position, caught as they are

[66] San Francisco *Chronicle,* May 12, 1969.

between the Chinese world of their elders and that of their contemporaries. Many of these young people do not even speak Chinese and flush unhappily when the Chinese waiters snigger at them, calling them "Jook Sing," a term of contempt, as the youth mispronounce the names of the dishes they order in the Chinatown restaurants.

For most of their life, the "Jook Sing" generation has "thought white," believed in being accepted as part of the white world. Only now are increasing numbers of them beginning to question the values of the white world, groping for answers as to how they may relate their Oriental heritage to being Americans. As they search for those answers, clinging together in small clusters on campuses, they are discovering that most Americans only perceive of the Chinese heritage as the Chinatown façade, its food and services.

The young Chinese rebels cannot melt into the great American pot—nor do they want to. They feel that the old world of Chinatown and the new world of America are equally unacceptable. The struggle for self-definition, for a Chinese identity, will bring them into conflict with both structures.

Introduction to Chinese Documents

No ethnic group in America has been more reticent about revealing itself and its reactions to the white world than the Chinese. The Chinese, perhaps out of traditional pride, have been reluctant to tell how they felt about the white barbarians among whom they lived. And they have been equally reluctant to speak with non-Chinese about the internal problems of their communities or what can only be described as the atrocities committed against them in the past by whites.

This reticence has not been shared by the whites—torrents of the most virulent anti-Chinese propaganda were a hallmark of America during the late nineteenth and early twentieth centuries. Here are examples of both the Chinese and white versions of how the Chinese have lived in America.

(1)

Agreement between Atu the Cook and Jacob Leese*

This contract, between Jacob Leese, a California merchant, and Atu, a cook, is typical of the agreements made in the nineteenth century between Chinese workers and their American employers.

ARTICLES OF AGREEMENT made, entered into and concluded this [28th] day of [July,] in the Year of Our Lord, One thousand Eight hundred and [Forty nine] Between [Jacob P. Leese Esq. of Monterey] of the one part and [Atu, chinaman] of the other part, Witness that for the consideration hereinafter contained on the part of the said [Jacob P. Leese Esq] he the said [Atu] doth hereby covenant, promise and agree with, and to the said [Jacob P. Leese Esq] that he the said [Atu] will proceed in and on board of a certain [Brig] or Vessel called the [*Eveline*] whereof [Cooper] is Master now lying in the Harbor of Hongkong, and about to proceed on a voyage to [San Francisco] a Port or Ports, on the West Coast of America, and that he will any where in that Country, for the space or period of [(3) three] Years from the date of his arrival at the Port of destination, work as [a cook] or otherwise to the best of his knowledge and ability, under the orders and directions, of the said [Jacob P. Leese Esq] or any other person holding this Contract. And that he the said [Atu] will keep and provide himself with all the necessary, and proper tools of his trade, and will also find, and provide his own clothing. And that he will not do or assist to do or direct or aid in any manner whatsoever any work or busi-

* "Agreement between Atu the Cook and Jacob Leese," in *Papers of Jacob Leese* (California Historical Society, July 28, 1849).

ness, other than, that ordered or directed by the said [Jacob P. Leese Esq] or any other persons to whom this contract may be transferred. And these presents further witness that in consideration of the covenants herein before contained on the part of the said [Atu]—he the said [Jacob P. Leese Esq] doth hereby for himself his Heirs Executors, and Administrators covenant promise, and agree with, and to the said [Atu—] that he his Survivors or Substitutes shall and will afford to him a passage in the above mentioned Vessel, to the West Coast of America, and shall, and will as soon as he shall have entered upon such work or trade of [a cook] as aforesaid furnish and provide him with lodgings, and suitable provisions, and food for, and during the said space or period of [(3) three Years,] and that the said [Atu] is to be paid for his work at the rate of [($15) Fifteen] Dollars per month payable monthly in the due, and proper fulfillment, and completion of their said agreement, and covenants herein before contained, the said wages to be computed for the period of [(3) three] Years from the date the said [Atu] shall arrive at the Port of destination. And it is hereby agreed by and between the said parties hereto that the said [Atu] shall not receive any wages until, and after the Sum of [Thirty ($30)] Dollars advanced to the said [Atu—] shall have been paid off, and satisfied, and the said [Atu] doth hereby acknowledge the receipt of the said advance so made to him by the said [Jacob P. Leese Esq] And it is hereby further agreed, that in case the said [Jacob P. Leese Esq] or his substitute *not requiring* the services of the said [Atu] at any time during the said period of [(3) three] Years he the said [Jacob P. Leese Esq] or his substitute shall be at liberty to cancell this Contract on giving to said [Atu] One Month's notice, and from and after the expiration of such one Month's notice, this contract shall be null and void.

(2)

To His Excellency Governor Bigler from Noman Asing*

The following letter was published in the *Daily Alta California* of May 5, 1855. Governor Bigler of California was the first governmental official to advocate the exclusion of the Chinese.

TO HIS EXCELLENCY GOV. BIGLER

Sir: I am a Chinaman, a republican, and a lover of free institutions; am much attached to the principles of the government of the United States, and therefore take the liberty of addressing you as the chief of the government of this State. . . . the effect of your late message has been thus far to prejudice the public mind against my people, to enable those who wait the opportunity to hunt them down, and rob them of the rewards of their toil. . . .

I am not much acquainted with your logic, that by excluding population from this State you enhance its wealth. I have always considered that population was wealth; particularly a population of producers, of men who by the labor of their hands or intellect, enrich the warehouses or the granaries of the country with the products of nature and art. You are deeply convinced you say "that to enhance the prosperity and preserve the tranquility of this State, Asiatic immigration must be checked." This, your Excellency, is but one step towards a retrograde movement of the government. . . . It was one of the principal causes of quarrel between you (when colonies) and England; when the latter pressed laws against emigration, you looked for immigration; it came, and immigration made *you what you are*—your nation what it is. It transferred you at once from childhood to manhood and made you great and respectable

* "To His Excellency Gov. Bigler," in *Daily Alta California* (San Francisco: May 5, 1855).

throughout the nations of the earth. I am sure your Excellency cannot, if you would, prevent your being called the descendant of an immigrant, for I am sure you do not boast of being a descendant of the red man. But your further logic is more reprehensible. You argue that this is a republic of a particular race—that the Constitution of the United States admits of no asylum to any other than the pale face. This proposition is false in the extreme, and you know it. The declaration of your independence, and all the acts of your government, your people, and your history are all against you.

It is true, you have degraded the Negro because of your holding him in involuntary servitude, and because for the sake of union in some of your states such was tolerated, and amongst this class you would endeavor to place us; and no doubt it would be pleasing to some would-be freemen to mark the brand of servitude upon us. But we would beg to remind you that when your nation was a wilderness, and the nation from which you sprung *barbarous,* we exercised most of the arts and virtues of civilized life; that we are possessed of a language and a literature, and that men skilled in science and the arts are numerous among us; that the productions of our manufactories, our sail, and workshops, form no small share of the commerce of the world; and that for centuries, colleges, schools, charitable institutions, asylums, and hospitals, have been as common as in your own land. . . . And we beg to remark, that so far as the history of our race in California goes, it stamps with the test of truth the fact that we are not the degraded race you would make us. We came amongst you as mechanics or traders, and following every honorable business of life. You do not find us pursuing occupations of degrading character, except you consider labor degrading, which I am sure you do not; and if our countrymen save the proceeds of their industry from the tavern and the gambling house to spend it on farms or town lots or on their families, surely you will admit that even these are virtues. You say "you desire to see no change in the generous policy of this government as far as regards Europeans." It is out of your power to say, however, in what way or to whom the doctrines of the Constitution shall apply. You have no more right to propose a measure for checking immigration, than you have the right of sending a message to the Legislature on the subject. As far as regards the color and complexion of our race, we are perfectly aware that our population have been a little more tan than yours.

Your Excellency will discover, however, that we are as much allied to the African race and the red man as you are yourself, and that as far as the aristocracy of *skin* is concerned, ours might compare with many of the European races; nor do we consider that your Excellency, as a Democrat, will make us believe that the framers of your declaration of rights ever suggested the propriety of establishing an aristocracy of *skin*. I am a naturalized citizen, your Excellency, of Charleston, South Carolina, and a Christian, too; and so hope you will stand corrected in your assertion "that none of the Asiatic class" as you are pleased to term them, have applied for benefits under our naturalization act. I could point out to you numbers of citizens, all over the whole continent, who have taken advantage of your hospitality and citizenship, and I defy you to say that our race have ever abused that hospitality or forfeited their claim on this or any of the governments of South America, by an infringement on the laws of the countries into which they pass. You find us peculiarly peaceable and orderly. It does not cost your state much for our criminal prosecution. We apply less to your courts for redress, and so far as I know, there are none who are a charge upon the state, as paupers.

You say that "gold, with its talismanic power, has overcome those natural habits of non-intercourse we have exhibited." I ask you, has not gold had the same effect upon your people, and the people of other countries, who have migrated hither? Why, it was gold that filled your country (formerly a desert) with people, filled your harbors with ships and opened our much-coveted trade to the enterprise of your merchants.

You cannot, in the face of facts that stare you in the face, assert that the cupidity of which you speak is ours alone; so that your Excellency will perceive that in this age a change of cupidity would not tell. Thousands of your own citizens come here to dig gold, with the idea of returning as speedily as they can.

We think you are in error, however, in this respect, as many of us, and many more, will acquire a domicile amongst you.

But, for the present, I shall take leave of your Excellency, and shall resume this question upon another occasion which I hope you will take into consideration in a spirit of candor. Your predecessor pursued a different line of conduct towards us, as will appear by reference to his message.

I have the honor to be your Excellency's very obedient servant.

Noman Asing

(3)

Chinese Cannot Testify in California Courts: People v. George W. Hall, 1854*

The Supreme Court of the State of California, in this 1854 decision, refused to allow the testimony of Chinese in court. As a result of this decision, many Chinese were murdered and robbed by whites who knew that they were immune from prosecution for their crimes.

People v. *George Hall*

The People, Respondent, v. George W. Hall, Appellant

Witness—Persons Incompetent—Section 394 of the Civil Practice Act provides: "No Indian or Negro shall be allowed to testify as a witness in any action in which a white person is a party."

Idem.—Section 14 of the Criminal Act provides: "No Black, or Mulatto person, or Indian shall be allowed to give

* People v. George W. Hall, 4 Cal. 399 (1854).

evidence in favor of, or against a White man." *Held,* that the words, Indian, Negro, Black, and White, are generic terms, designating race. That, therefore, Chinese and all other peoples not white, are included in the prohibition from being witnesses against Whites.

Mr. Chief Justice Murray delivered the opinion of the Court. Mr. J. Heydenfeldt concurred.

The Appellant, a free white citizen of this State, was convicted of murder upon the testimony of Chinese witnesses.

The point involved in this case, is the admissibility of such evidence.

The three hundred ninety-fourth section of the Act Concerning Civil Cases, provides that no Indian or Negro shall be allowed to testify as a witness in any action or proceeding in which a White person is a party.

The fourteenth section of the Act of April 16, 1850, regulating Criminal Proceedings, provides that "No Black or Mulatto person, or Indian, shall be allowed to give evidence in favor of, or against a white man."

The true point at which we are anxious to arrive is, the legal significance of the words, "Black, Mulatto, Indian and White person," and whether the Legislature adopted them as generic terms, or intended to limit their application to specific types of the human species. . . .

The words of the Act must be construed in *pari materia.* It will not be disputed that "White" and "Negro" are generic terms, and refer to two of the great types of mankind. If these, as well as the word "Indian," are not to be regarded as generic terms, including the two great races which they were intended to designate, but only specific, and applying to those whites and Negroes who were inhabitants of this continent at the time of the passage of the Act, the most anomalous consequences would ensue. The European white man who comes here would not be shielded from the testimony of the degraded and demoralized caste, while the Negro, fresh from the coast of Africa, or the Indian of Patagonia, the Kanaka, South Sea Islander, or New Hollander, would be admitted, upon their arrival, to testify against white citizens in our courts of law.

To argue such a proposition would be an insult to the good sense of the Legislature.

The evident intention of the Act was to throw around the citizen a protection for life and property, which could only be secured by removing him above the corrupting influences of degraded castes.

It can hardly be supposed that any Legislature would attempt this by excluding domestic Negroes and Indians, who not unfrequently have correct notions of their obligations to society, and turning loose upon the community the more degraded tribes of the same species, who have nothing in common with us, in language, country, or laws.

In using the words "no Black or Mulatto person, or Indian shall be allowed to give evidence for or against a White person," the Legislature, if any intention can be ascribed to it, adopted the most comprehensive terms to embrace every known class or shade of color, as the apparent design was to protect the white person from the influence of all testimony other than that of persons of the same caste. The use of these terms must, by every sound rule of construction, exclude every one who is not of white blood. . . .

The word "White" has a distinct signification, which *ex vi termini,* excludes black, yellow, and all other colors. It will be observed, by reference to the first section of the second Article of the Constitution of the State, that none but white males can become electors. . . . On examination of the constitutional debates, it will be found that not a little difficulty existed in selecting these precise words, which were finally agreed upon as the most comprehensive that could be suggested to exclude all inferior races. . . .

The same rule which would admit them to testify, would admit them to all the equal rights of citizenship, and we might soon see them at the polls, in the jury box, upon the bench, and in our legislative halls.

This is not a speculation which exists in the excited and

over-heated imagination of the patriot and statesman, but it is an actual and present danger.

The anomalous spectacle of the distinct people, living in our community, recognizing no laws of this State, except through necessity, bringing with them their prejudices and national feuds, in which they indulge in open violation of law; whose mendacity is proverbial; a race of people whom nature has marked as inferior, and who are incapable of progress or intellectual development beyond a certain point, as their history has shown; differing in language, opinions, color, and physical conformation; between whom nature has placed an impassable difference, is now presented, and for them is claimed, not only the right to swear away the life of a citizen, but the further privilege of participating with us in administering the affairs of our Government.

For these reasons, we are of the opinion that the testimony was inadmissible.

(4)

"Memorial of the Chinese Six Companies to U. S. Grant, President of the U.S.A."*

Unable to appeal to their own government for help, the Chinese Six Companies wrote to President Ulysses S. Grant to ask for protection against the atrocities then being committed against them. This Memorial recounts the many prejudices held by the whites and the Chinese answers to them. The Chinese even suggest limiting their own immigration as a means of mitigating such prejudices.

* "Memorial of the Chinese Six Companies to U. S. Grant, President of the U.S.A.," in B. E. Lloyd, *Lights and Shades in San Francisco* (San Francisco: A. L. Bancroft & Co., 1876).

TO HIS EXCELLENCY U. S. GRANT, PRESIDENT OF THE UNITED STATES OF AMERICA

Sir: In the absence of any Consular representative, we, the undersigned, in the name and in behalf of the Chinese people now in America, would most respectfully present for your consideration the following statements regarding the subject of Chinese emigration to this country:

We understand that it has always been the settled policy of your honorable Government to welcome emigration to your shores from all countries, without let or hindrance. The Chinese are not the only people who have crossed the ocean to seek a residence in this land. . . .

American steamers, subsidized by your honorable Government, have visited the ports of China, and invited our people to come to this country to find employment and improve their condition. Our people have been coming to this country for the last twenty-five years, but up to the present time there are only 150,000 Chinese in all these United States, 60,000 of whom are in California, and 30,000 in the city of San Francisco.

Our people in this country, for the most part, have been peaceable, law-abiding, and industrious. They performed the largest part of the unskilled labor in the construction of the Central Pacific Railroad, and also of all other railroads on this coast. They have found useful and remunerative employment in all the manufacturing establishments of this coast, in agricultural pursuits, and in family service. While benefiting themselves with the honest reward of their daily toil, they have given satisfaction to their employers and have left all the results of their industry to enrich the State. They have not displaced white laborers from these positions, but have simply multiplied the industrial enterprises of the country.

The Chinese have neither attempted nor desired to interfere with the established order of things in this country, either of politics or religion. They have opened no whiskey saloons for the purpose of dealing out poison and degrading their fellow-men. They have promptly paid their duties, their taxes, their rents, and their debts.

It has often occurred, about the time of the State and general elections, that political agitators have stirred up the minds of the people in hostility to the Chinese, but formerly the hostility has usually subsided after the elections were over.

At the present time an intense excitement and bitter hostility against the Chinese in this land, and against further Chinese emigration, has been created in the minds of the people, led on by His Honor the Mayor of San Francisco and his associates in office, and approved by His Excellency the Governor, and other great men of the State. These great men gathered some 20,000 of the people of this city together on the evening of April 5, and adopted an address and resolutions against Chinese emigration. They have since appointed three men (one of whom we understand to be the author of the address and resolutions) to carry that address and those resolutions to your Excellency, and to present further objections, if possible, against the emigration of the Chinese to this country.

It is charged against us that not one virtuous China-woman has been brought to this country, and that here we have no wives nor children. The fact is, that already a few hundred Chinese families have been brought here. These are all chaste, pure, keepers-at-home, not known on the public street. There are also among us a few hundred, perhaps a thousand, Chinese children born in America. The reason why so few of our families are brought to this country is because it is contrary to the custom and against the inclination of virtuous Chinese women to go so far from home, and because the frequent outbursts of popular indignation against our people have not encouraged us to bring our families with us against their will. Quite a number of Chinese prostitutes have been brought to this country by unprincipled Chinamen, but these at first were brought from China at the instigation and for the gratification of white men. And even at the present time it is commonly reported that a part of the proceeds of this villainous traffic goes to enrich a certain class of men belonging to this honorable nation—a class of men, too, who are under solemn obligations to suppress the whole vile business, and who certainly have it in their power to suppress it if they so desired. A few years ago, our Chinese merchants tried to send these prostitutes back to China, and succeeded in getting a large number on board the outgoing steamer, but a certain lawyer of your honorable nation (said to be the author and bearer of these resolutions against our people), in the employ of unprincipled Chinamen, procured a writ of habeas corpus, and brought all those women on shore again, and the courts decided that they had a right to stay in this country if they so desired. Those women are still here, and the only remedy for this evil, and also for the evil of Chinese gambling, lies, so far as we can see, in an honest and impartial administration of municipal government, in all its details, even including the Police Department. If officers would refuse bribes, then unprincipled Chinamen could no longer purchase immunity from the punishment of their crimes.

It is charged against us that we have purchased no real estate. The general tone of public sentiment has not been such as to encourage us to invest in real estate, and yet our people have purchased and now own over $800,000 worth of real estate in San Francisco alone.

It is charged against us that we eat rice, fish, and vegetables. It is true that our diet is slightly different from the people of this honorable country; our tastes in these matters are not exactly alike, and cannot be forced. But is that a sin on our part of sufficient gravity to be brought before the President and Congress of the United States?

It is charged that the Chinese are no benefit to this country. Are the railroads built by Chinese labor no benefit to the country? Are the manufacturing establishments, largely worked by Chinese, no benefit to this country? Do not the results of the daily toil of a hundred thousand men increase the riches of this country? Is it no benefit to this country that the Chinese annually pay over $2,000,000 duties at the Custom house of San Francisco? Is not the $200,000 annual poll-tax paid by the Chinese any benefit? And are not the hundreds of thousands of dollars taxes on personal property, and the foreign miners' tax, annually paid to the revenues of this country, any benefit?

It is charged against us that the Six Chinese Companies have secretly established judicial tribunals, jails, and prisons, and secretly exercise judicial authority over the people. This charge has no foundation in fact. These Six Companies were originally organized for the purposes of mutual protection and care of our people coming to and going from this country. The Six Companies do not claim; nor do they exercise any judicial authority whatever, but are the same as any tradesmen or protective and benevolent societies. If it were true that the Six Companies exercise judicial authority over the Chinese people, then why do all the Chinese people still go to American tribunals to adjust their differences, or to secure the punishment of their criminals? Neither do these companies import either men or women into this country.

It is charged that all Chinese laboring men are slaves. This is not true in a single instance. Chinamen labor for bread. They pursue all kinds of industries for a livelihood. Is it so then that every man laboring for his livelihood is a slave? If these men are slaves, then all men laboring for wages are slaves.

It is charged that the Chinese commerce brings no benefit to American bankers and importers. But the fact is that an immense trade is carried on between China and the United States by American merchants, and all the carrying business of both countries, whether by steamers, sailing vessels or railroads, is done by Americans. No China ships are engaged in the carrying traffic between the two countries. Is it a sin to be charged against us that the Chinese merchants are able to conduct their mercantile business on their own capital? And is not the exchange of millions of dollars annually by the Chinese with the banks of this city any benefit to the banks?

We respectfully ask a careful consideration of all the foregoing statements. The Chinese are not the only people, nor do they bring the only evils that now afflict this country. And since the Chinese people are now here, under solemn treaty rights, we hope to be protected, according to the terms of this treaty; but if the Chinese are considered detrimental to the best interests of this country, and if our presence here is offensive to the American people, let there be a modification of existing treaty relations between China and the United States, either prohibiting or limiting further Chinese emigration, and, if desirable, requiring also the gradual retirement of the Chinese people now here from this country. Such an arrangement, though not without embarrassments to both parties, we believe would not be altogether unacceptable to the Chinese government, and doubtless it would be very acceptable to a certain class of people in this honorable country.

With sentiments of profound respect,

Lee Wing How,
President Sam Yup Company
Lee Chee Kwan,
President Yung Wo Company
Law Yee Chung,
President Kong Chow Company
Chan Leung Kok,
President Wing Yung Company
Lee Cheong Chip,
President Hop Wo Company
Chan Kong Chew,
President Yan Wo Company
Lee Tong Hay,
President Chinese Young Men's Christian Association

(5)

"Be Cautious–Meats Handled by Chinese"*

BE CAUTIOUS!

A DUE RESPECT FOR A NATURAL prejudice against using

MEATS

Handled by Chinese,

and kept in their

Unventilated Dens

until sold for market use, has decided us to advertise the fact that we

SELL NO MEATS

that have been handled by

CHINAMEN.

Black Point Packing and Provision-House Cash Market,

532 MARKET STREET,

Opposite Second.

This notice put out by a butcher shop in San Francisco in the 1870s played upon the whites' fear of Chinese filth.

(6)

The Chinese at Home and Abroad, 1885*

The following selection from *The Chinese at Home and Abroad* by Willard B. Farwell illustrates the subjugation of Christian teachings as well as the Declaration of Independence to racial hatred. It was printed in 1885 with "A Report by

* "Be Cautious—Meats Handled by Chinese," Bancroft Library Scrapbook (Berkeley: University of California).

* Willard B. Farwell, *The Chinese at Home and Abroad, Together With the Report of the Special Committee of the Board of Supervisors of San Francisco, on the Condition of the Chinese Quarter of That City* (San Francisco: A. L. Bancroft & Co., 1885).

a Special Committee of San Francisco Supervisors" which reported on the slum conditions of Chinatown. However, instead of attributing responsibility for these conditions to the predominantly white owners of the buildings, they blamed the innate depravity of the Chinese who were forced to live there because of white hostility.

The evidence as to the manners and habits of the Chinese at home is conclusive. Conceding all that may be said in their praise as to their habits of industry and their frugality, there can be no doubt or question that this, the oldest known civilization in the world, is rotten to the core with vice and crime, with sensuality and lust, with the universal indulgence in all the baser passions, and no better motive for their industrious inclination than the love of money, than sordid, unfeeling avarice. It is in proof that there is no human abomination or cruelty that they do not practice. That they are a race to which the attribute of gratitude for favors or kindness bestowed upon them is unknown. That contact with Christianity, when they emigrate to the very strongholds of Christianity itself, leaves but a trace of impression upon the outward surface of their lives. That for every human soul converted from their ranks to the Christian faith, they plant a hundred vices in our midst and scatter the seeds of disease that render thousands of lives but chapters of misery, leaving out of view the perdition of the hereafter which our Christian faith sternly attaches to their sin. . . .

That the banners of Christianity and Christian civilization may be advanced throughout the remotest confines of the Chinese Empire by never ceasing missionary work upon Chinese soil itself, may well be our prayer and our faith. But that these people should be invited to our shores in countless thousands in the hope and expectation of Christianization here, is a proposition too horrible to the physical, moral and religious well-being of our own people to be thought of—judging from the frightful evidence which the presence of the thousands who are already here have furnished in the story of their lives so far, and the faithful picture of their condition at present wherever they are gathered together in communities among us. . . . the time has come, and the issue is joined; the contest must be made. Two races, standing face to face with each other, between whom, as history thus far shows, there can be no assimilation, are contending for industrial supremacy upon this Continent. Can any rational mind doubt where the victory will rest, unless the broad ocean that separates the two continents which each inhabit shall be declared an impassable barrier across which the invading race shall not pass? The American sentimentalists who find in "The Declaration" certain immutable principles which it would shock their very natures to see trenched upon, who live and die in the political faith that all men are born free and equal, that ours is a land which divine wisdom has set apart as an asylum for the oppressed of all nations, who believe in the universal brotherhood of man, will do well to study the picture of the "Chinese at Home," thus far furnished them in the preceding statement of the case. They will continue to do well by examining all that is to follow, showing how perfectly successful the race has been in transplanting their idolatry, their vices, their diseases, and all their contaminating influences in immigrating to these shores. . . .

In speaking of the improvement that has taken place in the general appearance of "Chinatown" since your Committee commenced its investigations, we would not be understood as saying that the condition of the locality is in any sense what it should be in point of cleanliness. Our effort is to point out the fact that, as compared with what it was four months ago, it presents an improved aspect. The difference is one of degree, however, and even in its bettered aspect, in its byways, its slums, and its purlieus, its habitations, some of its places of business and places of amusements, it is today the filthiest spot inhabited by men, women, and children on the American continent.

All great cities have their slums and localities where filth, disease, crime, and misery abound; but in the very best aspect which "Chinatown" can be made to present, it must stand apart, conspicuous and beyond them all in the extreme degree of all these horrible attributes, the rankest outgrowth of human degradation that can be found upon this continent. Here it may truly be said that human beings exist under conditions (as regards their mode of life and the air they breathe) scarcely one degree above those under which the rats of our waterfront and other vermin live, breathe, and have their being. And this order of things seems inseparable from the very nature of the race, and probably must be accepted and borne with—must be endured, if it cannot be cured—restricted and looked after, so far as possible, with unceasing vigilance, so that, whatever of benefit, "of degree," even, that may be derived from such modification of the evil of their presence among us, may at least be attained, not daring to hope that there can be any radical remedy for the great, overshadowing evil which Chinese immigration has inflicted upon this people.

Your Committee have found, both from their own and individual observations and from the reports of their surveyors, that it is almost the universal custom among the Chinese to herd together as compactly as possible, both as regards living and sleeping-rooms and sleeping-accommodations. It is almost an invariable rule that every "bunk" in Chinatown (beds being almost unknown in that locality) is occupied by two persons. Not only is this true, but in very many instances these bunks are again occupied by "relays" in the day time, so that there is no hour, night or day, when there are not thousands of Chinamen sleeping under the effects of opium, or otherwise, in the bunks which we have found there.

Not only have your Committee found that the rule is for two persons to each "bunk," and relays of sleepers through the day in many, if not most instances, but women and children seem also to be stowed away in every available nook and corner, without reference to any special accommodation being provided for them. . . . The frequent custom with this people is to have the brick and mortar bench where cooking is carried on, the sink, always more or less filthy, and an open, filthy, bad-smelling water-closet, all adjoining each other in the same room, or under the same cover. Frequently a space at the end of this cooking range —if we may call it so—is used as a urinal, the only outlet from which is the absorption of and seepage through some earth placed there for that purpose, while the intermingling odors of cooking, sink, water-closet and urinal, added to the fumes of opium and tobacco smoke and the indescribable, unknowable, all-pervading atmosphere of the Chinese quarter, make up a perfume which can neither be imagined nor described. This is no exaggeration, nor is it a fancy sketch. It is one of the common features of life in Chinatown. . . . In the basement on the east side of Bartlett Alley, in what is known as the Dog Kennel, filth and its accompanying stenches reign supreme. A blind woman and several dogs and cats live in the kennel in a state of wretched squalor that baffles description, while the rear space is occupied by water-closets without traps, leading into what receptacle no one knows, the whole area and surroundings being wet, moldy, and rotten. The lowest grade of prostitution guards the entrance to this den on either side, and the hideous visages that peer through the wickets help to add to the general aspect of degradation and misery that reigns below.

The basement of the next building adjoining is a twin specimen in filth and methods of violation of the sanitary regulations which we have quoted.

At 714 Jackson street, in the basement, occupied by seven Chinese prostitutes and two children, there are no water-closets, and the slops and filth generated in this underground slum are flung into the street as an extra generous contribution to the rotting garbage that daily accumulates there, or disposed of in other ways unknown to your Committee. . . .

The atmosphere at night in these crowded dens—many of which, it will be seen, are in cellars—when the occupants are in possession, is something indescribably horrible; especially when vitiated by the smoke of opium and tobacco, the effluvia from surrounding filth, and the exhalations from the bodies of the Celestials who inhabit them. . . .

It is from such pest-holes as these that the Chinese cooks and servants who are employed in our houses come. Cleanly though they may be, in appearance, while acting in the capacity of domestic servants, they are nevertheless born and reared in these habits of life. The facility with which they put on habits of decency when they become cooks and servants simply adds other testimony to their ability to adapt themselves to circumstances when it is their interest to do so. But the instinct of the race remains unchanged; and when the Chinese servant leaves employment in an American household he joyfully hastens back to his slum and his burrow, to the grateful luxury of his normal surroundings, vice, filth and an atmosphere of horror. . . .

The "opium lay-out" is found in nearly every sleeping-room in Chinatown, and is nearly as common as the tobacco pipe; but these dens are for the general accommodation of those who have no sleeping bunks and conveniences for opium-smoking of their own, and who therefore frequent these resorts to indulge in the habit.

The bunks are occupied night and day, and the spectacle of pallid men in a condition of death-stupor, wrapped in the dirty rags which constitute their bedding, may be witnessed in these dens any day from 10 A.M. to 2 P.M. . . .

The use of opium is so general among the Chinese that no visitor to Chinatown, night or day, can enter many sleeping-rooms without finding men indulging in the habit. Nor will the explorer travel far without finding them under every stage of its influence down to the dead stupor such as would seem to furnish fit subjects for the coroner and the morgue rather than as beings to whom life is ever to return again.

(7)

Anti-Chinese Riots*

A librarian at the Oregon Historical Society, answering a request for information about a specific massacre of Chinese in the 1880s, sent this page of the index to the *Oregonian* with a letter stating that she was not certain which massacre was meant and remarked that the 1880s were "indeed, troubled years for the Chinese" in Oregon.

CHINESE RIOTS,
Chinese always aliens, O-Mar. 22, 1882 (ed.);
not desirable as citizens, O-Nov. 11, 1880 (ed.);
assaults upon Chinese, Sept. 7, 1885, Squawk Valley; Sept. 11, 1886,
Chinese quarters burned at Coal Creek Mine, King County; Nov. 3, 1885, 200 Chinese driven out of Tacoma;
details of assaults, O-Nov. 12, 1885, p. 8;
ordered to "go" at Olympia, Feb. 9, 1886;
Seattle under martial law, Feb. 1886; troops sent to Seattle under General John Gibbon, Nov. 8, 9, 1885; proclamation by Pres. Cleveland, O-Nov. 8, 1885, p. 8; troops fire on mob at Seattle, Feb. 7, 1886; soldiers there from Vancouver;
Chinese assaulted at Tacoma and Seattle, O-Nov. 12, 1885, p. 8, 1/3 col.;
anti-Chinese meetings, Portland, Feb. 12, 13, 1886; procession, Feb. 21, 1886;
driven out of Oregon City Woolen Mills, Feb. 22, 1886; O-Mar. 5, 1886, p. 3;
driven from Albina, Feb. 28, 1886; from Mt. Tabor, Mar. 4, 1886; O-Mar. 6,
1886, p. 3; Chinese raided at Guild's Lake, Mar. 12, 1886;
dynamite attempt in North Portland, Mar. 12, 1886;
agitators arrested, O-Mar. 5, 1886, p. 3, 250 w.;
measures of protection, O-Mar. 1, 1886, p. 3; meeting of citizens to suppress lawlessness called for, Mar. 16, 1886, O-Mar.

* "Chinese Riots," *Index to the Oregonian* (1850).

14, 1886; two militia companies organized, Mar. 24, 1886; rioters indicted by U.S. Grand Jury, Mar. 29, 1886; arrests made, construction of armory contract let, May 10, 1887;
assaults at Mount Tabor, O-Mar. 6, 1886, p. 3, 200 w.;
mass meeting against agitators, O-Mar. 15, 1886, p. 5, 200 w.;
attack on Chinese washhouse, Portland, Mar. 23, 1886; Chinese shanty burned in East Portland, Mar. 24, 1886; dynamite attack in East Portland, July 7, 1886; assault upon Chinese laundry, East Portland, Aug. 22, 1886; dynamite attack, Sept. 9, 1886;
driven from work on Northern Pacific, O-Aug. 18, 1886, p. 3, 200 w.;
agitation against Chinese, O-Dec. 4, 1890 (ed.); O-Feb. 16, 1886 (ed.);
O-Mar. 20, 1886 (ed.); incited by Governor Pennoyer, O-Jan. 26, 1891 (ed.)

(8)

Evils of Mongolian Immigration, 1892*

On April 21, 1892, the Honorable Charles Felton of California addressed the United States Senate on the evils of Mongolian immigration, justifying the exploitation of the yellow race and white superiority as "nature's law."

Mr. President, The people of the Pacific Coast do not desire to maltreat, to persecute, or to deport the Chinese now within our borders. They recognize their rights under the treaty to remain and enjoy them until they voluntarily leave, and hence do not desire to interfere with them. But we would and will, if possible, prevent the further incoming of this race or the return of those who shall voluntary [sic] leave.

We would have this nation follow nature's laws and integrate a higher type of our civilization, one more dis-

* "Speech in the Senate of the U.S., Thursday, April 21, 1892," by Hon. Charles Felton, in *Evils of Mongolian Immigration—The Chinese Question* (Berkeley: University of California, Bancroft Library).

tinct, special, more American, and would protect its evolution from all danger, real or threatened. We would first take care of ourselves, recognizing that in so doing we were making our "greatest contributions to the welfare of humanity."

In other words, Mr. President, we would not permit the purity and sweetness of our national waters to be contaminated or polluted by the mingling of its pure streams with the impure from any source whatsoever. We would first use of them whatever portion we require and then permit them to flow on and to the fullest extent possible purify the noxious streams of less fortunate conditions.

(9)

Roundup in Boston, 1906*

The *Atlantic Monthly* of January, 1906 described a raid by the United States Immigration officials upon the Chinese community of Boston. This was one of many such brutal roundups practiced by government officials in the early twentieth century in the hope of deporting illegal immigrants. Some were discovered, but at the price of great cruelty and with total disregard for the rights of the law-abiding majority. A Chinese diplomat in Washington, who had been falsely arrested and tied by his queue to a fence, committed suicide because of the dishonor to which he had been submitted.

The following narrative is condensed from the newspapers of that city. At about half past seven o'clock on the evening of Sunday, October 11, 1902, a number of United States officials of Boston, New York, and other cities charged with the administration of the Chinese exclusion

* "The Chinese Boycott," John W. Foster, The *Atlantic Monthly* (Jan., 1906).

laws, assisted by a force of the local police, made a sudden and unexpected descent upon the Chinese quarter of Boston. The raid was timed with a refinement of cruelty which did greater credit to the shrewdness of the officials than to their humanity. It was on the day and at the hour when the Chinese of Boston and its vicinity were accustomed to congregate in the quarter named for the purpose of meeting friends and enjoying themselves after a week of steady and honest toil. The police and immigration officials fell upon their victims without giving a word of warning. The clubs, restaurants, other public places where Chinese congregated, and private houses, were surrounded. Every avenue of escape was blocked. To those seized no warrant for arrest or other paper was read or shown.

Every Chinese who did not at once produce his certificate of residence was taken in charge, and the unfortunate ones were rushed off to the Federal Building without further ceremony. There was no respect of persons with the officials; they treated merchants and laborers alike. In many cases no demand was made for certificates, the captives were dragged off to imprisonment, and in some instances the demand was not made till late at night or the next morning, when the certificates were in the possession of the victims at the time of their seizure.

In the raid no mercy was shown by the government officials. The frightened Chinese who had sought to escape were dragged from their hiding-places, and stowed like cattle upon wagons or other vehicles, to be conveyed to the designated place of detention. On one of those wagons or trucks from seventy to eighty persons were thrown, and soon after it moved it was overturned. A scene of indescribable confusion followed, in which the shrieks of those attempting to escape mingled with the groans of those who were injured.

The case of one old man was particularly sad. In the upsetting of the wagon two of his ribs were broken, and he was otherwise bruised and injured. The attending physician made oath that his age was such that the injury might develop pleurisy or other serious complication as the result of his injuries. The rough usage to which he was subjected was a great strain upon his feeble frame, weakened by age. When the raid burst upon the Chinese quarter, he had just come downstairs from his lodgings when he was caught in the police drag-net. He informed the officers that his certificate was in his trunk upstairs, and that he could lay his hands on it without loss of time. But he was not permitted to go to get his papers even under guard, but was thrown into the overloaded wagon. The result was that this innocent man, who under treaty had a perfect right to reside in the country free from molestation, was made to suffer untold tortures in body and mind, in order that the immigration and police officers might satisfy their thirst for sensational activity.

About two hundred and fifty Chinese were thus arrested and carried off to the Federal Building. Here they were crowded into two small rooms where only standing space could be had, from eight o'clock in the evening, all through the night, and many of them till late in the afternoon of the next day. There was no sleep for any of them that night, though some of them were so exhausted that they sank to the floor where they stood. Their captors seemed to think that they had to do with animals, not human beings. Some of them were released during the night, when relatives brought their certificates or merchants were identified. But the greater part were kept till the next day, when the publicity of the press brought friends, or relief through legal proceedings.

One of the Boston journals reported that the Federal judge, who had a case set for hearing in an adjoining room the next morning, had to adjourn to another part of the building because of the foul exhalations from the overcrowded prison pen. It would hardly be believed that the "Black Hole of Calcutta" could at this day have an imitation in such an enlightened community.

So strong was the indignation of the respectable citizens of Boston, that a large public meeting was held in Faneuil

Hall to denounce the action of the immigration officials and the police. Prominent men who took part did not hesitate to refer to that action in the strongest terms as a brutal outrage, a disgrace to the city; and the resolutions adopted assert that the Chinese were seized without warrant of law, and, after being brutally handled, were placed in close and ignominious confinement; and they declare that the lawless acts of the officials are dangerous to liberty and in defiance of constitutional rights—arbitrary, unwarranted, and outrageous.

It was announced by the immigration officials that their raid was organized under the belief that there were a number of Chinese in Boston and its vicinity unlawfully in the United States, and this method was adopted for discovering them. The official report of the chief officer soon after the event showed that two hundred and thirty-four Chinese were imprisoned, that one hundred and twenty-one were released without trial or requirement of bail, and that only five had so far been deported, but that he hoped that he might secure the conviction and deportation of fifty; as a matter of fact, however, the deportations fell much below that number. But even if these men were unlawfully in the country, they were entitled to humane treatment, and, above all, to the orderly process and application of the law. The act of Congress prescribes "that any Chinese person . . . found unlawfully in the United States or its Territories *may be arrested upon a warrant issued upon a complaint,* under oath, filed by any party on behalf of the United States," etc.

(10)

How He Was Taught Civilization*

The San Francisco *Chinese Defender,* published for a few months in 1910 and 1911, printed this ironic letter from Ah Sing, describing his experiences with the immigration service and in the city.

* "How He Was Taught Civilization," in *Chinese Defender,* Vol. I, No. 6 (Feb., 1911).

To Editor of Chinaman Defender:

Me come from China heathen country four months ago; now me learn how to be civilized. I tell you how me learn.

First when I come on steamer they take me to Angel Island, and then have one doctor man try see what he can find the matter. He try very hard every day—one time take me from bed midnight and catch blood from my ear. Some Chinaman very much frighten that way; one man doctor first give medicine, and one day more man die, me no no what matter that way: all little boys very much frighten, many boys sick all kinds trouble; me not care, maybe die, all right; bye and bye two weeks doctor no try any more. Then three weeks more they talk my case, ask me maybe more 100 questions, like who my grandmother, how much teeth my grandfather, how many fish my village pond have—oh, lots questions. Two weeks more talk me some more questions, because my friend who come talk to help me make mistake, not know how much fish that pond or something. Bye and bye, two weeks more, make more than two months steamer come here, they talk me all right take me go San Francisco; me very glad, for me get scared for some man he appeal head city Washington he stay Angel Island maybe four and five months, and little boys stay there long time and me think me no like my little boy stay that kind place so long. Then one man he be there ninety-one days then he die—me think more better die stay there too long and eat different kind food all same prison.

Then me go Chinatown—too much no good white lady live there; my friend talk me all no good lady policeman send live in Chinatown; then all no good white man go there see her; this way teach Chinaman be good Christian man, make Chinaman's children heap smart see that kind people, hear all men swear and see them smoke and get drink too much.

My friend he show me maybe like do something no matter what, they like Chinaman be civilized man and pay money, then no trouble; me think lot of men make lot of money from Chinaman—that the civilized way. My friend get good job; he no can keep; Union may say no more Chinaman can clean saloon Slavonian more cheap. Then my cousin he be arrested but man no take him prison; four, five days keep him somewhere else; they talk he no right stay this country; bye and bye he get lawyer, costs lots money; then they say make mistake, catch wrong man, and let him go. What can he do—he lost lot of work. Oh, me sabbe what kind man civilized man now.

Yours respectively,

Ah Sing.

(11)

Story of Wong Ah So–Chinese Prostitute*

Because almost all of the immigrants to the United States from China were men who had left their families behind, their lives were frustrated ones, especially sexually. Women were brought over by various ruses to live in Chinatown and work as prostitutes.

I was born in Canton Province, my father was sometimes a sailor and sometimes he worked on the docks, for we were very poor.

I was nineteen when this man came to my mother and said that in America there was a great deal of gold. Even if I just peeled potatoes there, he told my mother I would earn seven or eight dollars a day, and if I was willing to do any work at all I would earn lots of money. He was a laundryman, but said he earned plenty of money. He was very nice to me, and my mother liked him, so my mother was glad to have me go with him as his wife.

I thought that I was his wife, and was very grateful that he was taking me to such a grand, free country, where everyone was rich and happy.

When we first landed in San Francisco, we lived in a

* "Story of Wong Ah So—Chinese Prostitute," in *Orientals and Their Cultural Adjustment* (Nashville, Tenn.: Fisk University, Social Science Institute, 1946).

hotel in Chinatown, a nice place, but one day, after I had been there for about two weeks, a woman came to see me. She was young, very pretty, and all dressed in silk. She told me that I was not really Hucy Yow's wife, but that she had asked him to buy her a slave, that I belonged to her, and must go with her, but she would treat me well, and I could buy back my freedom, if I was willing to please, and be agreeable, and she would let me off in two years, instead of four if I did not make a fuss. She said that so I would be quieter about it. I did not believe her, I thought that she was lying to me. So when Hucy Yow come I asked him why that woman had come and what she meant by all that lying. But he said that it was true; that he was not my husband, he did not care about me, and that this was something that happened all the time. Everybody did this, he said, and why be so shocked that I was to be a prostitute instead of a married woman. I asked him, "What is a prostitute? Am I not your wife?" And he said, "Couldn't I just say that you were my wife? That does not make it so. Everybody does this sort of thing. The woman gave me money just to bring you over."

I was in that life for seven months, and then I was released. I don't know just how it came about, but I know it was through a friend of my father's that I met at a banquet.

It was a party given by the Tong men, where slave girls are invited, who sit and eat and drink with the men. Suddenly I saw a friend of my father's come in, a man who had seen me less than a year ago. Although I was all dressed up so grand he recognized me, and the first chance he had, he came and asked me, "Are you not so and so's daughter?"

. . . About ten days after the party and the interview with this man I was rescued and taken to the mission. . . .

I am learning English and to weave, and I am going to send money to my mother when I can. I can't help but cry, but it is going to be better.

(12)

Sojourners—1954*

After the Communist Revolution in China, the United States forbade Chinese who had scientific or technical training to return to their homeland. This letter by twenty-six Chinese students was sent to President Eisenhower appealing for permission to return to China.

August 5, 1954

The President
The White House
Washington, D.C.

Dear Mr President:

We the undersigned are a number of many Chinese students who have been engaged in the study of engineering, medical or natural science for various lengths of time in the United States.

After the completion of certain stages of academic studies, some of us have applied for exit permits either to go back to China or to go to other places. Invariably these applications were refused, and we were told by the immigration authorities that none of the few thousands of Chinese students in the field of technical sciences would be allowed to leave. Hence, with a feeling of futility, the rest of us refrained from applying for exit permits.

In the seeking of knowledge and wisdom, some of the undersigned have had to leave behind their beloved wives and children. In most of the cases the painful separation has already lasted seven years, and their return is being denied. The plight of others, although not married, is by no means less tragic. Distressed and unsettled, we are forced to let slip

* "Letter to the President, Aug. 5, 1954," Rose Hum Lee, *The Chinese in the United States of America* (Hong Kong: Hong Kong University Press, 1960).

through our fingers the best years of our lives. Our parents back home find that sons and daughters are no longer a source of joy, not to mention the lack of succor and solace in cases of want and sickness. Instead of being able to repay their selfless parental love with love, we have distressed them with the possibility that they might never see us again. In these years of absence from home all of us have suffered an ever increasing agony that verges on despair, since no immediate return could be foreseen.

Having been well received by various people we have met in the United States and having observed at first-hand a democracy at work, under which human rights are being held sacred, we feel all the more that preventing us from leaving this country can at best be attributed to a temporary expediency, especially when the persons concerned are guilty of no crime and the sole reason for restraining their departure is their acquisition of technical training. We would respectfully point out that the technical training we have received here involves no code of secrecy; indeed, the spreading of scientific knowledge and technical know-how has been the very spirit of the great tradition of this country ever since its establishment. Unfortunately, the policy of preventing the departure of Chinese students has merely created hardship and misery for the innocent.

Recently we have learned from the newspapers that fifteen Chinese students are to be released. We sincerely appeal to you, Mr President, to make it possible for any Chinese student to be allowed to leave the United States whenever he so chooses, and we petition you to revoke the restraining order. In doing so we do not believe that the security of this great nation would be in any way endangered. On the contrary, we are of the opinion that by so doing a firmer bond of friendship and understanding will be established between our two peoples. We are hopeful, Mr President, that you will give your most serious consideration to our urgent appeal.

Most respectfully yours,
Signed
A group of 26 students

(13)

Poverty Conditions in Chinatown, 1964*

The official Six Companies myth of Chinatown's prosperity and lack of social problems is questioned by the following report made in 1964 to the California Legislature.

STATEMENT BY LARRY JACK WONG, REPRESENTING THE CHINATOWN-NORTH BEACH DISTRICT COUNCIL BEFORE THE CALIFORNIA LEGISLATURE ASSEMBLY INTERIM SUBCOMMITTEE ON ECONOMIC OPPORTUNITY

Mr. Chairman and Members of The Subcommittee:

We are grateful for this opportunity afforded The Chinatown–North Beach District Council of San Francisco to testify before you.

The employment situation in Chinatown is serious, although it is very difficult to obtain sufficient exact figures [to substantiate the facts]. The State Department of Employment estimates that for the month of October, 1964 some 700 members of the Chinese community had active unemployment insurance claims. This indicates only a small portion of the problem, however, because many do not submit claims and because so much of the real difficulty is caused by under-employment, or employment in the most poorly paying occupations.

There is a large group of unskilled, non-English-speaking men whose employment opportunities are limited to being dishwashers in Chinese restaurants, doing janitorial work, and other jobs at the minimum wage level, which simply does not enable them to support a family. In an effort to make ends meet, both parents in the family go to work: both at jobs that are minimal in terms of wages and hours, and often, especially for the women, are seasonal and part-time

* "Poverty Condition in Chinatown as of Dec. 8, 1964," by Larry Jack Wong, Statement before the California Legislature Assembly; Interim Subcommittee on Economic Opportunity.

and temporary. The employment, however, interferes with their ability to take advantage of any educational opportunities to learn English or to secure job training for better employment, and they are caught in this treadmill of trying to get enough money week by week to support the family.

In census tract A-13, 10 percent are families with an annual income of less than $2,000 and 24 percent with an annual income less than $4,000. In census tract A-14, 12 percent are families with an income under $2,000 annually, and 33 percent under $4,000. Census tract A-15 shows 16 percent and 30 percent respectively. Census tract A-16 shows 4 percent and 37 percent respectively. These four census tracts are most representative of the Chinatown community. These are compared with the whole of San Francisco, which shows 8 percent and 13 percent respectively.

The total male unemployment rate in the Chinese community is 8.5 percent, 11.1 percent, 15.6 percent, and 16.1 percent respectively in the same four census tracts. The total unemployment rate in San Francisco is 6.7 percent. . . . Chinatown is the third largest area of poverty in San Francisco—40 percent of the families have income under $4,000 a year. The Chinese are the most segregated in terms of deprived families—97 percent of Chinatown's 705 deprived families are Oriental. The unusual pattern of families with older fathers and parents with a low level of education—the median of school years completed in the core census tracts run from .9 years to 6.1 years.

Chinatown has been recognized as one of the pockets of poverty in San Francisco. The income level in many families and for many individuals is very low.

The only way that a substantial breakthrough can be made is by providing opportunity for the necessary basic education in English, for job training, and job placement in employment that can hope to go beyond the level at which they are now caught. More adequate employment would, of course, have an effect upon the economy of the community as a whole in raising the living standard, making better conditions for the children to grow up in, and raising the general level of prosperity.

Chinatown seems to suffer from a general assumption on the part of the major community that it has no great problems. Those of us who work and live in the community are aware that there are very real and deep problems. The one discussed here is very real, serious, and handicapping, and a long-term contributor to the continuing poverty of the area.

The Chinese community has traditionally been looked upon as a community of proud people, who responsibly and adequately take care of its own. Indeed, there is much truth in this popular concept. The pride and community effort may have too long misled too many and caused too much neglect too often. The problem of unemployment in Chinatown is too serious, too oppressive, too captivating to be sheltered by either pride or passiveness.

The problem of unemployment and poverty is too great and too complex for any individual community to solve alone. In this regard, we must make mention of two additional related problems, equal employment opportunities and motivation. It is a general fact that since World War II equal employment opportunities have been made available to Chinese-Americans in many areas. However, there is still a difficulty among Chinese-Americans to gain membership in all craft unions. Too many unions just recently admitted their first Chinese member. Though these unions purport to disavow any discrimination, the fact is there are very few qualified Chinese admitted to their apprentice program or into their union. Few qualified Chinese have been appointed to meaningful federal, state, and city offices and commissions. This has contributed to the perpetuation of an attitude that a Chinese cannot really gain full rights and opportunities in a white man's country. Such an attitude is still whispered and hinted from generation unto generation. Such attitude, no matter how limited in scope, when slightly and even accidentally supported, greatly stifles motivation.

(14)

The Chinese Demand Change

The effects of the Civil Rights Movement and the consciousness generated throughout the 1960s by both radical and liberal reform led some Chinese to begin a kind of muckraking campaign in Chinatown to try to break down the facade of the united-prosperous-inscrutable covering that masked the deep social and racial problems of Chinese Ghettos.

The first two documents were circulated at the San Francisco Chinese New Year's Festival in 1969; the third is from a report on conditions in Chinatown in San Francisco, sponsored by the Economic Opportunity Office.

STATEMENT AND DEMANDS BY CONCERNED CHINESE FOR ACTION & CHANGE FEBRUARY 14, 1969

It is common knowledge that we, the Chinese, were subjected to blatantly discriminatory legislation and incessant vilification and abuse in this country over the last 120 years. Many of our forefathers were forced to return to China. Those who stayed were squeezed into tight ghettoes, segregated not only physically, but also socially, politically, and economically. Today, economically most of our people are limited to those occupations which do not bring us into direct competition or confrontation with whites. Politically, we have no share in government and no power to abolish injustice and bring about social changes. Physically and socially, our contact with the rest of the society is kept at a minimum. In short, most of the approximately 70,000 Chinese in San Francisco remain very much victims of segregation and outright disregard. Social and economic problems in our community remain unnoticed and unattended to by those in power.

Today, we members of the Chinese community from all walks of life have come out to the Board of Education to zero in on one of the most crucial problems—the problem of education. We are here to call to the attention of the Board, the city, state and federal governments our needs and grievances and to demand that the Board take immediate and effective steps toward the full implementation of our twelve demands. . . . We . . . demand immediate action be taken toward the implementation of the following demands!!

1) Establish a multi-service English Language Clearinghouse and Center for all recent immigrant families. a) For immigrant adults: intensive language training, vocational guidance and classes on social and medical services available in the city. b) For immigrant school-age children: intensive language classes using ESL method prior to placement in actual schools, bilingual classes at all levels also prior to placement. c) A professional staff to man this center and coordinate needed services.

2) Incorporate Asian studies, whenever possible, into existing curriculum at all grade levels.

3) Initiate the following courses: a) history of Asian-Americans, b) Chinatown, and c) Cantonese and Mandarin. All these courses to be taught by qualified Oriental teachers.

4) Recruit qualified Chinese immigrant teachers into the S. F. Unified School District.

5) Actively enlist principals, counselors and teachers, preferably of Oriental descent, who understand and identify with the Chinese Community.

6) Place qualified Oriental college students and members of the Chinatown–North Beach Area Youth Council to tutor, counsel, and work with students in and out of schools in our area.

7) Involve and consult the Chinese Community in all

aspects of education, e.g., appointment of principal, selection of counselor, development of new programs, etc.

8) Increase Chinese adult education classes for occupational, vocational and professional competence; basic language and literacy education, prerequisite for employment and skill training, be provided for those who previously were not given the right and opportunity to such education.

9) Assign additional compensatory education classes to our schools.

10) Establish sufficient pre-school centers in Chinatown–North Beach area.

11) Alleviate existing overcrowded conditions in schools serving our Community.

12) Declare Chinese New Year's Day a school holiday.

CHINATOWN AND THE CHINESE*

Chinatown is at once many things to many people. To thousands of ignorant *tourists and visitors,* it is the closest thing to visiting "exotic" China and for watching the strange "Chinese creatures" at work. For *store-keepers, restauranteurs, "sweat" shop- and land-owners,* it is a sure place for making easy money off the disadvantaged Chinese, commanding respect of the poor, and making-believe that they are living in China. For the *Bay Area middle-class Chinese and Chinese college students,* it is a place for Chinese grocery and occasional Chinese dinners. But, for *the majority of Chinatown residents,* especially the recent immigrants, it is a concentration camp where they must fight for minimum survival means and where their way of life is poverty and degradation.

Chinatown is unquestionably a ghetto in every sense of the word. Cultural and language barriers have prevented the over-crowded population from seeking employment outside of the confines of Chinatown. High unemployment

* "Chinatown and the Chinese," by L. Ling-chi Wang, of Intercollegiate Chinese for Social Action at San Francisco State College.

and under-employment rates provide fertile ground for small-time opportunist businessmen to exploit at will the helpless and the poor of their own race to the fullest extent. Seventy-five cents per hour and 10-13 hours of work per day are common practices in Chinatown. Substandard housing, tuberculosis, suicide, mental illness, and juvenile delinquency are widespread in spite of constant efforts to hide these phenomena and to discredit and sometimes violently suppress those who try to expose the problems and seek government help.

Historical injustice committed against the Chinese in the U.S., Chinese traditionalism and ethnocentrism are among the factors contributing to the existing deplorable ghetto conditions in Chinatown. *But the social expectation of the predominant white society also plays a crucial role* in determining the behavior and fate of the Chinese in the U.S. Chinese people have always been considered hard-working, inscrutable, patient, quiet, non-militant people with lasting endurance and self-respect.

In short, Chinese are expected to be super-human and take the worst in stride. This popular Chinese myth is held by both the white and the Chinese alike. The Chinatown establishment especially uses it as a means of suppressing and exploiting the humble, the weak and the meek; Chinese college students use it as an excuse for tolerating social injustice and for not asserting their rights as U.S. citizens; middle-class Chinese employ it as a self-righteous weapon against those who protest social injustice. In other words, the desire to live up to the popular expectation has crippled the entire Chinese population, including the Chinese college students, preventing them to think and act independently. . . . We Chinese act the way we are expected to act.

As long as those who "made it" maintain a hands-off "Uncle Tom" attitude, the Chinese will continue to be exploited by our own "warlords" and the majority white society, and Chinatown's problems will forever be neglected by the government. As for the foreign-born Chinese college students who take pride in so-called Chinese culture and "identity," they had better re-examine critically their values and attitude and start thinking on their own because they are among those who are perpetuating the Chinese myth and destroying any opportunity for Chinatown to pull out of its degrading conditions. The problems in Chinatown are our problems. *We must free ourselves from the tyranny of this Chinese myth, to solve our problems.*

Endurance, working hard, patience, and quietness are good virtues in any society, especially in China, but when they become a license for exploitation and governmental negligence, as we now witness in San Francisco, they ought to be re-examined in the light of the American political, social, and economic reality. Chinese people have much to contribute to the American society, but what good is it to talk about cultural and scientific contributions if basic human needs are not being met and our people are being subjected to sub human conditions?

"MENTAL HEALTH PROBLEMS AND CULTURAL CONFLICTS"*

Health Problems: Physical/Mental Health Indices

It can be seen that with cramped housing, high unemployment, low education, and a sizeable older population, the Chinatown–North Beach area would have many physical and mental health problems. Quantitative statistics on many of these problems are still difficult to accumulate because of cultural differences. For example, while the Chinese are slowly accepting institutional aid in matters of employment and welfare, they continue to be reticent where health is concerned, preferring to take care of their own, often until it is too late for help. A few qualitative studies which we have, however, do give a fair indication of the major problems.

A 1965 Public Health survey showed that the Chinese

* "Mental Health Problems and Cultural Conflicts," in report from Chinatown Economic Opportunity Council.

have the highest incidence of tuberculosis in the city and that the death rate (21.2 percent) for them is still three times that of the whites and Negroes. Heart disease and cancer, the two leading causes of death in all groups, account for nearly half (49.5 percent) of the Chinese deaths. The high death rates in these incidences is easily attributable to the failure to seek and/or inability to get timely medical attention.

A recent survey (February 1967) conducted by the Chinatown–North Beach Office of the Economic Opportunity Council indicated that of those polled, 34 percent had never had a complete physical examination—and this, in spite of the fact that 53 percent were immigrants and therefore had to have a physical examination before entering the United States. Dental and eye care fared even worse; over half had never had either a dental or eye examination. Twenty-three percent of those who had a dental examination and 29 percent of those who had an eye examination had them over five years ago and have had none since. The study also showed that 40 percent of the new immigrants that arrived in San Francisco within the last year had received health services through one of the two area EOC delegate agencies with referral services. (Health Screening and Treatment and Self-Help for the Elderly.)

If the Chinese have a tendency to neglect their physical disabilities, they also have a compulsion to hide their mental problems. San Francisco's Chinese have a suicide rate that is nearly three times that of the national rate (37/10,000 as against 11/10,000). The majority of this number were immigrants who were unable to make the adjustment to their new environment.

In a 1964 study, Dr. Stanley Wang, a psychiatric resident at Langley Porter Clinic, stated that the bulk of his Chinese patients came to the hospital with overt manifestations of their illnesses. His sample study of eighty-eight patients showed that 72 percent were either schizophrenic or psychotic and that 10 percent were serious suicidal attempts.

Of this group 62.5 percent were first admissions to any psychiatric hostpital. He found that most of his group fell into low socio-economic classes with less than high school education. Over 70 percent had significant language difficulties in English, and over half of these confronted a profound barrier in a clinical setting on admission. He further added that he got some remarkably positive responses from patients who found that he spoke their language.

Mental Health Problems and Cultural Conflicts

The mental and emotional problems of the Chinatown residents cover the whole span of those in other communities outside, such as the lack of communication between parent and children; child development problems; juvenile delinquency; marital discord; the isolation and loneliness of the old; and so on. However, these mental ills, serious and damaging as they may be in American society, are severely intensified for the Chinese in so far as they have never been beset by such problems in their former cultural context before and thus are totally unprepared to counter them. Parents and children in Chinatown are not only alienated by the different values brought about by changing times but their inabilty to communicate directly results from the stultifying language barrier. The second-generation Chinese children born on American soil are generally unable to speak Chinese while their parents cannot express themselves adequately, or at all, in English. The youth feels that the values clung to by his parents are of the "Old Country," and that they "don't know anything." Losing identity with his parents, rejecting what they stand for, and their expectations of him, he is left at the mercy of the bewildering practices of American teenagers to which he is exposed in real life as well as from the larger-than-life images bombarding him from advertisements, movies, radio, and television. In families where both parents work, the young have no family life to go back to after school. These family problems arising out of language and cultural barriers, set in the hot-bed of economic and cultural poverty, lead to the depletion of values and motivation for the young. Without the sense of "something of value" they often result in school failures, drop-outs, and juvenile delinquency.

The younger Chinese children, between infancy and about the age of five, suffer perhaps the most gravely of all precisely because they are maltreated when they are still totally defenseless. These first impressions and knowledge gained about the world may last, however submerged, to haunt them for the rest of their lives. Many infants and young children in Chinatown are neglected or literally abandoned for long periods, by working mothers who board them out with women that are untrained for this function.

Old age with all its attendant feelings of being neglected and no longer useful to their families and to society, are sharply increased for the elderly Chinese because, for them, there has never been a tradition of isolation and loneliness for the old such as exists in the United States. On the contrary, traditionally, these are their golden years, the "best years of their lives" when honor and tribute are automatically paid to them in respect to their age. These dispossessed, in terms of dignity, have suffered the greatest loss of all. They have fallen from the pinnacle of social status given to old age in China to the abyss of the no-longer-socially-useful, in America the disowned. Outcasted by their grown-up children who have their own children to look after, and unable to find work, these elderly people without home and job often develop mental disturbances such as psychosomatic disorders, and deep depressions with suicidal tendencies.

THE JAPANESE

The Post Office Building in downtown San Francisco is an old, ugly structure covering half a large city block. There, on February 21st and 23rd, 1942, in a crowded room, a select committee of the House of Representatives listened to testimony about whether or not the Japanese-American population of the West Coast should be evacuated and, if so, how the evacuation should be carried out. The committee held similar hearings in Los Angeles, Portland, and Seattle, the major centers of the Japanese population. More than 85 percent of the Japanese in the United States lived in the West at that time.

Late in the afternoon of the second day's session, James M. Omura, a floral worker who also published a magazine with a small circulation, appeared before the committee. Omura was dressed in his work clothes, since he had come to the hearing directly from his job and had not had time to change.

He spoke earnestly to the committee, almost desperately,

pleading with them not to proceed with the plans to remove the Japanese.

It is doubtlessly rather difficult for Caucasian Americans to properly comprehend and believe in what we say. Our citizenship has even been attacked as an evil cloak under which we expect immunity for the nefarious purpose of conspiring to destroy the American way of life. . . .

I would like to ask the Committee: Has the Gestapo come to America? Have we not risen in righteous anger at Hitler's mistreatment of the Jews? Then, is it not incongruous that citizen Americans of Japanese descent should be similarly mistreated and persecuted? . . .[1]

Omura expressed his anger at the leaders of the Japanese-American Citizens League, an organization founded in 1930 of second-generation Japanese-Americans born in the United States or Hawaii. These people were known as Nisei and, of course, they were citizens. ". . . I have been consistently opposed to the Japanese-American Citizens League," Omura said. ". . . I have felt that the leaders were leading the American-born Japanese along the wrong channels. . . ."[2]

The wrong channels to which Omura referred were evident at the hearings. All the JACL representatives, including its national secretary, Mike Masaoka, testified that the Japanese-Americans were willing to accept evacuation to prove their loyalty to the United States. "I think sincerely," stated Masaoka, "if the military say 'Move out,' we will be glad to move. . . ."[3] Masaoka also asked that "The Japanese American Creed," which he had written, become part of the committee's record as an additional sign of the loyalty of the JACL. The creed began with:

I am proud that I am an American citizen of Japanese ancestry for my very background makes me appreciate more fully the wonderful advantages of this Nation. I believe in her institutions,

[1] Select Committee Investigating National Defense Migration, San Francisco Hearings, February 21 and 23, 1942, Part 28, p. 11231, 77th Congress, 2nd sess., Washington, 1942.
[2] *Ibid.*, pp. 11229, 11230.
[3] *Ibid.*, p. 11148.

ideals and traditions; I glory in her heritage; I boast of her history; I trust in her future. . . . I am firm in my belief that American sportsmanship and attitude of fair play will judge citizenship and patriotism on the basis of action and achievement and not on the basis of physical characteristics. . . .[4]

The tone of the creed and the willingness of the JACL to accept the degradation of evacuation were consistent with the organization's general character. Most of the Nisei for whom Masaoka spoke had grown up trying to prove that they were more American than Japanese. They had gone to American schools, dressed in American clothes, played American sports; they spoke very little Japanese and that only at home with their families. They were aware that anti-Oriental prejudice existed because they were daily victims of it, but they had convinced themselves that only by accepting and conforming to the standards of white America could they break through the social, political, and legal barriers which kept them from full participation in American life. So despite the discrimination practiced against them, despite the fact that intermarriage with Caucasians was legally prohibited, despite the fact that they were barred from many public places, they cherished the American citizenship which their parents, the Issei (first generation), had been denied by law. Above all, they were, like the Chinese, fearful of calling too much attention to themselves by making demands for the rights associated with citizenship. The JACL had many opponents within the community and was not widely supported. It was attacked as being made up of Nisei (second generation) who only wanted to be accountants.

The Japanese-Americans were told to move out. The criterion used to determine who was to be forced from their homes, businesses, and communities was a simple one: anyone, citizen or alien, who had "A Japanese ancestor, regardless of degree." In some places they were given less than forty-eight hours' notice. The evacuation was supported and welcomed by West Coast legislators, judges,

[4] *Ibid.*, pp. 11138–39.

politicians, newspaper editorialists, businessmen, veterans' organizations, and the overwhelming majority of the white population. Even most of the liberal press and commentators were for it.

The evacuation, with all its anguish and heartache, intensified the bitter quarrel within the Japanese community between those who agreed with Omura and those who accepted the JACL position.

"America, the standard bearer of Democracy, has committed the most heinous crime in its history!" said Joseph Yoshisuko Kurihara in a rage. Kurihara, who opposed the JACL, was a Nisei, born in Hawaii in 1895. He was a veteran of World War I and a very successful businessman; furthermore, he was active in civic and veterans' groups and very proud of being an American. He had never been to Japan in his life and had never shown the slightest interest in anything Japanese until the evacuation. Kurihara responded with fury to the removal decree and tried, unsuccessfully, to convince other Nisei they ought to resist it. "These boys claiming to be the leaders of the Nisei were a bunch of spineless Americans. Here I decided to fight them and crush them in whatever camp I happened to find them. I vowed that they would never again be permitted to disgrace the name of the Nisei as long as I was about."

The initial impetus for Japanese immigration to the United States was the need for cheap labor. Prior to 1885 only a handful of Japanese had come to the United States; the census for 1860 lists no Japanese, that for 1870 only 55, and the one for 1880 less than 200. But, from 1885 when labor emigration from Japan was legalized, to 1924 when Oriental exclusion became part of immigration law, more than 200,000 Japanese came to the United States directly from Japan. Thousands more came to the mainland from Hawaii.

From the start the immigration of Japanese to the United States met with a negative response. In 1886 one California politician proclaimed: "Wherever the Japanese have settled, their nests pollute the communities like the running sores of leprosy. They exist like the yellow, smoldering discarded butts in an over-full ashtray, vilifying the air with their loathsome smells, filling all those who have the misfortune to look upon them with a wholesome disgust and a desire to wash."[5]

The wholesome disgust felt by that politician was an expression of the fear felt by many white Americans, particularly in the West, about "The Yellow Peril." Before the Japanese arrived, that fear had been reserved for the Chinese. But with the influx of Japanese, the white xenophobes believed another loathsome and dangerous foe was flooding their country with the intent of destroying its civilization.

The West of the late nineteenth century was still a frontier culture. Whites had settled it by conquering the Indians and Mexicans. Their contempt for the nonwhite losers was reinforced by the American military adventure in the Philippine Islands during the Spanish-American War of 1898. "Damn, damn, damn the Filipinos, cross-eyed, Kakiak Ladrones," were the words to a song white American soldiers sang as they brutally occupied the Philippine Islands, killing the brown-skinned men who opposed them.

Some westerners actually believed that billions of Asian "coolies" were waiting for the first opportunity to descend like a plague of locusts upon America. And in the case of the Japanese, settlers on the frontier were frightened not only by the sheer number of possible immigrants but by the prospect of competing with their already recognized industrial skills, tenacity, and willingness to work long hours for low pay.

The use of the Japanese as cheap labor provided a legitimized outlet for the contempt most white Americans felt for nonwhites. That contempt infused all of white American society from the lowest paid workers to the richest corporation presidents. A typical university view of Orientals, for instance, was expressed by a Stanford pro-

[5] Dr. C. C. O'Donnell in "The Japanese Must Go," quoted in the *Pacific Citizen*, December 20–27, 1968, p. 2A.

fessor of sociology in 1900. He said the Japanese, like the Chinese, were always willing to work for lower wages than Caucasian workers and were content with their lower standard of living. He also said that they were so committed to the authority figure of the Emperor they could never understand American democracy[6] and were therefore unassimilable.

The Japanese response to the anti-Oriental pressures and prejudices of whites was initially determined by the structure of the dominant white American society to which they had come and by the social and economic system of Japan at the time they emigrated. The basic feature of Japanese life at the time of the emigration was its status system, in which individuals knew and accepted the roles to which they had been born. The concept of social mobility was nonexistent in Japanese culture at that time. The primary social unit was the tightly structured family which reflected the same authoritarian and hierarchical patterns of the larger Japanese society.

The Japanese who came to the United States had been born into this rigid structure, and brought with them their concept of *on*—a great sense of pride and obligation to their families, villages, and the Japanese nation. They also brought a great need to be respected by others for their willingness to fulfill these obligations and a great need to exercise self-control lest they disgrace the family, village, or the Emperor. These traditional Japanese values conflicted sharply with the values of the American West where most of the immigrants settled. And because the Japanese were never given the opportunity to fully integrate into American life, the sense of *on* was reinforced, and so continued to exist long after the immigrants had settled.

Forbidden to live where they wished, they lived in segregated communities. Denied employment, except in menial jobs or in occupations suffering from shortages in labor, they created service industries for their own communities. Sneered at by most whites, they organized hundreds of

[6] *Pacific Citizen*, Dec. 20–27, 1968, p. 2A.

language, social, religious, and political groups. Japanese-language newspapers flourished and the immigrants' American-born children attended Japanese schools. Since the first generation of immigrants were not permitted to become citizens, they maintained close ties to Japan and looked to it for protection. In 1906 the Japanese Government protested the closing of Japanese schools in San Francisco. Thirty years later, Japanese farmers in Arizona and California turned to the Japanese Government after they were threatened with death and fire for daring to buy farms in white communities.

Unlike their fellow immigrants in Hawaii, the Japanese in the United States were never more than a tiny minority of the population, actually less than one-tenth of one percent. Even though almost all of the Japanese were concentrated in ten counties, in the three major West Coast cities, they were always outnumbered by the whites who surrounded them. Thus the Japanese were isolated from the larger community. They were forced to organize in defense of their own interests. In 1900 the Mayor of San Francisco, acting on a rumor that the city was threatened by an attack of the bubonic plague, quarantined the Chinese and Japanese sections of the city. The Japanese protested, charging that the quarantine was politically motivated and designed to put them out of business. They also protested that they had been unfairly treated by officials of the city's health bureau.

To protect themselves from any recurrence of such incidents in the future, the Japanese in San Francisco organized the first Japanese Association, which hired plainclothes men as guards. Similar organizations were set up in other Japanese communities. In Denver the local Association equipped all its members with whistles to be blown if they were physically attacked by whites; presumably they would then be rescued by armed gangs employed by the Association.

The Associations were primarily composed of businessmen and farmers, the top level of Japanese immigrants, who dominated the internal life of the communities. Their domination was based on the old, rigid class and caste structure of Japan which was carried over into Japanese life in the United States.

From self-defense, however, San Francisco's Association moved on to other objectives. One of them was ". . . to elevate the character of every Japanese resident in America; to promote his or her happiness and prosperity, and to cultivate a better understanding between our people and the American people."[7] They also attempted to change anti-Japanese laws. In 1901 the governor of California told the State Legislature that "At present the peril from the Chinese labor finds a similar danger in the unrestricted immigration of Japanese laborers."[8]

About the turn of the century California's legislature did adopt a resolution calling for the restriction of Japanese immigration. In 1904 the American Federation of Labor's national convention demanded that the Chinese Exclusion Laws be used against the Japanese as well. A few months later, Samuel Gompers, President of the A.F. of L., typically described a Japanese socialist visiting the United States as "a presumptuous Jap" who had a "lecherous mouth whose utterances show this mongrel's perverseness, ignorance, and maliciousness. . . ."[9]

Gompers refused to allow any Chinese or Japanese to join the labor unions. In 1903 in Oxnard, California, Japanese sugar-beet workers led a strike against their employers, charging starvation and bad treatment. They were joined by Mexican workers, and together they won an increase in wages and improvements in working conditions. After forming a union, they applied for membership in the American Federation of Labor. The reply from the union, received by the Mexican secretary J. M. Larraras, stated, in part: "Your union must guarantee that it will under no circumstances

[7] E. Manchester Boddy, *Japanese in America.* Los Angeles: Published by author, 1921, p. 73.

[8] Governor Henry T. Gage, quoted in *Pacific Citizen, op. cit.*

[9] Samuel Gompers, *Journal of the American Federation of Labor,* May, 1905.

accept membership of any Chinese or Japanese." Larraras wrote back:

> Your letter . . . in which you say the admission with us of the Japanese Sugar Beet and Farm Laborers into the American Federation of Labor can not be considered, is received. I beg to say in reply that our Japanese brothers here were the first to recognize the importance of cooperating and uniting in demanding a fair wage scale. . . .
>
> They were not only just with us, but they were generous when one of our men was murdered by hired assassins of the oppressors of labor, they gave expression to their sympathy in a very substantial form. In the past we have counseled, fought and lived on very short rations with our Japanese brothers, and toiled with them in the fields, and they have been uniformly kind and considerate. We would be false to them and to ourselves and to the cause of unionism if we now accepted privileges for ourselves which are not accorded to them. We are going to stand by men who stood by us in the long, hard fight which ended in a victory over the enemy. We therefore respectfully petition the A.F. of L. to grant us a charter under which we can unite all the sugar beet and field laborers of Oxnard without regard to their color or race. We will refuse any other kind of a charter except one which will wipe out race prejudices and recognize our fellow workers as being as good as ourselves.[10]

This was an exceptional situation in which members of two minority groups combined to fight for their rights. More often than not the Japanese were left to stand alone.

Many of the forces opposed to Japanese immigration joined together in 1905 to organize the Asiatic Exclusion League. The League's basic objectives were clear: "The preservation of the Caucasian race upon American soil and particularly upon the Western soil thereof, necessitates the adoption of all possible measures to prevent or minimize the immigration of Asiatics to America."[11]

Primary support for the League came from the trade unions, who organized it and always dominated its affairs. The League did not restrict its activities to fighting against

[10] Philip D. Foner, *History of the Labor Movement in the United States.* New York: International Publishers, 1947–55, Vol. III, p. 277.
[11] *Pacific Citizen, op. cit.*

immigration, however. It promoted boycotts of every Japanese enterprise that competed with those operated by whites; it also promoted boycotts of white businesses that employed Japanese workers, described by the League as "coolie hordes of . . . mongolized mongrels. . . ."[12]

A 1909 West Coast labor newspaper headline read, "UNLESS PEACE AND PROTECTION ARE SECURED BY TIMELY LEGISLATION, CHRISTIAN CIVILIZATION AND THE WHITE RACE ARE DOOMED."[13]

Even though the trade unions took the lead in fighting against the "coolie hordes," their position was buttressed by many other groups and individuals. The secretary of the California Board of Charities and Correction told a national convention of welfare groups in 1909 in a discussion on "Oriental Immigration": "Talk of assimilation is nonsense. The white peoples coming to this country will unite into a homogeneous race. . . . But sooner will the red and black race be assimilated with the Future American than will the yellow. . . . The foundation of this Republic is the Christian home, and a solemn duty is laid upon us for its preservation. The only safety lies in refusing admission to all branches of the Mongolian race."[14]

West Coast newspapers, too, spoke out vigorously against Japanese immigration. The editor of the San Francisco *Chronicle* wrote in the *Annals of the American Academy of Political and Social Science* that the opposition to the Japanese

> . . . is very general and there is not the slightest doubt that if a vote on exclusion were taken it would, after a brief campaign of education, be as nearly unanimous as that cast against Chinese immigration in 1879, when less than four-tenths of one per cent of the qualified electors of California voted in favor of continuing the admission of Chinese laborers. The motives that contributed

[12] *Proceedings of the Asiatic Exclusion League,* January, 1908, p. 13.

[13] *Organized Labor,* February 20, 1909.

[14] W. Almont Gates, "Oriental Immigration on the Pacific Coast," in *Pamphlets on Japanese Exclusion.* Berkeley: Phelan Collection of the University of California, Vol. 2, pp. 11–12.

to that result would again operate in the case of the Japanese and in a much more powerful manner, because the people are profoundly convinced that only by their exclusion can the white man's civilization be preserved on the Pacific coast.[15]

The San Francisco newspapers ran articles with headlines such as:

"JAPANESE WOMEN A MENACE TO AMERICAN WOMEN"
"BROWN ASIATICS STEAL BRAINS OF WHITES"
"BROWN MEN ARE AN EVIL IN THE PUBLIC SCHOOLS"[16]

Anti-Oriental groups in the West stressed the fact that Americans living in the eastern part of the United States did not understand the dimensions of the Asiatic problem. United States Senator Francis G. Newlands of Nevada warned in 1909 that "Confronting our Pacific Coast lies Asia, with nearly a billion people of the yellow and brown races, who, if there were no restrictions, would quickly settle upon and take possession of our entire western coast and intermountain region."[17]

The three leading political parties in California were unanimous in supporting anti-Oriental legislation. Early in the twentieth century a plank in the Republican Party platform stated the party's faith in the "unswerving opposition of the People of California to the further admission of Oriental laborers." The Democratic Party called for "The

[15] John P. Young, "The Support of the Anti-Oriental Movement," *Annals of the American Academy of Political and Social Science,* Vol. XXXIV, No. 2, Sept., 1909, p. 18.

[16] *Pacific Citizen, op. cit.*, p. B4.

[17] Francis G. Newlands in the *Annals of the American Academy of Political and Social Science, op. cit.,* p. 270. The Senator, who believed "The race question is the most important one now confronting the nation," also had definite convictions about the blacks. He wrote: "As to the black race, we have already drifted into a condition which seriously suggests the limitation of the political rights heretofore, perhaps mistakenly, granted them, the inauguration of a humane national policy which, by co-operative action of the nation and the southern states, shall recognize that the blacks are a race of children, requiring guidance, industrial training, and the development of self-control, and other measures designed to reduce the danger of that race complication, formerly sectional, but now rapidly becoming national." *Ibid.,* p. 289.

exclusion of all Asiatic labor" and the prevention of "Asiatics who are not eligible to citizenship from owning land in California." Even the Socialist Party opposed the "mass immigration and importation of Mongolian or East Indian labor. . . ."

Anti-Asiatic groups did not stop with attempts to limit immigration, but carried on an active program of hostility towards the Japanese who were already in the United States. In some places the Japanese were beaten in the streets and their businesses and homes set on fire. Mr. M. Sugawa, a shoemaker at 1172a Divisadero Street in San Francisco, reported that on

> August 17, 1906 ,at 8:40 P.M., as I was passing on Sutter Street, near Scott, three boys, 21 or 22 years of age, attacked my person. I nearly fainted. Upon rising to my feet, they again assaulted me. This time they smashed my nose. I grabbed the coat of one of the trio, and after having my nose dressed at one of the nearby hospitals, I went home. The next day a policeman came, requesting me to give up the coat. I at first refused, but finally, upon his assuring me that it would be deposited at the police station, I gave it up. I reported the matter to the police. When the case came up for trial the youngster was dismissed on the plea of insufficiency of evidence.

In another typical report, a grocery clerk named I. Ikuda said,

> As I was driving my wagon on Davis Street, between Vallejo and Broadway, five or six laborers, apparently over 28 years old, appeared from the baggage cars and threw potatoes and egg plants at me and my horse. Soon they began throwing pieces of brick, and I was forced to turn back a block or so. Since September 8 such incidents occurred five times. None of these events were reported to the police, because it would be of no avail.

Most western states passed legislation forbidding intermarriage between Asiatics and Caucasians.

Such intense hostility dominated the early years of Japanese immigration to the United States. In part, it was because several national groups were competing in a dynamic area. But many of the problems the Japanese encountered were carried over from the conflicts engendered by Chinese immigration approximately fifty years earlier. Influenced to a certain extent by the racism of nineteenth-century anthropology, Californians tended to conceive of their state as white man's territory.

Opposition to the Japanese continued over a span of many years. As late as 1933 the California Joint Immigration Committee, whose members included state officials and representatives of the American Federation of Labor, the American Legion, and the Native Sons of the Golden West, was still warning that

> . . . absolute exclusion of Asiatics in the future is vital to California. The Gentlemen's Agreement, announced as a plan for rigid restriction of Japanese immigration, was to be carried out by Japanese good faith instead of enforced by U.S. law. . . . Today over one-third of Hawaii's total population is Japanese; over two-thirds is Asiatic. Hawaii, a United States Territory, is lost to the white race. . . . It is admitted that the Japanese are mentally, morally and physically the equal of Caucasians, but racial differences and racial pride, social conditions and ineligibility to citizenship make them hopelessly unassimilable. . . . Exclusion of ineligibles casts no reflection on the mental, moral and physical fitness of those excluded. They are excluded because their unassimilability makes them a danger to the political health of the nation, as immigrants deficient physically would offer danger to the physical health of its citizens. . . .[18]

Although the mainland Japanese community resented the treatment from whites, none of the numerous Japanese-language newspapers on the West Coast took the aggressive role enacted by *Hawaii Hochi,* a newspaper published for the Japanese living in Hawaii. Whenever the mainland community found itself in difficulty, it first tried limited self-protection and then, as a last recourse, sought help from Japan. In some cases Japan did help.

California's 1903 school law, Page 37, Article 10, "Primary and Grammar Schools," Section 1662, says, "Trustees

[18] The California Joint Immigration Committee Answers the Two Leading Proponents of Quota, November 13, 1933. Pamphlet in Bancroft Library, University of California, Berkeley, California.

shall have the power to exclude all children of filthy or vicious habits, or children suffering from contagious or infectious diseases, and also to establish separate schools for Indian children, and for the children of Mongolian or Chinese descent. When such separate schools are established, Indian, Chinese or Mongolian children must not be admitted into any other schools."

In 1906 San Francisco city authorities attempted to segregate Japanese children into one school. The Japanese Government formally protested to the American Government. President Theodore Roosevelt, who feared the incident might lead to war, successfully pressured the city authorities into rescinding the ruling. "I am horribly bothered about the Japanese business," Roosevelt wrote his son. "The infernal fools in California and especially San Francisco insult the Japanese recklessly and in the event of war, it will be the nation as a whole that will bear the consequences."[19]

After Roosevelt's tactic, the Japanese and Corean [*sic*] Exclusion League wired Mayor Schmitz of San Francisco:

> . . . Sovereign rights must not be bartered away for promises, and should not be basis for compromise. We will not yield one iota of our rights as a sovereign people, regardless of cost of consequence. If President wants to humiliate American flag, let him tell California's Governor and Legislature to repeal the law, but he cannot coerce free Californians to bow in submission to the will of the Mikado. Roosevelt's power will not make one white man out of all the Japs in the Nipponese Empire. California is the white man's country, and not the Caucasian graveyard.

Roosevelt, however, was actually opposed to any large-scale immigration of Japanese. He was convinced that the best way to avert it was not by attacking the Japanese in the United States, but by dealing with the Japanese Government. He negotiated a treaty with Japan in 1907 limiting further immigration. The treaty, which became known as the "Gentlemen's Agreement," provided that the Japanese

[19] A. W. Griswold, *Far Eastern Policy of the United States*. New York: Harcourt, Brace & Co., 1938, p. 251.

government would issue passports only to ". . . such of its subjects as are non-laborers or are laborers who, in coming to the continent, seek to resume a previously acquired domicile, to join a parent, wife or children residing therein, or to assume active control of an already possessed interest in a farming enterprise located in this country. . . ."[20] The Agreement also prohibited those Japanese whose passports were valid only for Mexico, Canada, and Hawaii from traveling to the U.S. from those places. Immigration dropped from 10,000 a year to 2,500. It did not rise again until 1910 when immigration authorities began to interpret more liberally those provisions of the Agreement stating that members of an immigrant's family could join him in America. That provision led to the practice of bringing over "picture brides" from Japan.

The new, liberal approach of the immigration authorities was their response to the continuing demand for Japanese labor by American employers. In the United States, as in Hawaii, there was a conflict between those who wanted the Japanese as cheap labor and those who opposed them for the same reason. As a result of this conflict some illegal immigration went on, perhaps with the secret cooperation of the immigration authorities.

The fact that some of the Japanese were illegal immigrants influenced the community's response to the white world: the possibility of jail or deportation forced the illegal immigrants to be cautious and to suffer abuse rather than retaliate and attract the attention of government officials.

The first Japanese in the United States worked at the marginal jobs: laying railroad ties and performing menial service tasks in mining towns and lumber camps. As those jobs disappeared, many Japanese immigrants fanned out into the rural areas where they became day workers for farmers. Soon Japanese men—and women—became a source of mobile labor, supplied to the farmers by a contractor, or "Jap boss" as the whites called him. The "Jap

[20] Henry Steele Commager, ed., *Documents of American History*. New York: Appleton-Century-Crofts, Inc., 1950, p. 225.

boss" provided living quarters, food, and a small wage to his workers, moving them from place to place to do the back-breaking work whites refused to do.

This system brought a reasonably stable labor force to the task of harvesting California truck crops. To the newly arrived Japanese immigrant who spoke no English, the paternalistic boss system offered employment, counseling, sustenance, and some continuity with his life in Japan.

Because the Japanese were skilled at making things grow, they increasingly occupied land in the valleys. They turned arid land nobody else wanted into green, productive areas. In the desert they would sink a well, plant trees, and soon begin to market cash crops. They drained the marshy lands, introduced irrigation systems, and reclaimed marginal properties.

Their success in agriculture added new fuel to the fires of anti-Orientalism; while the California growers were delighted to have the Japanese available as a stable, trustworthy work force, they were bitterly resentful of those Japanese who became competitors.

So a law was passed in 1913 in California prohibiting aliens "ineligible for citizenship" from owning land or from leasing land for more than three years; another land law was passed in 1920 by popular vote that extended the prohibitions against land ownership to corporations and trustees. Those laws struck at the base of the Japanese economy—farming. The alien land laws attempted to prevent the first-generation Japanese immigrants from legally owning land. But with the cooperation of some whites who had an economic stake in Japanese farmers, the law was evaded. After the 1913 law was passed, Japanese farms were put into the names of corporations of whites who acted as trustees. Then the 1920 law was enacted, stopping up this loophole. Immigrants then put their farms under the legal ownership of their American-born children.

By this time the Issei, or first generation, were convinced they would never be allowed citizenship. In 1912 the U.S. Supreme Court ruled that Takao Ozawa, who had applied for citizenship in Hawaii, was ineligible because, although "well qualified by character and education for citizenship," he had been born in Japan and was not Caucasian. To justify the government's refusal to grant citizenship to Ozawa, the Solicitor General of the United States argued in the Court that "The men who settled this country were white men from Europe and the men who fought the Revolutionary War, framed the Constitution and established the Government, were white men from Europe and their descendants. They were eager for more of their kind to come and it was to men of their own kind that they held out the opportunity for citizenship. . . ."

The Court agreed with the Solicitor General, stating that the exclusion of Orientals from citizenship was "a rule in force from the beginning of the Government, a part of our history as well as our law, welded into the structure of our national policy by a century of legislative and administrative acts and judicial decisions. . . ."[21]

The Japanese paid a heavy penalty for the low status forced upon them by the immigration and land laws. They managed to evade the laws but this made it difficult to seek legal redress for grievances, since the price of taking such action might be exposure. The traditional Japanese distrust of outsiders was thus reinforced; any white person asking questions might be dangerous.

In 1924 Congress passed another Immigration Act that reaffirmed the ineligibility of foreign-born Japanese immigrants for citizenship and halted Japanese immigration almost completely. By this time, the dominant responses to white society were fixed. The older generation, the Issei, knew that American citizenship was not open to them and tended to identify more with Japan than with America; Japan was not only their mother country, it was their only country. They were guests in America and not very welcome guests at that. Whatever rights they had were at the sufferance of the white society in which they lived.

Inevitably, then, some Issei tried to duplicate the life they

[21] Ozawa v. U.S., 260 U.S. 178 (1922), p. 187.

or their parents had lived in Japan. They spoke only Japanese, ate Japanese food, observed all the old Japanese customs. Many sent their children back to Japan for at least some education in the Japanese way of life. When the children returned, they were called Kibei. The Issei operated politically through the Japanese Associations which maintained formal ties with Japan and its consuls. The Association processed immigration matters, assisted indigents, encouraged adult education, and sponsored Japanese-language schools for Nisei children as a way of bridging the generation gap.

The Association had a quasi-official function—representing ghetto interests to the outside world and Japan. In addition, the Japanese in America organized *kenjinkai,* groups primarily social in origin and purpose. *Kens* were to be found in Japanese communities all over the West Coast. They expressed the impulse of the community to stick to its own kind; the *ken* members shared a common speech and a nostalgia for their heritage and geographical origin; they also arranged marriages and employment.

It was inevitable that many of the American-born, the Nisei, would come into conflict with their elders and try to develop their own life styles. The conflict was muted, however, since it was difficult to shake off the old ways they had been brought up to respect. "During my childhood," said one Nisei in a typical report, "the Issei considered that socials and dances among the Nisei were taboo. There was also a general taboo against the Nisei smoking or dating out. The Nisei fellows couldn't date out girls of certain families and we couldn't even go over there for a social visit because of the parents' attitude. These girls were married by arrangement in the Japanese manner and I think that most of the Nisei in our area accepted this practice. Those who rebelled were ostracized for their action."[22]

Inevitably, the Nisei view of how to deal with difficulties they encountered in the Caucasian-dominated world was

[22] Dorothy Swaine Thomas, with Charles Kikuchi and James Sakoda, *The Salvage*. Berkeley: University of California Press, 1952, p. 157.

affected fundamentally by the experiences of their parents. The Nisei set up in 1930 an organization of their own, the Japanese-American Citizens League; like the older Japanese Association, it tried to avoid any direct confrontation with the white world. Its main activities were social, its politics conservative.

"Most of the Nisei students were children of small Issei businessmen and a very few of them were proletarian," reported one observer, himself a Nisei. "That is why the bulk of the Nisei were so conservative. Before the war, the JACL was a very innocuous group and not socially conscious at all. It played the middle of the line on all political issues."[23] Politically, the JACL attempted by discreet lobbying to build up pressure against discriminatory legislation and to perform public relations for the Japanese community by politely interpreting it to the world outside. At the same time it educated the Nisei students in Americanism.

Occasionally, however, some act of anti-Japanese hostility forced even the JACL to take a different stance. In 1934 the homes of Japanese farmers were bombed in Arizona. In 1935 increasing bitterness threatened the Japanese farmers of Tulare County, California, and the JACL, together with the Japanese Association, had to turn to the Japanese Government for help. But during the Sino-Japanese War in the 1930s the JACL refused to take a positive stand in support of or opposition to the Japanese Government. Ultimately, though, as World War II approached, the JACL began an anti-Japan campaign.

The mainstream of America was never open to the Nisei, despite their efforts to be more American than the whites they emulated. Most employment, except for menial jobs, was closed to them. If they were hired for white-collar work, they were the first to be fired; only rarely were they able to advance above low-level positions, no matter how professionally they were trained. College graduates worked

[23] *Ibid.*, p. 330.

for long hours at low pay as domestic servants and fruit-stand clerks, and in laundries. Except for a few cartoonists, art teachers, and entertainers, most Nisei were forced to turn to their own communities for employment, which brought them back into conflict with their Issei elders. The Nisei girls had a little more opportunity: nurses' jobs, for example, were open for them.

The frustrations of the Nisei were enormous, tantalized as they were by an America that proclaimed equal opportunities for all its citizens, but refused to grant those opportunities to the Japanese. And nearly all the Nisei encountered some form of direct aggression in their daily lives, beginning in their childhood.

One Nisei writer recalls: "The first time that I ran into the epithet 'Jap,' "

> I was six years old, living in Green Valley, California, when a bully riding on a horse pulled up to the school grounds, where we were playing and yelled "Japs" and proceeded to charge his horse into us. . . .
>
> A little later in Sacramento when I was 7 or 8 . . . I awoke very early to go down and take a peek [at a carnival]. The flap in the tent was open and an unshaved man was sitting in front of a fire boiling water for coffee. Suddenly, he picked up a paring knife and chased me, saying he was going to cut off the ears of this "Jap"! He chased me all the way home. . . .

Every Nisei was always aware of being a Nisei, always conscious of being different, of being considered inferior. For some Nisei even Pearl Harbor and the evacuation into detention centers came as a welcome lifting of the burden they had been carrying.

"The war came with terrible suddenness, even more violently broke the shell in which we lived," said one.

> In my heart I secretly welcomed the evacuation because it was a total escape from the world I knew. Even when the men took me away to the tarpapered barracks I felt for the first time in my life a complete sense of relief. The struggle against a life which seemed so futile and desperate was ended. Never again would I

have to live it, never again see it, never again be haunted by its spectres.

This was relief. It was no solution.[24]

The shock waves set off by the bombing of Pearl Harbor were disastrous for every person of Japanese ancestry living in the continental United States. All the old hostilities toward Orientals surfaced. "No Japs Allowed" signs reappeared in public places, Nisei were fired from their jobs and denounced in the mass media. The Chinese began wearing buttons saying "I Am Chinese," and the Koreans wore ones stating "I Am Korean," lest they be mistaken for the Japanese enemy.

The United States Government moved immediately against Japanese-Americans. The FBI took hundreds of Japanese into custody and Nisei servicemen were discharged from the military.

One response of the United States Government to Pearl Harbor was to freeze in the banks the assets of enemy aliens—Italians and Germans, as well as Japanese. Enemy aliens were visited by a representative from the Immigration Service who had the power to relax restrictions on their assets and on their freedom to travel after determining their loyalty. Sometimes this determination involved no more than a simple interview; sometimes it involved arrest.

The money of all the Japanese was frozen in the banks and their credit abolished. Private industry reacted just as viciously. Milk deliveries were cut off, for example. The Japanese had to use cash for all purposes, cash they could only get by selling their possessions for tiny sums paid by unscrupulous buyers. And even with cash, they could not buy groceries or clothing easily, because some merchants were afraid to sell goods to them—it might be considered trading with the enemy.

After the initial raids by the Immigration Service, some Caucasian friends of the Japanese came to their aid, offer-

[24] Bradford Smith, *Americans from Japan.* Philadelphia & New York: J. B. Lippincott Co., 1948, p. 243.

ing them support. Life and business returned almost to normal in the Japanese ghettos. The Japanese people were certain no further hostilities would be visited upon them like those at the outbreak of the war with Germany in 1914.

Military officials and federal authorities made assurances that the Japanese-Americans were neither a threat to United States security nor an impediment to the war effort. Officials acted quickly to protect the Little Tokyo in Los Angeles. One policeman there commented that the Japanese were much better citizens than those who were throwing stones at the neat Japanese stores and homes.

Yet, within two months public opinion shifted radically because of a heavy anti-Japanese campaign by the press and political leaders. The public mood became ugly, and there was loud talk of sending the Japs back where they came from. Another war for democracy again unleashed the racism in America.

Political pressure was put on the military to intern all Japanese as enemy aliens. A West Coast Congressional delegation recommended that "all persons of Japanese lineage" be evacuated from California, Oregon, and Washington. Governor Cuthbert B. Olson of California warned that "if nothing is done, the people may take things into their own hands," and Mayor Fletcher Bowron of Los Angeles added his official voice to the growing clamor for the evacuation of all Japanese.

Veterans' organizations like the American Legion and the Veterans of Foreign Wars were, of course, among those who demanded that all Japanese, citizens and aliens alike, be interned. Chambers of Commerce up and down the coast joined in the chorus, supported by even more prestigious groups like the Merchants and Manufacturers Association of Los Angeles.

Strident cries for evacuation also came from those white Americans who had the most to gain financially from their patriotic demand—the white farmers. For years they had been watching for an opportunity to take over the lands which had been transformed by the hardworking Japanese from deserts and rocky terraces into productive farms.

"We're charged with wanting to get rid of the Japs for selfish reasons," said the managing director of a growers' association in California in 1942:

> We do. It's a question of whether the white man lives on the Pacific Coast or the brown men. They came into this valley to work and they stayed to take over. . . . They undersell the white man in the markets. . . . They work their women and children while the white farmer has to pay wages for his help. If all the Japs were removed tomorrow, we'd never miss them in two weeks, because the white farmers can take over and produce everything the Jap grows. And we don't want them back when the war ends, either.[25]

Significantly, plans for the evacuation of the Japanese were opposed by growers in the northern part of California who depended upon Japanese farm workers to harvest their grapes, asparagus, tomatoes, and grains.

The tempo of hysteria was quickened, too, by the ever-increasing support the evacuation concept received in the mass media. The Hearst press, always on the lookout for "The Yellow Peril," naturally advocated evacuation, and the august Los Angeles *Times* suggested that, since "A viper is nonetheless a viper wherever the egg is hatched," no distinction could be made between alien Japanese and those born in the United States. The *Times* proposed to "treat them all as potential enemies."

The old anti-Orientalism of the American Federation of Labor burst into the open again, now made respectable by the war. In September of 1942, the annual convention of the California State Federation of Labor went on record as commending the Native Sons of the Golden West for its work in anti-Oriental agitation. It pointed out, however, that "the true credit for the agitation against Oriental

[25] Quoted in the Supreme Court Decision, Koramatsu v. U.S., from *The Saturday Evening Post,* May 9, 1942, p. 66.

immigration should go where it belongs—to the pioneers of the trade union movement . . . who in and out of season preached the gospel of exclusion of Orientals."[26]

Even Walter Lippmann, the liberal columnist, argued in favor of the evacuation of all Japanese, whether or not they were American citizens.

Earl Warren, then Attorney General of California, said:

> . . . The consensus of opinion among the law-enforcement officers of this State is that there is more potential danger among the group of Japanese who are born in this country than from the alien Japanese who were born in Japan. . . . I believe we are just being lulled into a false sense of security and that the only reason we haven't had a disaster in California is because it has been timed for a different date. . . . Our day of reckoning is bound to come in that regard. . . .[27]

(To this day Warren's correspondence and files on that remarkable period are not available for publication.)

The Commanding General of the Western Defense Command, John L. DeWitt, reported to the Secretary of War that "The Japanese race is an enemy race and while many second and third generation Japanese born on United States soil, possessed of United States citizenship, have become 'Americanized,' the racial strains are undiluted. . . . It, therefore, follows that along the vital Pacific Coast over 112,000 potential enemies, of Japanese extraction, are at large today."[28] Furthermore, General DeWitt had his explanation as to why no single act of sabotage had taken place on the West Coast despite the presence of over 112,000 "potential enemies": "The very fact that no sabotage has taken place to date," stated the General, "is a

[26] *Proceedings of the Forty-Third Annual Convention of the California State Federation of Labor,* September 21–25, 1942, p. 226.

[27] Select Committee Investigating National Migration, *op. cit.,* pp. 11012, 11014.

[28] Jacobus ten Broek, Edward N. Barnhart, Floyd W. Matson, *Prejudice, War and the Constitution.* Berkeley: University of California Press, 1954, p. 110.

disturbing and confirming indication that such action will be taken."[29]

The organized growers, having long been covetous of Japanese-owned farms, began petitioning their congressmen and agitating for the evacuation of the Japanese "before it is too late." The racism of some of the California congressmen approached the intensity of classic southern demagoguery. They denounced public officials who offered protection to Japanese and disbelieved statements by military officials claiming that the Japanese posed no threat. After all, hadn't Pearl Harbor caught the military off guard?

The most fantastic rumors swept California. For example, it was asserted as fact that Nisei soldiers serving at Fort Ord shouted "Banzai!" and burned their barracks upon hearing of the strike on Pearl Harbor. And Japanese farmers were supposed to have planted their crops in arrow patterns to direct Japanese air strikes on military installations. Japanese gardeners supposedly told their employers, "You'll be working for me when the war is over!"

In the early days of 1942, when a Japanese invasion appeared imminent, life in the Japanese ghettos took on a nightmarish quality. Rumors flew thick and fast, just as they did through the Caucasian communities, wreaking havoc on the lives of the Japanese. No one could plan for even a week ahead.

All Japanese shared the feelings of fear and confusion in the face of the evacuation threat and vigilante violence. Rumors of anti-Japanese actions spread throughout the communities, as well as wild stories of widespread sabotage carried out by Japanese-Americans in Hawaii and on the West Coast. In their common plight, the Japanese turned to each other as they had never done before. Many of those with *hakujin* (Caucasian friends) found those friends as bewildered as they were.

[29] U.S. Army, Western Defense Command and Fourth Army, *Final Report: Japanese Evacuation from the West Coast*. Washington: Government Printing Office, 1943, p. 34.

Many Japanese were angry; the young ones because they had convinced themselves they were Americans as good as any others; the older ones were bitter at seeing the work of their lives wiped out and their children betrayed.

Their fear, anger, and bitterness were accompanied by a profound sense of frustration because they felt there was nothing *they* could do to change the direction of their lives. The Nisei, especially, felt they were the helpless victims of a prejudice many of them had convinced themselves was disappearing. In a larger sense, they were victims of a war fought between Japan and the United States for the empire of Southeast Asia. That conflict dated as far back as the 1904–05 Russo-Japanese War when the U.S. Government sided with the Russians under the assumption that Japan was the more formidable threat to the United States.

Both countries, of course, used the rhetoric of patriotism to enlist popular support. In the case of the Japanese, the attack on Pearl Harbor was headlined as sneaky, brutal, and barbaric—methods of attack supposedly typical of the Japanese personality. If they pulled a sneak attack on Pearl Harbor, reasoned the press and public, they were certain to do worse in California.

Because of their tenuous position, the Japanese needed an agency through which to deal with the American authorities. Because the government had chosen the JACL as the organization with which it would make arrangements and through which it would communicate its plans for American Japanese, the JACL became the focal point of the ghetto. The JACL became the U.S. Government's interpreter to the Japanese community. The Issei organizations, the older Japanese Associations, lost influence as the JACL gained.

The accommodationist JACL accepted evacuation and relocation plans developed by the authorities. It became, in fact, the official liaison between agencies involved in evacuation procedures and the Japanese communities. It cooperated with all the government intelligence agencies and assisted the FBI in making loyalty assessments of the Japanese. Because many Issei spoke no English, they were dependent upon their Nisei children (many of whom belonged to JACL) to translate the implications of war with Japan to them.

Within the communities the JACL continued to advocate acceptance of any policy proposed by the U.S. Government. Its members were convinced that acceptance was the only way Japanese-Americans could prove they were truly American. Some Japanese, however, like Joseph Y. Kurihara, wanted to resist the evacuation and believed the communities ought to organize to protest against being treated as the enemy. When the U.S. Army took over responsibility for the Japanese on the West Coast, Kurihara had "expected that at least the Nisei would be allowed to remain. But to General DeWitt, we were all alike. 'A Jap's a Jap, Once a Jap, Always a Jap.' . . . I swore to become a Jap 100 percent and never to do another day's work to help this country fight this war. My decision to renounce my citizenship there and then was absolute."[30]

Even those Nisei who were most pliant and most willing to cooperate with the Caucasian authorities to prove their loyalty were scarred by the terrible shock of being interned solely because of their ancestry.

In anticipation of the evacuation order, many Japanese along the coast picked up their belongings and moved inland. By mid-March of 1942, 9,000 Japanese had moved out of the restricted zones along the coast. The inland communities, without exception, would not accept them. There was no room for them, no work, and no place to live. The logic was that if the Japanese were saboteurs on the coast, could they not just as well contribute to the Emperor's war effort inland? If the Japanese might blow up a naval installation, might they not poison the water supply of Fresno or Bakersfield?

By the end of March, the Army made plans for the immediate evacuation of the Japanese to assembly centers,

[30] Allan R. Bosworth, *America's Concentration Camps.* New York: W. W. Norton & Co., 1967.

to await construction of relocation camps in the hinterland.

One persistent rumor that destroyed peace of mind in those days—it even followed ghetto residents into the camps—was that the Japanese were to be interned as hostages to insure the future well-being of American war prisoners. That rumor had some basis in fact when it became apparent that the United States in cooperation with the Peruvian Government had transported by ship and air nearly two thousand Peruvian Japanese from South America to internment camps in Texas. The Peruvian Japanese, many of them married to Peruvian women, had been part of the Japanese emigration to South America in 1900 in response to the demand for cheap labor on the plantations. After Pearl Harbor these immigrant laborers were arrested by the Peruvian police and turned over to American MPs for shipment to the United States. One important reason for this maneuver was that the Peruvian Japanese could be held for possible exchange for Americans interned in Japan.

In the United States the Peruvian Japanese were kept in camps, under the provisions of the Enemy Alien Act of 1798, until the end of the war. Then a dispute broke out among government agencies over their legal status. Neither the State Department, which had made the original arrangements for their forced deportation, nor the Justice Department, which had supervised their internment, wanted the responsibility for them any longer. The Peruvian Government refused to take them back, and they did not want to go to Japan. They were turned over to the Immigration Service which maintained they were not eligible for American citizenship because they were illiterate in English and Hebrew (in order to pass the Immigration Service tests, they had to know one or the other) and because they had entered the United States without credentials or passports. The latter was certainly true since they had actually been kidnapped by the Peruvian and United States governments. Some years later, after many legal battles, waged by two attorneys, Wayne Collins and Theodore Tamba they were finally granted the right to remain in the United States.

Despite the JACL's belief that Japanese-Americans would not be judged "on the basis of physical characteristics," the criterion used to determine who was to be removed was precisely that: all persons, citizens and aliens alike, who had "a Japanese ancestor, regardless of degree" were evacuated. (The Nazis used only one-eighth Jewish ancestry as the criterion for removal to their concentration camps.)

So 112,000 West Coast Japanese were moved, on notice as short as forty-eight hours in some cases and ranging up to two weeks in others. When these thousands of bewildered men, women, and children boarded the buses, trains, and trucks that transported them to the assembly centers, they were allowed to take with them only as much baggage as they could carry. They left behind hundreds of millions of dollars worth of land, stores, cars, household goods, and personal possessions, which they were forced to sell at a tiny percentage of their real value to greedy and unscrupulous speculators. One aspect of the plight of the evacuees is illustrated in part of a letter to the authorities. ". . . I own a refrigerator which I purchased about five months ago, I am almost half finished with the payment. What do you think I should do? The ladies here are all debating too. Whether to return it or still keep payment on it. Is it worth it? I sure hate to lose it, because I've paid so much on it already. Please let me know? . . ."

Kurihara, the resister, described in the most bitter terms the evacuation process at Terminal Island where families were given only forty-eight hours to sell their possessions and leave for the camps:

> It was really cruel and harsh. To pack and evacuate in forty-eight hours was an impossibility. Seeing mothers completely bewildered with children crying from want and peddlers taking advantage and offering prices next to robbery, made me feel like murdering those responsible without the slightest compunction in my heart.

The parents may be aliens but the children are all American citizens. Did the government of the United States intend to ignore their rights regardless of their citizenship? Those beautiful furnitures which the parents bought to please their sons and daughters, costing hundreds of dollars, were robbed of them at the single command, "Evacuate!" Here my first doubt of American Democracy crept into the far corners of my heart with the sting that I could not forget. Having had absolute confidence in Democracy, I could not believe my very eyes what I had seen that day. America the standard bearer of Democracy had committed the most heinous crime in its history.[31]

The War Relocation Authority was created to find relocation camps for the Japanese, but since no community would accept the camps, they were opened in the most desolate, windswept areas of California, Arizona, Colorado, Utah, and Arkansas. A single camp in New Jersey accommodated all the East Coast Japanese.

General DeWitt stretched the authority of the President's Executive Order to detain the Japanese and establish the Wartime Civilian Control Administration. Fifteen assembly centers were chosen, by the WCCA, near the ghettos—usually race tracks or large fairgrounds. At Santa Anita, for example, 13,000 residents from the Los Angeles area camped in hastily constructed barracks or horse stalls converted for human habitation. Life in the assembly centers was a temporary phase of the detention. It was assumed that the camps would be temporary places of confinement, until the Japanese could be relocated in communities outside the restricted zones.

The War Relocation Authority camps turned out to be a curious mixture of concentration camp and welfare state. The internees were to be given an opportunity to demonstrate their loyalty to the United States through jobs which would contribute to the war effort. Health and hospital services were provided, as well as communal dining areas.

[31] Dorothy Swaine Thomas and Richard S. Nishimoto, *The Spoilage*. Berkeley & Los Angeles: University of California Press, 1946, pp. 367–68.

Counseling services were offered by kindly WRA staff as part of a plan to accustom internees to their new life.

Camp life was at first pleasant for some, despite their griping. For the first time, many Issei men had the leisure to indulge in pastimes they had always valued. Women were freed from the drudgery of life in the ghettos or on the farms. They were not faced with the necessity of making decisions affecting their lives, since that responsibility now resided with a paternalistic bureaucracy.

Work in the camps was not forced labor; if the inmates did not like conditions of camp life, they struck or did not cooperate; due process usually accompanied efforts to discipline camp insurgents; families were kept together. Most important, no effort was made to shatter the strong Japanese identities of the inmates.

Attempts at indoctrination were half-hearted and mostly verbal. The nationalistic pro-Japanese Kibei who flaunted makeshift Japanese flags and shouted "Banzai!" were segregated. Life in the camps, for three or more years, was no idyll. But it never approached the horrors of the European concentration camps. Some administrators at the Tule Lake Segregation Camp, in California, for example, resigned when the Army put tanks outside the gates, protesting that a concentration camp atmosphere was being generated.

Many Japanese entered the camps in a spirit of good will and cooperation with WRA authorities. They viewed the barren countryside, the absence of comfortable facilities, and the crowding of whole families into a single room as problems they had to overcome. They set about making the countryside bloom, and fashioning homes from old lumber and makeshift tools.

The experience began to sour, though, as issue after issue reopened the wounds and humiliations of the evacuation. By mid-June, 1942, the good will that well-meaning liberal WRA administrators had brought to their jobs was spent.

The camps became like prisons, fenced off by barbed wire, with military sentinels stationed in towers at spaced intervals. Passes were required for whites to enter or leave the camps. In most relocation camps the guards were merely tokens of authority; in others major outbreaks occurred. At Poston, Arizona, and Manzanar and Tule Lake in California, the inmates revolted, led strikes, and refused to cooperate.

The old, dormant conflicts within the Japanese communities broke out into the open but always over some present, important issue. The poor conditions and low wages exacerbated the tensions. JACL leadership counseled that working for $16 per month was a demonstration of patriotism—but white workers outside the camps were earning inflated wartime wages. At Tule Lake a field-workers' strike over working conditions became a general strike when authorities brought in strikebreakers and gave them choice wages and excellent food. The Army arrested the strike leaders and confined them without formal charges for the duration of the war.

At Manzanar, a camouflage-net factory was opened. Originally the factory offered competitive wages, but when word spread outside the camps that the Japanese were going to earn more than American soldiers, such a howl went up that the WRA quickly backed down. Even the promised $16 per month rarely materialized. Finally the factory was abandoned.

Work assignments in the camps were made on the basis that each inmate would do what he was best prepared for as his contribution to camp life. This meant that the Issei, who were mostly small businessmen and farmers, had few of the skills suitable for the prestige jobs. Those jobs—running the newspaper, camp administrative tasks, and clerical assignments—went to the Nisei. The Issei filled the service jobs as dishwashers, cooks, and janitors.

Another abrasive feature of camp life was its government. The prevailing WRA ideology was that the camps would be run democratically, with eventual self-government for the inmates; there would also be indoctrination into the values of the American way of life. To this end—and also to prevent outside meddling—official WRA policy discouraged Japanese national pastimes, the celebration of Japanese customs, and the use of the Japanese language. Japanese schools, for so long an important feature of ghetto life, were forbidden. English was to be the official language in all camp affairs. The effect of these policies was to disfranchise the Issei as a class and to hand over power to the Nisei, thus alienating the Issei even more from camp affairs. Ultimately the Americanization policy hampered efforts of the camp administration to integrate the Issei into American life.

The response of the Japanese to the restrictive rules of the WRA was to organize themselves.

At Manzanar the Issei refused to take their exclusion from camp government without a fight. They dominated the small, block councils, which selected representatives to the larger councils and had the power to veto measures. When, for example, the larger councils attempted to pass a resolution to assist the Office of War Information in making propaganda broadcasts to Japan, the Issei vetoed the measure.

Unions of kitchen and field workers were organized. Leaflets and manifestoes mysteriously appeared on the walls of the baths and dining commons denouncing real or imagined traitors, protesting conditions in the camps, interpreting the rulings of the WRA. These interpretations took on anti-American, pro-Japanese tones.

The Issei saw conditions of camp life as proof that they would never be accepted as American citizens or returned to their old status as friendly aliens in American society. Many romanticized life in Japan as they remembered it and made plans to resettle there after the war. Some Kibei, aggressively pro-Japanese from the outset, agitated for recognition as Japanese aliens from the camp administration. They attempted to maintain relations with the Japanese Government through the Spanish consuls.

But the greatest tension and conflict was among the Nisei. The evacuation had shattered the patterns of their lives and broken their faith in America and their image of themselves as Americans.

Violence broke out at Manzanar. The nationalistic and secret Blood Brothers emerged, writing threatening letters to the *inu* (the dogs) who had betrayed their fellow Japanese. They beat or intimidated real and imagined informers. The militants began a campaign to discredit the Manzanar Citizens Federation which they claimed was the old accommodationist JACL leadership in sheep's clothing. The militants urged as many camp inmates as possible to fight the administrators. Many families were caught between the pressure to resist from the militants and the pressure to cooperate from the administrators and their accommodationist Nisei helpers. The insurgents were certain the collaborators had an active relationship with the FBI and other intelligence operations that seemed omnipresent in the camps; they were also convinced that reports of their meetings found their way into the files of the camp administration.

When one alleged informer was beaten and another had to hide for his life under a hospital bed, camp authorities arrested a suspect and secretly whisked him away from the camp. They did not charge him with a specific crime. Camp inmates rose up *en masse* and marched on the administration. Organizers of the march refused to disperse the crowd until the suspect was released or his rights of due process upheld. National Guardsmen attempted to disperse the crowd with tear gas, but the gas wafted away in the wind. One Guardsman was heard to exhort other soldiers to "Remember Pearl Harbor!" Suddenly the soldiers fired on the crowd, killing two young Nisei. Others were hurt in the ensuing melee.

The insurrection ended when its leadership was isolated and removed to special segregated units at Tule Lake. There the rebel leaders were dumped in with avowedly pro-Japanese aliens from other camps for the duration of the war.

Affairs in the camps came to a head in January of 1943 with the efforts to relocate the Japanese again. They were to be moved out of the camps and settled in occupations and homes in the interior. During the spring and summer of 1942, more than 1,500 work furloughs were granted to inmates for farm work. Several thousand Japanese college students returned to school through programs established by the American Friends Service Committee in cooperation with eastern universities. But permanent relocation was delayed inordinately; the process of screening for loyalty was so cumbersome that few placements were made for permanent positions in civilian life. At best Nisei found that the only work open to them was teaching Japanese at the United States Army language schools.

The relocation of Nisei who had demonstrated their loyalty to the United States by collaborating with authorities left crucial leadership gaps in the camps. Ironically, the gaps were often filled by radicals. The Army's plan to organize a special, segregated Nisei unit to fight against the Germans was especially abrasive to many in the camps. A team of Army recruiters toured the camps in early 1943; it frequently met with hostility.

Young Nisei wanted to know why the units were to be segregated and why the Nisei could not go into the Navy as well. They wanted to know why only one Nisei sergeant accompanied the recruiting team; they suggested that if the team included a Nisei captain it would have much more luck. The Army had hoped to raise 3,500 volunteers; it recruited only 1,250.

As a complement to recruitment, the WRA had attempted to register all inmates. Registration meant expressing loyalty. By signing a pledge of allegiance to the United States and swearing that one's loyalties to the Emperor of Japan had ceased, an inmate became eligible for future removal from the camps.

The WRA assumed that inmates would rush to sign the pledge and gladly exchange life in the camps for the outside world. What the Authority did not recognize was that life in the camps, however dictated and regimented, was at least stable and secure. Many Japanese were terrified at the thought of leaving the relative security of the camps for the frightening, racist world outside.

Furthermore, blaring newspaper accounts describing the United States' war against bandy-legged, yellow-skinned, evilly-grinning fiends made internees fearful of rejoining American life outside the camps. (Nineteenth-century characterizations of "The Yellow Peril" seem almost gentle compared to the horrific stereotypes of the twentieth.) Rumors flew about the fate of Japanese at the hands of West Coast vigilante groups. In California, where word had spread that the Japanese were to return, the same patriots who had engineered the evacuation renewed their vociferous, well-publicized efforts to prevent the return. Even Mayor Fiorello La Guardia of New York, a longtime liberal, protested against the release of "the Japs" from the camps to live in the East.[32]

Twenty-eight percent of the Nisei and Kibei inmates of the camps refused to sign the loyalty oath; refused, in effect, to give up any claim to Japanese citizenship. At Manzanar 52 percent refused; at Tule Lake 49 refused; at Topaz, Utah, 32 percent refused. These refusals reflected a high level of politicalization in those camps. Those who refused became known as the "no-noes," because they said no to swearing allegiance to the United States and no to forswearing allegiance or obedience to the Japanese Emperor. "My American friends . . . no doubt must have wondered why I renounced my citizenship," said Kurihara, who became a "no-no." "This decision was not that of today or yesterday. It dates back to the day when General DeWitt ordered evacuation. It was confirmed when he flatly refused to listen even to the voices of the former World War Veterans and it was doubly confirmed when I entered Manzanar. . . ."[33]

The many Nisei who refused to register had various reasons for their actions. Many feared a yes would mean

[32] *Pacific Citizen*, October 25, 1968.
[33] Thomas and Nishimoto, *op. cit.*, p. 369.

they would have to leave the security of the camps for the hostile outside world. Others believed a yes would split up families and push the vulnerable Issei (average age 52) out into hostile circumstances.

Some preferred to sit out the war in the camps, firm in their conviction that Japan would win. They did not want to jeopardize their relations with a possible new regime by a premature pledge of loyalty to the United States.

Some simply refused to register as a matter of principle, having seen enough of the empty promises of American democracy. These Nisei refused to succumb to coercion by camp administrations despite the threat of being indicted under the Espionage Act.

Even after the war had ended some were still so bitter that 8,000 of them joined in emigrating from the United States to Japan. Those who remained quietly re-entered American life without fanfare. Many did not return to the West Coast, but started new lives in the cities to which they had been released from the camps. During the postwar years, the raw wounds left by the evacuation slowly healed, but the scars did not entirely disappear. ". . . the great majority of the Nisei seem to be incapable of being completely integrated now, so that the process may have to carry on into the next generation," said one Nisei girl discussing the reactions of her generation soon after she had left a camp:

> It seems that the Nisei find it impossible to live without their own group now and they insist upon having their segregated dances and affairs regardless of future consequences. . . .
>
> . . . there is no denying the fact that I am Nihonjin. I might as well accept the fact, because I will never be accepted in Caucasian society no matter how hard I try. Very few Nisei will ever be able to do that. We just have to go along and make the best of things. . . . There is no use dreaming that all of the prejudices and discriminations are going to suddenly vanish.[34]

Nor did they vanish. In 1967 a poll revealed that more than 50 percent of Californians who knew about the forced

[34] Thomas, Kikuchi, and Sakoda, *op. cit.*, p. 504.

evacuation *still* approved of it.[35] In 1954, however, twelve years after the evacuation, Congress shamefacedly admitted that the country had done an injustice to the Japanese-Americans. It held a series of hearings to determine whether or not the government should repay even a small portion of the hundreds of millions of dollars Japanese-Americans had lost as a result of their internment during the war. During the hearings one California congressman admitted that he had been wrong in his wartime suspicions about the loyalty of the Japanese. "As time went by," said the congressman, "it gradually became obvious that the Japanese were not in fact disloyal." The congressman generously conceded that the behavior of the Japanese had demonstrated "they were just as loyal as those whose skin was white."[36]

No one on the West Coast protested, publicly, the congressman's casual equation of loyalty with skin color. But in one part of the United States such a statement could not have been made without creating a furor in the Japanese community. In Hawaii, Japanese-Americans have pursued a different path from the one taken by their counterparts on the U.S. mainland, a path ending with the election of Daniel Inouye, a Japanese-American, to the United States Congress in 1960.

THE JAPANESE IN HAWAII

In 1960, in Hawaii's first poststatehood election, Daniel Inouye was elected to the United States House of Representatives, thus becoming the first American of Japanese

[35] Japanese American Research Project, University of California at Los Angeles.

[36] Hearings before Subcommittee #5 of the Committee on the Judiciary, House of Representatives, 83rd Congr., 2nd Sess. San Francisco, August, 1954; Los Angeles, September, 1954. Washington: Government Printing Office, 1954, Serial #23, p. 6.

descent to enter Congress. Inouye was an appropriate choice for the post. He was a Nisei born in Hawaii, and a decorated war veteran from the all-Nisei 442nd "Go for Broke" Battalion who had lost an arm in combat. Today Inouye is one of two senators from Hawaii and was a strong supporter of American military activities in Southeast Asia. He is, most importantly, a living proof that it is possible in Hawaii for a person of Japanese descent to attain one of the highest offices in the land.

But it was not always like this for those of Japanese descent in Hawaii.

From the day the first Japanese were brought to Hawaii to work on the sugar plantations until after World War II, they were treated with suspicion, as second-class citizens. Ultimately they became the largest nonwhite minority group in the multiracial Islands. But they did not achieve power by the sheer force of their numbers alone. Unlike the Japanese on the mainland, one segment in the Japanese-Hawaiian community fought for its rights against what the editor of the *Hawaii Hochi,* a popular Japanese newspaper, called, in 1926, the "insufferable arrogance" of the Anglo-Saxons. If that fight had not taken place, Daniel Inouye probably would not have become a United States senator. "What is the use of insisting that one is an 'American citizen' if he does not act like one?" wrote Fred Kinza-buro Makino, the editor of the *Hawaii Hochi.* Makino, the son of an English father and a Japanese mother, had come to Hawaii in 1899. To him, being an American citizen meant helping Japanese plantation workers organize unions, going to jail for assisting strikes, starting law suits against discriminatory actions, and protesting unfair trials. It also meant urging, in his newspaper, that the Japanese community act on its own behalf and defend its own interests . . . "when the young Japanese are able to look their white brothers squarely in the eye and tell them to 'get out of the way,' they will find out whether there is any race discrimination that can hinder them or keep them from success."[37]

[37] *Hawaii Hochi,* July 24, 1926.

The first Japanese immigrants to Hawaii quickly discovered there was race discrimination. In the middle of the nineteenth century, the developing sugar industry was desperately in need, said the *Planters Monthly,* of ". . . cheap labor, which means in plain words, servile labor."[38] Robert C. Wylie, a *haole* who had become Hawaii's foreign minister, wrote to American businessmen in Japan in 1865 telling them of his own needs as a sugar planter: "We are much in want of them (laborers). I myself could take 500 for my own estates. Could any good agricultural laborers be obtained from Japan or its dependencies. . . . If so send me all the information you can and state at what cost per head they could be landed here and if their wives and children could be induced to come with them. . . ."[39]

The Japanese were brought to the Islands because the Chinese laborers who had come to Hawaii proved unsatisfactory and left the plantations as soon as possible for the cities. Negroes were feared because they were considered unruly. So planters put pressure on the Hawaiian Government to make an immigration agreement with Japan, and a treaty was finally signed in 1866 opening up immigration.

In 1868, one hundred and fifty Japanese came to the Islands after a great deal of wrangling between the Japanese Government and the planters over the conditions under which the laborers were to work and over their right to leave their jobs and return to Japan. The government charged that much of the recruiting operation was illegal; relations between Japan and Hawaii became strained. (Hawaii was not a part of the U.S. until 1898.)

For their part, this first small group of Japanese workers discovered a great discrepancy between the working conditions they had been promised and the virtual enslavement they experienced. In addition to conditions similar to medieval prison life, on some plantations the men were docked a quarter of a day's pay if they were ten minutes late to work.

[38] Lawrence H. Fuchs, *Hawaii Pono: A Social History.* New York: Harcourt, Brace & World, Inc., 1961, p. 206.

[39] Hilary Conroy, *The Japanese Frontier in Hawaii, 1868–1898.* Los Angeles and Berkeley: The University of California Press, 1953, p. 8.

If they broke tools at work, they had to pay for them; if they were sick—due to their "own imprudence"—they were fined; and if they left the plantation without permission on any working day, they were fined two days' pay for each day of absence.

Contract laborers in Hawaii were bound by the Masters and Servants Act of 1850, which exacted severe penalties, including jail sentences for workers who broke their contract or tried to leave the plantation before their contractual time had expired. The Act helped create a form of slavery. Furthermore, contracts for the indentured workers were bought and sold, and workers who disobeyed overseers or owners were flogged or jailed.

Reports on the ill-treatment of the workers went back to Japan and were publicized there.

Conditions for the Japanese on the Hawaii plantations in 1866 had not improved very much over what they had been earlier. Financially the workers were wiped out and therefore unable to return to Japan as they had originally planned. Fines were imposed on them, their pay docked, and illegal assessments charged against them. They had to pay bribes to their overseers, they lost money at gambling, and had difficulty in obtaining the 15 percent of their pay due at the expiration of their contracts.

Faced with these conditions and the impossibility of changing them, the Japanese sought strength by making an effort to preserve some aspect of their Japanese identity. But to do this, the plantation laborers had to resist owners and overseers in matters large and small. The sugar growers were only interested in increasing production. They opposed Japanese-language schools on the plantations; they also tried to get their workers "to desist from pickled preparations" and to eat meat instead—in their judgment a meat diet was required to make their employees able to carry out their arduous labor.

Paradoxically, because of the need to discharge obligations of *on* and the strong sense of self-pride and demand for self-respect that went with it, the Japanese workers tried to change the living conditions imposed on them. Their first attempts were very polite. Here is a typical demand:

Dear Sir:
We have the pleasure to express our keen appreciation of your past kindness and favor, and it is particularly pleasing to recollect that we have taken part in the development of the Oahu Sugar Company. . . . It shall be our fondest and most cherished hope to continue to help the development and progress of your plantation . . . we look back upon the past with pleasure and pride, and look forward with hope and enthusiasm. . . . Therefore it has become our painful burden to hereby respectfully present to you our request for reasonable increase of wages.[40]

During the 1890s there were several disturbances protesting the abuse of laborers by *lunas*—overseers—(who were almost always *haoles*). After the abolition of the contract system at the time of annexation by the United States in 1898, workers were freer to emigrate to the mainland or to organize themselves to better their lives.

Finally, in the 1900s, Japanese workers began to organize unions rather than rely on outbursts of protest to get higher wages and improved working conditions. Strikes were organized around the question of discrimination in wages paid to Japanese laborers, who were always paid less than workers of other nationalities doing the same jobs. The Japanese got $18.00 a month in 1909; the Portuguese $22.00 or $23.00.

One Japanese newspaper in Honolulu said:

If a laborer comes from Japan and he performs the same quantity of work of same quality within the same period of time as those who hail from opposite side of the world, what good reason is there to discriminate one as against the other. It is not the color of the skin or hair, or the language that he speaks, or manner or custom, that grow cane in the field. It is labor that grows cane, and the more efficient the labor the better the crop the cane field will bring. We demand higher wages of planters in the full confidence of the efficiency of our labor, and, also in the equally full confidence in the planters' sense of justice and equity in all things

[40] Fuchs, *op. cit.*, p. 118.

that pertain to human affairs, especially in the delicate relation between capital and labor.[41]

The newspaper's confidence in the planters' sense of justice and equity turned out to have little foundation in reality. The planters' immediate response was to fight any attempt at unionization by the Japanese workers, jailing them if necessary. The police were under the planters' control and were openly used to break any strikes. During one strike in 1905 on the island of Maui, 1,700 Japanese left work and were fired on by the police, who killed one worker and injured two others. A few years later, when thousands of Japanese struck on Oahu, their leaders were arrested by the police and put in jail. It was in one such strike that Fred Makino, then operating a drugstore, was jailed for helping strikers. Makino's office was broken into and his safe stolen.

The planters' bitter resistance to unionization was based on more than their fear of monetary loss; a deep-seated racial contempt for all Orientals affected their every decision.

Hoales were as convinced of their Anglo-Saxon superiority over Orientals as southern white planters had been convinced of innate Negro inferiority. Their beliefs were supported by such distinguished senators as Henry Cabot Lodge and Albert Beveridge as well as by the outspoken carrier of the white man's burden, Theodore Roosevelt. To the planters, Oriental workers were only the means to an end—their labor was needed to produce sugar—and not entitled to any more consideration than that given any machine to keep it running properly. Of course some plantation owners treated their workers with a measure of consideration, just as some southern slave owners took care of their slaves. However, such care stemmed from a sense of *noblesse oblige* toward an inferior race rather than a recognition of their workers' rights.

[41] Gavan Daws, *The Shoal of Time.* New York: The Macmillan Co., 1968, p. 304.

Haoles regarded the Japanese and other Orientals as "coolies" who had to be dealt with by force. A "coolie" would see a compromise "as a sign of fear" proclaimed the *Pacific Commercial Advertiser,* the voice of the white planter: "Yield to his demands and he thinks he is the master and makes new demands; use the strong hand and he recognizes the power to which, from immemorial times, he has abjectly bowed. There is one word which holds the lower classes of every nation in check and that is Authority."[42]

The Anglo-Saxon sense of superiority manifested itself in innumerable ways. White workers received three to four times the wages of Orientals with exactly the same skills; Oriental workers could never rise above a certain level of minor administrative work. Schools for Oriental children were not provided on many plantations and residential segregation was strictly observed. At the social level, little contact was possible in the early 1900s between whites and Orientals. There was no incentive for whites to intermarry with Oriental Hawaiians, the reason being that the Orientals had no land.

The white view of the Oriental as an inferior created a colonial society in which any white person, no matter how low in status, was higher in the social order than any Oriental, no matter how high he was in the Oriental community. The Japanese who lived in the cities, for example, related to whites only as domestic servants or gardeners, and never socially. No white family was too poor to have Japanese servants. Even educated Japanese professionals were cut off from any real contact with the white world that dominated life in the Islands.

The Japanese were prevented from making any changes in their conditions through politics—the Hawaiian Constitution of 1887 did not extend the voting privilege to Orientals. When the monarchy was overthrown in 1893 and the Republic established, the same principle of exclusion was carried over. The whites were in complete control. They

[42] Fuchs, *op. cit.,* p. 208.

refused Orientals all political rights, fearing their growing numbers.

The situation was bound to produce conflict. The planters needed the Japanese as laborers, but their importation had eventually created the largest non-Caucasian group in the Islands. They far outnumbered the whites. The Japanese were unwilling to accept the inferior status imposed on them by the *haoles*.

The Honolulu *Advertiser,* a powerful voice in the *haole* community, commented on the growing demands of one Japanese group:

> A more obstreperous and unruly lot of Japanese than Waipahu is cursed with, is not to be found in these Islands. . . . The Japanese consul, once all-powerful among laborers of his race in Hawaii, meets insults and threats on every hand. . . . To discharge every Jap and put on newly-imported laborers of another race would be a most impressive object lesson to the little brown men on all the plantations. . . . It would subdue their dangerous faith in their own indispensability. So long as they think they have things in their own hands, they will be cocky and unreasonable. . . . Ten or fifteen thousand Portuguese and Molokans in the fields would make a vast difference in the temper of the Japanese.[43]

But no Portuguese or Molokan workers were available. The *haoles* were forced to remain dependent upon their Japanese workers; at the same time they were determined to prevent the Japanese from dominating the Islands. If that were to happen it would disrupt the order of the class and color lines which made life so pleasant and profitable for whites.

The *haoles* dominated the legislature and made a concerted effort to shut down the Japanese-language schools. A typical pronouncement against Japanese-language schools was issued by the Aloha Chapter of the Daughters of the American Revolution. It proclaimed that its members were ". . . unequivocally opposed to all practices within the borders of the United States of America subversive to the peace and order of our Nation and the undivided allegiance

[43] *Ibid.,* p. 210.

of our people and unalterably opposed to all foreign-language schools of whatever nationality." Instead of language schools, the DAR adopted ". . . a firm stand for Americanism in its truest and loftiest form, and for one language—that of our heroic Revolutionary ancestors who gave their fortunes and their lives that the United States might live and prosper, and one flag—'Old Glory'."[44]

Any attempt by a Japanese to gain citizenship through naturalization was obstructed. Japanese strike leaders were blacklisted. Japanese religious temples and shrines were described as threats to Christianity. The Japanese press was attacked, and a law was passed prohibiting publication of any material that might stir up distrust between different races or between aliens and citizens. The segregated social, political, and cultural life of the Japanese was now claimed as evidence that they were unassimilable and therefore incapable of ever becoming Americans. Since whites refused to give the Japanese any opportunity to participate in society, the Orientals were forced to turn inward and develop their own special sense of identity.

Initially some Japanese-language schools had been set up on the plantations, because the workers believed they would return one day to Japan and also needed to educate their children in the language. Even after plans to return were abandoned, the schools were continued, as a link to Japan and as an expression of pride in being Japanese, by those who left the plantations for the cities. Religion flourished for the same reasons. The Japanese immigrants built Buddhist temples and Shinto shrines. They continued to eat Japanese food and began importing Japanese goods in quantities. Japanese holidays were observed and visits by Japanese warships were occasions for great rejoicing. Japanese newspapers flourished and Japanese culture became an integral part of their new life. Intermarriage with whites was regarded as a grave violation and betrayal of the community's mores.

Yet despite the strong sense of solidarity that bound all

[44] Daws, *op. cit.*, p. 309.

the Japanese together, sharp differences of viewpoint existed in the community, particularly over the first strikes by plantation workers, which were models of decorum and good behavior by mainland standards. Polite or not, the strikes were opposed by the conservatives in the Japanese community who were convinced that the way to secure their future was to accept the role imposed on them and not stir up undue enmity from whites.

This view was reinforced by the uncertain legal status of the Japanese, even after annexation to the United States. The Naturalization Act of 1790, the original law covering the right of aliens to become American citizens, had given that right to "Any alien, being a free white person. . . ." After the abolition of slavery, the law was changed to include "aliens of African nativity and persons of African descent." Congress had made other changes over the years, but they were procedural. Except for that one notable exception, naturalization was still open to whites only. Even after Hawaii became an American territory, the Japanese immigrants were deprived of any opportunity to become citizens. The fact that some illegal immigration had taken place did not help matters for it meant that calling undue public attention to their plight might end in deportation.

Three responses to anti-Orientalism developed among the Issei or first generation of immigrants. Initially all three centered around the Nisei, who in increasing numbers were being educated in public schools where they were exposed to the rhetoric of so-called American equality.

One group of Issei lived as displaced persons and urged the Japanese to ignore whites as much as possible. In their minds the Japanese were guests in the country of the whites, and one never behaved rudely toward one's host, no matter how badly treated. These followers of *Yamato Damashii* (the traditional life of Japan) were in conflict with their own children who had been born in the Islands, as well as the two other groups of Issei. They were angry with those of their children who became *furyoshonin* (pool-hall bums) or *abura-mushi* (cockroaches), the word used for Nisei girls who dated without their parents' approval or went out with Caucasians.

The second Issei group was convinced that the anti-Japanese attitude of the *haoles* was created by the behavior of the Japanese who participated in strikes or tried to prevent the closing of the language schools. Led by Takie Okumura, a Christian missionary, this faction was called the New Americans. It opposed Buddhism and urged the Japanese youth to remain on the plantations. Okumura traveled all over the Islands, pointing out the things which he felt caused his people to be disliked by the Americans:

> (a). Living conditions, manners, and habits and customs are so persistently Japanese. Some Japanese scorn the manners and customs of this country in which they are mere sojourners. . . .
>
> (b). Religious conditions. America is a country of religious freedom. But can the American people sit quietly by and gaze at the rapidity with which their country is being repaganized. Idols are being imported. Temples are being erected in every nook and corner of the Territory, and pagan rites are being held. Traditional Sunday observances are giving way to noisy festivals and wrestling tournaments at the temples and shrines.
>
> (c). Japanese children who should be taught and trained into good American citizens are being taught Japanese ideas and ideals. . . .
>
> (d). Since last year's school agitation, the sentiment of the community is gradually crystallizing against Japanese in general. This year's plantation laborer's strike did not remain a mere capital-labor dispute. It has turned out to be a terrific clash between the American people and the Japanese. . . .[45]

Okumura and his party spoke against the forming of unions and the conducting of strikes by Japanese workers. Okumura visited many plantations, explaining to the workers their duties to the plantation owners and to Hawaii. "And," said Okumura to the laborers, "above everything else remember that 'YOU ARE GUESTS OF THIS LAND' and be very careful in everything that you do."[46]

[45] Takie Okumura and Umetaro Okumura, "Hawaii's American-Japanese Problem: Report of the Campaign 1921–1927." No place, date, or publisher given, pp. 4–5.

[46] *Ibid.*, p. 20.

The third group of Issei rejected Okumura's concept. Led by Fred Makino, editor of the *Hawaii Hochi,* these Issei were convinced that the Japanese would achieve equality only by fighting for their rights; they were unwilling to remain invisible. At the same time they were unwilling to give up those elements of Japanese culture which they believed were important. "The effects of such a practice," Makino warned in his paper, "will be far-reaching and dangerous in the extreme for it will engender bitterness and hatred in the hearts of those who are crushed down under the wheel of a White Oligarchy."[47]

The *Hawaii Hochi* and its supporters not only led the successful fight to keep the Japanese-language schools open, but resisted the white oligarchy's attempts to discriminate against Orientals. When five Japanese teachers were refused entry to the Islands, Makino appealed and won a favorable decision. When a Japanese youth was accused of murder, the *Hochi* fought for his right to a fair trial. When the Hawaiian Immigration Office established the practice of having a Christian minister conduct mass weddings for the "picture brides" and their husbands, even though most of the couples were Buddhists or Shintoists, Makino attacked the weddings as a violation of human rights.

And when the United States Government gave citizenship to all aliens who had fought in World War I with the exception of the Japanese, Makino and his group took the case to court and got the decision reversed. But neither Makino nor any other Issei were able to achieve naturalization rights for the other Japanese who sought citizenship.

The dispute over the correct policy to be followed by the Japanese community in Hawaii continued on through the 1920s and 1930s. When the Nisei generation grew old enough to vote, the area of disagreement shifted from education to politics. In the 1920s the Japanese of Hawaii represented only 3 percent of the voting population; ten years later they were more than 25 percent of the voters.

[47] *Hawaii Hochi,* July 22, 1926.

Despite this extraordinary increase in voting power, they had little influence and few appointed jobs. In the early 1930s, less than 2 percent of the appointed positions in government went to Japanese; even in the 1940s, when the Japanese were nearly 30 percent of the voting population, they held only 3 percent of the government posts.

The conservatives in the Japanese community bitterly opposed any overt expression of "Yellow Power," such as pressuring for jobs or bloc voting for the few eligible Japanese candidates who ran for office. The conservatives were still uneasy about their status and still conscious of being "guests in the house." They were concerned that organized political action against the *haoles* might bring down on them some form of punishment. "If we expect to be true Americans in spite of our ancestry, we must be Americans in every way. We must associate with Americans and adopt their ideals, customs and traditions," explained a Japanese student in an essay submitted in a contest sponsored by one of the conservative Japanese-language newspapers. To the conservatives, being an American meant not indulging in bloc voting or supporting Japanese candidates against *haoles*.

To the militant members of the community, such policies spelled disaster. They were convinced that the only way *haoles* would respect the Japanese would be for the Japanese to go on fighting for their rights. To prove the validity of their position, they insisted that anti-Japanese discrimination was not any less despite the conservatives' refusal to act more aggressively. Furthermore, the militants asserted, if the Japanese voted for the same candidate, the *haoles* would accuse them "of having voted in a racial bloc, and on the other hand, if they happened to stagger their votes, they are spoken of as lacking in cooperative spirit. . . ."[48]

On the whole, the conservatives dominated the Japanese community; but, as the militants observed, their policies did not bring about the desired results. The *haoles* continued their attacks on the Japanese. And the Japanese found

[48] Fuchs, *op. cit.*, p. 134.

themselves increasingly isolated—first by the Sino-Japanese War, which created deep hostility toward Japan in every segment of Hawaiian society, and then by the hostilities between Japan and the United States which culminated in war between the two countries.

The attack on Pearl Harbor brought the latent hostility against the Japanese to the surface. The *haoles* were now joined by the Filipinos, Chinese, Koreans, and Hawaiians, all of whom had their own special grievances against the children and grandchildren of the Rising Sun.

Immediately after the bombing, the Islands were put under martial law. During the next few weeks, wild rumors flew around that the local Japanese had cut arrows in the sugar cane fields to direct the Japanese fliers toward Pearl Harbor, that they had blocked traffic on December 7th to prevent American soldiers from defending Pearl Harbor, that they had sent signals to saboteurs, that they had poisoned the water supply. There was even a rumor that they had ambushed some American soldiers.

None of this, of course, was true, but the stories spread anyway. There was pressure for the internment of all the Japanese on the Islands—not just those arrested by authorities because of overt sympathies with Japan or suspected activities in that country's behalf.

But internment of all the Japanese in the Islands presented an enormous problem of logistics. There was no place to intern the 160,000 Issei and Nisei in the Islands, as some people had proposed, and shipping space was not available to send them back to the U.S. mainland. Internment presented another serious problem: those 160,000 Japanese made up one-third of the population, and to put them in camps meant eliminating the Islands' major labor supply, especially in the skilled trades. For a number of obvious reasons internment was not a rational possibility and the Hawaiian Japanese were permitted to remain in their homes. But they suffered anyway, since nearly everyone in Hawaii distrusted them.

"A Jap is a Jap even after a thousand years and can't

become Americanized." This was the sentiment of one *haole* leader, who expressed what many *haoles* and other groups believed about the Japanese in Hawaii. As a result, all Japanese—including Nisei—had difficulty in finding war work. The Japanese community decided to take whatever steps were necessary to prove its loyalty: they gave up their language schools, the older people stopped wearing kimonos and sandals, and the Japanese societies disbanded. The Army censored the Japanese-language newspapers and radio programs.

The Army had problems of its own in deciding what to do with 1,400 Nisei who were members of the National Guard. Finally it was decided to send them to the mainland where they were trained under *haole* officers. Ultimately they became part of the famous Nisei 442nd Regimental Combat Team and 100th Battalion. A justification for the Army's creation of these units was contained in a memorandum sent to General George Marshall, the Chief of Staff, which stated that setting up such a unit might have

> . . . a profound propaganda effect upon certain other peoples, who at present, are more or less unfriendly to the cause of the United States due to the Japanese allegation that this is a racial war. Considering the fighting qualities which enemy Japanese have demonstrated there is no reason to believe that combat units of a high degree of effectiveness could not be developed from loyal personnel of this class. In furtherance of this belief it is reasonable to assume that a particularly high degree of spirit and combativeness could be developed in such an organization due to the desire of the individuals therein to demonstrate their loyalty to the United States and to repudiate the ideologies of Japan.[49]

The memo combined the racial stereotype about the fighting qualities of the enemy Japanese with the observation that those same qualities could be harnessed for the American side of the war. American-born Japanese, especially those from Hawaii, would be very eager to demonstrate their loyalty by going into combat.

The Army was right about that. The 442nd became one

[49] Daws, *op. cit.*, p. 350.

of the most effective and certainly one of the best-publicized fighting units in the Allied cause. Its casualty rate was three times higher than the average and it received more unit and individual awards than any other comparable combat group. Eventually the unit even fought under Nisei officers.

The Hawaiian-born Japanese who fought in the war and witnessed the deaths of their friends in combat were determined to change things in the Islands when they returned. "We have helped win the war on the battlefront," said one of their leaders, "but we have not yet won the war on the homefront. We shall have won only when we attain those things for which our country is dedicated, namely equality of opportunity and the dignity of man."

When they did return to Hawaii, the Nisei veterans began the homefront battle by entering politics and running for office. During the war not a single Nisei had been in the Territorial Legislature, but in 1946 five went into the House and one to the Senate. By 1952 representation in the legislature was divided equally between *haoles* and Nisei. Almost all of the Japanese were Democrats. Today, three of Hawaii's four Representatives in Congress are Nisei; they are a powerful force in politics within the state as well.

The Hawaiian-Japanese have demonstrated how an ethnic group can achieve power and prestige in America. The requirements are simple. The group must be large enough to make an economic and political impact; it must be willing, at some point in its history, to wage a tough fight for its rights; and ultimately its members must become indistinguishable from white Americans.

Such is the price that must be paid for acceptance. Until now, most Hawaiian-born Nisei, and their sons and daughters, the Sansei, have been willing to pay it. Only recently has there been stirring within the community a questioning of whether perhaps the price has been too high, too much of the past lost.

Today a few young Americans of Japanese descent in Hawaii are beginning to search for a link to their special Asian identity. But this group is still small and it seems unlikely that it will grow in size or influence within the near future—too many Nisei and Issei are satisfied with America and their place in the Islands' sun.

WE STILL CAN'T BE SURE

Japanese self-segregation continues today. But on the mainland a new interest in Asian history and culture has developed; Asian-American student and political groups have been organized. These groups participate, along with blacks and Mexican-Americans, in the campus rebellions that have marked American university life in the late 1960s.

"What we hate to recall," wrote Mrs. Kats Kunitsugu, a columnist for a Japanese-American newspaper, in 1968, "is not so much the hardships that the war and evacuation brought to us, but the vast sense of alienation we suffered when we were like the man without a country. And perhaps we are reluctant about evoking those days gone by because we still can't be 100 percent sure that the possibility of rejection is as remote as it appears today."[50]

The anxiety expressed by Mrs. Kunitsugu was echoed in 1969 by a Japanese actor, George Takei. ". . . when World War II happened, the soul of the Japanese was broken down. Anything Japanese about us was suspect. Even those who could speak Japanese pretended they couldn't. We have this legacy of insecurity." But today the Japanese in America are beginning to fight, openly, against the "legacy of insecurity," as the Noguchi case proved.

The Noguchi controversy arose in 1967 in Los Angeles when Dr. Thomas Noguchi, then Deputy County Coroner, wanted to become Chief Coroner. Although he had qualified in the Civil Service examinations, officials of the two Los Angeles medical schools traditionally associated with the Coroner's Office publicly declared him unacceptable.

[50] *Pacific Citizen,* December 20–27, 1968.

However, Dr. Noguchi's appointment was approved by the County Board of Supervisors. Later, some friction developed between Noguchi and the County Chief Administrative Officer, L. S. Hollinger.

In March of 1969, according to Noguchi, Hollinger gave him an ultimatum: that Noguchi resign as Chief Coroner and accept, at no reduction in pay, a position as chief pathologist at a county hospital. Noguchi, in traditional Oriental fashion, first chose to resign, accept the new position, and avoid taking a stand. After conversations with his wife and friends, however, he changed his mind, rescinded his resignation before it had been acted upon, and engaged lawyers to help him. The Supervisors voted unanimously to dismiss him from his post after Hollinger lodged charges of insanity and cruelty against him. Noguchi appealed for a Civil Service hearing so that he could confront his accusers and defend himself.

During the hearings, evidence showed that some of the behavior questioned by the prosecution was clearly attributable not to insanity, but to his Japanese culture. (For example, an almost perpetual smile.) Many witnesses for the prosecution were unable to recall specific information about the charges and it was revealed that Hollinger had not corroborated the allegations against Noguchi which turned out to have been made by dissatisfied employees working in the Coroner's Office.

The Commissioners' verdict was that Dr. Noguchi should be reinstated as Chief Medical Examiner-Coroner with full back pay. That decision was "blue skies and banana splits with all the trimmings," one happy Japanese-American wrote, and the community rejoiced. But there were afterthoughts with the rejoicing. Jeffrey Matsui of the Japanese-American Citizens League in Los Angeles, commented upon the reaction of his people:

"At first the charges were a little frightening. . . . But as we watched the charges and found that there was no foundation, we couldn't believe what was happening. . . . I don't think those charges could have been levelled at anyone except an Oriental—the power-crazed man smiling over the bodies. The intention was to scare people like World War II days." Japanese-Americans felt that the role of their ad hoc organization, J.U.S.T.—Japanese United in the Search for Truth—was important in securing a fair hearing for Noguchi and they worried that, without it, justice would not have prevailed. Dr. Harry Kitano, a sociologist at U.C.L.A., commented, after the reinstatement of Dr. Noguchi: "It is really a dramatic change. I would say that if this had happened ten years ago they would have acquiesced. . . . I once said that if a wartime evacuation situation occurred again, the Japanese would merely go again. After this incident, I'm not so sure. The vast majority might try to resist."

But despite Dr. Kitano's suggestion that the Japanese are ready to claim their rights, the Japanese still show fundamental doubts about their own status. At the victory dinner given by J.U.S.T. following the reinstatement of Dr. Noguchi, a table was reserved for the newsmen who had covered the trial, with place cards to show where they were to sit. Ironically, though, when representatives of the two Japanese papers arrived and went to join their colleagues at the press table, there were no place cards for them. One of them later commented: "To me, this was another instance of the Japanese acceptance of white supremacy. It was another expression of an attitude that white is automatically better than yellow, brown or black unless proven otherwise, a self-denigration resulting from decades of brainwashing. . . ."[51]

Some Japanese-American students were among the strongest supporters of Dr. Noguchi. In the late 1960s, these students began to band together with those of Chinese, Korean, and Filipino ancestry in militant Asian-American organizations on campuses and in cities. Now they picket, sponsor peace marches, and publish newspapers. The war in Vietnam has stirred their consciousness of racism at home and abroad, and they are painfully aware of their

[51] *Kashu Mainichi,* Los Angeles: Sept. 5, 1969.

history in the United States. "Remember Manzanar" signs wave in peace marches, and articles describing the camps appear often in their papers.

They have no desire to imitate their elders, whom they consider "silent" and "whitewashed." A voice for the young Oriental is *Gidra,* a newspaper published in Los Angeles whose name is taken from that of a Japanese "Godzilla the Monster," part worm and part dragon. In a review of a book sponsored by the JACL, entitled *Nisei, The Quiet American, Gidra* concludes "In this time of political, social, and moral crises in America, old and new problems demand radical approaches, not tired orations. And so having had their testament for posterity written, we bid the old guard to retire as 'quiet Americans.' "

Introduction to Japanese Documents

Like the Chinese, the Japanese in America paid a heavy price for being Orientals. But the Japanese, unlike the Chinese, fought back more openly and argued more openly among themselves over whether to accommodate or to resist the white world's culture and standards.

The bombing of Pearl Harbor and the subsequent evacuation of the Japanese into camps forced the community to face its dilemma. It has not yet resolved the question of its identity, as these documents testify, and however bland a response the Japanese give today to questions about their experiences in the internment centers, the documents illustrate the hatred caused by their being singled out and for the treatment given them.

(1)

The Story of Torikai—A Businessman*

In 1946, the Social Science Institute of Fisk University published a study of "Orientals and Their Cultural Adjustments." The series included the story of Torikai, a businessman, who had lived in the United States for twenty-five years. He described the bitterness he felt at the treatment he had received from white Americans.

When I first came to America I made up my mind to be a real American, so I would not speak Japanese at all or eat Japanese food, or wear Japanese clothing, or do anything Japanese. My own countrymen called me "Kito" meaning "foreigner." I did it, because I thought that to be successful in America I must be American, but now I have changed. I got no success here, all time trouble. Americans do not treat us right. We try hard to be American but Americans say you always Japanese. Irish become American and all time talk about Ireland; Italians become Americans even if do all time like in Italy; but Japanese can never be anything but Jap. That is what they say. It is not fair so why should we try to be like Americans? Americans all time call us "Charley" and I don't like that at all. Why should they call us Charley? They don't call everyone else in stores "Charley." We all got name and store got name. Americans say, "But we don't know your name," and I say, "Then don't call us anything; if you do not know other American's name you do not say 'Charley.' " I *hate* that name and sometimes when men come into store and call me that I won't take their trade. It is insult! Some ignorant Japanese do not care, they think it is American way to be friendly, but it isn't. It is only insult. We do not like to be called *Jap* either. White children and white lady come in to use tele-

* Fisk University Social Science Institute, "Orientals and Their Cultural Adjustments" (Nashville, 1946).

phone and I hear them say to someone they are at a Jap's place. I tell them not to come back any more if that is what they are going to call me; they are family of tailor next to me and know my name and know name of store so why not use it?

I don't go among Americans any more like I used to. I know I am not wanted. Even go way down to South Seattle to get hair cut because white men in some barber shops say bad things about Japanese. I am tied down by store; stay open until twelve o'clock every night and still can't make living; I eat here but when I have chance I go and have Japanese food. No use try to be American, we all have to go back to Japan some day. Maybe not all Japanese feel like that but that is how I feel.

I was married to a white woman at one time but my married life was not very happy and ended in a divorce. This experience did not tend to elevate my opinion of Americans. The best type of Americans do not intermarry. I guess it is very hard for American girl to marry Japanese and be happy unless she is content to find all her happiness in her home. She is considered outcast among most Americans and that is hard. Street-car conductors make remarks that are not nice and neighbors say to my wife, "If you like Japanese so well why don't you go down into the Japanese section to live where there are more of them?" If you ask my advice about marrying Japanese man I would not give it to you. Some get along very well and some not get along at all. Don't know much about children, that not in my experience, but think most of them very bright. Queer thing about American law about guardian of children. Japanese father cannot be guardian because he is Oriental but mother can be guardian if she is white even if she is alien.

(2)

Proceedings of the Anti-Japanese Laundry League, 1909*

The Anti-Japanese Laundry League flourished on the West Coast during the first decade of the twentieth century. It was supported by the press, some of the business community, and most of the trade unions. The following excerpts are from the report made by the business secretary of the San Francisco branch of the League in 1909.

It was brought to our notice that a number of Japanese Laundry Ads were being published in the National Theater program, and with the view of having same removed we communicated with the publisher, Mr. W. E. Valencia. Our arguments presented in this way availed us nothing. We then communicated with each individual advertiser in said program asking them to write Mr. Valencia to the effect that their ad would be withdrawn unless those of the Japanese were eliminated. This they did, and as a result Mr. Valencia communicated with us promising to remove all Jap Ads at the expiration of their contracts. The last of these have just expired, and we have reminded him of his promise.

One of the most important accomplishments has been the enlistment of the moral support of practically every Union man and woman in San Francisco, and we are indebted to the Building Trades and the Labor Councils for having passed resolutions recommending that all affiliated unions instruct their members not to patronize Orientals or patrons thereof. In response many of the Unions have covered the recommendation by passing laws punishable by fines. . . .

* Pamphlets on Japanese Question, Bancroft Library, University of California, Berkeley.

In conclusion, I desire to submit for your favorable consideration the following: That this convention, in conjunction with the outside League, concentrate its efforts and energy against all saloons and business houses who are known to patronize or employ Orientals, and suggest that all such places who are loyal to us be supplied with a large and *attractive* official card with the inscription "WE DO NOT EMPLOY OR PATRONIZE ASIATICS" printed thereon.

We believe, Mr. President and Delegates, that if that plan is adopted many of our friends would soon learn to look for the sign, and spend their money in such places, instead of those institutions who did not display such a sign.

(Signed) Nelson Elliott.
H. Lumina.
F. Mazet.
John LaFargue.
Alfred S. Edwards.

(3)

Joe Kurihara–Experiences in California*

"Repatriate" might very well be the title of Joe Kurihara's life from the time he was born in Hawaii. An American citizen who fought with the American Army in World War I, he was interned during World War II, and left America a bitter man to live in Japan after the War ended. In this excerpt from his life story, told by him during his internment days at Tule Lake Center in California, Kurihara describes his first experiences in California after he arrived from Hawaii.

. . . My early experiences in Sacramento were of appalling nature. While walking on K Street from the Depot

* Dorothy Swaine Thomas and Richard S. Nishimoto, *The Spoilage* (University of California Press, Berkeley and Los Angeles, 1946).

toward the Japanese district, suddenly a fairly well-dressed person came and kicked me in the stomach for no reason whatever. Luckily it glanced as I instinctively avoided it.

I watched his next move, maneuvering into position to fight it out the best I could. A crowd started to gather but no sooner than it did, another person came out of a saloon in front of which we were about to tackle, stopped this public show. I went my way feeling terribly hurt.

In this same city of Sacramento, as my friend and I were walking in the residential district, a short distance away from the Japanese center, something came whizzing by, and then another and another. We noticed they were rocks being thrown at us by a number of youngsters. As we went toward them, the boys ran and hid. Feeling perplexed, I asked my friend, "Why do they attack us in such a manner?" He answered, "It's discrimination." No such thing ever happened where I came from. It was disgusting. I felt homesick for my good old native land, Hawaii.

. . . Unexpectedly my friend from Sacramento called and persuaded me to go East, Michigan as destination. He vouched to me that the American people East of Chicago are very friendly and kind. They do not discriminate just because we are Japanese. . . . I could not believe it, but the news was very tempting after experiencing much unpleasantness for two years. Giving no further thought to the venture, I agreed and the next day we took a cab to the ferry and ordered our tickets to Chicago. . . . At the end of our destination, we hired a cab and directed him to a Japanese hotel. On the way, a very pleasant sight had greeted our eyes. A Japanese boy was walking down the street with an American girl, arm in arm. My friend, noticing it, exclaimed, "See what I told you? They don't discriminate us out here. They are very sociable!" I couldn't believe it, but I simply had to.

(4)

Governor Stephens' Message to the American Secretary of State, 1920*

In 1920, the Oriental "problem" was still very much alive; the press was agitating about it, continuously, and great pressures were exerted upon all government agencies to restrict Asian immigration. But, by then, the Chinese had been replaced by the Japanese as the greatest menace to American civilization. Here are sections from a report from Governor W. M. Stephens of California analyzing the situation for the United States Secretary of State.

(This official report ranks alongside of Reports of the Immigration Commission [1910] and the Hearings before the Committee on Immigration and Naturalization, House of Representatives [1920], as the outstanding official reports in recent times. Mr. Kiichi Kanzaki, General Secretary of Japanese Association of America, comments: "As to the spirit of the letter, all of us who have had an opportunity of reading it agree that it was written with the utmost cordiality and frankness and without enmity toward the people of Japan or the Japanese in California. Unfortunately, Governor Stephens was led to draw his conclusions from data which were, in many instances, inaccurate and were presented by unscientific methods. It is a serious duty of the leaders of both peoples to consider the problem dispassionately, basing their conclusions on authentic facts and seeking a solution for the best interest of all."—From *California and the Japanese,* published by the Japanese Association of America, 44 Bush Street, San Francisco, April, 1921.)

* E. G. Mears, *Resident Orientals on the American Pacific Coast: Their Legal and Economic Status,* Chicago: University of Chicago Press, 1928.

STATE OF CALIFORNIA
GOVERNOR'S OFFICE
SACRAMENTO, June 19, 1920

Hon. Bainbridge Colby,
Secretary of State,
Washington, D.C.

. . . These Japanese, by very reason of their use of economic standards impossible to our white ideals—that is to say, the employment of their wives and their very children in the arduous toil of the soil—are proving crushing competitors to our white rural populations. The fecundity of the Japanese race far exceeds that of any other people that we have in our midst. They send their children for short periods of time to our white schools, and in many of the country schools of our state the spectacle is presented of having a few white children acquiring their education in classrooms crowded with Japanese. The deep-seated and often outspoken resentment of our white mothers at this situation can only be appreciated by those people who have struggled with similar problems.

It is with great pride that I am able to state that the people of California have borne this situation and seen its developing menace with a patience and self-restraint beyond all praise. California is proud to proclaim to the nation that despite this social situation her people have been guilty of no excesses and no indignities upon the Japanese within our borders. No outrage, no violence, no insult, and no ignominy have been offered to the Japanese people within California. . . .

California harbors no animosity against the Japanese people or their nation. California, however, does not wish the Japanese people to settle within her borders and to develop a Japanese population within her midst. California views with alarm the rapid growth of these people within the last decade in population as well as in land control, and foresees in the not distant future the gravest menace of serious conflict if this development is not immediately and effectively checked. Without disparaging these people of just sensibilities, we cannot look for intermarriage or that social interrelationship which must exist between the citizenry of a contented community.

It may be an exquisite refinement, but we cannot feel contented at our children imbibing their first rudiments of education from the lips of the public school teacher in classrooms crowded with other children of a different race. They do not and will not associate in that relationship prevalent elsewhere in the public schools of this country. We recognize that this attitude is too deep-seated to remove. And we recognize that with this attitude goes the necessity of Japanese isolation and that inevitable feeling which socially a proscribed race always develops. . . .

The Japanese, be it said to their credit, are not of servile or docile stock. Proud of their traditions and history, exultant as they justly are at the extraordinary career of their country, they brook no suggestion of any dominant or superior race. Virile, progressive, and aggressive, they have all the race consciousness which is inseparable from race quality. And it is just because they possess these attributes in such marked degree and feel more keenly the social and race barriers which our people instinctively raise against them that they are driven to that race isolation and, I fear ultimately will reach that race resentment, which portends danger to the peace of our state in the future. . . .

I trust that I have clearly presented the California point of view, and that in any correspondence or negotiations with Japan which may ensue as the result of the accompanying report, or any action which the people of the state of California may take thereon, you will understand that it is based entirely on the principle of race self-preservation and the ethnological impossibility of successfully assimilating this constantly increasing flow of Oriental blood.

I have the honor to remain,

Yours very respectfully,

Wm. D. Stephens
Governor of California

(5)

A Farmer's View of the Question*

The Japanese-American farmers in California were among the people affected most seriously by the anti-Oriental pressure on the West Coast. In this document, George Shima, President of the Japanese Association of America in Stockton, California, states the position of his organization. The year was 1920.

I am a farmer, who has devoted his life to the development of the delta district of the Sacramento Valley, and know little of politics, diplomacy, or international questions. But it seems to me the part of wisdom and common sense to look upon the treatment of the local Japanese as a purely local matter, which should be considered quite independently of Japanese policy in the Far East.

We live here. We have cast our lot with California. We are drifting farther and farther away from the traditions and ideas of our native country. Our sons and daughters do not know them at all. They do not care to know them. They regard America as their home.

We have little that binds us to Japan. Our interest is here, and our fortune is irrevocably wedded to the state in which we have been privileged to toil and make a modest contribution to the development of its resources. What is more important, we have unconsciously adapted ourselves to the ideals and manners and customs of our adopted country, and we no longer entertain the slightest desire to return to our native country.

The devotion of local Japanese to California is evidenced in their conduct during the war. To the third Liberty Loan, for instance, the Japanese in this state contributed

* E. G. Mears, *Resident Orientals on the American Pacific Coast: Their Legal and Economic Status.* Chicago: University of Chicago Press, 1928.

$761,000, and to the fourth Liberty Loan $1,200,000. A very large percentage of the Japanese in California have joined the American Red Cross. In Contra Costa County, I am told, there is almost no Japanese family which has not joined the Red Cross. . . .

It seems to me wrong and unjust to propose various measures, calculated to oppress and inflict hardship upon the local Japanese, for the purpose of checking Japanese immigration.

I don't like the man who puts the cart before the horse. If the present immigration arrangement with Japan is not satisfactory, there is the right way to find a remedy, and the right way is not to abuse and oppress the local Japanese, who are neither responsible for nor in a position to control Japanese immigration.

To a practical farmer, who has all his life been guided by horse sense and little else, it would seem that there should be and is a way to adjust the Japanese question without stirring up bad blood everywhere by unnecessary agitation. The Japanese in California have not lost their heads. They are calm and quiet, and are willing to listen to any reasonable proposition for readjustment. That is why I say this agitation is unnecessary.

Just recently the board of directors of the Japanese Association, of which I have the honor to be the president, has adopted a resolution urging the abolition of "picture marriage." On December 17, the Japanese government announced that on and after February 25, 1920, it will stop issuing passports to "picture brides." All this shows that the Japanese are always conciliatory and solicitous for friendly relations with America and in particular the people of California.

The constant exploitation of the Japanese question makes it well-nigh impossible for self-respecting Japanese to live in California. The result, I fear, is that eventually only the undesirable class of Japanese, who care not a straw for self-respect or dignity, will remain here. Certainly this can not be the condition which California wishes to establish.

Both wisdom and justice demand that such a condition should not be permitted to prevail.

We are living in an extraordinary age. It may be that we are standing upon the threshold of a new era. Whether we like the League of Nations or not, we must admit that the world is entering upon a new age, in which the idea of just and fair play is going to be the dominant note in human dealings. If we do not strive and contribute a widow's mite to the realization of such an age, all the bloodshed and all the sacrifices of the late war have been in vain.

This is a practical view of a practical farmer.

(6)

Ozawa v. United States, 1922*

Takao Ozawa lived in Hawaii where he applied for American citizenship in 1914. His application was denied and his case was eventually taken to the United States Supreme Court, which decided in October, 1922, to uphold the denial. Here are sections of the Court's decision which embodied the arguments made on Ozawa's behalf, the answers of the government's attorneys, and the Court's own opinion.

Ozawa's attorneys argued: ". . . The origin of the Act of 1906 shows that it was intended to be a complete scheme for naturalization, the test being 'fitness for citizenship,' with no discrimination against Japanese. Message of President Roosevelt, December 5, 1905, 40 Cong. Rec. pt. 1, p. 99. This policy, announced by President Roosevelt, has been steadily followed in legislation in respect both to naturalization and immigration, including the Immigration Act of 1917.

"These acts show the traditional policy of the United States to welcome aliens, modified only by restrictions

* *Takao Ozawa v. United States,* 260 U.S. 178 (1922).

against contract laborers, those morally, mentally, and physically unfit for citizenship and the Chinese, but with no restrictions against the Japanese race.

"Numerous Chinese Exclusion Acts have been passed; but there is no line in any statute before or since 1875 which indicates any intention to classify the Japanese with those excluded or to discriminate against them in any way.

"This Court in a recent case, in reviewing the history of the Immigration Acts, has held that the purpose of applying these prohibitions against the admission of aliens is to exclude classes (with the possible exception of contract laborers) who are undesirable as members of the community, even if previously domiciled in the United States. . . .

"The Immigration Act of 1917, and the circumstances of its passage in Congress, show the clear intention of that body to make no declaration that Japanese are excluded from naturalization. Any other construction would be violative of the existing treaty with Japan. . . .

". . . The Japanese are 'free.' They, or at least the dominant strains, are 'white persons,' speaking an Aryan tongue and having Caucasian root stocks; a superior class, fit for citizenship.

"The Japanese are assimilable.

"Congress in repeating without qualification the words 'white persons' has left the subject in great uncertainty. All authorities without exception agree on dismissing the idea of white as a characteristic to be demonstrated by ocular inspection. If it is sought to interpret it as an ethnological term, authorities are so conflicting that it opens the way to serious inequalities of application. To apply the ambulatory definition which some of the learned judges have adopted, is to rob the law of all definiteness and to leave it to the whim of the particular judge or court. The only safe rule to adopt is to take the term as it undoubtedly was used when the naturalization law was first adopted, and construe it as embracing all persons not black, until the Act of 1870, and after that date, as having no practical significance. If this would run counter to the intention of Congress, that body can readily amend the act so as to make clear the legislative intention. But the subject certainly should not be left in the uncertain state in which it now is. . . ."

The Government maintained: ". . . The men who settled this country were white men from Europe and the men who fought the Revolutionary War, framed the Constitution and established the Government, were white men from Europe and their descendants. They were eager for more of their kind to come, and it was to men of their own kind that they held out the opportunity for citizenship in the new nation. It is quite probable that no member of the first Congress had ever seen a Chinese, Japanese, or Malay.

". . . It is a matter of common knowledge that for many years Japan, and to a somewhat less degree, China, maintained a policy of isolation, and this policy continued from the middle of the seventeenth century until the Perry Expedition in 1853. American thought and statesmanship were directed toward Europe, not toward Asia. It was Europe and its 'set of primary interests' with which Washington was concerned in his farewell address and it was against interweaving our destiny with that of any part of Europe, or entangling our peace and prosperity in the toils of European ambitions that he warned his countrymen. It was European trade that was sought and, beyond doubt, European immigration which was desired and expected. Citizenship has always been deemed a choice possession, and it is not to be presumed that our fathers regarded it lightly, to be conferred promiscuously according to a 'catch-all' classification. It could only be obtained by those to whom it was given, and the men of 1790 gave it only to those whom they knew and regarded as worthy to share it with them, men of their own type, white men. This does not imply the drawing of any narrow or bigoted racial lines, but a broad classification inclusive of all commonly called white and exclusive of all not commonly so called. This has been the rule followed by the courts, and the cases already cited, many of which show exhaustive research and wealth of learning, leave very little to be said. A reading of the opinions of the judges who have written in these cases reveals impressive unanimity in one respect. Each person admitted, with the single exception of the Filipino . . ., was admitted because he was deemed as matter of fact to be white; each person refused was refused because he was deemed as matter of fact not to be white. The ethnological discussions have covered a wide range of most interesting subjects particularly in the borderline cases, the Syrian case . . . and the Armenian case. . . . But the present case can not be regarded as a doubtful case. The Japanese is not, and never has been, regarded as white or of the race of white people.

"While the views of ethnologists have changed in details from time to time, it is safe to say that the classification of the Japanese as members of the yellow race is practically the unanimous view. Unless it could be demonstrated that the Japanese were of the white race, ethnological differences would be unimportant, even if otherwise relevant. . . .

Mr. Justice Sutherland delivered the opinion of the Court.

"The appellant is a person of the Japanese race born in Japan. He applied, on October 16, 1914, to the United States District Court for the Territory of Hawaii to be admitted as a citizen of the United States. His petition was opposed by the United States District Attorney for the District of Hawaii. Including the period of his residence in Hawaii, appellant had continuously resided in the United States for twenty years. He was a graduate of the Berkeley (California) High School, had been nearly three years a student in the University of California, had educated his children in American schools, his family had attended American churches, and he had maintained the use of the English language in his home. That he was well qualified by character and education for citizenship is conceded.

"The District Court of Hawaii, however, held that, having been born in Japan and being of the Japanese race, he was not eligible to naturalization under §2169 of the Revised Statutes, and denied the petition. . . .

"It is the duty of this Court to give effect to the intent of Congress. Primarily this intent is ascertained by giving the words their natural significance, but if this leads to an unreasonable result plainly at variance with the policy of the legislation as a whole, we must examine the matter further. We may then look to the reason of the enactment and inquire into its antecedent history and give it effect in accordance with its design and purpose, sacrificing, if necessary, the literal meaning in order that the purpose may not fail. . . . We are asked to conclude that Congress, without the consideration or recommendation of any committee, without a suggestion as to the effect, or a word of debate as to the desirability, of so fundamental a change, nevertheless, by failing to alter the identifying words of §2169, which section we may assume was continued for some serious purpose, has radically modified a statute always heretofore maintained and considered as of great importance. It is inconceivable that a rule in force from the beginning of the Government, a part of our history as well as our law, welded into the structure of our national polity by a century of legislative and administrative acts and judicial decisions, would have been deprived of its force in such dubious and casual fashion. . . .

". . . Is appellant, therefore, a 'free white person,' within the meaning of that phrase as found in the statute? . . .

". . . The appellant, in the case now under consideration, however, is clearly of a race which is not Caucasian and therefore belongs entirely outside the zone on the negative side. A large number of the federal and state courts have so decided and we find no reported case definitely to the contrary. These decisions are sustained by numerous scientific authorities, which we do not deem it necessary to review. We think these decisions are right and so hold.

"The briefs filed on behalf of appellant refer in complimentary terms to the culture and enlightenment of the Japanese people, and with this estimate we have no reason to disagree; but these are matters which cannot enter into our consideration of the question here at issue. We have no function in the matter other than to ascertain the will of Congress and declare it. Of course there is not implied—either in the legislation or in our interpretation of it—any suggestion of individual unworthiness or racial inferiority. These considerations are in no manner involved. . . ."

(7)

Address to Laborers, 1923*

Takie Okumura was a Christian minister, who was convinced that the anti-Japanese sentiment in the Hawaiian Islands would disappear only if the Japanese would "Forget the idea 'Japanese'." He traveled around the plantations, during the 1920s, speaking to the Japanese laborers and urging them to be on their good behavior. Here are excerpts from the speech he made to the workers.

I am very glad to see so many of you here tonight. I wish to take this opportunity of thanking you for your kind and hearty assistances during the past two years.

You well remember that I have thus far emphasized three points, namely:

a) Forget the idea "Japanese" and always think and act from the point of view of the American people, so long as you live and work under the protection of America, and enjoy many unique privileges, blessings, and opportunities.

b) Inasmuch as your children were born in Hawaii, and expect to live here permanently and work shoulder to shoulder with the American people, you should educate

* Takie Okumura and Umetaro Okumura, *Hawaii's American-Japanese Problem, Report of the Campaign, 1921–1927.*

your children into a good and loyal element which places the interest of this community above everything else. If you dislike to have your children live and work in Hawaii, if you prefer them to be educated into Japanese, if you prefer your children to become an element which has not the slightest interest in the affairs of this community, you should send them back immediately to Japan, and have them educated in that country, for when they grow up, they will become not assets, but liabilities of this country.

c) Your pressing duty today is to build up character and efficiency, and be recognized by the plantation managements as really reliable laborers. You are in direct contact with the business interests of the American people, and therefore you have a greater responsibility than the Honolulu Japanese. It is perfectly foolish to talk about "cooperation" or "cordial relations," if you are not ready and willing to go more than half-way and help the American people in building up this land. . . . WE ARE GUESTS OF THIS LAND. If you constantly follow this principle, you would not err, you would not become a great nuisance to any community.

As to the right of laborers to organize, no one has any objection. It is a right of laborers. But in all the labor organizations of America and England there are three essential aims: cultivating high character, increasing the laborer's efficiency, and mutually helping each other. A labor organization which loses sight of these aims is a menace to the community. If an organization holds fast to these aims, and actually elevates the character of its members and increases their efficiency as workmen, no one would have anything to say in opposition. Look at the so-called labor union which has sprung up among the Japanese community! It was purely an organization founded not for the above aims, but for the strike, or the higher wage agitation. . . .

All the so-called capital-labor disputes in America or England are disputes between the same countrymen. In America, the capitalists are Americans and the laborers are also Americans. In England, the capitalists are English, and the laborers are also English. But here in Hawaii the situation is entirely different. The capitalists are American people, and the majority of laborers are Japanese. Therefore the disputes are bound to become racial. The last strike was a good example. Many Japanese said, if Japanese lose in this strike, they cannot lift up their head any more; therefore, every Japanese should show his real *Yamato Damashii* and fight it out. The strike agitators appealed to the Japanese spirit and united their countrymen. The capitalists, on the other hand, said they cannot allow the Japanese to do what they please and control the industry; therefore, they must fight to the last ditch, whatever the cost. Then what was the loss? To the Japanese laborers, the tremendous amount of money lost was terrible. But they suffered a far greater loss than money. They have lost the confidence of the last thirty years. . . . I want to hear from you what you have to say, what grievances you have on this plantation. Now is the time to speak out very frankly. If you have any complaint, speak it out. If you harbor any grievance constantly, you would not become happy, and you would not be able to work contentedly. And such grievance would constantly irritate you, and would become in the end a source of trouble.

You are all working on a plantation, which is after all a big family. You are a member of a big family. Then is it not your duty to settle any point of difference or question within your family, and not by bringing in outside men, or precipitating an unnecessary agitation? One of the great weaknesses of Japanese is lack of frankness. Cultivate a quality of frankness. If you are not frank, how can anyone understand your trouble? How can anyone help you? You would have to be always miserable. Plantations would always play square with you, if you go right to the office and talk over your trouble frankly.

But above everything else remember that YOU ARE GUESTS OF THIS LAND, and be very careful in everything that you do.

(8)

Editorials from *Hawaii Hochi**

The *Hawaii Hochi* was the newspaper owned and edited by Fred Makino, whose approach to the problem of Japanese rights was almost directly the opposite of Okumura's. Here are two typical editorials from *Hochi,* published during the 1920s.

PRACTICING WHAT THEY PREACH!

The English language dailies of Honolulu have, on many occasions, given voice to the fervent praise of the American-born Orientals, who make up such a large proportion of our varied population. Editorially and in signed articles they have urged racial tolerance and harmony, denying most emphatically that there is any race problem in Hawaii. . . .

The young Orientals have taken them at their word, and have come to believe that their Asiatic blood does not act as a bar to their progress here in Hawaii. In the schools and at the University, in the clubs and the YMCA, the young people have discussed the question of race discrimination and "color line" and have come to the conclusion that here in Hawaii all the racial barriers are down, and that a man is judged according to his ability and given the opportunity to which he is entitled, regardless of whether his skin is white or yellow or brown.

Theoretically, these are very fine sentiments and there is no doubt that the expresssion of them has caused the editorial breasts to swell with the consciousness of virtue, and has brought the warm glow of self-appreciation into the barren hearts of many of our English writers. But as a cold business proposition, where facts count for more than theories, it is *all bunk!* These sanctimonious English newspapers use such sentiments only to serve their own ends and

* *Hawaii Hochi,* July 17, 1926 and July 24, 1926.

to fool their readers. When it comes to practicing what they preach,—that is a different thing altogether.

The *Honolulu Advertiser,* according to the statements made to this paper by those who have had occasion to test its sincerity, has stated frankly that it is against the policy of the paper to employ reporters of Oriental blood. Ability to write and speak English correctly did not enter into the question at all. The reason was told bluntly and to the point! *Orientals were not wanted!*

The same thing holds true of the *Star Bulletin* though that paper was not honest enough to give its reasons in so many words. But the fact remains that its policy has been and is now to refuse to employ Orientals as reporters, no matter what their journalistic qualifications may be. The stories told by some of the young Americans of Oriental blood should bring the blush of shame to the cheeks of their white brothers. Honest, industrious, capable boys have been told by white employers that they would not have an Oriental in the establishment. They have been told that if they were Portuguese or part-Hawaiian they could go to work at once but that *Orientals were not wanted!*

What is the explanation? Why do these Anglo-Saxons preach so feelingly about race equality and tolerance and the meeting of the East and West, and then, in their insufferable arrogance, give the lie direct to all their teachings by practicing the very intolerance and prejudice in discrimination which they condemn?

What is the psychological reason for this condition? And what will be its future effect upon the next generation of Americans in Hawaii? Is there a deliberate conspiracy to force the Orientals back to a position of servile inferiority? Is Hawaii planting the seeds of a terrible caste system which will wreck her civilization?

These are some of the questions that need to be answered frankly and openly, if we are to justify our proud position before the world as the "Melting Pot of The Pacific."

HOW ABOUT THE JAPANESE?

One of our Haole friends, commenting on a recent editorial in this paper relative to the "superiority complex" of the Anglo-Saxons here in Hawaii, admitted the general truth of our statements regarding the danger that lies in the establishment of a Nordic caste system, but disclaimed the responsibility, placing the blame on the Japanese themselves.

"You told us the truth about our Nordic egoism," he said, "But *how about the Japanese?* Why don't you tell them about their *inferiority complex?"*

It is true that we have perhaps devoted more attention to the mote in our brother's eye than we have to the beam in our own. For this we offer the usual excuse—that it is easier to see! But if we are to be of service to our friends and true to our own ideals we must use the surgeon's scalpel with steady and impartial hand, even though we cut to the quick.

Our Haole friends are right. If there is race discrimination here in Hawaii on the part of the Anglo-Saxons against the Orientals, it is as much the fault of one as it is of the other. Speaking of the Japanese in particular, the attitude of the younger generation of Hawaiian-born really invites discrimination.

It is not wholly their fault, but they occupy an uncomfortable halfway position between the old culture of the Japanese and the new culture of the Americans, and they are neither altogether of the one or of the other. What, in the older generation, was the deference and courtesy of the stranger in the presence of his host, has become in the young Japanese an obsequiousness that is almost servile and that is wholly foreign to the American standards.

As Japanese, they are extremely sensitive to slights and are always looking for them. Naturally, they find them, in many cases where they were not intended at all. And their reaction is to accept with meekness the aggressive domination of their white brothers, thus lowering themselves and creating in their own minds what amounts to an "inferiority complex."

The young Japanese born in Hawaii are not as a rule as aggressive as their parents. They lack that quality of combativeness that is called "pep" or "spunk." They do not attack and overcome opposition with a spirit of their white brothers. They are in every way as well qualified to win success, but they do not assert themselves. They lack the fighting instincts that have given the Japanese their dominant position in the Orient and the Anglo-Saxons their leadership in the Occident.

And always there is present in their minds the idea that they are discriminated against. They resent it, but they do not rise to the obstacle and surmount it. If they spent half the energy in fighting back that they spend in pitying themselves, they would find that the barrier before which they halt could be brushed aside as readily as a wall of straw.

What is the use of insisting that one is an "American citizen" if he does not act like one? To be an American citizen is nothing in itself. There are thousands that are not worth the powder to blow them off the earth. It is the individual behind the citizen that counts, the mere accident of birth means nothing as a guarantee of character. No one can demand respect or consideration just because he was born in this country, if he has not the quality that make others respect him.

We have been told by some of those who "do not employ Orientals" that the reason is not because they are of a different race or because they are looked down upon, but because experience has taught that they do not deliver the goods in certain lines of endeavor. And it is this very attitude which we have been criticizing that is the obstacle to their success.

Perhaps there is something in this objection to the young Orientals, after all. If there is, surely they ought to know it and not continue to blame "race discrimination" for what may be really their own fault. At any rate, the matter should be studied seriously and an effort made to overcome any tendency to a racial "inferiority complex." This is as dangerous and as fraught with peril as the Nordic caste complex which we made the subject of our previous criticism.

We have an idea that when the young Japanese are able to look their white brothers squarely in the eye and tell them to "get out of the way!" they will find out whether there is any race discrimination that can hinder them or keep them from success!

(9)

Joe Kurihara–Duty Before Pleasure*

After migrating from Hawaii to the mainland United States, Joe Kurihara continued in his efforts to become part of the American scene, to "make it" in the traditional ways open, presumably, to all poor people who wanted to better themselves.

. . . My first impression was of San Francisco, the atmosphere was not too pleasant. However, I decided to weather it through. For two years, I have borne patiently the distasteful word, "Jap." Never had I heard this word Jap in the islands, but here in California it was almost a universal title, used to address the Japanese. Many times, trying to be broad-minded, I soothed my feelings by interpreting it as an abbreviation of the word Japanese, but when an ugly expression is manifested by the speaker, I felt very, very unpleasant. Disregarding the conditions, I pursued my studies for two years, taking care of a boiler for board and room. . . .

. . . Having successfully completed my course at California Commercial College, I was now employed as part-time bookkeeper by the Bay City Produce Company, receiving $80 per month. The path so far was rough and hard. Many, many times, I went with only two meals a day. To work through school is not an easy task. It requires super-human determination to accomplish one's aim to work and support oneself through college. My body

* Japanese Relocation Papers, Bancroft Library, University of California, Berkeley, Calif.

trembled and I experienced fainting spells frequently during those trying days of 1920.

I saw boys and girls heading for picture shows while I had to stay in and study. I saw people going to a picnic party while I had to work. It really was discouraging at times but I felt and knew, to succeed I must deny all pleasures however painful it may be.

Eighty dollars per month was more than ample for me to meet all expenses at the Southwestern University. The day of reckoning came in June 1924. It was unquestionably the greatest and the most glorious day of my life when I donned the cap and gown to receive my Bachelor of Commercial Science Degree, together with the Certificate of Accountancy. I graduated in three-and-a-half years by attending through all summer vacations. It was my motto: "Duty before pleasure." I will not rest until I succeed.

(10)

Experiences of Orientals in America*

Kurihara's early belief that if he worked hard and studied seriously he would be accepted in American life was shared by many other Japanese-Americans. But, very quickly, they discovered that the reality of their daily lives had very little to do with the rhetoric of equality. The following excerpts are from the life stories of Orientals gathered by the Fisk University project.

First, an American-born Japanese speaks:

I was born in America and I am happy to call myself a native of this soil, but because of my race and physical make-up and differences from the Occidental I have been denied the full opportunity as a citizen of this country. It is sad to think that the Orientals are looked down upon just

* Fisk University Social Science Institute, "Orientals and Their Cultural Adjustments" (Nashville, 1946).

because of the physical appearances. There are many other foreigners here under the American flag, but because of their physical similarity with the Americans they can have the freedom of doing as they please. . . .

When I entered the University of Southern California in 1927 my ideas changed very quickly because of the treatment I received here. It seems more or less that the professors and the students treat the Oriental students with some kind of a pity, and not with understanding, that was my first impression and I resolved to show them I came here to study and not to be pitied because I am a Japanese. . . . In my sophomore year, I began to dislike the Americans bitterly as I never did before. This feeling was the result of trouble arising from the house problem in Belvedere. I bought a bungalow in Belvedere district so that my parents and I could live respectfully, until I graduate, and thinking we can sell it when we will return to Japan. It was only two weeks when two gentlemen came to us and asked us politely, but not too cordially, to leave the house as we cannot live among white people. White people! I suppose white people were Jewish, Italians, Russians, and low-class Europeans. This was my first experience with a real conflict between foreigners against foreigner. And to imagine that respectable gentlemen visit us at nine o'clock in the night. . . .

Japanese are not served by the American barber. I have known many cases. When I came to this country, my friend said to us that I could not be served by an American barber. I wondered. One day I went to an American barber for trial. There were eight seats in the room. One man was on a seat. Five men were talking about daily news, but nobody said to me to take the seat and to serve for me for about one hour. At last I left there for Japanese barber.

Japanese are not served by high-class American restaurants. One time I went to a big restaurant in San Francisco for trial and I was refused. . . .

Last year was a peaceful one for me—we rented a house in Boyle Heights, the owner being a Jewish couple who delight in charging us a very high rent. But in order to avoid further trouble and experience another disappointment and discomfort, we are staying there temporarily until my graduation. During my junior year I made many good friends among the American people, they came to treat me with equality and with interest, but somehow I feel more comfortable talking with my own people. And I am studying very hard with the ambition to be an editor, when I go back to Japan. I shall, I know, be able to write some good points of America and the bad points. There are still hundreds of students back there with the desire to come here and study in reality the Christian life in America. But I know many of them shall be disappointed to know that America is not true to the laws of equality and the Statue of Liberty.

After my graduation from Harvard I tried to get a position in the East but was unable to secure one after a month's effort. I had conferences with representatives of several of the big electrical concerns but was repeatedly told that I would encounter difficulties because I was not a citizen. I am now elevator boy in a large apartment house in Los Angeles. I do not enjoy this work because there is no future to it, but I am working here because I can have some money which will enable me to go to New York to try my fortune again. If I can make no headway in the East I will return to Japan where I am quite certain of finding suitable employment. My father has suggested that I return at once to Japan but I prefer to remain here at least for a few years. . . . At times I have felt rather discouraged but then I have said to myself that it is the natural thing to expect that the Americans should favor members of their own group and not select members of the Yellow Race ahead of them.

Whenever a Japanese has made a place for himself he has been accepted, as was Dr. Noguchi, who is with the Rockefeller Institute, but there are few places open to the mediocre members of the Yellow Race.

I came to California because I wanted, in the first place, to understand the nature of anti-Japanese feeling and the true condition of Japanese in California; and my purpose in coming to this country was to understand true America and to introduce her to Japan.

The first thing that surprised me when I arrived at San Francisco in 1919, was the gigantic advertisement of "Join the Navy," because I never thought that America was so eager to emphasize that line. Seeing that big advertisement I could not help laughing at the honest movement in Japan regarding the disarmament, or the peace of the world, which was aroused by America's declaring the world peace. At the same time I was compelled to think that America would become a more militaristic country than any other countries in the world in future. . . .

It is most difficult to comprehend the movement of anti-Japanese in the Christian country like America.

The bias social condition is the greatest difficulty in getting adjusted to America. . . .

A girl in Oakland High School was elected as the representative of the graduates by the faculty of the high school, but she was opposed by some of the graduates and their parents. Consequently she was forced to give up to play her part.

Japanese and American-born Japanese cannot enjoy themselves in the public swimming pool. About a half-month ago a Grammar School boy was brought to a swimming pool, but he was not allowed to swim because of his father's nationality.

Japanese cannot play at public tennis court. When I and my friends went to the tennis court in San Francisco, we could not be allowed to play there. . . .

Strictly speaking I have not realized my ambition yet (to understand the true America) because the social attitude of Americans toward Japanese betrays all what I thought about before. Of course, I am greatly pleased to find the Democratic spirit of America. On the other hand, I am threatened to see the systematized anti-Japanese feeling. So I cannot still understand America. I thought that America was Democracy itself. . . .

I am in favor of intermarriage. Intermarriage is the essence of social interaction and of eternal peace. Only by this is racial problem solved in the most peaceful way.

(11)

The Japanese-American Creed*

Almost nine months to the very day before Pearl Harbor, Senator Elbert Thomas of Utah introduced into the *Congressional Record* "The Japanese-American Creed." The "Creed" had been written by Mike Masaoka, a young Nisei who was one of the leaders of the Japanese-American Citizens League. The "Creed" expressed the Niseis' belief in America and their conviction that they would be accepted as full citizens by all Americans.

I am proud that I am an American citizen of Japanese ancestry for my very background makes me appreciate more fully the wonderful advantages of this nation.

I believe in her institutions, ideals, and traditions; I glory in her heritage; I boast of her history; I trust in her future. She has granted me liberties and opportunities such as no individual enjoys in this world today. She has given me an education befitting kings. She has entrusted me with the responsibilities of the franchise. She has permitted me to build a home, to earn a livelihood, to worship, think, speak, and act as I please—as a free man equal to every other man.

Although some individuals may discriminate against me, I shall never become bitter or lose faith for I know that such persons are not representative of the majority of the American people.

* U.S. Congress, *Congressional Record,* Vol. 87, Part II, 77th Congress, 1st Session (May 9, 1941).

True, I shall do all in my power to discourage such practices, but I shall do it in the American way; aboveboard, in the open, through courts of law, by education, by proving myself to be worthy of equal treatment and consideration. I am firm in my belief that American sportsmanship and attitude of fair play will judge citizenship and patriotism on the basis of action and achievement, and not on the basis of physical characteristics.

Because I believe in America, and I trust she believes in me, and because I have received innumerable benefits from her, I pledge myself to do honor to her at all times and in all places; to support her constitution; to obey her laws; to respect her flag; to defend her against all her enemies, foreign and domestic; to actively assume my duties and obligations as a citizen, cheerfully and without any reservations whatsoever, in the hope that I may become a better American in a greater America.

(12)

Kurihara Attempts to Enlist*

After the outbreak of war between the United States and Japan, the Japanese-American Citizens League was intent upon demonstrating the patriotism of its Nisei members by cooperating, fully, with all the agencies of the United States Government. And individual Niseis, like Joe Kurihara, tried to enlist in the armed forces. Here Kurihara tells of what happened to him when he offered his services to the government.

Immediately following the declaration of war on Japan, December 7, 1941, I resigned my navigation post at the company's offices in Los Angeles, California. . . .

I thought that my qualifications might stand me in good stead as a navigator for planes and their pilots ferrying cargos across the Atlantic to England and Russia. At that

* Dorothy Swaine Thomas and Richard S. Nishimoto, *op. cit.*

early date I had had no indication, as yet, that my Japanese features and Japanese ancestry were going to work hard against every enlistment effort I was to make. I was still thinking, naturally, in terms of an American and as an American.

I first went to the Consolidated Aircraft Corporation in Los Angeles to present my idea and to present my qualifications. I was told to "come back and see us later," and there followed many days of going back and seeing them, and there was much stalling and still I had not even been able to get myself granted an initial interview.

. . . [Consolidated] told me in no uncertain terms that my chances of being connected, even remotely, with their or any other war efforts were very slim.

In spite of all of this I still felt that I should and must keep on trying, and so I went to the Los Angeles shipyards and offered my services as a laborer. I didn't know a thing about shipbuilding, but in those days that wasn't so necessary. They needed manpower, and if I was accepted I would still be doing some little thing constructive. . . . The result of this shipyard interview, however, was even worse and more discouraging than were the interviews at Consolidated. They told me bluntly that they didn't want me and further, they didn't want anyone of Japanese ancestry. I felt like saying—and maybe I did, I don't remember—"But I am not a Japanese. I am an American and an American citizen and I'm a veteran of twenty-six-months overseas duty in the last war." It was no use, however. . . .

It was an awful feeling, this first realization that my own government did not even consider me American. It considered me a Japanese and, further a Japanese ready and willing to sell it out. I knew, too, by this time, that I had been and still was being watched, every hour of every day by the Bureau of Investigation—the "police" of the only government I ever had, or served or claimed. . . .

(13)

A Teenager's Attitude Toward Evacuation*

The months following the outbreak of war were filled with uncertainty and anguish for all the Japanese: rumors about their future fate swept the communities. The older generation, those born in Japan and therefore prohibited by law from becoming citizens, were resigned to the possibility they might be interned; the younger generation of American-born Nisei could not believe that they, too, would be treated as enemy aliens. Here a sixteen-year-old high-school girl, Rhoda Nishimura, describes her reactions to the evacuation order.

On the day our evacuation orders came out in Berkeley, I was elated to think orders had finally broken the suspense but on the other hand I saw a dark future. It was in one of my most melancholy moments that one of my teachers came up to me and discussed with me my attitude regarding evacuation. The last words are ones I shall remember when I feel like pouring out words of contempt toward the U.S. government. She said to me: "To win this war everyone in the U.S. must make sacrifices. Your sacrifice is a much harder one than most of us have to bear. As a citizen always remember that this is your part in the war. . . ."

I admit that my thoughts were none too pleasant during the period of quarantine. With the police department making its appearance every few hours, I really felt like a prisoner. The fence and the sentry marching back and forth just a few steps from the door strengthened the feeling of confinement. I was certain that a prisoner in the isolation ward of San Quentin couldn't be worse off. And then I got to thinking. We aren't the only ones going through such

* *Japanese Relocation Papers,* Bancroft Library, University of California, Berkeley, California.

trying days. The people in Greece are starving. In China there are famines each year. When an air-raid siren goes off in Europe putting out lights is an elementary thing. There an air raid signal means running for shelter and much anxiety over the safety of a dear one. But do you not think in comparison to life in other suffering nations, our existence here in America though in camp is a much easier one? Would we not take a Pollyanna attitude and say that nothing can be so bad it can't be worse?

Since it is necessary that we spend the duration in camp, why not take it on the chin? Many men have given their lives for their country since December 7. They gave their all for their native land. Let us drop our ill feelings and take on this life in camp as our duty in this war as loyal Americans.

(14)

Life in the Camps*

> The experience of being forced into the internment camps was shattering for many of the Japanese, especially the young Nisei. The following documents are excerpts from letters, reports, and interviews of Nisei about their experiences and reactions to the camps.

. . . It is still hot in Poston. Having no cooling system, we have no way to escape the heat except, perhaps, by taking frequent cold showers. We are too often denied even that because at least once a week, the water system goes wrong, and water is shut off for various lengths of time. We then don't have even drinking water then, there being no emergency water line.

Food is terrible. I am getting tired of breakfast consisting of mush, toast without butter or jam, and coffee. We occa-

* *Japanese Relocation Papers,* Bancroft Library, University of California, Berkeley, California.

sionally have corn flakes or shredded wheat. We seldom have fruits. We miss greens.

The medical situation has improved somewhat after the head physician was forced to resign. What precipitated it was the death of two new-born babies. The Japanese doctors under him requested cooling systems for rooms where babies are kept in the hospital. The head physician refused, saying it was unnecessary. As a consequence, at least two babies died in the room in a temperature of 108 degrees. The doctors pronounced death due to dehydration. One of the babies' mothers grabbed a pair of shears and attacked the head doctor. It was her first baby.

There were other instances of deliberate misconduct on the part of the medico and a firm pressure was put to the administration by the evacuees through their representatives. The head doctor resigned. The significant part of it was that there was nothing done until the evacuees got their dander up. The administration either took the attitude of protecting the head doctor, or "I don't know" attitude. . . .

It makes me smile a wry smile when I read in the American papers (for instance, the *Arizona Republic,* editorial for August 19) about how well the Japanese in America are being treated. Our life is that of slow torture. The queerest part of American democracy is that it is torturing its own citizen because he happens to have Japanese blood in him while German and Italian aliens go scot free. I haven't heard a sensible explanation of that phenomena yet, excepting those not very complimentary to America. . . .

I am working as an adult education leader. We are spreading the information on cooperatives. We have four specialists from New York to help us. They will be with us for about a month. My pay is $16 a month. Only professionals like doctors, registered nurses, and a few others get the top pay of $19 a month. It seems queer to see the hospital white nurses getting good wages while the Japanese nurses doing the same work get only $19. . . .

At first, some of the Caucasians evidently held on to the

idea that they can treat the Japanese as they would Indians who had never been out of the reservation. They quickly found out their error.

Within the bounding limits prescribed by the Army and the War Relocation Authority, the government within this camp is administered by the "City Council" elected by the evacuees. Every evacuee over sixteen years of age was allowed to vote. . . .

Prospect of college students leaving for college is very dim. Army approved only seventeen out of 150 colleges willing to accept Japanese.

Regards.

. . . Left Fresno at 8:55 this morning and reached the Assembly Center at about 9:10 A.M. We first stopped at the registrar's office to be checked and registered. Our bags and pockets were searched, to my surprise. For what? I don't know. Luckily we all passed. I mean nothing was taken from us. Then our baggage was inspected from corner to corner. What a feeling I had when they went through our personal belongings. . . .

When I first entered our room, I became sick to my stomach. There were seven beds in the room and no furniture nor any partitions to separate the males and the females of the family. I just sat on the bed, staring at the bare wall. For a while I couldn't speak nor smile. Well, after getting over with my shock, I started to get the baggage in. . . .

Then we wanted to know where our rest rooms were. This was too much for me. There is no privacy. I just can't explain how it is, but it's worse than a country privy. After it's been used a couple of times, there is a whole stack of flies. Once you open the door the flies can be seen buzzing around; it is like a nest of bees. We just couldn't go in there, so we excavated. The hospital being facilitated with flush toilets, we sneaked in. Then we tried the showers, which are not so bad except that there is no privacy. Well that's that for the day's happening.

As to what I think of camp life; I think it's hell. That's the only word I could think of to describe it.

I've done a great deal of thinking since we came here and after nearly a month in this "new life," I find it terribly discouraging. Conditions in some ways have improved, for example the pre-school nursery schools have been started and from this past Monday six-to-eight year olds are having classroom activity from 8:45 A.M.–11:30 A.M. daily. It consists of community singing—Americanization and group play activities, mostly—some books (texts from Alameda County school system), crayons, pencils, and paper were expected so as the supplies come in the children will have more to work with. . . .

We had a "Town Hall" meeting tonight and representative people who have been responsible for camp functioning . . . spoke on a panel. It seems that the big reason why we cannot get any results or to make any changes is due to a bottleneck caused by the Tanforan Administration. The milk problem—the canteen problem—the diet and menu problem—the lack of sufficient laundry—bathing and toilet facilities, etc. etc. The chief and biggest worry is that we have really no self-government. The administration controls all of our liberties to the extent where everything is actually limited to their dictates. . . .

We are constantly aware of this sort of regimentation and regulation and our feeling is that of confinement and held as a sort of prisoner for no other crime than that we were unfortunately of Japanese descent. . . .

One inhumane incident occurred yesterday, a mother of five children—dying—and members of the family could not see her as they had too much red tape to wade thru. While the administrative heads were considering whether the family should be allowed to visit their mother, she passed away—none of them knew whether they could notify relatives on the outside after the tragic incident occurred. As it happens the hospital is only a twenty minute ride away from Tanforan. The family was notified about three hours prior to her death—you can see what bitterness this sort of thing creates. I simply cannot sleep nights—thinking of the injustice of everything.

As an American, I revolt because it was my understanding that we were sacrificing our homes, our life that we had worked and planned for our children and ourselves—as a patriotic duty. Evacuating for military reason and all such reasons which I question now. I challenge any American to stack up their record against any of us and see if we hadn't been as good or better Americans in *deed* and to think today—we and our children (third- and fourth-generation Americans—who have to live in this country after this mess is over) have to be confined in concentration camps—If we are to really be victorious fighting for the preservation of democracy and the American way of life, we had better review the constitutionality of all this right here in U.S.A. If we feel this way now—I wonder how we shall feel two years or three years hence. Really when I see small children and growing youngsters—I can't stand this life.

Every Nisei . . . was extremely annoyed when he was reminded by some visiting Caucasian that he had been placed in the assembly center "for his own protection." Also, without exception, everyone was highly indignant at the practice of focusing floodlights from twelve watch-towers on camp every night from twilight to dawn. When informed by the administration that the searchlights had been installed to protect us from outsiders who might leap over the fence to injure us, his usual retort was: "Why should the lights be focused on the barracks and not on the outer fence as a logical procedure?" Similarly, there was keen resentment against the barbed-wire fence surrounding camp and many a time I watched a novice throwing rocks at it to discover if the wires were actually charged.

No systematic study was made of the attitudes of little children but the narrating of a few stray incidents might be of some aid in identifying them. One afternoon in late June, I heard a great commotion behind my barrack and on investigation perceived a group of twelve boys about six to ten years of age shouldering wooden guns and attacking a "Japanese fort" while lustily singing "Anchors Aweigh." . . . Similarly, in the blackout of May 24, little children raced down our street yelling at the top of their lungs: "Turn off your lights! The Japs are coming!"

A Nisei mother once told me with tears in her eyes of her six-year-old son who insisted on her "taking him back to America." The little boy had been taken to Japan about two years ago but was so unhappy there that she was compelled to return to California with him. Soon afterwards they were evacuated to Santa Anita, and the little boy in the absence of his Caucasian playmates was convinced that he was still in Japan and kept on entreating his mother to "take him back to America." To reassure him that he was in America she took him to the information center in her district and pointed to the American flag but he could not be consoled because Charlie and Jimmie, his Caucasian playmates, were not there with him in camp.

It is also interesting to note that whenever little children sang songs these were not Japanese folksongs but typically American songs like "God Bless America," "My Country 'Tis of Thee," "My Old Kentucky Home," "Row, Row, Row Your Boat," "Jesus Loves Me," and other songs known to every American child. The "Americanness" of the Sansei may serve to identify the character of their Nisei parents.

When 1,500 work orders were sent out by the Personnel Office to U.S. citizens above the age of sixteen a day before the camouflage project was opened, approximately 800 were reported to have refused to work. Some excused themselves by claiming that they were allergic to the dye on burlap strips or to the lint which fell off from them, but at least half of that number was said to have refused on principle. They felt that they were really "prisoners of war" and that the U.S. government had no right to appeal to them to aid in the war effort on a patriotic note. The battle cry during the camouflage strike of June 16–17 seemed to be: Give us the treatment accorded other American citizens and we will gladly cooperate in completing the number of nets requested by the U.S. Army. . . .

The majority of the center residents were convinced that the extreme unpopularity of the JACL [Japanese-American Citizens League] would prevent its functioning after the war. They referred to it as a "thing of the past." Most of the Nisei claimed that they had been "sold down the river" by the JACL leaders and indicated a great desire to "get even" with them. With reference to their utterances in the Tolan hearings they declared: "They were self-appointed representatives of the Nisei and not our true leaders." Their dislike for the organization was so great that during the riot of August 4 many of the former JACL leaders received unwelcome visits and their apartments had to be protected by the military police. One of the primary causes for their unpopularity was that many felt that JACL members had turned in names of "dangerous" Japanese to the FBI not for patriotic but mercenary reasons. In my walks through camp certain persons were frequently pointed out to me as former JACL members who had received twenty-five dollars a head for each Japanese they had sent to a detention camp. They were shunned by the rest of the population like lepers. By ridiculing and ignoring them they hoped to discipline other *inu* or dogs who might develop in camp.

There was a pronounced feeling among the Japanese at Santa Anita that the Caucasians in a camp suffered a definite superiority complex and were totally unsympathetic toward their problems. Many of the Nisei contended that practically all of the W.C.C.A. [Wartime Civil Control Administration] officials if they did not say so outright implied in their actions that "after all, they're all Japs here whether citizens or not."

. . . Whenever any friction occurred in camp it was blamed on the Jews who were said to entertain hatred toward the Japanese. Thus whenever bad meals were served in the mess halls they were attributed to the Jewish stewards and to a Jewish concern which had contracted to supply food to the mess halls. Even after the administration announced officially that the food supply came direct from the quartermasters' corps in San Bernardino, the rumor persisted that a Jewish company had subcontracted it from the army and was making profits on it. They claimed that the meals served could not cost fifty cents a head as allotted by the army and that someone—in all probability the Jews—was deriving profits from it.

This hostility toward Jews acquired from the general American public was enhanced in pre-evacuation days when a number of the Main Street Jews in Los Angeles bought up the majority of the Little Tokyo stores at ridiculous prices while the more unscrupulous members of their group "robbed" non-English-speaking Japanese of their homes and furniture. How many of the atrocities reported to have been committed by the Jews were true or not I was unable to ascertain but a prominent member of the Federal Security Bank in Los Angeles informed me that a number of them had reached their attention and they were employing legal means to apprehend them.

(15)

Kurihara in the Camps*

Kurihara's bitterness at the treatment of the Japanese, the circumstances found in the camps, coupled with his hatred for the Japanese-American Citizens League, led him to become a leader and to organize against the administration and the collaborationists at Manzanar.

The desert was bad enough. The mushroom barracks made it worse. The constant cyclonic storms loaded with sand and dust made it worst. After living in well furnished homes with every modern convenience and suddenly forced to live the life of a dog is something which one cannot so readily forget. Down in our hearts we cried and cursed this

* Dorothy Swaine Thomas and Richard S. Nishimoto, *op. cit.*

government every time when we were showered with sand. We slept in the dust, we breathed the dust; and we ate the dust. Such abominable existence one could not forget, no matter how much we tried to be patient, understand the situation, and take it bravely. Why did not the government permit us to remain where we were? Was it because the government was unable to give us the protection? I have my doubt. The government could have easily declared Martial Law to protect us. It was not the question of protection. It was because we were Japs! Yes, Japs!

After corralling us like a bunch of sheep in a hellish country, did the government treat us like citizens? No! We were treated like aliens regardless of our rights. Did the government think we were so without pride to work for $16.00 a month when people outside were paid $40.00 to $50.00 a week in the defense plants? Responsible government officials further told us to be loyal and that to enjoy our rights as American citizens we must be ready to die for the country. We must show our loyalty. If such is the case, why are the veterans corralled like the rest of us in the camps? Have they not proven their loyalty already? This matter of proving one's loyalty to enjoy the rights of an American citizen was nothing but a hocus-pocus.

(16)

A Nisei Who Said "No"*

In February, 1943, the Army submitted a questionnaire to all male evacuees. Question 28 was "Will you swear unqualified allegiance to the United States of America and faithfully defend the United States from any or all attack by foreign or domestic forces, and forswear any form of allegiance or obedience to the Japanese em-

* War Relocation Authority Communication Analysis Section: Community Analysis Notes No. 1. Jan. 15, 1944.

peror or any other foreign government, power or organization?"

Those men who answered "No" to the question were taken from the camps in which they had been interned and segregated at the Tule Lake Center. The following document is a set of verbatim notes taken during a hearing in which a young Nisei told a hearing board why he had answered "No."

HEARING BOARD MEMBER: I see you have always lived in this country.

NISEI: Yes.

HBM: Are you a dual citizen?

NISEI: No, I am an American citizen only.

HBM: In February, during the army registration, you said "No" to Question 28 according to our record. Did you understand the question?

NISEI: I guess I did understand the question.

HBM: And do you want to change the answer or do you want the "No" to stand?

NISEI: I'll keep it "No."

HBM: What does that mean? (The boy stands there. His lips are quivering but he does not speak.)

HBM: Do you want to talk about it? Something is bothering you.

NISEI: What is bothering me could not be answered by any one person in particular.

HBM: Don't you want to tell us? Perhaps there is something that we can do. If you say "No," you are giving away your American citizenship. Is that what you want to do? Feel free to talk. We're not here to argue with you but we want to help you.

NISEI: What I was thinking. I thought that since there is a war on between Japan and America, since the people of this country have to be geared up to fight against Japan, they are taught to hate us. So they don't accept us. First I wanted to help this country, but they evacuated us instead of giving us a chance. Then I wanted to be neutral but now that you force a decision, I have to say this. We have a Japanese face. Even if I try to be American I won't be entirely accepted.

HBM: What is this about "the Japanese face" deal? Up to today we haven't heard this expression, and today we hear it all over this block. Have you been reading Mary Oyama's article in *Liberty?*

NISEI: I read Mary's article. It doesn't say much. It just tells about the conditions of leaving our homes, about the hardships we suffered and how well we took them. But that was just the beginning. A great deal has happened since then that she says nothing about.

HBM: What do you plan to do?

NISEI: I planned to stay in this country before the war. I planned to be a farmer.

HBM: What about your folks?

NISEI: They figure they'll stay here if I do or they'll go to Tule Lake if I do.

HBM: Is it that some of your friends are going to Tule Lake? Are you being influenced by the talk of friends?

NISEI: No, my best friend is going to stay here.

HBM: Then what is at the bottom of this?

NISEI: If I would say "Yes," I'd be expected to say that I'd give up my life for this country. I don't think I could say that because this country has not treated me as a citizen. I could go three-quarters of the way but not all the way after what has happened.

HBM: Would you be willing to be drafted?

NISEI: No, I couldn't do that.

HBM: That's all. I see that you have thought about it and that your mind is made up. (Nisei goes out.)

HBM: I feel sorry for that boy. Some of them I don't feel sorry for.

(17)

Kurihara Renounces U.S. Citizenship*

Joe Kurihara played a leading role in the organization of the "Blood Brothers" insurrection at Manzanar, which resulted in the deaths of two inmates when inmates stormed the administration building to insist that a captive be released in 1943. Kurihara expatriated himself to Japan after the war. He sailed November 24, 1945 from Seattle, on the first ship carrying the repatriates to Japan. They were mostly American citizens, but after two years in concentration camps, Japan was their chosen country.

My American friends . . . no doubt must have wondered why I renounced my citizenship. This decision was not that of today or yesterday. It dates back to the day when General DeWitt ordered evacuation. It was confirmed when he flatly refused to listen even to the voices of the former World War Veterans and it was doubly confirmed when I entered Manzanar. We who already had proven our loyalty by serving in the last World War should have been spared. The veterans asked for special consideration but their requests were denied. They too had to evacuate like the rest of the Japanese people, as if they were aliens.

I did not expect this of the Army. When the Western Defense Command assumed the responsibilities of the West Coast, I expected that at least the Nisei would be allowed to remain. But to General DeWitt, we were all alike. "A Jap's a Jap. Once a Jap, always a Jap." . . . I swore to become a Jap 100 percent, and never to do another day's work to help this country fight this war. My decision to renounce my citizenship there and then was absolute. . . .

It is my sincere desire to get over there as soon as possible to help rebuild Japan politically and economically.

* Dorothy Swaine Thomas and Richard S. Nishimoto, *op. cit.*

The American Democracy with which I was infused in my childhood is still unshaken. My life is dedicated to Japan with Democracy my goal.

(18)

Japanese-American Citizens League Hymn

After the war ended, many Japanese attempted to resume the pattern of their lives. But they were not the same people and much of what they had done in the past was closed to them. They tried to forget the camp experience: the post-war Japanese-American Citizens League hymn dwelt on the future.

There was a dream my father dreamed for me
A land in which all men are free—
Then the desert camp with watchtowers high
Where life stood still, mid sand and brooding sky
Out of the war in which my brothers died—
Their muted voices with mine cried—
This is our dream that all men shall be free!
This is our creed, we'll live in loyalty,
God help us rid the land of bigotry
That we may walk in peace and dignity.

(19)

Evacuation–The Pain Remains*

EVACUATION—THE PAIN REMAINS was the headline on a column by Kats Kunitsugu in the *Pacific Citizen,* the official weekly of the Japanese-American Citizens League. In the column, she writes about a question asked of her by another Nisei: "Are Nisei parents reluctant to talk about the Evacuation with their kids? Do they avoid talking about what happened twenty-five years ago, especially their feelings about it?"

* Kats Kunitsugu in *Pacific Citizen,* Dec. 20–27, 1968.

I didn't feel that we were "reluctant" or that we "avoided" the question. It seems to me that most Nisei parents were willing enough to discuss the Evacuation if their children brought the topic up because it was being talked about in their social studies class or something. Of course, it all happened a long time ago, and I don't think we make it a point to bring the topic up.

Last night I stayed up until all hours reading *Chusei Toroku,* which recounts the Evacuation experience with the focus on Questions 27 and 28—the so-called loyalty questions. Taisuke Fujishima, the 34-year-old Japanese author who gained notice for his "Kodoku no Hito," a *roman à clef* of Prince Hirohito, whose classmate he was at the Peers' School, explains that he became intrigued with the Evacuation story when he stayed here about four months in 1966.

What fascinated him was "the Pacific War" as seen from the American side, the United States' treatment of Japanese Americans during that war and most importantly, the reaction of the Japanese Americans to their treatment.

Fujishima calls his book a "semi-documentary." The documentary part recalls the overt anti-Japanese mood of the West Coast rooted in its Wild West history and fanned by self-righteous white supremacists and exploding in hysteria after the Japanese attack on Pearl Harbor. Much of the material is from Allan Bosworth's *America's Concentration Camps* (which incidentally is now out in pocket-book form, published by Bantam Books) and accounts published in the *Rafu Shimpo* and the Los Angeles metropolitan dailies.

The "Semi" part comes in his use of the "Toyo Miyamura" family as well as a couple of Kibei as fictional characters to attempt to plunge more deeply into the question of loyalty. Evidently he relies on extensive interviews with Li'l Tokio photographer Toyo Miyatake for material, although there is no acknowledgement of the fact in his epilogue where he lists other sources.

Obviously the device was used to add more personal human interest to what otherwise would be a rather formidable parade of "kanji" in a narrative of impersonal events.

But pursued in only a sketchy and superficial manner that contains neither the attention to the telling minutiae that characterized Walter Lord's *The Longest Day* nor the searching, penetrating insight into what makes a human being tick that characterized Truman Capote's *In Cold Blood,* the book fails to live up to the importance of its theme.

For the theme is important. It is Jobian. With Questions 27 and 28, human beings, caught in a web of circumstances, were forced to decide where their loyalty lay . . . to ties of flesh and blood or to a gut feeling of belonging to the land of their birth, regardless of its treatment of them. To what extent did personal experience influence the final decisions of those caught in the web? The theme cries for a great novel with a strong, multi-faceted central character with whom we can identify as a human being, not simply as a representative Issei or Nisei figure.

Aside from my evaluation of *Chusei Toroku* as a literary achievement, I found that the book, because it is written in Japanese, conveys the Issei mood much better than books on the Evacuation written in English. And getting back to Masamori Kojima's query I mentioned at the beginning of this column, I have to admit more honestly that the pain remains from those days.

What we hate to recall is not so much the hardships that the war and Evacuation brought to us but the vast sense of alienation we suffered when we were like the man without a country. And perhaps we are reluctant about evoking those days gone by because we still can't be 100 percent sure that the possibility of rejection is as remote as it appears today.

(20)

Asian-American Political Alliance Statement, 1968*

Now, a new wind is blowing through the Japanese-American community. Just as all the other minority groups are looking at themselves differently than they have in the past, a new spirit is found among Japanese-Americans, especially the younger ones. In September, 1967, young Orientals in California, both Chinese and Japanese, formed the Asian-American Political Alliance. Here is a statement issued by the Alliance dealing with the role played by Dr. S. I. Hayakawa during the protracted strike at San Francisco State College in 1969.

We, the Asian-American Political Alliance, hereby give our unequivocal support to the courageous struggle being waged at San Francisco State College by the Black Students Union and the Third World Liberation Front. We condemn the violent police-state tactics which are being used, almost with relish, by the newly appointed president, S. I. Hayakawa, whom we regard as the worst possible type of "yellow Uncle Tom."

Although he is of our own race, we have no sympathy for someone who is so obviously allowing himself to be used to carry out the well-known repressive and anti-intellectual policies of Ronald Reagan. To us he has become a shameful symbol of the emasculation that Asian-Americans have undergone in the hands of this white racist society.

Hayakawa's recent statements reveal to us he has descended from the human level to that of a machine-like symbol manipulator. He expresses his concern for the rights of the majority of 17,500 white students, but at the same

* *Rafu Shimpo*. Los Angeles, December 9, 1968.

time shows a complete lack of compassion for the rights of the long-oppressed minorities.

Such a reaction does not surprise us for we are aware that he has publicly stated that he had no emotional feelings about the incarceration of his people in concentration camps during World War II—one of the more flagrant instances of disregard for the rights of a minority in this country's history.

To those of us who suffered through this unforgettable trauma, that statement is incredible! We can only conclude that he is either completely insensitive to human suffering, or he is a complete fool.

We are also compelled to repudiate Hayakawa when he says, "In a very profound sense, I stand in the middle. I am neither white nor black." To us he is also not yellow! In the past he has expressed his profound inability to identify with his own race—perhaps it is because he has been trying so hard to be white!

Yet, he now finds it convenient to use his color to help him become, in his words, "a channel to bring blacks and whites together." Does he believe that his reputation as an internationally recognized semanticist gives him license for such outrageous hypocrisy?

We of AAPA have spoken out on this issue for we feel that the maxim, "Silence is consent," is particularly relevant to Asian-Americans. The time has come for Asian-Americans to break that silence. We therefore wish to make it unequivocally clear that Hayakawa does not speak for AAPA, and that he is in fact being blatantly hypocritical when he implies that he is speaking for the Asian-American communities.

We reject Hayakawa as one of our own, and we have no doubts that he will in the end be rejected as president of San Francisco State College.

THE PUERTO RICANS

They think that Puerto Ricans are so easy-going and lazy that they would never fight an armed struggle like black people.

Yoruba, Minister of Information, Young Lords

Poverty in modern nations is not only a state of economic deprivation, of disorganization, or of the absence of something. It is also something positive in the sense that it has a structure, a rationale, and defense mechanisms without which the poor could hardly carry on. In short, it is a way of life, remarkably stable and persistent. . . .

Oscar Lewis in *La Vida*

"Que bonita bandera. . . ." ("How beautiful the flag is. . . .")

From the Puerto Rican National Anthem

All over New York City, stores and service agencies have signs in the windows, *"Se habla español."* In San Juan, Puerto Rico, the window signs say, "English spoken." An island housewife tells her husband, "Me voy al downtown pa'cer mi laundry," and in a clothing store on the Lower East Side of New York, another Puerto Rican housewife argues in Spanish and broken Yiddish about the price of a coat with a shop owner who answers her in Yiddish and broken Spanish.

San Juan and New York, Ponce and Chicago, Arecibo and Trenton, New Jersey—these cities are so connected with each other that no analysis of the place of Puerto Ricans in the United States is possible except in terms of dualities.

There are two Puerto Ricos. In one of them, United States sailors roam the streets of San Juan picking up whores while battalions of tourists visit the more than forty swank hotels, each with its elaborate gambling casino. For every tourist and sailor there are two whores, three beggars, and scores of barefoot kids. Pimps and cab drivers steer the sightseer to all the goodies once so easily available in Havana.

San Juan today is not fully comparable to what Havana was under Batista, and Puerto Rico is materially better off than it was thirty years ago. But, despite the over-all progress, a vast gap exists between the poor and the middle class, and another between them and the rich. More than 90,000 people in San Juan live in horrible slums, and the average yearly rate of decline in the slum population is less than one-half of 1 percent.[1]

The other Puerto Rico has been lavishly praised by the celebrators of America. "Island of promise," "a study in economic development," "a land of wonders," "the quiet revolution," "a bridge to freedom," "a success story"—these phrases are the titles of books written by Americans

[1] Oscar Lewis, *La Vida: A Puerto Rican Family in the Culture of Poverty—San Juan and New York.* New York: Random House, 1965, p. xiv.

congratulating themselves on having established a bastion of free enterprise and anti-Communism in the Caribbean. But in 1950, while Puerto Rico was being hailed as an example of American success, two Puerto Ricans killed a White House guard in an unsuccessful attempt to assassinate President Truman.

One of them, Oscar Collazo, had lived in the United States for sixteen years. Three years after the incident he told the judge who had just sentenced him to die: "Anything I may have done, I did for the cause of my country. I use this last plea for the right of my country to be free. Even if I die today, and I realize the Americans have a right to kill me, they will never be able to kill the ideals I stand for."

The same motives and emotions that had brought Collazo to the point of killing a White House guard burst forth again in 1954, when three Puerto Ricans entered the halls of Congress screaming, "Puerto Rico is not free." They were bearing the Puerto Rican flag and, as *Time* put it, "jabbering in Spanish." They fired their weapons at the Congressmen, wounding five of them. The explanation for the attack was found in a note written by Lolita Labron, one of the three attackers. "Before God, and the world, my blood claims for independence of Puerto Rico. My life I give for the freedom of my country. This is a cry for victory in our strugle [sic] for independence." On the back of the note was written: "I take responsible for all."[2]

There are contradictions existing within Puerto Rican enclaves in the United States. Puerto Rican immigrants are pursuing traditional means to status and power. Their economic conditions are improving, and Herman Badillo, a man of Puerto Rican descent, has been elected Bronx borough president and ran in a primary election for mayor of New York. At the same time, Puerto Ricans in the mainland United States cities suffer the same anguish as all nonwhites when they realize they are not full Americans and perhaps never will be.

[2] *Time*, March 15, 1954 and May 8, 1954.

That knowledge is accepted in *El Barrio*. Oscar Lewis quotes a bitter Puerto Rican man in *La Vida:*

I want to be buried in Puerto Rico because that's my country. Even if I do live in New York, I never forget my country. . . . I don't want to die here because if no one claims the body, it's sent—know where?—to the Women's Jail. To a hospital they have there, where they make experiments. . . . I want my body given to the School of Tropical Medicine in Puerto Rico but not to anybody here. Let them take their own pricks and make experiments with them. If somebody's going to use my body, let it be Puerto Rican doctors in Puerto Rico. At least, they are *hispanos*. But not here. Shit! I don't care what happens here. I'm only interested in what goes on in my own country, in what happens to Puerto Ricans who belong to my race. Nobody else matters to me.

OUR OWN COLONY

"We have a record of conquest, colonization and expansion unequalled by any people in the Nineteenth Century. We are not to be curbed now."

Henry Cabot Lodge, 1895

"American law, American order, American civilization, and the American flag will plant themselves on shores hitherto bloody and benighted, but by these agencies of God henceforth to be made beautiful and bright."

Sen. Albert J. Beveridge of Indiana, 1895

In 1898, to the surprise of most Puerto Ricans, the United States invaded and annexed their tiny island; four hundred years of Spanish colonial rule ended and United States colonial rule began. The Spaniards had left all their traditions behind: language, culture, illiteracy, poverty, corruption, and exploitation. They also left behind the burdens of bureaucracy and Catholicism. The Spanish influence had been diluted by the importation of African slaves brought in as a labor force. The blacks mixed their rhythms and rituals with Spanish culture to produce a pagan-tinged Catholicism that was an anathema to Spaniards and their Church.

Most Puerto Ricans shed few tears over the Spanish exodus. Few resisted the American soldiers since neither the American nor Puerto Rican people anticipated any colonization. The commanding general of the United States invading forces, Nelson A. Miles, announced shortly after he arrived:

> We have not come to make war upon the people of a country that for centuries has been oppressed, but, on the contrary, to bring you protection, not only to yourselves but to your property, and to bestow upon you the immunities and blessings of the liberal institutions of our Government. This is not a war of devastation, but one to give all within the control of its military and naval forces the advantages and blessings of enlightened civilization.[3]

In 1898 the language of American politics was benevolent, superior, and filled with promises of the advantages of democracy. The Puerto Ricans had no reason to believe that the United States would colonize them. Each territory on the North American continent had eventually become a state. It was assumed that if this were not going to be the case with Puerto Rico, the United States would withdraw, and the island would become independent.

But the Americans had decided that the day of the overseas empire had arrived. "The world," said President Grover Cleveland in 1893, "should be open for our ingenuity and enterprise."[4] Although American expansionism reached new ideological heights during the 1890s, American policy had always been to view the Caribbean as an integral part of the economy and defense of the United States. From the time of Thomas Jefferson, the American

[3] *Documents on the Constitutional History of Puerto Rico,* Washington, D.C., Office of Puerto Rico, 1948, p. 55.

[4] William A. Williams, *The Contours of American History*. New York: World Publishing Co., 1961, p. 320.

fear that the Caribbean might fall into the hands of powers stronger than Spain motivated much of American diplomacy. Several times during the nineteenth century, proposals to annex Caribbean territory were formulated by various secretaries of state, only to be defeated by Congress. The Monroe Doctrine of 1823 established a unilateral principle that the western hemisphere was not for European colonization. In 1895, Secretary of State Richard Olney issued a dispatch spelling out precisely what the Monroe Doctrine implied: "The United States is practically sovereign upon this continent, and its fiat is law upon the subjects to which it confines its interposition."[5]

During the 1890s the United States established its dominance in the Caribbean by intervening militarily in, or occupying Cuba, Santo Domingo, Haiti, and then Puerto Rico. While these acts occurred, debate took place in Congress between "imperialists" and "anti-imperialists." The debate had nothing to do with the principle of extending United States influence, only with how that extension should best be executed. The "imperialists" were old-fashioned colonialists who argued that Europe had gotten a head start, and the United States ought to catch up. The "anti-imperialists" sought to avoid the expense of colonial administration and to use American economic power to extend the country's influence.

The depression of the 1890s convinced key American officials, and much of the population as well, that expansion was the only solution for internal economic problems of overproduction and insufficient markets for surplus commodities and capital. The Congressional discussion, carried by the yellow press, and a rising tide of racism, reached all levels of the population. Even the labor movement under Gompers and the farmers' associations were urged to join in the great cause. America would at last become a formidable world power.

Spain was the weakest and most vulnerable of the foreign powers in "our sphere," and it was relatively easy to invent

[5] *Ibid.*, p. 34.

a cause for war with her in 1898. The end result was the United States' control of most of the Caribbean. Those countries not occupied by marines were influenced by their presence in the vicinity and by their obvious readiness to invade at any sign of instability.

For two years Puerto Rico remained under United States military rule, since no colonial office existed and Congress was unwilling to grant statehood to a people who were colored and spoke a foreign language. Nevertheless, the Puerto Ricans were reassured by military governors that they would at least have autonomy if statehood was not granted. General George W. Davis, a military governor, published an explanation of U.S. policy in Puerto Rican newspapers. He wrote that "under the American Constitution . . . the people themselves are to make and enforce their own laws" and that his administration would provide "a form of government resembling, as respects the superior branches, the Territorial form heretofore applied in the United States to those portions of the national domain in a transition stage or one preparatory to full statehood and membership in the National Union."[6] Those who read the papers were undoubtedly pleased to hear that "Every step taken by the commanding general in changing the existing order of things has for its ultimate, and indeed its primary object, the adaptation of the laws and administration to suit the change that may soon come and which all desire; that is, complete territorial autonomy."[7] A hint of what was actually to come lay in another part of his circular, where he again referred to territorial autonomy, but qualified it with, "should such be enacted by Congress."

The American promises of self-government were soon revealed as a camouflage for colonialism. The Foraker Act, or First Organic Act, which set up a form of government for Puerto Rico under U.S. rule, was in force from May of 1900 to March of 1917. Congress labeled it a temporary

[6] *Documents on the Constitutional History of Puerto Rico, op. cit.*, pp. 59–60.

[7] *Ibid.*, p. 60.

act, but seventeen years elapsed before it was replaced. Under the Foraker Act, Puerto Rico had less autonomy than under Spanish rule; America was unwilling to grant self-government to an "inferior" people. The Puerto Rican "farming class is about on a par with the poor darkies down South," wrote Mr. F. Tennyson Neely, "and varies much even in race and color, ranging from Spanish white trash to full-blooded Ethiopians."[8]

One of the framers of the Treaty of Paris, which ended the Spanish-American War, was Whitelaw Reid. He spoke often and frankly about the newly acquired territories. In an article entitled "The Territory With Which We Are Threatened," he wrote:

> The chief aversion to the vast accessions of territory with which we are threatened springs from the fear that ultimately they must be admitted into the Union as States. . . . In no circumstances likely to exist within a century should they be admitted as States of the Union. Their people come from all religions, all races—black, yellow, white, and their mixtures—all conditions, from pagan ignorance and the verge of cannibalism to the best product of centuries of civilization, education, and self-government, all with equal rights in our Senate and representation according to population in our House, with an equal voice in shaping our national destinies—that would, at least in this stage of the world, be humanitarianism run mad, degeneration and degradation of the homogeneous, continental Republic of our pride too preposterous for the contemplation of serious and intelligent men.[9]

Reid warned the members of the Massachusetts Club:

> . . . the enemy is at the gates . . . he may gain the citadel.[10] . . . it is for you to say how Massachusetts would relish having this mixed population, a little more than half colonial Spanish, the rest negro and half-breed, illiterate, alien in language, alien in ideas of right, interests, and government, send in from the mid-Atlantic, nearly a third of the way over to Africa, two Senators to balance the votes of Mr. Hoar and Mr. Lodge; for

[8] Gordon K. Lewis, *Puerto Rico: Freedom and Power in the Caribbean.* New York: M. R. Press, 1963, p. 575.

[9] Whitelaw Reid, *Problems of Expansion.* New York: The Century Co., 1900, pp. 13–14.

[10] *Ibid.*, p. 205.

you to say how Massachusetts would regard the spectacle of her senatorial vote nullified. . . . The republican institutions I have been trained to believe were institutions founded, like those of New England, on the Church and the school-house. They constitute a system only likely to endure among a people of high virtue and high intelligence. . . . Such are its complications and checks and balances and interdependencies . . . that it is a system absolutely unworkable by a group of tropical races.[11]

PUERTO RICANS BECOME LIMITED CITIZENS

In 1917 the Puerto Ricans were granted United States citizenship and a Bill of Rights, although the U.S. Commissioner and Congress could nullify those rights at any time. Fewer than 300 people refused American citizenship and maintained their Puerto Rican citizenship. They could not vote or hold office. Certain changes were made in the government, but the Executive Branch, composed primarily of Americans appointed by the President, retained most of the power. The law was "deliberately designed, as its author Senator Jones acknowledged in the Senate hearings on the bill, to check the elective element."[12] Only those who understood English could be jurors in the District Court of Puerto Rico; this, of course, eliminated most Puerto Ricans.[13]

Not all rights of American citizenship were extended, however, as Jesus Balzac discovered in 1922 when he appealed for a trial by jury, claiming the 6th Amendment. Puerto Rican law did not provide for jury trials in cases such as his and the U.S. Supreme Court, in deciding his case, said, "Congress has thought that a people like the

[11] *Ibid.*, p. 205, pp. 208–09.
[12] Gordon Lewis, *op. cit.*, p. 109.
[13] *Documents on the Constitutional History of Puerto Rico, op. cit.*, p. 77.

Filipinos or the Puerto Ricans, trained to a complete judicial system which knows no juries, living in compact and ancient communities, with definitely formed customs and political conceptions, should be permitted themselves to determine how far they wish to adopt this institution of Anglo-Saxon origin, and when. . . ."[14]

The Supreme Court went on to distinguish between courts in the United States and the court set up for Puerto Rico. "The resemblance of its jurisdiction to that of true United States courts . . . does not change its character as a mere territorial court." Democracy in the United States was real and that in Puerto Rico illusory, the Supreme Court implied. "The Constitution . . . contains grants of power and limitations which in the nature of things are not always and everywhere applicable, and the real issue was . . . which of its provisions were applicable."[15]

So the Puerto Ricans, although citizens, had only certain "applicable" rights; although free of Spain, they still had no power to govern themselves. All in all, what had they gained by the release from Spanish tyranny? "The Puerto Rican patriot," wrote Gordon Lewis, "as he looked at the political institutions and the constitutional status with which the Congress had saddled his country, might have been forgiven for suspecting that, with the transfer from Spain to the U.S. thus effected, the new presbyter had turned out to be but old priest writ large."[16] The United States, for racial reasons, had relegated the Puerto Ricans to the rank of second-class citizens.

There were several differences between the new ruler and the old; one of the most important was economic. In the name of security, Spain had sacrificed economic opportunities by refusing to allow its possessions to trade with other nations, thereby keeping Puerto Rico tied to its economy. But the United States regarded its new possession as a potential source of great wealth.

[14] Balzac v. People of Puerto Rico, 258 U.S. 298 (1922).
[15] *Ibid.*
[16] Gordon Lewis, *op. cit.*, p. 112.

CHEAP LABOR

In 1901 Governor Charles H. Allen wrote in his annual report: "When the American capitalist realized that there is a surplus of *labor accustomed to the Tropics,* and that the return of capital is exceedingly profitable, it is my feeling that he will come here . . . to make at least five spears of grass to grow where one had grown before, to *the immense and permanent prosperity* of the Island."[17]

Businessmen, hoping to discover a source of cheap labor, wrote several thousand letters to the United States consul in San Juan inquiring about opportunities for investment. In an astonishingly short time, Americans had bought up most of the land and controlled most of the industry. By 1930 absentee owners in the United States controlled all shipping between the island and the mainland, as well as 80 percent of the tobacco industry and 60 percent of the sugar. By 1920 it was estimated that 70 percent of the total profits of the sugar industry went to foreigners. Throughout the island big firms bought out the small. Sugar cultivation took up larger and larger portions of the arable land, while the raising of subsistence food and coffee declined. The 500 Acre Law, passed as part of the Foraker Act of 1900, forbade ownership of more than that amount of land by anyone. Sugar companies and others lobbied hard for the repeal of this law, while at the same time evading it. Since there were no provisions for the enforcement of the law, evasion was both successful and widespread. Secretary of the Interior Harold Ickes, in a letter to Duncan N. Fletcher in January 15, 1935, summed up the effect of the high-profit, low-wage sugar industry in Puerto Rico:

[17] *Annual Report* of the Governor of Puerto Rico to the Secretary of War. Washington, D.C.: U.S. Government Printing Office, 1901, as cited by Gordon Lewis, *op. cit.,* p. 88.

Puerto Rico has been the victim of the laissez-faire economy which has developed the rapid growth of great absentee owned sugar corporations, which have absorbed much land formerly belonging to small independent growers and who in consequence have been reduced to virtual economic serfdom. *While the inclusion of Puerto Rico within our tariff walls has been highly beneficial to the stockholders of those corporations, the benefits have not been passed down to the mass of Puerto Ricans. These on the contrary have seen the lands on which they formerly raised subsistence crops given over to sugar production while they have been gradually driven to import all their food staples, paying for them the high prices brought about by the tariff. There is today more widespread misery and destitution and far more unemployment in Puerto Rico than at any previous time in its history.*[18]

The impact of highly developed capitalism on Puerto Rican society brought significant changes in the social structure—the decline of the estate owner, the rise of the managerial class, the proletarianization of the lower classes. Employees were dependent on the companies for housing and for credit, as well as for work. Many were driven to the cities where they became slum dwellers and squatters. Major decisions affecting the lives of Puerto Ricans were made in board rooms on the mainland.

With economic exploitation came cultural imperialism. To survive and prosper, it was necessary for the Puerto Rican to accommodate himself to the Americans who governed and owned his island. One way was to adopt American ways and attitudes. "The political pilgrimage to Madrid was succeeded by that to Washington."[19] Command of English became important. In fact, some Puerto Ricans who had been leading political figures before annexation, lost their influence because of an inability to master the new language.

Such efforts to please began with the invasion of the island in 1898. A war correspondent described how Puerto Ricans "struggled with the names of historic Americans and

[18] Gordon Lewis, *ibid.*, p. 92. Author's italics.
[19] *Ibid.*, p. 104.

besought lessons in the language so they could speak admiringly of Washington or Jackson without saying 'Hor-heh Vash-ing-tone' or 'Hen-eral Alexhandro Haxone.' "[20] Especially at first, politicians harangued audiences with eulogies of the American flag and the American way, with accompanying depreciations of anything Puerto Rican. Puerto Ricans learned English; Americans did not learn Spanish.

The middle and upper classes became caught between the two cultures, with little they could call their own. Eventually the Americans provided them with neon signs, soda fountains (instead of coffee houses), Mother's Day, frantic lunch hours, the need to struggle for money and status—and progress.

Those who had money and position were not anxious to lose them. This desire not to offend was, of course, well received in Washington. One governor of Puerto Rico observed: "I found it the tendency of Congressmen . . . to accept the thesis that all Puerto Ricans wanted to be like Americans in everything, even to having Puerto Rico become a state of the Union, which gave them (the Congressmen) a comfortable feeling of superiority. . . ."[21]

The United States kept tight control of the educational system. From 1905 to 1916, English was the official language in all public schools. "Patriotic songs were almost the first English language lessons in the schools. . . . School officials and schoolteachers—Puerto Ricans—led in the fostering of this spirit."[22] One teacher, speaking at a meeting, said, "I am glad tonight that I can speak to you from a platform draped in the glorious Stars and Stripes. We love that flag—the flag that our grandfathers hid in their garrets and secretly venerated but which now, thank God, floats over all the schools of our beloved island home."[23] Dr. M. C. Brumbaugh, the first American Commissioner of Educa-

[20] Trumbull White, *Puerto Rico and Its People*. New York: Frederick A. Stokes Co., 1938, p. 30.
[21] Rexford Tugwell, *The Stricken Land*. Garden City, New York: Doubleday and Co., Inc., 1947, p. 41.
[22] White, *op. cit.*, p. 62.
[23] *Ibid.*, p. 63.

tion, boasted in 1900 that "the average Puerto Rican child already knew more about Washington, Lincoln, Betsy Ross, and the American flag than did the average child in the United States."[24]

Under Spanish rule education had been restricted to the upper classes. Before 1898 about 80 percent of the population was illiterate[25] and less than 10 percent of the children of school age attended classes. The Americans constructed a system of free public schools for all. Since no money from the mainland was used, and since the Puerto Ricans had to begin with virtually nothing, the task was difficult. And, to make the difficult almost impossible, Puerto Ricans were instructed to model their school system on that of Massachusetts. English was, in most grades, to be the language of instruction. (While education in urban areas progressed remarkably well, education in rural areas lagged far behind. By about 1940, approximately two-fifths of the population still did not have secondary schooling.)

In the schools the language question was bound up with loyalty to the United States. English was insisted upon—not as a second language, but as the official language of the schools. Thus, a child who had spoken Spanish from infancy and whose parents read Spanish newspapers, had to learn long division in English. His teacher was usually poorly educated and only barely able to speak English, let alone teach in it.

One of the most important factors in the President's choice of a commissioner of education was the man's attitude toward the primacy of the English language. At least one nominee was refused confirmation because members of the Senate felt he was not strong enough on the language question. Because of the enormous power vested in his office, a new commissioner was able to, and often did, change existing educational policies to suit his own prefer-

[24] Earl Parker Hanson, *Puerto Rico, Land of Wonders*. New York: Alfred A. Knopf, 1960, p. 248.

[25] Vincenzo Petrullo, *Puerto Rican Paradox*. Philadelphia: University of Pennsylvania Press, 1947, p. 48.

ences and prejudices. Curriculums were changed, and then changed again, as commissioners came and went. A school system was established, but few children learned.

Puerto Rican resistance to American cultural domination of their island began with their refusal to learn English.

When control of education was given to the islanders in 1948, Spanish became the primary language, and interest in learning increased dramatically. By 1957, according to a United Nations report, Puerto Rico had the highest percentage of its population enrolled in school of any country in the world, although many were on half-day sessions. The quality of education, however, was still low.

RESISTANCE

The nineteenth century marked the decline of the Spanish Empire. As the spirit of independence spread through Latin America, Puerto Rican political leaders remained the least aggressive in the Hispanic colonial domain. In 1868, when Cuba's first bloody war for independence broke out in Oriente Province and spread to the rest of the island, Puerto Ricans responded with a brief revolt in the mountain village of Lares. It was quickly smashed. (Today, that revolt has taken on far greater significance than it may have actually had at the time.) There had been no tradition of militant resistance to the Spanish in Puerto Rico, as there had been in Cuba. When the United States took possession of the island, however, a serious but poorly organized struggle for independence began.

In 1898, after the U.S. invasion, the *Liga de Patriotas Puertorriqueños,* led by Eugenio Maria de Hostos, asked for a plebiscite in the hope of achieving independence for the island. Nothing came of the request. In 1900 a petition was presented to Congress asking that Puerto Rico be ceded back to Spain rather than remain under the government of the United States.[26]

The main issue was independence. From time to time leaders emerged who wanted Puerto Rico to sacrifice the supposed economic advantages of United States domination for the freedom to govern itself. But a strong anti–United States position was difficult to maintain, because of official and unofficial repression, and because of the seductive promises of American democracy. "Wait," counseled United States officials. "You will have your freedom as a state, and you will not have to lose any money."

The Puerto Rican bourgeoisie were not anxious to be displaced; they urged cooperation with the United States in discouraging radical movements among the workers and rural people. The long Spanish rule had left most Puerto Ricans detached from politics and unaccustomed to the idea of creating their own identity through independence. Despite these handicaps, leaders for independence emerged. They were linked to a larger Latin American tradition, although many were champions of independence for only a brief period in their careers.

In 1915 José de Diego, an *independentista* leader, presented a resolution to an assembly of the Union Party condemning any concession of United States citizenship to Puerto Ricans and advocating independence as the goal of the party. His move was blocked by Luis Muñoz Rivera, the United States resident commissioner at that time.

Luis Muñoz Marin, who was governor from 1948 to 1964 and presided over Operation Bootstrap, felt during the 1930s that independence was the only solution for his country. ". . . I want my people to *want* independence. It is degrading for a lot of colonial subjects not to want to be free. They don't assert themselves. They can't. Let them once want independence, and they will begin to assert themselves . . . as of now, independence is the only solution."[27]

[26] San Francisco *Examiner,* March 4, 1900.
[27] Hanson, *op. cit.,* p. 88.

In 1937 Muñoz Marin was expelled from the Liberal Party for espousing independence. At that time, he was regarded as an enemy by the United States. Later Muñoz Marin changed his thinking; Washington pumped money into the island during the New Deal, so he began to feel it was necessary to remain subject to North American sovereignty in order to benefit from its financial generosity.

The most important resistance and the most significant independence movement on the island was led by Pedro Albizu Campos, who is acknowledged today as Puerto Rico's martyr for independence. A Harvard graduate, he is usually described by American writers as "a bitter man who hates the United States venomously," or as "a fanatical visionary." These descriptions express the disbelief that a rational man could accuse the United States of being an imperial power and want Puerto Rican independence. The United States Government took Albizu Campos seriously. As a result, the nationalist spent most of the later years of his life in federal penitentiaries.

In 1917, with law degree in hand, Albizu Campos had first registered for the draft in Cambridge; he then transferred to Puerto Rico where he thought he would not be segregated. But he was assigned to an all-black regiment which did manual labor and garrison duty in Puerto Rico and Panama during "The War to Make the World Safe for Democracy." Albizu became a lieutenant. After the war, he began a career in journalism exposing the United States as an imperialist power. He maintained that the United States had no legal right to rule Puerto Rico, since Spain had had no right to cede Puerto Rico to the United States according to the Treaty of Paris designed by Woodrow Wilson. Furthermore, the people of Puerto Rico had never ratified the U.S. takeover.

Albizu Campos began his anticolonial struggle in much the same fashion as earlier *independentistas,* like José Martí, had begun theirs. He traveled, wrote for popular audiences, and pleaded the case for Puerto Rican independence before the League of Nations. In 1927 and 1928, he toured Latin America where anti-American feelings provided a basis for widespread support for his movement. In Puerto Rico he became the acknowledged leader for independence.

Campos expounded "his reasoned criticism of American colonialism,"[28] castigated the Americans for the wretched poverty in which most of his people lived, and pointed out the pitiful incompetence of most of the governors. He gained a large following in the 1930s, especially since the poor conditions in Puerto Rico were made much worse by the 1929 depression.

By 1930 Campos had become the leader of the Nationalist Party, which was dedicated to the achievement of independence. He had the support of many other groups and his speeches were well received. He hoped to achieve a solid base of support in the island elections of 1932, declare Puerto Rico a republic, and break forever from Yankee imperialism. But Albizu received only 5 percent of the vote; others of his party polled only 2 percent. After the election he changed tactics, maintaining that fair elections were impossible under the colonial system. From that time on he ignored the electoral process completely. His followers wore uniforms in public and accepted violence as a possible means of achieving their goal.

According to the analysis of the 1932 election by most American writers, Albizu had not won the sympathy of the mass of voters. Albizu and his followers claimed that the voters had been tricked by false promises from the United States. The New Deal rhetoric had come to Puerto Rico, they claimed, and masked the true interests of the Puerto Rican people. Token measures such as the Federal Emergency Relief Administration and the Puerto Rican Relief Administration were seen as imperialist tactics. They also denounced the Liberal Party, which Albizu claimed was Yankee-controlled and insincere in its platform for independence:

[28] Lewis, *op. cit.*, p. 406.

. . . imperialism created these federal agencies, placed in its [the Liberal Party] hands Yankee millions. . . . This Yankee divisionist plan couldn't be clearer. On the one hand, they maintained the division between Coalitionists and Liberals, reviving the hatred and the budgetary war between the two. On the other hand they initiated a convenient division in the leadership of the Liberal Party. . . . The result was treason and reformism, reaction and glorification of imperialism, maintaining control over the island's budget . . . through the control by federal agencies. Imperialism prepared a long range division of the country.[29]

Juan Antonio Corretjer, an associate of Albizu Campos, wrote:

The axiom of each empire for maintaining rule over a subject people is always the same: divide and rule. By instituting the electoral battle, imperialism divided Puerto Ricans and will keep them separated until Puerto Ricans shatter the machine, uniting themselves to struggle outside of electoral processes. Elections are Yankee imperialism's weapon of political domination. By accepting elections Puerto Ricans accept United States domination over their country.[30]

In October of 1935, Albizu gave a speech denouncing Franklin Delano Roosevelt, the existing Puerto Rican political parties, and the passivity of the students at the University of Puerto Rico. Under U.S. influence, he claimed, Puerto Rican boys were becoming effeminate and the girls immoral. At a subsequent meeting of hostile students, there was a clash between police and Nationalists. What took place is not clear. A carload of Nationalists either did or did not try to break up the meeting, did or did not open fire. There was no dispute, however, over the fact that police opened fire on the Nationalists, killing at least four (up to twenty in one account). Several days later Albizu gave a funeral oration in which he ordered the United States out of Puerto Rico, threatened to resort to arms, and began to recruit Cadets of the Republic.

[29] Juan Antonio Corretjer, *La Lucha por la Independencia de Puerto Rico.* San Juan: Publicaciones de Union del Pueblo pro Constituyente, 1949, pp. 67–68.
[30] *Ibid.,* p. 107.

An anti-Albizu writer reports the fiery leader as saying, in speeches throughout Puerto Rico, "Nationalists should prepare themselves with arms suitable not for picking teeth, but for shooting well. . . . If the Insular Police fire on Nationalists, then the Nationalists must kill a North American for every countryman who dies. . . . The enemies of the Republic must be punished by cutting off their heads and piercing their hearts with daggers. It does not matter if some Nationalists must die."[31]

Whether or not Albizu actually said the above words is irrelevant (he has denied several of the speeches attributed to him by writer Wenzell Brown); his followers acted as though he had. A Nationalist newspaper blared: "Arm yourselves, arm yourselves, arm yourselves; pistols, pistols, pistols; rifles, rifles, rifles; bullets, bullets, bullets; dynamite, dynamite, dynamite; find there, Puerto Ricans, the sole truth of today and tomorrow."[32] The Nationalists assassinated the chief of the Insular Police, an American. The two who were suspected of the killing were immediately apprehended. They were murdered in a police station.

Albizu Campos gave another fiery speech. A few weeks later, he walked into a police station and offered to surrender, saying he had heard he was to be arrested. His offer was declined. The next day he was arrested; Nationalist headquarters all over the island were raided; one rifle was found. Albizu was charged with sedition and conspiracy. (Under Puerto Rican law, there is no such crime as sedition. Furthermore, the entire case was handled in such a way as to outrage the American Civil Liberties Union and liberals in the United States, who contributed funds for Albizu's defense.)

While testifying in his own defense, after repeatedly denying hostility to the United States, he was overcome with patriotic emotion and "suddenly declared that he was more than willing to use force if the United States refused

[31] Wenzell Brown, *Dynamite on Our Doorstep*. New York: Greenberg Publishers, 1945, pp. 69–70.

[32] From *La Palabra,* alleged organ of the Nationalist Party in Puerto Rico, as appearing in *Time,* August 10, 1936, p. 20.

to withdraw from the island. That apparently convinced the jury that Albizu was a dangerous man."[33] He was found guilty and sentenced to ten years in the federal prison in Atlanta. Subsequent appeals, going all the way up to the Supreme Court, failed, and Albizu went to jail. The jury that convicted him was composed of ten Americans—some of whom knew no Spanish—and two Puerto Ricans.

After Albizu's conviction there was an atmosphere of great tension, which exploded in the Palm Sunday Massacre in Ponce on March 21, 1937. The Nationalists had obtained a permit and announced a parade. At the very last minute the permit was revoked. The police surrounded the gathering; a shot was fired, and a slaughter began that killed and wounded many people. Wenzell Brown, an American resident of Puerto Rico hostile to the Nationalists, wrote: "The pent-up rage of years drove the police into berserk slaughter. They killed and killed and killed—without regard for age or sex or opportunity for defense. They even killed members of the police in their own cross-fire."[34] Even children were riddled with bullets by the police.

Arthur Garfield Hays, who headed an investigation of the incident, wrote:

> When we started our investigation, we objected to the title "Committee for Investigation of the Ponce Massacre." We designated the Ponce tragedy as the "Ponce Affair," or "melee," or "riot," or by other words, which would indicate our desire to consider the matter objectively. After hearing the evidence, we have come to the conclusion that the people of Ponce have given this tragedy the only possible title: this was the *Ponce Massacre*—and deserves the title even more because it occurred in times of peace.[35]

The governor of Puerto Rico at the time of the massacre was a Southern gentleman named Blanton Winship. The year before the massacre, on July 4, 1936, he said, "Noisy advocates of unrest and disorder should be repudiated and be persuaded to abandon the errors of their ways." Win-

[33] *Time,* Aug. 10, 1936.
[34] Brown, *op. cit.,* p. 90.
[35] *Ibid.,* p. 96.

ship's method was to increase the number of police, buy military equipment such as machine guns and tear gas, and give the police intensive indoctrination against the advocates of independence. The governor forbade Nationalist public meetings; a police-state atmosphere prevailed. Winship proved so incompetent, however, that he was forced to resign; another political hack was sent back to the mainland.

It is difficult for Americans to take seriously a dark-skinned Latin who challenges this country; it is equally difficult for them to understand how deeply resented and hated the United States is in much of the Third World. They tend to view Albizu's politics as a personal response to injuries suffered because of his dark skin (inherited from his black mother). One commentator said of him: ". . . Pedro was a smart youngster, his schoolboy career was creditable, and he was regarded as a promising half-caste boy." Earl Parker Hanson concluded that Campos' hatred for the United States[36] was produced by the race issue and his illegitimacy. He cannot understand that as a Puerto Rican, Albizu was also a Latin American and inherited an anti-colonial tradition of independence, as well as a firmly based anti-U.S. outlook.

The United States committed the "crime of colonialism" in Puerto Rico, and although most American writers have refused to acknowledge any serious defects in our policies there, a few have. Waldo Frank, one of Simón Bolívar's biographers, wrote that Puerto Ricans "sense vaguely that an injury to their ethos has been done already, and that no constitution of independence can efface it."[37]

In 1947, after serving several years in prison, Albizu Campos returned to Puerto Rico. Again he urged the cause of independence and again he was arrested and tried, this time for inciting to murder during the 1950 revolt. He was pardoned by Governor Muñoz Marin in 1953. After sev-

[36] Hanson, *op. cit.*, p. 70.

[37] Waldo Frank, "Puerto Rico and Psychosis," *The Nation*, March 13, 1954.

eral Puerto Ricans shot up the U.S. House of Representatives in 1954, Campos was sent back to prison, where he died in 1965.

Those who dismiss Albizu Campos as a deranged fanatic do not take into account the distortion to human personality produced by colonial rule in Puerto Rico. Many of the complications and conflicts that exist in Puerto Ricans today, both on the island and in the United States, can be traced to injustices perpetrated by the governing power on the island, and to American attitudes toward the "little brown brothers" whose land we seized in 1898.

"A ROSE IN SPANISH HARLEM . . . GROWS UP IN THE STREET, THROUGH THE CONCRETE."

In Chicago, in 1969, young Puerto Ricans marched through the streets protesting the murder of one of their group, the Young Lords, by an off-duty policeman. Many of them wore buttons saying *"Tengo Puerto Rico en mi Corazón."* Asked what the button meant, Cha Cha Jiménez, leader of the Young Lords Organization—once a street gang, now a militant activist group akin to the Black Panthers—responded, "It says I have Puerto Rico in my heart. Understand that we're still a colony, controlled by the United States. A governor was allowed to be elected by the people in 1947 . . . 1898 to 1947, that's a long time. And the governor now, to us, is nothing but an uncle tom, a person that advocates statehood. We've been fucked over for so long, as a colony."[38]

Little did Albizu Campos dream that his ideas would be revived by young men and women, many of them born in

[38] *The Movement,* July, 1969, p. 5.

the United States, who were once teenage hoodlums. In most Puerto Rican communities throughout the country, there are movements similar to the Young Lords. They are dedicated to Puerto Rican independence and to the revolutionary ideals espoused by the Third World Liberation Front. But the vast majority of Puerto Ricans in the United States are apathetic; they accept their poverty and the culture it spawns. It is a culture that came into existence with the large-scale Puerto Rican migration, especially to New York City.

In 1910 only 500 Puerto Ricans lived in New York; in 1920, 7,000 were listed; and in 1930 there were 45,000. By 1940 the Puerto Rican population in New York had reached 70,000, with most of it in East Harlem. With the introduction of low-priced air travel and an increasing demand for labor at the end of World War II, Puerto Rican immigration shot up. By 1950 almost 200,000 Puerto Ricans lived in New York and by 1961 census figures revealed there were more than 600,000. By then, the mass migration had come to an end. The Puerto Rican population has now spread to New Jersey, Pennsylvania, Massachusetts, and Chicago. Initially the Puerto Ricans came to work and earn enough money to return to the island. Some accomplished this mission, but the vast majority stayed longer than they planned before returning, becoming annual or biannual commuters as the air-fare rates dropped. Others resigned themselves to a permanent life in New York, a life of poverty different from the one they had known in San Juan.

Spanish Harlem was the first of the *barrios* in New York. Hundreds of thousands of Puerto Ricans packed into a few square blocks; the streets teemed with people and refuse, rats and roaches ran wild, and health and vice statistics kept pace with the data on vermin. Puerto Ricans and blacks from the South shared the misfortune of coming to New York as the last of the immigrant groups. By the late 1920s, the Italians and Jews had moved to the Bronx and Brooklyn and the dilapidated tenements they left behind became the homes of the newly arrived Puerto Ricans and blacks.

One of the problems that became more intense for Puerto Ricans after moving here was that of skin color. About one-quarter of the Puerto Ricans in New York are black. And although Puerto Rico is relatively free from color bias, the Puerto Ricans who moved to New York have picked up some of America's attitudes. For example, the dark-skinned Puerto Ricans are more despised than the light-skinned.[39] In addition, drug addicts among the Puerto Ricans are generally darker of skin. Unlike Cuban blacks, dark-skinned Puerto Ricans possess little consciousness of their African past. In Cuba, runaway slaves had set up several all-black villages which they protected with arms; in Puerto Rico, there was little armed resistance on the part of runaway slaves. This lack of identification with their negritude was due, in part, to the gradual process of assimilation in which color lines on the island were all but erased. American colonization, however, re-established them to some degree.

Another problem is that Puerto Rican kids, like black children, are forced to mature early. Their so-called sexual promiscuity, for one thing, disturbs white teachers and officials. Puerto Rican parents try to protect their daughters' virginity, but the slum tenements cannot contain the adolescents' energy during the spring, summer, and fall months. As a result, there are many illegitimate births, especially among teenagers; Puerto Ricans also tend to marry early.

Life in the Spanish-speaking ghettos was always grim, hard, and exhausting. The poet Garcia Lorca said it well; he wrote: ". . . From behind the grey walls / I hear nothing else but the lament."[40] For new arrivals, the gray poverty of New York replaced the greener misery of Puerto Rico. Although unemployment and poverty were greater in

[39] Piri Thomas, *Down These Mean Streets*. New York: Alfred A. Knopf, 1967; *Patricia Cayo Sexton, Spanish Harlem*. New York: Harper & Row, 1965.

[40] Sexton, *ibid*., p. 14.

Puerto Rico, many New York residents maintained family and cultural ties to the island, visiting there and returning to New York if the money ran out.

This practice continued until the end of the 1950s. Then the mass migration stopped as Puerto Rican unemployment in New York rose almost to the level of that in San Juan. Puerto Ricans returning to the island were able to obtain better jobs there because of skills and training acquired in New York.

Puerto Ricans living in New York have had difficulty establishing a political focus, because of weak community ties, and because New York required a literacy test in English for voting eligibility. Less than 50 percent of Spanish Harlem voted in the 1960 election, for example.

Although almost a million Puerto Ricans now live in New York and its environs, they have no newspaper of their own. The Spanish-language dailies with the largest circulations are owned by one Anglo.

In the mid-1960s, no institution in Spanish Harlem bore the name of a Puerto Rican, the kind of oversight blacks have already corrected. Ironically, on the Lower East Side of New York—once a Jewish, now a heavily populated Puerto Rican neighborhood—Peretz Square (named after a Jew) is called Perez Square by the Puerto Ricans.

During the post–World War II period, Puerto Ricans were a source of cheap labor in New York. In 1950, 64.5 percent of all Puerto Rican workers were men and women in blue-collar jobs and 20 percent were service workers; only 15 percent had white-collar jobs. The 1950 employment figures for female Puerto Rican and white workers showed an astonishing disparity—more than 80 percent of all the Puerto Rican women were employed as factory hands, primarily in the garment trades.

By 1960 a shift had taken place. White-collar employment among all Puerto Ricans had risen to 19 percent primarily among clerical and sales categories. The proportion of managers, proprietors, and officials had dropped by nearly 1 percent. Blue-collar employment remained the same, but service workers had dropped by 3 percent. The percentage of female Puerto Rican workers in factories had dropped to 72 percent, a sizeable drop from 1950.

This shift in the employment of Puerto Ricans has been accompanied by a sharp increase in the number of Puerto Ricans on New York's welfare rolls, especially among young Puerto Rican mothers, whose rate of births is five times higher than that of whites. (It is possible that the money saved by New York employers using Puerto Ricans as cheap labor is offset by the Welfare Department expenditures.)

In Spanish East Harlem the average family income is always very much lower than the average in New York City. This explains why Puerto Ricans live in dilapidated housing[41] and suffer acute stress from disease, sexual perversion, and drug and alcohol abuse. In East Harlem one-third of the pregnant mothers in 1963 received no prenatal treatment; fifty-nine apartments had more than 1,319 housing violations. The most disturbing feature of Puerto Rican and black tenements, however, was the rat population and the lack of heat on the coldest winter days.

AH—TO LIVE IN A REPUBLIC

In Puerto Rico, the United States applied an "enlightened" colonial policy; it provided a façade of a Constitution (it could be revoked by Congress) and an electoral system. It bought off some Puerto Rican leaders, cajoled others, and jailed those it could not control. Journalists and scholars provided a smoke screen of words and images to convince Puerto Ricans and mainlanders that all was going well and that we were not a typical colonial power. The United States divided and ruled, extracted wealth and manpower,

[41] From The Women's Club of New York, Inc., *Maintaining Decent Dwellings: A Study of Code Enforcement in Five New-Law Tenements,* New York: April, 1963, cited *ibid.,* p. 197.

and policed the island for 70 years—all the while pouring out pro-American propaganda.

The native culture was ruthlessly destroyed, and the new authorities engendered shame and guilt in their subjects. Industrial American culture was transplanted to the Caribbean—the commercialism, the racism that makes black Puerto Ricans inferior to *mestizos,* and *mestizos* inferior to whites. The tranquility of the hot Caribbean midday was interrupted by the supermarket-supersales-life.

The Puerto Rican middle class, imitating its American counterpart, became stereotyped colonial *compradors.* They were filled with optimism by statistics that showed the Puerto Rican economy was prospering. Statistics on crime, vice, mental health, suicide, and insanity—to say nothing of the continuing high-unemployment rate—were passed over as minor problems that would be solved when Americanization became complete.

The United States undermined all original sources of identity—in government, education, language, politics, and religion. It was impossible for the majority of Puerto Ricans ever to attain any sense of American identity. The Puerto Rican entered the United States as a "spic" or a "nigger" or both. Incapable of active resistance, many Puerto Ricans responded to racism by developing the sense of *puertorriqueñidad*—a vague, often nostalgic and mythologized longing for the culture experienced by their fathers and grandfathers. Gordon Lewis notes that *puertorriqueñidad* is "itself an expression of the inferiority complex, for a social group that possess real self-assurance is under no felt necessity to announce it publicly. That is why, perhaps, Americans praise themselves whereas the English merely permit others to praise them."[42]

Eduardo Seda, a Puerto Rican scholar, and Oscar Lewis have agreed that while the Puerto Rican population has multiplied threefold, it has lost perhaps two-thirds of what made it culturally unique. What is left of its heritage is

[42] Gordon Lewis, "Culture of Poverty or Poverty of Culture." *Monthly Review,* September, 1967, Vol. 19, no. 4, p. 51.

daily-life habits and attitudes. Today, however, these represent not the old culture so much as the culture of poverty which has replaced it, a culture shared by most colonized people. The best of Puerto Rican culture has been distorted by its encounter with American, and some Puerto Ricans now question whether American culture is superior to the ways of their island.

Joseph Monserrat, a prominent Puerto Rican, asked this question: "Is a culture that has for four centuries been able to maintain the individual dignity, value and worth of all of its members (despite differences in race and class) a deprived or disadvantaged culture when compared with one that has been striving to achieve these values and has not yet been able to do so?"[43]

This question expresses the essence of Puerto Rican feelings about American cultural imperialism and its practitioners, the liberals. By labeling Puerto Ricans as deprived or disadvantaged and using a paternalistic approach to solve their problems, American liberals have been stripping away the Puerto Rican's sense of identity. Assimilation is the liberal policy concerning Puerto Ricans even though American society as a whole has shown its incapacity to absorb a colored, Spanish-speaking people as equals. The myth of the melting pot was fed to Puerto Ricans by social workers and liberal spokesmen, but most white Americans have little interest in Puerto Ricans. Many white teachers, and some black, accept the superiority of white, Anglo-Saxon values. Teaching these values to Puerto Rican children—as with Mexican, black, Indian, and Oriental children—leads to diminished self-esteem and confusion of identity. Often they drop out of school.

Generally Puerto Ricans go through the 8th grade in New York schools, at which point their potential for employment is determined. They are told, explicitly or implicitly, that they are worthless, since worth is determined by skin color, education, income, the ability to consume lavishly, and the approval of society. Their already weak self-

[43] *Ibid.*, p. 61.

image is further weakened by being labeled as deprived or disadvantaged. Often they fall into a life of drugs and crime or go on welfare, all of which do little to raise their self-esteem.

The paternalistic attitudes of government and private agencies and individuals have further reinforced Puerto Ricans' feelings of inferiority and have often resulted in removing some of the few cultural supports they have had. One example is the idea that removal of slums and construction of better buildings brings about improvements on every level of the inhabitants' lives. What the bulldozing proponents do not realize is that the old buildings represented more than just dilapidated structures; they represented their community, their stores, their familiar landscape, neighbors and friends. The new projects replaced the old physical community, and the people were dispersed throughout the city. This only served to increase the insecurity of the *barrio* residents. "I'm 23 years old," said one Puerto Rican, "and I've been living here (Spanish Harlem) all my life. I never been out of this neighborhood. To me this neighborhood is all right. People who have money—maybe it's a dump, as they call it, but this is my home."[44]

One of Oscar Lewis' most poignant characters is removed from her slum tenement to a housing project through a Puerto Rican welfare agency sponsored by New York City. She was more lonely and miserable than ever, because she was totally cut off from family and friends and familiar streets. However horrible her old life may have been, she preferred it to the new one in a city that did not, and never would, belong to her. Gordon Lewis, too, described slum clearance as "an act of war against the minority group, for it robs it of a vital emotional base."[45]

New York's Puerto Ricans have been, until recently, the most politically passive ethnic group in the city's history. Many of them considered themselves only as migrants. In

[44] *Ibid.*, p. 23.
[45] *Ibid.*, p. 48.

addition, they did not know enough English to pass the voting test. Perhaps a more important factor was that their expectations were low. But with the Civil Rights Movement, many young Puerto Ricans have become involved in militant action centering on the inequities in the *barrios,* especially the wretched school system. Some Puerto Ricans joined CORE, others found themselves involved in the Rent Strike Movement led by Jesse Gray, a black organizer, in 1964.

A still small but increasing number of young Puerto Ricans have begun to understand that their failure to "make it" in America is not because of their own inadequacies. It is because of what Oscar Lewis calls the culture of poverty, which they brought with them from San Juan to New York.

Oscar Lewis' Puerto Ricans are the best antidote to the myth that the United States has created a paradise in the Caribbean. The original Puerto Rican culture—Spanish, African, and colonial—has merged with the industrial capitalism of the American colonizer to produce a bastard stripped of the strengths of either. While constantly decrying America's ethos of consumption and anti-joy Protestant values, Puerto Rican women still use their savings to pay respects to John F. Kennedy's grave in Washington, the very symbol of the ambitious culture they despise. One Puerto Rican claims, "If I could be Governor of Puerto Rico or the Mayor of New York for five or ten minutes, I'd take a pistol and I'd shoot every Puerto Rican who has forgotten Spanish."

In the 1960s, with their new consciousness, the situation began to change for the Puerto Ricans. In 1969, Puerto Rican and black college and high school students manned the barricades at New York's City College and burned down several buildings. For these young Puerto Ricans, allied with blacks and other Spanish-speaking groups, the time for redemption had come. Albizu Campos became, once again, a symbol for resistance and revolution.

The factors that combined to produce the Puerto Rican

explosion can be found in the struggles of the 1960s, and in the victory of the Cuban Revolution which attracted growing numbers of young Puerto Ricans. Those who escaped from the culture of poverty and made it into the mainstream of American life and the university in particular, took on the leadership of the new resistance. Calling themselves members of the Third World and glorifying old Puerto Rican values and the Spanish language, they presented the American Establishment with a list of "non-negotiable demands" similar to those formulated by blacks, *chicanos,* and Indians. One major difference, however, was their call for Puerto Rican independence; they revived a movement that had been declared dead many times over by the popular press and the learned scholars who had celebrated the Puerto Rican miracle.

In Puerto Rico, after seventy years of pro-American education, a group of high school students have organized the Pro-Independence University Federation. In September of 1968, they made plans to celebrate the 100th anniversary of the *Grito de Lares,* the Puerto Rican uprising against Spanish colonial rule. Albizu Campos became their apostle for what they called the "highest level of revolutionary struggle."[46] The students involved came from those classes that had historically been the most loyal to American rule. Like their mainland counterparts, the middle-class Puerto Rican youths engaged the police—at first with words, then with bricks, rocks, and Molotov cocktails.

The riots were a shock to Americans, since reports of Puerto Rican resistance to U.S. rule had been limited to the 1954 terrorist attack on the House of Representatives. Few Americans knew that 60,000 Puerto Ricans refused to register under the Selective Service Law during World War II, or that more than 1,300 Nationalists and *independentistas* were in prison when the 1947 Constitution was adopted by plebiscite, or that a state of martial law was required to carry off the United States-directed election.

During the Cold War period, and especially after the

[46] *National Guardian,* September 28, 1968, p. 19.

victory of the Cuban Revolution, Puerto Rico acquired a new importance for Americans. "It plays a powerful role in the important matter of assuaging Latin America mistrust toward *el coloso del norte* and cementing inter-American relations," wrote one commentator. "Its people are today loyal to the United States as never before. . . ." Puerto Rico has "set an important example. . . . Thousands of visitors from all parts of the free world go to the island today, see what Puerto Rico has done and is doing, and return to their homes saying: 'This is America's answer to communism.' . . . In this they express Puerto Rico's greatest importance to the United States and to the modern world."[47]

The revival of a Puerto Rican independence movement has begun to prove that not all Puerto Ricans are loyal to the United States or committed to the Free World. During the Pan American games of 1963, much sympathy was expressed in Puerto Rico for Cuban athletes, and pro-Cuba demonstrations were squelched by the police. The American-controlled press of Puerto Rico has blamed the increasing cries for resistance and the violent anti-American and pro-independence movement on the traditional "handful of leftists and communists." However, the *Grito de Lares* celebration committee was headed by Catholic Bishop Antulio Parrilla, who has been pro-Castro and, like Albizu Campos, anti-electoral. Bishop Parrilla represents a multi-class force that is growing as Puerto Ricans return from New York, sick of America, to their island. Puerto Rican workers are beginning to realize that they have been raped, for the price of small material benefits.

In 1968, near the United States Peace Corps camp outside of Arecibo, an old farmer who had refused to learn English inquired about where the Peace Corps volunteers were going. He was told they were bound for the Dominican Republic. "Ah," he sighed, "a Republic. It must be wonderful to live in a Republic."

[47] Hanson, *op. cit.*, pp. 319–20.

The Puerto Ricans: Protest and the Fight for Independence

These documents show that not all Puerto Ricans are as enthusiastic about becoming "Americanized" as the celebrators of America believe. They are not intended to present a "balanced" picture of the Puerto Rican community, but simply to make clear that voices of dissidence and resistance have always existed—and still do—among the Puerto Ricans.

(1)

Que Bonita Bandera

The folk singer and collector Pete Seeger learned this patriotic song in 1955 from young Puerto Ricans living in New York. The name of the composer is unknown.

QUE BONITA BANDERA*

CHORUS:

Que bonita bandera,	How pretty the flag,
Que bonita bandera,	How beautiful it is,
Que bonita bandera, es la bandera Puertorriqueña.	How beautiful the Puerto Rican flag is.
Azul, blanca y colorada,	Blue, white and red,
y en el medio tiene una estrella,	with a star in the center,
Bonita, señores, es la bandera Puertorriqueña.	The Puerto Rican flag is beautiful, señores.
(Chorus)	

* *American Favorite Ballads, Tunes and Songs as Sung by Pete Seeger* (New York: Oak Publications, 1961).

Todo buen Puertorriqueño,	Every good Puerto Rican,
Es bueno que la defienda,	Is really good when he defends it,
Bonita, señores, es la bandera Puertorriqueña.	The Puerto Rican flag is beautiful, señores.
(Chorus)	
Bonita señora es,	What a beautiful señora she is,
Que bonita es ella,	She is pretty,
Que bonita es la bandera,	How beautiful is the Puerto
Puertorriqueña.	Rican flag.

(2)

Puerto Rican Independence Party Statement*

In this short statement, made in 1950, the Puerto Rican Independence Party stated its basic position.

The Puerto Rican Independence Party is organized for the essential purpose of working peacefully for the Constitution of the people of Puerto Rico in an independent, sovereign, and democratic republic.

[We] hold the present Government of Puerto Rico responsible for trying to impose upon the Puerto Rican people a political measure, a so-called Constitution, that amounts to a fraud on the legitimate rights of these people and which tends to confirm the colonial system in our homeland. Thus, we declare that this outrage to the dignity of the Puerto Rican people has led one of the world's most peaceful peoples into a state of turmoil and protest that has culminated in the present revolutionary movement.

In addition, we hold the present Government of Puerto Rico responsible because without having made a formal declaration of martial law (with the evident intention of

* "Aguadilla Statement for Independence—1950," in Robert William Anderson, *Party Politics in Puerto Rico* (Stanford: Stanford University Press, 1965).

diminishing before the world the importance of the Puerto Rican revolutionary movement) it has committed a long series of violations of civil guarantees, thereby illegally establishing in fact a state of martial law. . . .

We hold the Government of the United States of America responsible for the historic fact that throughout more than half a century of its domination in Puerto Rico it has refused to recognize the right of our people to . . . sovereignty. And at the end of this half-century it pretends (in collusion with the present insular colonial directors) to discharge its responsibility in Puerto Rico by the deception of a false Constitution.

The Puerto Rican Independence Party sends its profoundest respects to its fellow countrymen who have given and are giving their lives in the cause of Puerto Rican independence. . . . In its struggle, our party utilizes all the working instruments that the colonial regime puts in its hands for combatting and liquidating that regime.

(3)

Housing in New York City*

In 1963, housing among Puerto Ricans in New York City meant not individual family units, but apartments occupied by one or more families, even boarders, with everyone eating and sleeping in several shifts. The following passage cites a typical family experience.

Mrs. B., her husband, and her two children, Juan, 15, and Maria, 8, live with another family. For their own use they have one tiny room at the rear of a third-floor apartment. This room is off the kitchen and provides the cross-ventilation for the apartment. It is so small that a single bed and a folding cot completely fill the room. Mrs. B. and her

* John A. Burma, *Spanish Speaking Groups in the United States* (Chapel Hill: Duke University Press, 1954).

husband share the single bed and Juan sleeps on the cot, "within breathing distance" of his parents. Maria sleeps with the daughter of the other family. Mr. B. is employed as a laborer and earns $35.00 a week out of which he pays union dues, buys his lunches, pays his landlady $8.00 for the room, and supports his family. He contributes to the food bill, as the families eat together.

(4)

Revolt in Puerto Rico

The documents that follow—an interview with a leader of the Puerto Rican Independence Party and the Manifesto of the Armed Commandos of Liberation—illustrate both the seriousness and the revolutionary fervor of the Independence Movement.

Student Revolt in Puerto Rico*

Following is an interview between a leader of the Puerto Rican Pro-Independence University Federation (FUPI) who cannot be identified and Lois Reivich, a staff member of the North American Congress on Latin America.

Q: September 23 is the one-hundredth anniversary of the "Grito de Lares," the Puerto Rican uprising against the Spanish colonial regime. How are the FUPI and the MPI (Movimiento Pro-Independencia) planning to celebrate this and what relation will that have with your struggle today?

A: For us, as the organizations with the most radical position in the independence struggle, the celebration of the anniversary of Lares is an expression of the highest level of revolutionary struggle. In this century, this level of struggle was reached by the Nationalist Party, led by Albizu

* "Student Revolt in Puerto Rico," in *National Guardian* (September 28, 1968).

Campos in the 1940s and 1950s against U.S. imperialism. In the fifties, with the imprisonment of Albizu, the struggle entered a phase of decline manifested in electoral campaigns. In any colony, electoral activities are controlled by those who have the real power—in Puerto Rico, the U.S.—and such electoral activities are always used to hold back more advanced struggle. The MPI and the FUPI, the organizations of the sixties, have learned from the struggles for national liberation of other countries, particularly the Cuban Revolution.

The celebration has been organized by a committee headed by a militant Catholic bishop, Antulio Parrilla, who has been both pro-Cuban and anti-electoral politics. In a country which is overwhelmingly Catholic, having a bishop as leader has special importance. The FUPI is planning a student strike at the university on September 23, which has not been recognized as a national holiday. The FUPI, the high-school student organization, is collecting 50,000 signatures petitioning the governor to close all schools. If schools are not closed, students will boycott classes. Pro-independence supporters from all over the island will converge on the town of Lares. This is both a time to honor and learn from our history of struggle and to build our strength.

Q: What are the main programs that the FUPI will be working on this year at the university?

A: This school year began with a triumphant campaign in August against the university administration's approved increase in food prices in the cafeteria run by a U.S.–based corporation—Slater's. We first issued a report countering the argument for raising prices based on alleged losses as well as exposing the poor quality of food and service. As a first act of resistance, students piled trays high with food and left them unpaid at a cashier. The cafeteria workers who were organizing a union supported the students. A boycott was organized and the entrances to the cafeteria were blocked. In one incident, the university sent photographers to identify the students involved in order to suspend them. This intrusion ended with broken cameras and dishes and overturned tables and chairs. The following day, a Friday, Slater's offered the students a truce—a two-day recess—while they were to consult with their home office in Philadelphia. Following the Vietnamese lesson of holding out while the enemy decides to talk, we kept up the pressure and on Monday the vice president of Slater's, Hank Dyllae himself, came to negotiate. That evening prices were restored to their previous level. Much to the administration's dismay, we were also able to form an all-student committee with authority to supervise the cafeteria—check their books, and revise the quality of food sold.

A major part of our efforts this year will go to the struggle against ROTC at the University of Puerto Rico, as the physical presence of the "Yankee army" on campus. The campaign against ROTC goes back to 1960 when ROTC was obligatory for all students. In that year the first victory was won. ROTC was made voluntary. In the second phase of struggle, the aim is to have ROTC removed from campus altogether. We have stated that ROTC is in contradiction with our fundamental conception of a university—that we are not here to learn to kill in a U.S. war of aggression in Vietnam, rather we are here to learn to serve our country, Puerto Rico. This campaign gained impetus in 1967 when it was linked with the struggle for the right to picket and protest on campus. A series of mass pickets in defiance of an on-campus ban on picketing culminated in a disruptive demonstration at an ROTC marching review in May 1967. The administration was able to take advantage of the fact that school was over to expel forty-four students, since no opposition was possible during the vacation period.

The campaign against ROTC has so delegitimized it that today there are only 300 members when only a few years ago several thousand of the 20,000 students belonged. This year the tension in the issue has been heightened by the attempt of a U.S. army colonel to locate an army recruiting office on campus. The dean of students turned this down, remembering only too well the demonstrations across the

U.S. last year. Right-wing pressure has caused the administration to waver and the university rector, Jaime Benitez, favors giving the army an office. Any such move will be opposed strongly.

Q: Can you explain the events of September 27, 1967, which led to the confrontation with police at the University of Puerto Rico at Rio Piedras and what consequences this confrontation had for FUPI?

A: On September 27, a small group of reactionary students who have always acted as agents of the FBI and who never initiate their own political activity, published a slanderous leaflet accusing the FUPI of dealing in drugs. We immediately found the two persons distributing this leaflet, and made them leave the university. Later on many students gathered outside their pro-statehood office across from the main gates of the campus to demand proof of the accusations they had made. At that point about 300 police placed themselves between the students and the office and began to attack us. The students crossed the street and entered the campus with the police following. The students responded to the police violence with bricks and stones and much later Molotov cocktails. At the rector's request the police withdrew from the university. That night the students led a march to the police precinct to demand the release of fifteen arrested students. They were met by shots from the police—over their heads—and tear gas. The students withdrew to the university and tried to set up barricades to keep the cops off campus. The battle that ensued lasted until dawn when the governor of Puerto Rico ordered the police to withdraw.

Seven months after this happened, charges of conspiracy to riot, arson in the first and second degree, inciting to riot and damaging private property were brought against twenty-five students, in an attempt to victimize the FUPI leadership. Our trial will begin November 12, and the judge has already promised that this will be a nine-to-five affair for about three months. We have begun to organize a campaign to arouse support for our defense and we realize the importance of support from students in the U.S.

Manifesto of the Armed Commandos of Liberation*

CAL, clandestine bulletin of the Armed Commandos of Liberation, is born of the need to inform national public opinion how to militarily and effectively combat all the Yankee companies that rob the people of their sweat and labor. CAL will be a fuse ignited to explode in the hands of imperialism, to combat the bastard interests that reduce us to the abject colonial status we have today.

CAL will give precise instructions on how the people can defend themselves against the onslaught of the Puerto Rico Telephone Company and all the abuses of the Yankee monopolies which cruelly exploit our country. . . .

Regarding our organization, we wish to clarify one thing for the people: our entire organization is oriented toward inflicting the greatest possible damage in the ranks of our bitter enemies. No Yankee company should feel safe in Puerto Rico. Our entire campaign rests on sabotage. Therefore, for us, direct action, day by day, is the principal task.

For many years, the Puerto Rico Telephone Company monopoly (a subsidiary of the Yankee International Telephone and Telegraph Corporation) has been the most despised tentacle of the foreign octopus which strangles the Puerto Rican people. And for good reason: the Yankee Telephone company not only charges its customers excessive and outrageous rates, but also renders the worst service that a commercial enterprise could give.

The people have been clamoring for years to have this service taken over by the government, although the public services run by the colonial administrators are abysmal, as

* "Puerto Rico: Clandestine Press Revolutionary Instructions," in *Tricontinental* (Havana: April, 1969).

is proved by the abuse of the public by the Metropolitan Bus Authority, the River Freight Authority, and the Aqueduct and Sewer Authority. In spite of this, the people continue calling for the nationalization of the telephone system. They know that no matter how badly the local henchmen behave, they can never be as bad as the foreign exploiters.

Playing down the people's demand while trying to appear as a defender of it, the despicable traitor, Luis Muñoz Marin, and his party have threatened to transfer franchise of the operations of the Puerto Rico Telephone Company to another tentacle of the Yankee octopus. The Armed Commandos of Liberation (CAL) advise the traitor Muñoz, as well as his servile partisans and the other lackeys who share his ideas, that we will not tolerate such a brazen mockery of the people's interests and status. The telephone system should be nationalized; there is no alternative. We take the responsibility for seeing that whoever intends to make a mockery of the people's interests loses more than he tries to gain. Meanwhile, we exhort the people themselves to take the necessary reprisals to force the telephone company to give its customers more just treatment. Here are some recommendations:

1) Puncture the tires of the telephone company's official trucks. *2*) With a simple top from a soda bottle, or any other sharp instrument, scratch the paint on the vans until it is worn away. In this way, the monopoly is forced to spend the money they have robbed from the people on painting and repairing their vehicles. *3*) Pour at least a half-pound of sugar into the gas tank of any telephone company vehicle. It will not be able to move for a long time. *4*) Take your telephone off the hook and urge your neighbors to do likewise. This will paralyze the service in the entire neighborhood. *5*) Cut telephone lines, any telephone lines, with a pliers. This will force the telephone to spend money to repair them. *6*) Pull out the diaphragm of the mouthpiece of each public telephone you encounter in passing. These phones never work anyway, but in this way the telephone company will have to spend more to try to repair them. The operation entails no risk. 7) Fasten a completely dry rope (since water is a conductor of electric current) to a hook and throw this onto a telephone line you encounter in passing. Then tie the rope to the bumper of your car, start it and drive off with confidence. Pick up your instruments for the next occasion. *8*) With a hatchet—and gloves so as not to leave fingerprints—cut in two places the telephone trunk lines that go up the electric posts. Remember to throw the cut part a good distance away from the place where you carried out your patriotic work. Bear in mind that telephone trunk lines also run underneath or over bridges. Use your ingenuity.

Notice that all activity of this kind should avoid as much as possible causing communications problems for the establishments which serve the people. Therefore, be sure that the telephone lines thus sabotaged do not serve hospitals, public health units, schools, etc. We particularly recommend those that service the big Yankee businesses which are against nationalizing the telephone system, that is, against the urgent desires of the people.

(5)

Interview with Cha Cha Jiménez*

The following excerpts from an interview with Cha Cha Jiménez, from The Movement, *July, 1969, indicate the direction of some of the militant Puerto Rican youth groups. Jiménez is chairman of the Young Lords Organization, a Puerto Rican street gang whose members have become political activists.*

In 1962, a delegation from Puerto Rico went to the United Nations to ask the people of the world whether they thought Puerto Rico should be free or not. Everyone voted

* "Cha Cha Jiménez Interview," *The Movement,* Vol. 5, No. 6 (July, 1969).

that it should be free and independent but the United States. That same year they sucked $601 million out of Puerto Rico. We know what it's all about . . . they're fucking us over in Puerto Rico and over here. They call us citizens only when we get sent to war or something like that, when they want to use us. But we're not citizens of the United States, and we're going to fight. We want Puerto Rico to be free. We remember all the things that have been done to us. We won't forget them. . . .

The Cubans have this poster . . . saying we will destroy it from the outside, you from the inside. This is the same way we put it. We feel that we should stimulate revolution here in the mother country, as well as in the colony. There's organizations out there in Puerto Rico now, FUPI, MPI, that are fighting for liberation. We're just helping them. There's a nationalist party there, an independent party. The movement is growing in Puerto Rico. . . . People consider Puerto Ricans as passive . . . but as recently as 1950 there was a revolution in Puerto Rico. It's not known by the people; the mass media covers up everything. Lots of revolutionaries have come out of Puerto Rico. We relate to the class struggle because there's Puerto Ricans that are real black, then there's Puerto Ricans that are light-skinned like myself. We have to relate to poor people. We see it's some of our so-called own people that are fucking over us too, helping to keep us down. The ones that think they know everything, that want to talk for us. They want to say that they're our leaders. The ones appointed by the Mayors and the President. These are the ones keeping us down. So we have to relate to the class struggle.

A lot of people come over here, looking for a land of opportunity, for this dream. A lot of them come over to work on farms. There's a lot of Puerto Ricans working for $1.45 an hour right now. On farms. They're brought over there as slaves, even by their own people. People don't notice that. They don't speak the language. . . .

Puerto Ricans are a proud race, they don't like to admit

that they're poor. They come over here and save two or three hundred dollars, and then go back to visit Puerto Rico on the plane, usually buying the ticket on credit. Go to Puerto Rico, spend the two or three hundred dollars in about a week and then come back and leave the impression that they're living here a happy life and they're really not. They're just pretending. We have a lot of pretenders. It's basically pride. If we would just be sincere and let the people in Puerto Rico know what's happening, maybe we would get some changes.

Then there are the people who work for the city. Who want to organize this or that. Appointed by the mayor, the Uncle Toms, the bootlickers who've been sucking ass all their lives. They always want to be in the papers, want to put their face in everything. . . .

The Church has really fucked us over a lot. Saying it's a separate entity . . . when it's part of the United States . . . "how beautiful the United States is, how wonderful it is." They're helping it. Poor people grasp on to religion. They have to grasp on to something cause they're not free, not living a happy life, have to grab hold of something. People have been brainwashed by the Church.

We're talking about having a cultural center, a Puerto Rican cultural center. We got to include some black culture cause we got some blacks, we want to include some Chicano culture too cause we want to include all Latins. We want to invite the people from the white community. We'll educate them by giving them talks, by rapping to them, by showing films. We're trying to set up as many programs as we can to educate the people.

The Young Lords are going to try to get a little more ideology. We have to do this to educate the Latin community, not just Puerto Ricans, but also Chicanos, Cubans, South Americans, the whole Latin scene. We're trying to educate the people—we have to get more ideology. We're working with the Black Panther Party and other groups.

We look at the United States and we see lots of divisions. I see the Uncle Toms getting stronger every day. In the

Southwest some of them yelling Chicano power and not knowing what it's all about.

We're not so politically educated from books or anything, but we're educated from the streets, from being Puerto Ricans, from being different shades of skin.

And we see phony revolutionaries as a threat to the movement. If we don't get hip to which is the enemy and which is the friend, the movement is gonna be destroyed. And it's happening all over where there's people who say they're for revolution, say they want to stop this exploitation, but when it really gets down to the nitty gritty, when you say, would you give up your house, or this or that, they never want to give it up.

So they're really not for it. . . they just say it. They read all these books to prove they're so advanced. They're turning the revolution into some kind of new dance, or new car. Like on television they talk about revolutionary detergents, revolutionary soap, revolutionary toilet paper that explodes when you put it up to your ass. They're really not serious, not sincere when they talk about it.

Our people are poor, a lot of them are illiterate. There's opportunists who are out for themselves. This is why we need a vanguard Latin party, that can educate the people, the poor people, not just the Chicanos who have so called made it in the system. They've become pretty capitalistic, don't want to give up what they got.

We feel that we're revolutionaries and revolutionaries have no race. The system is the one that's using the tool to divide us. Revolutionaries are just revolutionaries. In Puerto Rico they have revolutionary nationalists who are fighting for the independence of Puerto Rico. We're poor and oppressed people here and we're fighting for the independence of the United States. We're fighting for freedom together . . . there's no other way to fight for it.

EXPANSION AS A WAY OF LIFE

George Washington counseled future generations of Americans against "entangling alliances." At the same time, John Quincy Adams warned his countrymen against seeking "foreign monsters abroad"; he was ignored.

Between 1789 and 1899 alone, more than 100 official armed interventions abroad were undertaken by the United States. Justifications for these armed interventions varied: "to protect U.S. interests during an insurrection" in Argentina in 1833; to "punish natives for attacking American exploring parties" in the Fiji Islands in 1840; "to punish a horde of savages who were supposed to have murdered the crew of a wrecked American vessel" in Formosa in 1867.

Such evidence destroys the myth of a peaceful, anticolonial America. In fact, the United States has believed, from her beginning as a nation, that she is endowed with special rights, enforceable by military means.

The history of American expansionism is directly linked to American racism. Almost every instance of armed intervention has been undertaken against a colored people including Latin Americans. If United States foreign policy is examined together with domestic policy, the theme of racism emerges more clearly. Zion in the Wilderness, Manifest Destiny, The American Mission, The American Century, all represent visions of a white America that rules the world; dreams for an empire.

From the time the American colonies revolted against the British Empire, America was viewed as an anticolonial nation, and she retained that image throughout the nineteenth century. America had no need to colonize Africa, Asia, and Latin America in the manner of the European powers. Instead, she inverted the idea of colonialism. Instead of sending white Americans to settle in the Congo or to exploit African resources through the use of that continent's cheap black labor, Americans imported African blacks to their own continent to work as slaves. Instead of conquering all of Mexico, Americans took some Mexican territory, and then used its resident population as cheap labor. It was cheaper and more rational to import quantities of Chinese and Japanese laborers than to colonize Asian territory, which had already been colonized anyway. And it should come as no surprise to discover that when colored peoples were imported to America they were treated as badly here as they had been by the European colonial powers in their native lands—or worse. Equality in the American democracy has always meant equality for white *men* only.

When overseas expansion became a national rallying cry, during the Mexican War period and later during the Spanish-American War, soldiers' songs were infused with blatant racism. During World War II—often called the battle for democracy—the armed forces not only segregated all nonwhites but, in addition, labeled the Japanese as monkeys, or worse. During the Korean and Vietnam wars, the word "gook" has been used to describe the "inferior" Oriental enemy.

So, when the Black Panthers, the Brown Berets, or the Red Guard talk of forging an alliance with the Third World and colored people all over the world, they are expressing an awareness of the basic facts of American history as well as its present state. Africans and Latin Americans, Asians and Indians, have been *the losers,* oppressed people, in all their contacts with white Americans, at home and abroad. Now, however, nonwhites are becoming aware of their position, and have begun to revive their own histories. In doing so, they have begun to achieve a sense of their own identity.

For the colored people in America, democracy and progress are not characteristic of American history; racism and oppression are. For every document showing the unfolding of democracy in the United States, they will now produce ten to show the unfolding of racism and imperialism. The nonwhites *have* always been *the losers,* and, except for periodic resistance, have always been ruthlessly suppressed. They accommodated to the inferior status forced upon them.

But the camouflage of democracy has been stripped away during the 1960s, and more and more nonwhites have been refusing to accept the rhetoric of good will and reason of American white society. They want not only a full share of what is rightfully theirs, but retribution for the hundreds of years of abuse. They want their true history acknowledged and recorded by white America.

But the dominant white society will not willingly yield to these new demands being made upon it at home. Nor will it easily yield to those people in other countries who insist upon their right to live outside the hegemony of the United States, no matter how benign that hegemony appears to be. And when, as in Vietnam, a colored people fights against America rather than surrender or accommodate, it must pay an awful price in death and destruction. The massacre of Vietnamese women and children at My Lai by American soldiers is only a modern version of the massacre of Indian women and children by American soldiers at Wounded Knee. The slogan "The only good 'Injun' is a dead one" has been supplanted by "If they're gooks, shoot first and then ask questions." Those cries for slaughter are rooted in white America's conviction that, underneath it all, white is right.

The domestic history of the United States has been rooted in racism. To correctly analyze her domestic history, the effects of racism on the American psyche must be taken into account. Furthermore, it is impossible to analyze her foreign policy without doing the same. American expansionism is inextricably linked to American racism.

(1)

No Entangling Alliances*

In the century following the Revolution, America's policy toward foreign involvements changed from the "hands off" attitude advocated by Washington and Adams to one of self-justifying imperialism, illustrated both by a clergyman's panegyric on the benefits of the Christian gospel in the Hawaiian Islands and President McKinley's account of how he decided that the United States would keep the Philippines.

It is our true policy to steer clear of permanent alliances with any portion of the foreign world, so far, I mean, as we are now at liberty to do it; for let me not be understood as capable of patronizing infidelity to existing engagements. I hold the maxim no less applicable to public than to private affairs that honesty is always the best policy. I repeat, therefore, let those engagements be observed in their genuine sense. But in my opinion it is unnecessary and would be unwise to extend them.

Taking care always to keep ourselves by suitable establishments on a respectable defensive posture, we may safely trust to temporary alliances for extraordinary emergencies.

* "George Washington's Farewell Address," in *Documents of American History,* ed. Henry Steele Commager (Appleton-Century-Crofts, Inc., 1958).

In Search of Monsters to Destroy*

The true American goes not abroad in search of monsters to destroy . . . [America] well knows that by once enlisting under other banners than her own, were they even the banners of foreign independence, she would involve herself, beyond the power of extrication, in all the wars of interest and intrigue, of individual avarice, envy, and ambition. She might become the dictatress of the world; she would no longer be the ruler of her own spirit.

The Lord Bless America†

Were it not for the light of the blessed Bible shining upon these shores, merchants, mechanics, planters, farmers, tradesmen, lawyers, physicians, judges, artisans, and citizens of foreign lands would not this evening be scattered throughout these islands in the peaceful pursuit of their various avocations. It is the wondrous influences accompanying the story of the Cross which has here dispelled the darkness of heathenism and transformed the pagan nation into a Christian community. The Lord of the Vineyard planted a goodly vine in these isles of the sea.

The Lord Says, "Keep the Philippines"‡

I walked the floor of the White House night after night until midnight; and I am not ashamed to tell you, gentlemen, that I went down on my knees and prayed Almighty God for light and guidance more than one night. And one night late

* "John Quincy Adams, July 4, 1821," in William Appleman Williams, *The Contours of American History* (New York: World Publishing Co., 1961).

† "Rev. A. O. Forbes," in Rev. Gulick and Mrs. Orramel Hinckley, *Pilgrims of Hawaii* (Fleming H. Revell Co., 1918).

‡ President William McKinley's explanation in 1898, quoted in Leon Wolff, *Little Brown Brother* (Doubleday & Co. Inc., Garden City, New York, 1961).

it came to me this way—I don't know how it was but it came; first, that we could not give [the Philippines] back to Spain—that would be cowardly and dishonorable; second, that we could not turn them over to France or Germany—our commercial rivals in the Orient—that would be bad business and discreditable; third, that we could not leave them to themselves—they were unfit for self-government, and they would soon have anarchy and misrule over there worse than Spain's was; and fourth, that there was nothing left for us to do but to take them all, and to educate the Filipinos, and uplift and civilize and Christianize them, and by God's grace do the very best we could by them, as our fellow-men for whom Christ also died. And then I went to bed, and went to sleep and slept soundly.

(2)

The Destruction of Sanctuaries in Florida*

One of the least-known and most infamous episodes in the history of developing white racism was the war conducted against the descendants of some Negroes who had escaped from slavery in South Carolina and settled in what was then Spanish territory in Florida, where they lived peacefully with the Seminole Indians. In a book published in 1858, Congressman Joshua Giddings described how these "exiles" were hunted down and slaughtered in 1816 under the orders of General Andrew Jackson. In the following excerpts from Congressman Giddings' book official U.S. disregard for "foreign frontiers" becomes clear. The "Seminole War" was a euphemism for an invasion of Spanish territory to destroy sanctuaries.

* Joshua Giddings, *The Exiles of Florida* (Gainesville, Fla.: University of Florida Press, 1964).

The pioneer exiles from South Carolina had settled here long before the Colony of Georgia existed. Several generations had lived to manhood and died in those forest-homes. To their descendants, it had become consecrated by "many an oft-told tale" of early adventure, of hardship and suffering; the recollection of which had been retained in tradition, told in story, and sung in their rude lays. Here were the graves of their ancestors, around whose memories were clustered the fondest recollections of the human mind. The climate was genial. They were surrounded by extensive forests, and far removed from the habitations of those enemies of freedom who sought to enslave them; and they regarded themselves as secure in the enjoyment of liberty. Shut out from the cares and strifes of more civilized men, they were happy in their own social solitude. So far from seeking to injure the people of the United States, they were only anxious to be exempt, and entirely free from all contact with our population or Government; while they faithfully maintained their allegiance to the Spanish crown.

Peace with Great Britain, however, had left our army without active employment. A portion of it was stationed along our Southern frontier of Georgia, to maintain peace with the Indians. The authorities and people of Georgia maintained social and friendly relations with the officers and men of the army. By means of Indian spies, the real condition of the Exiles was also ascertained and well understood. What means were used to excite the feelings or prejudices of the military officers against these unoffending Exiles, is not known at this day. Most of the officers commanding in the South were, however, slaveholders, and probably felt a strong sympathy with the people of Georgia in their indignation against them, for obtaining and enjoying liberty without permission of their masters.

General Gaines, commanding on the Southern frontier of Georgia, making Fort Scott his headquarters, wrote the Secretary of War (May 14), saying, "certain negroes and outlaws have taken possession of a fort on the Appalachicola River, in the Territory of Florida." He assured the Secretary, that he should keep watch of them. He charged them with no crime, imputed to them no hostile acts. He was conscious that they had taken possession of the fort solely for their own protection; but he styled them *negroes,* which, in the language of that day among slaveholders, was regarded as an imputation of guilt; and *outlaw* was supposed to be a proper term with which to characterize those who had fled from bondage and sworn allegiance to another government.[1]

For more than a year subsequently to the date of this letter, General Gaines made the Exiles a subject of frequent communication to the War Department. In this official correspondence, he at all times spoke of them as "runaways," "outlaws," "pirates," "murderers," etc.; but in no instance did he charge them with any act hostile to the United States, or to any other people or government.

Of these communications the Exiles were ignorant. They continued in peaceful retirement, cultivating the earth, and gaining a support for themselves and families. In the autumn of 1815, they gathered their crops, provided for the support of the aged and infirm, as well as for their children. They carefully nursed the sick; they buried their dead; they lived in peace, and enjoyed the fruits of their labor. The following spring and summer found them in this enviable condition.

While the Exiles living on the Appalachicola were thus pursuing the even tenor of their ways, plans were ripening among the slaveholders and military officers of our army for their destruction. A correspondence was opened by the Secretary of War with General Jackson, who commanded

[1] The reader will at once see, that these people were as much under the protection of Spain, as the fugitive slaves now in Canada are under the protection of British laws. They were as clearly Spanish subjects as the latter are British subjects. By the law of nations, Spain had the same right to permit her black subjects to occupy "Blount's Fort," that the Queen of England has to permit Fort Malden to be occupied by her black subjects. The only distinction between the two cases is, Spain was weak and unable to maintain her national honor, and national rights; while England has the power to do both.

the Southwestern Military District of the United States, holding his headquarters at Nashville, Tennessee. Various letters and communications passed between those officers in regard to this "Negro Fort," as they called it.

Power is never more dangerous than when wielded by military men. They usually feel ambitious to display their own prowess, and that of the troops under their command; and no person can read the communications of General Gaines, in regard to the Exiles who had gathered in and around this fort, without feeling conscious that he greatly desired to give to the people of the United States an example of the science and power by which they could destroy human life.

At length, on the sixteenth of May, General Jackson wrote General Gaines, saying, "I have little doubt of the fact, that this fort has been established by some villains for the purpose of rapine and plunder, and that it ought to be blown up, regardless of the ground on which it stands; and if your mind shall have formed the same conclusion, destroy it and return the *stolen negroes* and property to their rightful owners."[2]

Without attempting to criticize this order of General Jackson, we must regard a fort thus situated, at least sixty miles from the border of the United States, as a most singular instrument for the purpose of "rapine," or plundering our citizens. Nor could General Jackson have entertained any apprehensions from those who occupied the fort. The entire correspondence showed them to be *refugees,* seeking

[2] Perhaps no portion of our national history exhibits such disregard of international law, as this unprovoked invasion of Florida. For thirty years, the slaves of our Southern States have been in the habit of fleeing to the British Provinces. Here they are admitted to all the rights of citizenship, in the same manner as they were in Florida. They vote and hold office under British laws and when our government demanded that the English Ministry should disregard the rights of these people and return them to slavery, the British Minister contemptuously refused even to hold correspondence with our Secretary of State on a subject so abhorrent to every principle of national law and self-respect. Our government coolly submitted to the scornful arrogance of England; but did not hesitate to invade Florida with an armed force, and to seize the faithful subjects of Spain, and enslave them.

only to avoid our people; indeed, his very order shows this, for he directs General Gaines to return the "*stolen negroes* to their rightful owners." The use of opprobrious epithets is not often resorted to by men in high official stations: yet it is difficult to believe, that General Jackson supposed these Negroes to have been stolen; for, neither in the official correspondence on this subject, nor in the papers accompanying it, embracing more than a hundred documentary pages, is there a hint that these Negroes were "*stolen,*" or that they had committed violence upon any person, or upon the property of any person whatever. They had sought their own liberty, and the charge of stealing themselves, was used like the other epithets of "outlaws," "pirates" and "murderers," to cast opprobrium upon the character of men who, if judged by their love of liberty or their patriotism, would now occupy a position not less honorable in the history of our country than is assigned to the patriots of 1776.

Nor is it easy to discover the rule of international law, which authorized the Executive of the United States, or the officers of our army, to dictate to the crown of Spain in what part of his territory he should, or should not, erect fortresses; or the constitutional power which they held for invading the territory of a nation at peace with the United States, destroy a fort, and consign its occupants to slavery. But those were days of official arrogance on the one hand, and popular submission on the other. The exiles, or their ancestors, had once been slaves. They now were cultivating the richest lands in Florida, and possessed wealth; they were occupying a strong fortress. Many slaves during the recent war had escaped from their masters, in Georgia, and some were supposed to be free subjects of Spain, living in Florida; and if the Exiles were permitted to enjoy their plantations and property in peace, it was evident that the institution in adjoining States would be in danger of a total overthrow. These facts were apparent to General Jackson, as well as to General Gaines and the slaveholders of Georgia.

General Gaines only awaited permission from his superior to carry out the designs of the slaveholders, who had become alarmed at the dangers to which their "peculiar institution" was subjected. Upon the receipt of the order above quoted, he detailed Lieut. Col. Clinch, of the regular troops, with his regiment and five hundred friendly Creek Indians, under McIntosh, their principal chief, to carry out the directions of General Jackson. Colonel Clinch was directed to take with him two pieces of artillery, for the purpose of cannonading the fort if necessary.

This commencement of the first Seminole war was, at the time, unknown to the people of the United States. It was undertaken for the purposes stated in General Jackson's order, to "blow up the fort, and *return the negroes to their rightful owners.*" Historians have failed to expose the cause of hostilities, or the barbarous foray which plunged the nation into that bloody contest which cost the people millions of treasure and the sacrifice of hundreds of human lives.

On the twenty-fourth of July, Colonel Clinch commenced a reconnaissance of the fort. On the twenty-fifth, he cleared away the brush and erected a battery, and placed upon it two long eighteen-pounders, and commenced a cannonade of the fortress. At the time of this investment, there were about three hundred Exiles in the fort, including women and children, besides thirty-four Seminole Indians: yet in the official report of Colonel Clinch, he makes no mention of his fire being returned; nor does he say that any of his men were killed or wounded by the occupants of the fort. The cannonade was resumed, and the land and naval forces of the United States were engaged in throwing shot and shells for the purpose of murdering those friendless Exiles, those women and children, who had committed no other offense than that of having been born of parents who, a century previously, had been held in bondage. Mothers and children now shrieked with terror as the roar of cannon, the whistling of balls, the explosion of shells, the war-whoops of the savages, the groans of the wounded and dying, foretold the sad fate which awaited them. The stout-hearted old men cheered and encouraged their friends, declaring that death was to be preferred to slavery.

The struggle, however, was not protracted. The cannon balls not taking effect upon the embankments of earth, they prepared their furnaces and commenced the fire of hot shot, directed at the principal magazine. This mode proved more successful. A ball, fully heated, reached the powder in the magazine. The small size of the fort, and the great number of people in it, rendered the explosion unusually fatal. Many were entirely buried in the ruins, others were killed by falling timbers, while many bodies were torn in pieces. Limbs were separated from bodies to which they had been attached, and death, in all its horrid forms, was visible within that doomed fortress.[3]

Of three hundred and thirty-four souls within the fort, two hundred and seventy were *instantly killed;* while of the sixty who remained, only *three* escaped without injury. Two of the survivors—one Negro and one Indian—were selected as supposed chiefs of the allied forces within the fort. They were delivered over to the Indians who accompanied Colonel Clinch, and were massacred within the fort, in the presence of our troops; but no report on record shows the extent of torture to which they were subjected.

We have no reliable information as to the number who died of their wounds. They were placed on board the gunboats, and their wounds were dressed by the surgeons; and those who recovered were afterwards delivered over to claimants in Georgia. Those who were slightly wounded, but able to travel, were taken back with Colonel Clinch to Georgia and delivered over to men who claimed to have descended from planters who, some three or four generations previously, owned the ancestors of the prisoners. There could be no proof of identity, nor was there any court authorized to take testimony, or enter decree in such

[3] Monette says, "The scene in the fort was horrible beyond description. Nearly the whole of the inmates were involved in indiscriminate destruction; not one-sixth of the whole escaped. The cries of the wounded, the groans of the dying, with the shouts and yells of the Indians, rendered the scene horrible beyond description."

case; but they were delivered over upon *claim,* taken to the interior, and sold to different planters. There they mingled with that mass of chattelized humanity which characterizes our Southern states, and were swallowed up in that tide of oppression which is now bearing three millions of human beings to untimely graves.

(3)

Songs from the Spanish-American War

The following songs, all from the Spanish-American War, reveal the attitudes of American soldiers toward the peoples and the cultures of the lands which they invaded and annexed.

"Our" war against the Filipinos, who had established their own government after routing the Spaniards themselves, was the bloodiest in the history of the Philippine Islands, including World War II. Filipinos fought like tigers for their independence, and earned the hatred of Americans sent to overpower them.

The glorification of the Anglo-Saxon race and its superiority to all others was the theme of several songs written in 1898.

"TRAMP, TRAMP, TRAMP"*

Damn, damn, damn the Filipinos
Cross-eyed, Kakiak Ladrones,
And beneath the starry flag
Civilize 'em with a Krag†
And we'll all go back to our beloved homes.

* "Damn, Damn, Damn the Filipinos" (tune: "Tramp, Tramp, Tramp, The Boys are Marching.")

† Slang for the Krag-Jensen rifles, an extremely powerful weapon used by the U.S. Army in the Philippines.—Editor's Note.

DON'T YOU HEAR YOUR UNCLE SAM'L?*

Land of garlic and tortillas,
Land of xebecs and mantillas,
Land of mules and smuggled bitters,
Land of raisins and of fritters,
Land of Pedro and of Sancho,
Land of Weyler and of Blanco,
Land of bull fights and pesetas,
Land of dusky señoritas,
Land of manners stiff and haughty
Land of Isabella naughty,
Land of Boabdil and Hamil,
Don't you hear your Uncle Sam'l?
"Git!"

DEWEY, WHEN YO' COMIN' HOME?†

Mistah Dewey, like to know
When yo' comin' home?
Reckon dat yo' mus' go slow,
When yo' comin' home?
Sence de startin' ob dis war
Yo' is mighty popular,
Name yo' got done traveled far—
When yo' comin' home? . . .

Mistah Dewey, yo' has spunk,
When yo' comin' home?
Made dem Wienerwurstses shrunk,
When yo' comin' home?
Made dem Phillupeeners tame,
Made dem fo'iners walk lame,
Made Ol' Glory glad she came—
When yo' comin' home?

* In *Spanish-American War Songs,* comp. and ed. Sidney A. Witherbee (Detroit: Sidney A. Witherbee, Publisher, 1898).
† *Ibid.*

Mistah Dewey, ef yo' please,
   When yo' comin' home?
Swung dat banner to de breeze
   When yo' comin' home?
Ef dey 'sists to get too gay,
Nail it to de mast to stay,
Den jus' telyfone an' say
   When yo' comin' home?

—Baltimore *American*

IN HIS NAME*

From Cuba to the Philippines,
   A cry for rescue came;
As Macedonia of old:
   "Come! Help in Jesus' name!"

To those who sat in darkness,
   God sent His own Great Light;
So we, the Lord's own freemen,
   May take the message bright.

In bondage strong and cruel;
   God's blessed word withdrawn;
No hope for earth or heaven,
   Nor light of glorious dawn.

Tho' hollow-eyed and famished,
   For earthly bread and cheer,
Their need for Heavenly comfort
   Far greater doth appear.

To these "the least" who need us,
   God calls, "My truth proclaim."
Go! To the faint and fallen;
   Send peace through Jesus' name.

Can we, our best and dearest,
   To Christ this offering make?
The love of Christ constraineth.
   We can, for Jesus' sake.

—*M. Purdee Adams*

* *Ibid.*

THE ANGLO-SAXON*

What's the matter with old Europe, hear her mutterings and threats;
War's abroad and her passions are aflame;
She menaces John Bull to pay old scores and debts,
But to checkmate Uncle Sammy is the game.
Count on Sam, O! mother England when Europe wants to fight,
Should mad ambition overleap her sense;
The cherished Monroe doctrine will mount skyward like a kite;
He can march for either conquest or defense.

CHORUS:

Sing hey! for Britannia, sing ho; for Uncle Sam;
For kin to stand by kin is no disgrace;
Look out for their advance, Austria, Italy and France,
O! the Anglo-Saxon is the coming race.

The continental powers are balanced, so they say,
To guard against surprise or wily scheme;
All the while your scales, O, princess, are adjusted in the play
To make the Anglo-Saxon kick the beam.
The outstripped Latin race we cannot greatly blame,
Whichever way they turn, east or west,
The sleepless Anglo-Saxon has staked a mighty claim,
Always of the biggest and the best.

Sing hey! for Columbia, song ho! for Albion;
On every land their footsteps you may trace;
Round the globe their vessels roll; North and South from pole to pole,
O! the Anglo-Saxon's up and in the race.

Uncle Sammy is a giant who was never known to boast,
But he cautions you, my continental friend,
Not to twist the Lion's tail, nor approach the Eagle's roost,
Lest Britannia and Yankee Doodle blend.
The Dragon and St. George for a thousand years and more,
Have on many a sea and land fate defied;
While the Stars and Stripes float over and guard a mightier shore,
Than the ancient Roman Eagles in their pride.

* *Ibid.*

CHORUS:

Sing hey! on high C the Federal Eagle screams.
  Sing ho! for the Lion's double bass;
Ye will quickstep to changes beyond Boney's wildest dreams.
  To the music of the Anglo-Saxon race.

—*N. Albert Sherman*

(4)

Beveridge Trumpets Imperialism*

Albert J. Beveridge's speech, The March of the Flag, is a classic piece of pro-expansionist oratory. It was delivered at Indianapolis, Indiana, on September 16, 1898, before McKinley had made his decision to keep the Philippines. A year after making it, Beveridge was elected to the United States Senate from Indiana.

Distance and oceans are no arguments. The fact that all the territory our fathers bought and seized is contiguous is no argument. In 1819 Florida was further from New York than Porto Rico is from Chicago today; Texas further from Washington in 1845 than Hawaii is from Boston in 1898; California, more inaccessible in 1847 than the Philippines are now. . . . The ocean does not separate us from lands of our duty and desire—the oceans join us, a river never to be dredged, a canal never to be repaired.

Steam joins us; electricity joins us—the very elements are in league with our destiny. Cuba not contiguous! Porto Rico not contiguous! Hawaii and the Philippines not contiguous! Our navy will make them contiguous. [Admirals] Dewey and Sampson and Schley have made them contiguous, and American speed, American guns, American heart and brain and nerve will keep them contiguous forever.

But the Opposition is right—there is a difference. We did

* "Beveridge Trumpets Imperialism," in *The American Spirit—United States History as Seen by Contemporaries*, Vol. II, ed. Thomas A. Bailey (Boston: D. C. Heath & Co., 1963 & 1968).

not need the western Mississippi Valley when we acquired it, nor Florida, nor Texas, nor California, nor the royal provinces of the far Northwest. We had no emigrants to people this imperial wilderness, no money to develop it, even no highways to cover it. No trade awaited us in its savage vastnesses. Our productions were not greater than our trade. There was not one reason for the land-lust of our statesmen from Jefferson to Grant, other than the prophet and the Saxon within them.

But today we are raising more than we can consume. Today we are making more than we can use. Today our industrial society is congested; there are more workers than there is work; there is more capital than there is investment. We do not need more money—we need more circulation, more employment. Therefore we must find new markets for our produce, new occupation for our capital, new work for our labor. And so, while we did not need the territory taken during the past century at the time it was acquired, we do need what we have taken in 1898, and we need it now.

Think of the thousands of Americans who will pour into Hawaii and Porto Rico when the republic's laws cover those islands with justice and safety! Think of the tens of thousands of Americans who will invade mine and field and forest in the Philippines when a liberal government, protected and controlled by this republic, if not the government of the republic itself, shall establish order and equity there! Think of the hundreds of thousands of Americans who will build a soap-and-water, common-school civilization of energy and industry in Cuba, when a government of law replaces the double reign of anarchy and tyranny!—think of the prosperous millions that Empress of Islands will support when, obedient to the law of political gravitation, her people ask for the highest honor liberty can bestow, the sacred Order of the Stars and Stripes, the citizenship of the Great Republic!

What does all this mean for every one of us? It means opportunity for all the glorious young manhood of the republic—the most virile, ambitious, impatient, militant manhood the world has ever seen. It means that the resources and the commerce of these immensely rich dominions will be increased as much as American energy is greater than Spanish sloth; for Americans henceforth will monopolize those resources and that commerce.

(5)

A San Francisco Weekly Defends the Army, 1902*

In 1902, the San Francisco *Argonaut,* a weekly magazine, stated baldly the purposes of the United States regarding the Philippine Islands. The magazine was responding to criticism of American soldiers for their numerous and flagrant atrocities committed against the Filipino insurgents.

There has been too much hypocrisy about this Philippine business—too much snivel—too much cant. Let us all be frank.

WE DO NOT WANT THE FILIPINOS.

WE WANT THE PHILIPPINES.

All of our troubles in this annexation matter have been caused by the presence in the Philippine Islands of the Filipinos. Were it not for them, the Treaty of Paris would have been an excellent thing; the purchase of the archipelago for twenty millions of dollars would have been cheap. The islands are enormously rich; they abound in dense forests of valuable hardwood timber; they contain mines of the precious metals; their fertile lands will produce immense crops of sugar cane, rice, and tobacco. Touched by the wand of American enterprise, fertilized with American capital, these islands would speedily become richer than Golconda was of old.

* "A San Francisco Weekly Defends the Army," in *The American Spirit—United States History as Seen by Contemporaries,* Vol. II, ed. Thomas A. Bailey (Boston: D. C. Heath & Co., 1963 & 1968).

But unfortunately, they are infested by Filipinos. There are many millions of them there, and it is to be feared that their extinction will be slow. Still, every man who believes in developing the islands must admit that it cannot be done successfully while the Filipinos are there. They are indolent. They raise only enough food to live on; they don't care to make money; and they occupy land which might be utilized to much better advantage by Americans. Therefore the more of them killed, the better.

It seems harsh. But they must yield before the superior race, and the American syndicate. How shortsighted, then, to check the army in its warfare upon these savages; particularly when the army is merely carrying out its orders and the duly expressed wishes of the American people, as shown through their elections and their representatives.

Doubtless, many of the excellent gentlemen now in Congress would repudiate these sentiments as brutal. But we are only saying what they are doing. We believe in stripping all hypocritical verbiage from national declarations, and telling the truth simply and boldly. We repeat—the American people, after thought and deliberation, have shown their wishes. THEY DO NOT WANT THE FILIPINOS. THEY WANT THE PHILIPPINES.

It is no one party, no one class, that is responsible for our Philippine policy. It is the people of the United States. The Democratic Party shares equally the responsibility with the Republican Party. The Democratic Party voted for the war with Spain. Had it opposed the fifty-million [arms] appropriation, the war could not have taken place. The Democrats advocated the purchase of the Philippines. For a time, the confirmation of the Philippine treaty was in doubt. It was the direct personal lobbying of William J. Bryan with the Democratic Senators which led to the confirmation of the Philippine purchase, and which also led to the present bloody war. Mr. Bryan said at the time that he advocated the confirmation of the treaty in order to put "the Republicans into a hole." He has certainly put his country into a hole. Is he proud of his work?

We are all responsible. You, reader, are responsible. If you are a Republican, your party has made this action part of its national policy. If you are a Democrat, your party, by its vote in the House of Representatives, made the war possible, and by its vote in the Senate turned the scales for the purchase of the Philippines.

But if we, the people of the United States, are responsible for the Philippine campaign, the American army is not. The army is only seventy thousand out of seventy million. The army did not ask to go there. It was sent. It has fought for four years under tropic suns and torrential rains, in pestilential jungles and miasmatic swamps, patiently bearing the burdens placed upon it by the home country, and with few laurels to be gained as a result of hard and dangerous duty. Nearly every general officer returning from the Philippines has returned to either a wrecked reputation, newspaper odium, or public depreciation. Look at Merritt, Otis, Merriam, MacArthur, Funston. The best treatment that any of them has received is not to be abused. And yet, with these melancholy examples before them, our army toils on uncomplainingly doing its duty.

The army did not bring on the war. We civilians did it. The army is only doing our bidding as faithful servants of their country. And now that they have shown a perfectly human tendency to fight the devil with fire, we must not repudiate their actions, for their actions are our own. They are receiving the fire of the enemy from the front. It is shameful that there should be a fire upon them from the rear.

(6)

Instances of the Use of United States Armed Forces Abroad, 1798–1945*

On September 17, 1962, Secretary of State Dean Rusk presented a joint meeting of the Senate Committee on Foreign Relations and Armed Services with a list of American interventions abroad. He made the presentation to justify his request for passage of a resolution authorizing President Kennedy to use force against the Cuban revolution just prior to the "Missile Crisis" of October, 1962. The following document is that official list, compiled by the State Department. In it the direct relationship of domestic racism to foreign policy is outlined in stark clarity. The language is that of the State Department.

1798–1800—Undeclared naval war with France. This contest included land actions, such as that in the Dominican Republic, city of Puerto Plata, where marines captured a French privateer under the guns of the forts.

1801–1805—Tripoli. The First Barbary War, including the *George Washington* and *Philadelphia* affairs and the Eaton expedition, during which a few marines landed with United States Agent William Eaton to raise a force against Tripoli in an effort to free the crew of the *Philadelphia*. Tripoli declared war but not the United States.

1806—Mexico (Spanish territory). Capt. Z. M. Pike, with a platoon of troops, invaded Spanish territory at the headwaters of the Rio Grande deliberately and on orders

* "Instances of the Use of United States Armed Forces Abroad, 1798–1945," Hearing before the Committee on Foreign Relations and the Committee on Armed Services. 87th Congress, 2nd Session, Mon., Sept. 17, 1962.

from Gen. James Wilkinson. He was made prisoner without resistance at a fort he constructed in present-day Colorado, taken to Mexico, later released after seizure of his papers. There was a political purpose, still a mystery.

1806–1810—Gulf of Mexico. American gunboats operated from New Orleans against Spanish and French privateers, such as LaFitte, off the Mississippi Delta, chiefly under Capt. John Shaw and Master Commandant David Porter.

1810—West Florida (Spanish territory). Gov. Claiborne of Louisiana, on orders of the President, occupied with troops territory in dispute east of Mississippi as far as the Pearl River, later the eastern boundary of Louisiana. He was authorized to seize as far east as the Perdido River. No armed clash.

1812—Amelia Island and other parts of east Florida, then under Spain. Temporary possession was authorized by President Madison and by Congress, to prevent occupation by any other power; but possession was obtained by Gen. George Matthews in so irregular a manner that his measures were disavowed by the President.

1812–1815—Great Britain. War of 1812. Formally declared.

1813—West Florida (Spanish territory). On authority given by Congress, General Wilkinson seized Mobile Bay in April with 600 soldiers. A small Spanish garrison gave way. Thus we advanced into disputed territory to the Perdido River, as projected in 1810. No fighting.

1813–1814—Marquesas Islands. Built a fort on island of Nukahiva to protect three prize ships which had been captured from the British.

1814—Spanish Florida. Gen. Andrew Jackson took Pensacola and drove out the British with whom the United States was at war.

1814–1825—Caribbean. Engagements between pirates and American ships or squadrons took place repeatedly especially ashore and offshore about Cuba, Puerto Rico, Santo Domingo, and Yucatan. Three thousand pirate attacks on merchantmen were reported between 1815 and

1823. In 1822, Commodore James Biddle employed a squadron of two frigates, four sloops of war, two brigs, four schooners, and two gunboats in the West Indies.

1815—Algiers. The Second Barbary War, declared by our enemies but not by the United States. Congress authorized an expedition. A large fleet under Decatur attacked Algiers and obtained indemnities.

1815—Tripoli. After securing an agreement from Algiers, Decatur demonstrated with his squadron at Tunis and Tripoli, where he secured indemnities for offenses against us during the War of 1812.

1816—Spanish Florida. United States forces destroyed Nichols Fort, called also Negro Fort, because it harbored raiders into United States territory.

1816–1818—Spanish Florida: First Seminole War. The Seminole Indians, whose area was a resort for escaped slaves and border ruffians, were attacked by troops under Generals Jackson and Gaines and pursued into northern Florida. Spanish posts were attacked and occupied, British citizens executed. There was neither a declaration of war nor any congressional authorization, but the Executive was sustained.

1817—Amelia Island (Spanish territory off Florida). Under orders of President Monroe, United States forces landed and expelled a group of smugglers, adventurers, and freebooters.

1818—Oregon. The U.S.S. *Ontario,* dispatched from Washington, landed at the Columbia River and in August took possession. Britain had conceded sovereignty but Russia and Spain asserted claims to the area.

1820–1823—Africa. Naval units raided the slave traffic pursuant to the 1819 act of Congress.

1822—Cuba. United States naval forces suppressing piracy landed on the northwest coast of Cuba and burned a pirate station.

1823—Cuba. Brief landings in pursuit of pirates occurred April 8 near Escondido; April 16 near Cayo Blanco;

July 11 at Siquapa Bay; July 21 at Cape Cruz; and October 23 at Camrioca.

1824—Cuba. In October, the U.S.S. *Porpoise* landed blue jackets near Matanzas in pursuit of pirates. This was during the cruise authorized in 1822.

1824—Puerto Rico (Spanish territory). Commodore David Porter with a landing party attacked the town of Fajardo which had sheltered pirates and insulted American naval officers. He landed with 200 men in November and forced an apology.

1825—Cuba. In March, cooperating American and British forces landed at Segua La Grande to capture pirates.

1827—Greece. In October and November landing parties hunted pirates on the islands of Argenteire, Miconi, and Andross.

1831–1832—Falkland Islands. To investigate the capture of three American sealing vessels and to protect American interests.

1832—Sumatra, February 6–9. To punish natives of the town of Quallah Battoo for depredations on American shipping.

1833—Argentina, October 31–November 15. A force was sent ashore at Buenos Aires to protect the interests of the United States and other countries during an insurrection.

1835–1836—Peru, December 10, 1835–January 24, 1836, and August 31–December 2, 1836. Marines protected American interests in Callao and Lima during an attempted revolution.

1836—Mexico. General Gaines occupied Nacogdoches (Texas), disputed territory, from July to December during the Texan war for independence, under orders to cross the "imaginary boundary line" if an Indian outbreak threatened.

1838–1839—Sumatra, December 24, 1838–January 4, 1839. To punish natives of the towns of Quallah Battoo and Muckie (Mukki) for depredations on American shipping.

1840—Fiji Islands, July. To punish natives for attacking American exploring and surveying parties.

1841—Drummond Island, Kingsmill Group. To avenge the murder of a seaman by natives.

1841—Samoa, February 24. To avenge the murder of an American seaman on Upolu Island.

1842—Mexico. Commodore T. A. C. Jones, in command of a squadron long cruising off California, occupied Monterey, Calif., on October 19, believing war had come. He discovered peace, withdrew, and saluted. A similar incident occurred a week later at San Diego.

1843—Africa, November 29–December 16. Four United States vessels demonstrated and landed various parties (one of 200 marines and sailors) to discourage piracy and the slave trade among the Ivory coast, etc., and to punish attacks by the natives on American seamen and shipping.

1844—Mexico. President Tyler deployed our forces to protect Texas against Mexico, pending Senate approval of treaty of annexation. (Later rejected.) He defended his action against a Senate resolution of inquiry. This was a demonstration or preparation.

1846–1848—Mexico, the Mexican War. President Polk's occupation of disputed territory precipitated it. War formally declared.

1849—Smyrna. In July, a naval force gained release of an American seized by Austrian officials.

1851—Turkey. After a massacre of foreigners (including Americans) at Jaffa in January, a demonstration by our Mediterranean Squadron was ordered along the Turkish (Levant) coast. Apparently no shots fired.

1851—Johanna Island (east of Africa), August. To exact redress for the unlawful imprisonment of the captain of an American whaling brig.

1852–1853—Argentina, February 3–12, 1852; September 17, 1852–April (?) 1853. Marines were landed and maintained in Buenos Aires to protect American interests during a revolution.

1853—Nicaragua, March 11–13. To protect American lives and interests during political disturbances.

1853–1854—Japan. The "opening of Japan" and the Perry Expedition.

1853–1854—Ryukyu and Bonin Islands. Commodore Perry on three visits before going to Japan and while waiting for a reply from Japan made a naval demonstration, landing marines twice, and secured a coaling concession from the ruler of Naha on Okinawa. He also demonstrated in the Bonin Islands. All to secure facilities for commerce.

1854—China, April 4–June 15 or 17. To protect American interests in and near Shanghai during Chinese civil strife.

1854—Nicaragua, July 9–15. San Juan del Norte (Greytown) was destroyed to avenge an insult to the American Minister to Nicaragua.

1855—China, May 19–21 (?). To protect American interests in Shanghai. August 3–5 to fight pirates near Hong Kong.

1855—Fiji Islands, September 12–November 4. To seek reparations for depredations on Americans.

1855—Uruguay, November 25–29 or 30. United States and European naval forces landed to protect American interests during an attempted revolution in Montevideo.

1856—Panama, Republic of New Grenada, September 19–22. To protect American interests during an insurrection.

1856—China, October 22–December 6. To protect American interests at Canton during hostilities between the British and the Chinese; and to avenge an unprovoked assault upon an unarmed boat displaying the United States flag.

1857—Nicaragua, April–May, November–December. To oppose William Walker's attempt to get control of the country. In May, Commander C. H. Davis of the United States Navy, with some marines, received Walker's surrender and protected his men from the retaliation of native allies who had been fighting Walker. In November and December of the same year United States vessels *Saratoga, Wabash,* and *Fulton* opposed another attempt of William Walker on Nicaragua. Commodore Hiram Paulding's act of landing marines and compelling the removal of Walker to the United States, was tacitly disavowed by Secretary of State Lewis Cass, and Paulding was forced into retirement.

1858—Uruguay, January 2–27. Forces from two United States warships landed to protect American property during a revolution in Montevideo.

1858—Fiji Islands, October 6–16. To chastise the natives for the murder of two American citizens.

1858–59—Turkey. Display of naval force along the Levant at the request of the Secretary of State after massacre of Americans at Jaffa and mistreatment elsewhere "to remind the authorities (of Turkey) * * * of the power of the United States."

1859—Paraguay. Congress authorized a naval squadron to seek redress for an attack on a naval vessel in the Parana River during 1855. Apologies were made after a large display of force.

1859—Mexico. Two hundred United States soldiers crossed the Rio Grande in pursuit of the Mexican bandit Cortina.

1859—China, July 31–August 2. For the protection of American interests in Shanghai.

1860—Angola, Portuguese West Africa, March 1. To protect American lives and property at Kissembo when the natives became troublesome.

1860—Colombia, Bay of Panama, September 27–October 8. To protect American interests during a revolution.

1863—Japan, July 16. To redress an insult to the American flag—firing on an American vessel—at Shimonoseki.

1864—Japan, July 14–August 3, approximately. To protect the United States Minister to Japan when he visited Yedo to negotiate concerning some American claims against Japan, and to make his negotiations easier by impressing the Japanese with American power.

1864—Japan, September 4–14—Straits of Shimonoseki. To compel Japan and the Prince of Nagato in particular to permit the Straits to be used by foreign shipping in accordance with treaties already signed.

1865—Panama, March 9 and 10. To protect the lives and property of American residents during a revolution.

1866—Mexico. To protect American residents, General Sedgwick and 100 men in November obtained surrender of Matamoras. After three days, he was ordered by our government to withdraw. His act was repudiated by the President.

1866—China, June 20–July 7. To punish an assault on the American consul at Newchwang; July 14, for consultation with authorities on shore; August 9, at Shanghai, to help extinguish a serious fire in the city.

1867—Island of Formosa, June 13. To punish a horde of savages who were supposed to have murdered the crew of a wrecked American vessel.

1868—Japan (Osaka, Hiogo, Nagasaki, Yokohama, and Negata), mainly February 4–8, April 4–May 12, June 12 and 13. To protect American interests during the civil war in Japan over the abolition of the Shogunate and the restoration of the Mikado.

1868—Uruguay, February 7 and 8, 19–26. To protect foreign residents and the customhouse during an insurrection at Montevideo.

1868—Colombia, April 7, at Aspinwall. To protect passengers and treasure in transit during the absence of local police or troops on the occasion of the death of the President of Colombia.

1870—Mexico, June 17 and 18. To destroy the pirate ship *Forward,* which had been run aground about 40 miles up the Rio Tecapan.

1870—Hawaiian Islands, September 21. To place the American flag at half mast upon the death of Queen

Kalama, when the American consul at Honolulu would not assume responsibility for so doing.

1871—Korea, June 10–12. To punish natives for depredations on Americans, particularly for murdering the crew of the *General Sherman* and burning the schooner, and for later firing on other American small boats taking soundings up the Salee River.

1873—Colombia (Bay of Panama), May 7–22, September 23–October 9. To protect American interests during hostilities over possession of the government of the State of Panama.

1873—Mexico. United States troops crossed the Mexican border repeatedly in pursuit of cattle and other thieves. There were some reciprocal pursuits by Mexican troops into our border territory. The cases were only technically invasions, if that, although Mexico protested constantly. Notable cases were at Remolina in May 1873 and at Las Cuevas in 1875. Washington orders often supported these excursions. Agreements between Mexico and the United States, the first in 1882, finally legitimized such raids. They continued intermittently, with minor disputes, until 1896.

1874—Hawaiian Islands, February 12–20. To preserve order and protect American lives and interests during the inauguration of a new king.

1876—Mexico, May 18. To police the town of Matamoros temporarily while it was without other government.

1882—Egypt, July 14–18. To protect American interests during warfare between British and Egyptians and looting of the city of Alexandria by Arabs.

1885—Panama (Colon), January 18 and 19. To guard the valuables in transit over the Panama Railroad, and the safes and vaults of the company during revolutionary activity. In March, April, and May in the cities of Colon and Panama, to reestablish freedom of transit during revolutionary activity.

1888—Korea, June. To protect American residents in Seoul during unsettled political conditions, when an outbreak of the populace was expected.

1888–1889—Samoa, November 14, 1888–March 20, 1889. To protect American citizens and the consulate during a native civil war.

1888—Haiti, December 20. To persuade the Haitian Government to give up an American steamer which had been seized on the charge of breach of blockade.

1889—Hawaiian Islands, July 30 and 31. To protect American interests at Honolulu during a revolution.

1890—Argentina. A naval party landed to protect our consulate and legation in Buenos Aires.

1891—Haiti. To protect American lives and property on Navassa Island when Negro laborers got out of control.

1891—Bering Sea July 2–October 5. To stop seal poaching.

1891—Chile, August 28–30. To protect the American consulate and the women and children who had taken refuge in it during a revolution in Valparaiso.

1893—Hawaii, January 16–April 1. Ostensibly to protect American lives and property; actually to promote a provisional government under Sanford B. Dole. This action was disavowed by the United States.

1894—Brazil, January. To protect American commerce and shipping at Rio de Janeiro during a Brazilian civil war. No landing was attempted but there was a display of naval force.

1894—Nicaragua, July 6–August 7. To protect American interests at Bluefields following a revolution.

1894–1896—Korea, July 24, 1894–April 3, 1896. To protect American lives and interests at Seoul during and following the Sino-Japanese War. A guard of marines was kept at the American legation most of the time until April 1896.

1894–1895—China. Marines were stationed at Tientsin and penetrated to Peking for protection purposes during the Sino-Japanese War.

1894–1895—China. Naval vessel beached and used as a fort at Newchwang for protection of American nationals.

1895—Colombia, March 8–9. To protect American interests during an attack on the town of Bocas del Toro by a bandit chieftain.

1896—Nicaragua, May 2–4. To protect American interests in Corinto during political unrest.

1898—Nicaragua, February 7 and 8. To protect American lives and property at San Juan del Sur.

1898—Spain. The Spanish-American War. Fully declared.

1898–1899—China, November 5, 1898–March 15, 1899. To provide a guard for the legation at Peking and the consulate at Tientsin during contest between the Dowager Empress and her son.

1899—Nicaragua. To protect American interests at San Juan del Norte, February 22 to March 5, and at Bluefields a few weeks later in connection with the insurrection of Gen. Juan P. Reyes.

1899—Samoa, March 13–May 15. To protect American interests and to take part in a bloody contention over the succession to the throne.

1899–1901—Philippine Islands. To protect American interests following the war with Spain, and to conquer the island by defeating the Filipinos in their war for independence.

1900—China, May 24–September 28. To protect foreign lives during the Boxer rising, particularly at Peking. For many years after this experience a permanent legation guard was maintained in Peking, and was strengthened at times as trouble threatened. It was still there in 1934.

1901—Colombia (State of Panama), November 20–December 4. To protect American property on the Isthmus and to keep transit lines open during serious revolutionary disturbances.

1902—Colombia, April 16–23. To protect American lives and property at Bocas del Toro during a civil war.

1902—Columbia (State of Panama), September 17–November 18. To place armed guards on all trains crossing the Isthmus and to keep the railroad line open.

1903—Honduras, March 23–30 or 31. To protect the

American consulate and the steamship wharf at Puerto Cortez during a period of revolutionary activity.

1903—Dominican Republic, March 30–April 21. To protect American interests in the city of Santo Domingo during a revolutionary outbreak.

1903—Syria, September 7–12. To protect the American consulate in Beirut when a local Moslem uprising was feared.

1903–1914—Panama. To protect American interests and lives during and following the revolution for independence from Colombia over construction of the Isthmian Canal. With brief intermissions, United States Marines were stationed on the Isthmus from November 4, 1903–January 21, 1914, to guard American interests.

1904—Dominican Republic, January 2–February 11. To protect American interests in Puerto Plata and Sosua and Santo Domingo City during revolutionary fighting.

1904–1905—Korea, January 5, 1904–November 11, 1905. To guard the American Legation in Seoul.

1904—Tangier, Morocco. "We want either Perdicaris alive or Raisuli dead." Demonstration by a squadron to force release of a kidnapped American. Marine guard landed to protect consul general.

1904—Panama, November 17–24. To protect American lives and property at Ancon at the time of a threatened insurrection.

1904–1905—Korea. Marine guard sent to Seoul for protection during Russo-Japanese War.

1906–1909—Cuba, September 1906–January 23, 1909. Intervention to restore order, protect foreigners, and establish a stable government after serious revolutionary activity.

1907—Honduras, March 18–June 8. To protect American interests during a war between Honduras and Nicaragua; troops were stationed for a few days or weeks in Trujillo, Ceiba, Puerto Cortez, San Pedro, Laguna, and Choloma.

1910—Nicaragua, February 22. During a civil war, to

get information of conditions at Corinto; May 19–September 4, to protect American interests at Bluefields.

1911—Honduras, January 26 and some weeks thereafter. To protect American lives and interests during a civil war in Honduras.

1911—China. Approaching stages of the nationalist revolution. An ensign and ten men in October tried to enter Wuchang to rescue missionaries but retired on being warned away. A small landing force guarded American private property and consulate at Hankow in October. A marine guard was established in November over the cable stations at Shanghai. Landing forces were sent for protection to Nanking, Chinkiang, Taku, and elsewhere.

1912—Honduras. Small force landed to prevent seizure by the government of an American-owned railroad at Puerto Cortez. Forces withdrawn after the United States disapproved the action.

1912—Panama. Troops, on request of both political parties, supervised elections outside the Canal Zone.

1912—Cuba, June 5–August 5. To protect American interests in the Province of Oriente, and in Havana.

1912—China, August 24–26, on Kentucky Island, and August 26–30 at Camp Nicholson. To protect Americans and American interests during revolutionary activity.

1912—Turkey, November 18–December 3. To guard the American legation at Constantinople during Balkan War.

1912–1925—Nicaragua, August–November 1912. To protect American interests during an attempted revolution. A small force serving as a legation guard and as a promoter of peace and governmental stability, remained until August 5, 1925.

1912–1941—China. The disorders which began with the Kuomintang rebellion in 1912, which were redirected by the invasion of China by Japan and finally ended by war between Japan and the United States in 1941, led to demonstrations and land parties for protection in China continuously and at many points from 1912 on to 1941.

The guard at Peking and along the route to the sea was maintained until 1941. In 1927, the United States had 5,670 troops ashore in China and 44 naval vessels in its waters. In 1933, we had 3,027 armed men ashore. All this protective action was in general terms based on treaties with China ranging from 1858 to 1901.

1913—Mexico, September 5–7. A few marines landed at Ciaris Estero to aid in evacuating American citizens and others from the Yaqui Valley, made dangerous for foreigners by civil strife.

1914—Haiti, January 29–February 9, February 20–21, October 19. To protect American nationals in a time of dangerous unrest.

1914—Dominican Republic, June and July. During a revolutionary movement, United States naval forces by gunfire stopped the bombardment of Puerto Plata, and by threat of force maintained Santo Domingo City as a neutral zone.

1914–1917—Mexico. The undeclared Mexican-American hostilities following the *Dolphin* affair and Villa's raids included capture of Vera Cruz and later Pershing's expedition into northern Mexico.

1915–1934—Haiti, July 28, 1915–August 15, 1934. To maintain order during a period of chronic and threatened insurrection.

1916–1924—Dominican Republic, May 1916–September 1924. To maintain order during a period of chronic and threatened insurrection.

1917–1918—World War I. Fully declared.

1917–1922—Cuba. To protect American interests during an insurrection and subsequent unsettled conditions. Most of the United States armed forces left Cuba by August 1919, but two companies remained at Camaguey until February 1922.

1918–1919—Mexico. After withdrawal of the Pershing expedition, our troops entered Mexico in pursuit of bandits at least three times in 1918 and six in 1919. In August 1918, American and Mexican troops fought at Nogales.

1918–1920—Panama. For police duty according to treaty stipulations, at Chiriqui, during election disturbances and subsequent unrest.

1918–1920—Soviet Russia. Marines were landed at and near Vladivostok in June and July to protect the American consulate and other points in the fighting between the Bolsheviki troops and the Czech Army which had traversed Siberia from the western front. A joint proclamation of emergency government and neutrality was issued by the American, Japanese, British, French, and Czech commanders in July and our party remained until late August. In August the project expanded. Then 7,000 men were landed in Vladivostok and remained until January 1920, as part of an allied occupation force. In September 1918, 5,000 American troops joined the allied intervention force at Archangel, suffered 500 casualties and remained until June 1919. A handful of marines took part earlier in a British landing on the Murman coast (near Norway) but only incidentally. All these operations were to offset effects of the Bolsheviki revolution in Russia and were partly supported by Czarist or Kerensky elements. No war was declared. Bolsheviki elements participated at times with us but Soviet Russia still claims damages.

1919—Honduras, September 8–12. A landing force was sent ashore to maintain order in a neutral zone during an attempted revolution.

1920–1922—Russia (Siberia), February 16, 1920–November 19, 1922. A marine guard to protect the United States radio station and property on Russian Island, Bay of Vladivostok.

1920—China, March 14. A landing force was sent ashore for a few hours to protect lives during a disturbance at Kiukiang.

1920—Guatemala, April 9–27. To protect the American Legation and other American interests, such as the cable station, during a period of fighting between Unionists and the government of Guatemala.

1921—Panama-Costa Rica. American naval squadrons

demonstrated in April on both sides of the Isthmus to prevent war between the two countries over a boundary dispute.

1922—Turkey, September and October. A landing force was sent ashore with consent of both Greek and Turkish authorities, to protect American lives and property when the Turkish Nationalists entered Smyrna.

1924—Honduras, February 28–March 31, September 10–15. To protect American lives and interests during election hostilities.

1924—China, September. Marines were landed to protect Americans and other foreigners in Shanghai during Chinese factional hostilities.

1925—China, January 15–August 29. Fighting of Chinese factions accompanied by riots and demonstrations in Shanghai necessitated landing American forces to protect lives and property in the International Settlement.

1925—Honduras, April 19–21. To protect foreigners at La Ceiba during a political upheaval.

1925—Panama, October 12–23. Strikes and rent riots led to the landing of about 600 American troops to keep order and protect American interests.

1926–1933—Nicaragua, May 7–June 5, 1926; August 27, 1926–January 3, 1933. The coup d'état of General Chamorro aroused revolutionary activities leading to the landing of American marines to protect the interests of the United States. United States forces came and went, but seem not to have left the country entirely until January 3, 1933. Their work included activity against the outlaw leader Sandino in 1928.

1926—China, August and September. The Nationalist attack on Hankow necessitated the landing of American naval forces to protect American citizens. A small guard was maintained at the consulate general even after September 16, when the rest of the forces were withdrawn. Likewise, when Nationalist forces captured Kiukiang, naval forces were landed for the protection of foreigners November 4–6.

1927—China, February. Fighting at Shanghai caused American naval forces and marines to be increased there. In March, a naval guard was stationed at the American consulate at Nanking after Nationalist forces captured the city. American and British destroyers later used shell fire to protect Americans and other foreigners. "Following this incident additional forces of marines and naval vessels were ordered to China and stationed in the vicinity of Shanghai and Tientsin."

1933—Cuba. During a revolution against President Gerardo Machado naval forces demonstrated but no landing was made.

1940—Newfoundland, Bermuda, St. Lucia, Bahamas, Jamaica, Antigua, Trinidad, and British Guiana. Troops were sent to guard air and naval bases obtained by negotiation with Great Britain. These were sometimes called lend-lease bases.

1941—Greenland. Taken under protection of the United States in April.

1941—Netherlands (Dutch Guiana). In November, the President ordered American troops to occupy Dutch Guiana but by agreement with the Netherlands government in exile. Brazil cooperated to protect aluminum ore supply from the bauxite mines in Surinam.

1941—Iceland. Taken under the protection of the United States, with consent of its Government, for strategic reasons.

1941—Germany. Sometime in the spring the President ordered the Navy to patrol ship lanes to Europe. By July, our warships were convoying and by September were attacking German submarines. There was no authorization of Congress or declaration of war. In November, the Neutrality Act was partly repealed to protect military aid to Britain, Russia, etc.

1941–1945—Germany, Italy, Japan, etc. World War II. Fully declared.

1942—Labrador. Army-Navy air bases established.

Just as in 1962 Secretary Rusk presented the list of American interventions to justify President Kennedy's possible use of force against Cuba, so on June 23, 1969, Senator Everett Dirksen reinserted the list in the Congressional Record *to justify opposition to Congressional restraints on such actions.*

"One need only look," said Dirksen, "at the history of the use of force by the President, in his capacity as Commander in Chief, to see how many instances there have been where, for one reason or another, it had to be used."

The Dirksen list included four instances of intervention not carried in the Rusk list: "1950—Korean action; 1957—Lebanon; 1962—Cuba; 1964—Vietnam." Missing from the Dirksen insertion were the use of U.S. troops in Berlin from 1947 to the present day; in Guatemala in 1954; against Cuba in 1961, when the Air Force and Navy were involved; in the Dominican Republic in 1965. And a year after Senator Dirksen made his presentation to Congress, U.S. troops were sent into Cambodia, setting off one of the worst domestic crises in the history of the United States.

BIBLIOGRAPHY

The African Repository and Colonial Journal. Washington: Vol. XXII, No. 2. February, 1846.

Aguinaldo, General Emilio, and Albano, Vicente. *A Second Look at America.* New York: Robert Speller & Sons, Publishers, 1957.

Alexander, Arthur C. *Koloa Plantation, 1835–1935.* Honolulu: 1937.

Allen, Gwenfread. *Hawaii's War Years, 1941–45.* Honolulu: University of Hawaii Press, 1950.

American Friends Service Committee. *An Uncommon Controversy.* Published by the National Congress of American Indians, 1967.

Anderson, Robert William. *Party Politics in Puerto Rico.* Stanford: Stanford University Press, 1965.

Anderson, Major William H. *The Philippine Problem.* New York: G. P. Putnam's Sons, 1939.

Andrews, Charles M. *Colonial Period of American History.* New Haven: Yale University Press, 1934.

Annals of the American Academy of Political and Social Science, Vol. XXVIV, No. 2, September, 1909.

Aptheker, Herbert. *Nat Turner's Slave Rebellion: The Environment, The Event, The Effects.* New York: The Humanities Press, 1966.

"One Continual Cry": David Walker's Appeal to the Colored Citizens of the World: Its Setting and its Meaning. New York: The Humanities Press, 1965.

Asiatic Exclusion League. *Proceedings of the Asiatic Exclusion League.* San Francisco, January, 1909.

Bailey, Thomas A., ed. *The American Spirit—United States History as Seen by Contemporaries.* Boston: D. C. Heath & Co., 1963 & 1968.

Ball, Charles. *Fifty Years in Chains.* New York: H. Dayton, Publisher, 1859.

Bancroft, Frederic. *Slave Trading in the Old South.* New York: Frederick Ungar Publishing Co., 1959.

Bardolph, Richard. *The Negro Vanguard.* New York: Vintage Books, 1961.

Barth, Gunther. *Bitter Strength.* Cambridge, Mass.: Harvard University Press, 1964.

Beard, Charles A. *An Economic Interpretation of the Constitution of the United States.* New York: Macmillan Co., 1956.

Beatty, Willard W. *Education for Cultural Change.* Chilocco, Okla.: U.S. Department of the Interior, Bureau of Indian Affairs, 1953.

Beckett, Y. B. *Baca's Battle.* Houston: Stagecoach Press, 1962.

Bell, Irvin Wiley. "Out of the Mouths of Ex-Slaves." *Journal of Negro History,* Vol. XX, July, 1935.

Bennett, Lerone. *Before the Mayflower: A History of the Negro in America, 1619–1964.* Revised. Baltimore: Penguin Books, 1966.

Bishop, Rev. Artemas. "An Inquiry Into the Causes of Decrease in the Population of the Sandwich Islands." *The Hawaiian Spectator,* January, 1838.

Boddy, E. Manchester. *Japanese in America.* Los Angeles: published by author, 1921.

Bosworth, Allan R. *America's Concentration Camps.* New York: W. W. Norton and Co., 1967.

Brainerd, Cephas, and Warner, Eveline, eds. *New England Society Orations,* Vol. II. New York: The Century Co., 1901.

Brameld, Theodore. *The Remaking of a Culture.* New York: Harper & Bros., 1959.

Breitman, George, ed. *Malcolm X Speaks: Selected Writings and Statements.* New York: Grove Press, 1965.

Brown, Henry Box. *The Narrative of Henry Box Brown: Written by a Statement of Facts Made by Himself.* Boston: Brown & Stearns Publishers, 1849.

Brown, Wenzell. *Dynamite on Our Doorstep.* New York: Greenberg Publishers, 1945.

Bruce, John E. "Concentration of Energy." In the *Arthur B. Spingarn Collection of Negro Literature* at Howard University. Washington, D.C.

Bulosan, Carlos. *Sound of Falling Light: Letters in Exile.* Edited by Dolores S. Feria. Quezon City, The Philippines: 1960.

Burma, John A. *Spanish Speaking Groups in the United States.* Chapel Hill: Duke University Press, 1954.

Calderon, Enrique. *El Dolor de un Pueblo Esclavo.* New York: Azteca Press, 1950.

California Citizens Committee on Civil Disturbances in Los Angeles. *Report and Recommendations,* June 12, 1943.

California, Department of Industrial Relations, San Francisco. *Facts About Filipino Immigration into California,* April, 1930.

California, State Board of Health, Sacramento. *First Biennial Report, 1870–71.*

California Historical Society. *Neville Scrapbook,* Vol. 7, July, 1877.

Cash, W. J. *The Mind of the South.* Garden City, New York: Doubleday & Co., Inc., 1941.

Catterall, Mrs. Helen H., ed. *Judicial Cases Concerning Slavery and the American Negro.* Washington, D.C.: The Carnegie Institution of Washington, 1937.

Cayton, Horace. *Long Old Road.* New York: Trident Press, 1965.

Chai, Ch'u, and Chai, Winberg. *The Changing Society of China.* New York: Mentor Books, 1962.

Chief Flying Hawk. "The True Story of Custer's Last Fight." As told to M. I. McCreight (Tchanta Tanka). In *Chief Flying Hawk's Tales*. New York: Alliance Press, 1936.

Chinn, Thomas W., ed. *A History of the Chinese in California: A Syllabus*. San Francisco: Chinese Historical Society of America, 1969.

Chui, Ping. *Chinese Labor in California.* Madison, Wis.: State Historical Society of Wisconsin, University of Wisconsin Press, 1963.

Clark, Victor S. et. al. *Puerto Rico and Its Problems.* Washington, D.C.: The Brookings Institution, 1930.

Cochran, Thomas. *The Puerto Rican Businessman.* Philadelphia: The University of Pennsylvania Press, 1959.

Cohen, Felix. *The Handbook of Federal Indian Law.* Washington, D.C.: U.S. Government Printing Office, 1942.

Collier, John. *On the Gleaming Way.* Denver: Sage Books, Inc., 1962.

Commager, Henry Steele, ed. *Documents of American History.* New York: Appleton-Century-Crofts, Inc., 1958.

Communist Party of Puerto Rico. *The Case of Puerto Rico: Memorandum to the United Nations.* New York: New Century Publishers, 1953.

Conroy, Hilary. *The Japanese Frontier in Hawaii, 1868–1898.* Berkeley: The University of California Press, 1953.

Cook, James, and King, James. *A Voyage to the Pacific Ocean,* Vol. II. London: G. Nichol and T. Cadell Publishers, 1785.

Coolidge, Mary Roberts. *Chinese Immigration.* New York: Henry Holt & Co., 1909.

Corpuz, Onofre D. *The Philippines.* Englewood Cliffs, N.J.: Prentice-Hall Co., 1966.

Corretjer, Juan Antonio. *La Lucha por la Independencia de Puerto Rico.* San Juan, P. R.: Publicaciones de Union del Pueblo pro Constituyente, 1949.

Crichton, Kyle S. *Law and Order, Ltd.* Santa Fe, N.M.: New Mexican Publishing Co., 1928.

Cronon, Edmund David. *Black Moses.* Madison, Wisc.: University of Wisconsin Press, 1955.

Cross, Ira B. *A History of the Labor Movement in California.* Berkeley: University of California Press, 1935.

Cruse, Harold. *Crisis of the Negro Intellectual.* New York: W. R. Morrow & Co., 1967.

Culin, Stewart. "Chinese Secret Societies in the United States." *Journal of American Folklore,* July, 1890.

Cunningham, J. C. *The Truth About Murieta.* Los Angeles: Wetzel Publishing Co., 1938.

Current, Richard N., ed. *Reconstruction.* Englewood Cliffs, N.J.: Prentice-Hall Publishing Co., 1965.

Curtin, Philip D. *Africa Remembered: Narratives by West Africans from the Era of the Slave Trade*. Madison, Wisc.: University of Wisconsin Press, 1967.

Davis, David Brion. *The Problem of Slavery in Western Culture*. Ithaca, N.Y.: Cornell University Press, 1966.

Daws, Gavan. *The Shoal of Time*. New York: Macmillan Co., 1968.

Day, A. Grove, and Stroven, Carl, eds. *A Hawaiian Reader*. New York: Popular Library, 1961.

deBar, Gabriella. *José Vasconcelos and His World*. New York: Las Americas Publishing Co., 1966.

Delany, Martin R. *The Condition, Elevation, Emigration, and Destiny of the Colored Race*. Philadelphia: published by the author, 1852.

Diffie, Bailey W., and Whitfield, Justine. *Puerto Rico: A Broken Pledge*. New York: The Vanguard Press, 1931.

Dillon, Richard H. *The Hatchet Men*. New York: Coward McCann Publishing Co., 1962.

Dobie, Charles Caldwell. *San Francisco's Chinatown*. New York: D. Appleton-Century Co., 1936.

Dobie, J. Frank. *The Flavor of Texas*. Dallas: Dealey & Lowe Publishing Co., 1936.

Documents on the Constitutional History of Puerto Rico. Washington, D.C.: Office of the Commonwealth of Puerto Rico, 1948.

Donnan, Elizabeth. *Documents Illustrative of the History of the Slave Trade to America*. Washington, D.C.: The Carnegie Institution of Washington, 1935.

Downey, Fairfax. *Indian Wars of the United States Army, 1776–1865*. Garden City, N.Y.: Doubleday & Co., 1963.

Du Bois, William Edward Burghardt. *Black Reconstruction in America: An Essay Toward a History of the Part Which Black Folk Played in the Attempt to Reconstruct Democracy in America, 1860–1880*. Cleveland, Ohio: World Publishing Co., 1964.

Dusk of Dawn. New York: Schocken Books, 1968.

The Souls of Black Folk. Chicago: A. C. McClurg & Co., 1909.

El Grito: A Journal of Contemporary Mexican-American Thought. Berkeley: Quinto Sol Publications, Inc.

Elkins, Stanley. *Slavery: A Problem in American Institutional and Intellectual Life*. New York: Grosset & Dunlap, 1959.

Evans, Maurice. *Black and White in the Southern States*. London: Longmans, Green & Co., 1915.

Farb, Peter. *Man's Rise to Civilization*. New York: E. P. Dutton & Co., 1968.

Felt, Joseph B. *History of Ipswich, Essex and Hamilton*. Cambridge, Mass.: Charles Folsom Co., 1834.

Fergusson, Erna. *Our Southwest*. New York: Alfred Knopf, 1940.

Fiedler, Leslie. *The Return of the Vanishing American.* New York: Stein & Day, 1968.

Filipino Students Magazine, April, 1905.

Fisk University Social Science Institute. "Orientals and Their Cultural Adjustments." Nashville, Tennessee: 1946.

Fiske, John. *The Beginnings of New England.* Boston: Houghton Mifflin Co., 1889.

Fitzhugh, George. *Cannibals All! or Slaves Without Masters.* Cambridge, Mass.: Belknap Press of Harvard University, 1960.

Fleagle, Fred K. *Social Problems in Puerto Rico.* New York: D. C. Heath & Co., 1917.

Fogel, Walter. "Job Gains of Mexican-American Men." *The Monthly Labor Review,* October, 1968.

Foner, Philip D. *History of the Labor Movement in the United States,* Vol. III. New York: International Publishers, 1955.

Forbes, W. Cameron. *The Philippine Islands.* Cambridge, Mass.: Harvard University Press, 1945.

Fortune. "The Negro and the City." January, 1968.

Frank Waldo. "Puerto Rico and Psychosis," *The Nation,* March 13, 1954.

Franklin, John Hope, and Starr, Isidore, eds. *The Negro in 20th Century America.* New York: Vintage Books, Inc., 1967.

Fuchs, Lawrence H. *Hawaii Pono: A Social History.* New York: Harcourt, Brace & World, Inc., 1961.

Garvey, Marcus. *Marcus Garvey: Philosophy and Opinions.* New York: Universal Publishing Co., 1925.

Gates, W. Almont. *Oriental Immigration on the Pacific Coast.* Bound in *Pamphlets on Japanese Exclusion.* Berkeley: Phelan Collection of the University of California.

Genovese, Eugene. *The Political Economy of Slavery.* New York: Pantheon Books, 1965.

"The Legacy of Slavery and the Roots of Black Nationalism." *Studies on the Left,* Vol. 6, No. 6, 1966.

Giddings, Joshua. *The Exiles of Florida.* Gainesville, Fla.: University of Florida Press, 1964.

Glick, Clarence. *The Chinese Migrant in Hawaii.* Ann Arbor, Mich.: University Microfilms, Inc.

Golden, Harry. *Forgotten Pioneer.* Cleveland: World Publishing Co., 1963.

Goldfinch, Charles W. *Juan Cortina, 1824–1892: A Re-appraisal.* Brownsville, Texas: Bishop's Print Shop, 1950.

Goldman, Eric. *Rendezvous with Destiny.* New York: Vintage Press, 1958.

Gong, Eng Ying, and Grant, Bruce. *Tong War!* New York: Nicholas L. Brown Publishing Co., 1930.

Gonzalez, Nancie L. "The Spanish-Americans of New Mexico, a Distinctive Heritage." In *Mexican-American Study Project, Ad-*

vance Report, No. 9. Los Angeles: University of California, 1967.

Goveia, Elsa V. *Slave Society in the British Leeward Islands at the End of the 18th Century*. New Haven: Yale University Press, 1965.

Grant, Joanne. *Black Protest: Documents, History and Analysis from 1619 to the Present*. New York: Premier Fawcett, Fawcett World Library, 1968.

Greenway, John. "Will the Indians Get Whitey?" *National Review*, March 11, 1969.

Greenwood, Robert. *The California Outlaw*. Los Gatos, Calif.: The Talisman Press, 1960.

Griffith, Beatrice, *American Me*. New York: Houghton Mifflin Co., 1948.

Griswold, A. Whitney. *Far Eastern Policy of the United States*. New York: Harcourt, Brace & Co., 1938.

Gruening, Ernest. *Mexico and Its Heritage*. New York: The Century Co., 1928.

Gulick, Rev. and Mrs. Orramel Hinckley. *Pilgrims of Hawaii*. New York and Chicago: Fleming H. Revell Co., 1918.

Guzman, Ralph. *The Function of Ideology in the Process of Political Socialization: An Example in Terms of the Mexican-American People Living in the Southwest*. Unpublished manuscript, August, 1966.

Hackett, Charles William. *Revolt of the Pueblo Indians of New Mexico and Oterman's Attempted Reconquest, 1680–82*. Translation of original documents by Chairman Clair Shelby. Albuquerque, N.M.: University of New Mexico Press, 1942.

Hagan, William T. *Indian Police and Judges*. New Haven: Yale University Press, 1966.

Hanson, Earl Parker. *Puerto Rico: Land of Wonders*. New York: Alfred A. Knopf, 1960.

Hapgood, Hutchins. *A Victorian in the Modern World*. New York: Harcourt, Brace, 1939.

Harada, Tasaku, ed. *The Japanese Problem in California*. Printed for private circulation. San Francisco.

Harap, Louis, and Reddick, L. D. *Should Negroes and Jews Unite?* Negro Publication Society of America, 1943.

Heller, Celia S. *Mexican-American Youth*. New York: Random House, 1967.

Higham, John. *Strangers in the Land: Patterns of American Nativism, 1860–1925*. New York: Atheneum, 1963.

Hofstadter, Richard. *The American Political Tradition*. New York: Alfred A. Knopf, 1948.

Holt, John Dominis. *On Being Hawaiian*. Honolulu: Star-Bulletin Publishing Co., 1964.

Hoy, William. *The Chinese Six Companies.* San Francisco: Chinese Consolidated Benevolent Association, 1942.

Hughes, Langston, and Meltzer, Milton. *A Pictorial History of the Negro in America.* New York: Crown Publishing Co., 1956.

Hughes, Louis. *Thirty Years a Slave: Autobiography of Louis Hughes.* Milwaukee: South Side Printing Co., 1897.

Ichihashi, Yamato. *Japanese in the United States.* Stanford: Stanford University Press, 1932.

Iyenago, T., and Sato, Kenoske. *Japan and the California Problem.* New York: G. P. Putnam's Sons, 1921.

Jackson, Helen Hunt. *A Century of Dishonor.* Reprint. Minneapolis: Ross and Haines, Inc., 1964.

Jane, Cecil, trans. *Journal of Christopher Columbus.* New York: Clarkson N. Potter Publishing Co., 1960.

Japanese Relocation Papers. Bancroft Library, University of California, Berkeley.

Jay, William. *Causes and Consequences of the Mexican War.* Boston: Benjamin G. Mussey & Co., 1849.

Jenkins, William Sumner. *Proslavery Thought in the Old South.* Chapel Hill: University of North Carolina Press, 1935.

Jennings, John E. *Our American Tropics.* New York: Thomas Y. Crowell Co., 1962.

Johnson, Herbert B., D. D. *Discrimination Against Japanese in California: A Review of the Real Situation.* Berkeley: Press of the Courier Publishing Co., 1907.

Johnson, James Weldon. *Along This Way.* New York: Viking Press, 1933.

Black Manhattan. New York: Arno Press, 1968.

Jordan, Winthrop D. *White over Black.* Chapel Hill: University of North Carolina Press, 1968.

Josephy, Alvin M., Jr. *The Indian Heritage of America.* New York: Alfred A. Knopf, 1968.

The Nez Percé Indians and the Opening of the Northwest. New Haven: Yale University Press, 1955.

Kalaw, Maximo M. *The Case for the Filipinos.* New York: The Century Co., 1916.

Kamakau, S. M. *The Ruling Chiefs of Hawaii.* Honolulu: Kamehameha Schools Press, 1961.

Kardiner, Abram, and Ovesey, Lionel. *The Mark of Oppression: Explorations in the Personality of the American Negro.* Cleveland: World Publishing Co., 1962.

Katz, Shlomo, ed. *Negro and Jew, An Encounter in America.* New York: Macmillan Co., 1966.

Kawakami, K. K. *The Real Japanese Question.* New York: Macmillan Co., 1921.

Kelly, Marion. "Changes in Land Tenure in Hawaii." Unpublished M.A. thesis, University of Hawaii, Honolulu: 1956.

Korngold, Ralph. *Two Friends of Man.* Boston: Little Brown & Co., 1950.

Kraditor, Aileen S. *Means and Ends in American Abolitionism: Garrison and His Critics on Strategy and Tactics, 1834–50.* New York: Pantheon Books, 1967.

Kung, Shien-Woo. *Chinese in American Life.* Seattle: University of Washington Press, 1962.

Kuykendall, Ralph S. *The Hawaiian Kingdom, 1778–1854.* Honolulu: University of Hawaii, 1947.

Lam, Margaret M. "Racial Myth and Family Tradition-Worship Among the Part-Hawaiians." *Social Forces,* Vol. 14, No. 3, March, 1936.

Lasker, Bruno. *Filipino Immigration.* Chicago: University of Chicago Press, 1931.

Lee, Calvin. *Chinatown U.S.A.* Garden City, N.Y.: Doubleday & Co., 1965.

Lee, Rose Hum. *Chinese in the U.S.A.* Hong Kong: Hong Kong University Press, 1960.

Leiris, Michael. *Race and Culture.* Paris: UNESCO, 1958.

Lewis, Gordon. *Puerto Rico: Freedom and Power in the Caribbean.* New York: M. R. Press, 1963.

Lewis, Oscar. "The Culture of Poverty." *Scientific American,* Vol. 215, No. 4, October, 1966.

"Culture of Poverty or Poverty of Culture." *Monthly Review,* Vol. 19, No. 4, September, 1967.

La Vida: A Puerto Rican Family in the Culture of Poverty—San Juan and New York. New York: Random House, 1965.

Lewis, Tracy Hammond. *Along the Rio Grande.* New York: Lewis Publishing Co., 1916.

Liebow, Elliot. *Tally's Corner: A Study of Negro Streetcorner Men.* Boston: Little, Brown & Co., 1967.

Life of Joaquin Murieta, The Brigand Chief of California. San Francisco: Butler & Co., 1859.

Life of Kinzaburo Makino. Edited by the Compilation Committee for the Publication of Kinzaburo Makino's Biography. Printed in Japan: 1965.

Liliuokalani, Queen. *Hawaii Story by Hawaii's Queen.* Rutland, Vt. and Tokyo, Japan: Charles E. Tuttle Co., 1964.

Lincoln, C. Eric. *The Black Muslims in America.* Boston: Beacon Press, 1961.

Lind, Andrew W. *Modern Hawaii.* Honolulu: University of Hawaii Press, 1967.

Lloyd, B. E. *Lights and Shades in San Francisco.* San Francisco: A. L. Bancroft and Co., 1876.

Locke, Mary. *Antislavery in America.* Chapel Hill: University of North Carolina Press, 1961.

Los Angeles City Schools, Division of Instructional Services. *Angelenos Then and Now*. Publication No. EC—226, 1966.

Lyman, Stanford Morris. *The Structure of Chinese Society in 19th Century America*. Unpublished Ph.D. thesis, University of California, Berkeley: 1961.

McCague, James. *The Second Rebellion: The New York City Draft Riots of 1863*. New York: Dial Press, 1968.

McKee, Ruth E. *California and Her Less Favored Minorities*. Washington: War Relocation Authority, April, 1944.

McKenzie, R. D. *Oriental Exclusion*. Chicago: University of Chicago Press, 1928.

McReynolds, Edwin C. *The Seminoles*. Norman, Okla.: University of Oklahoma Press, 1957.

McWilliams, Carey. *Prejudice: Japanese-Americans, Symbol of Racial Intolerance*. Boston: Little, Brown & Co., 1944.

North from Mexico. Philadelphia: J. B. Lippincott Co., 1949.

Malcolm X Speaks: Selected Writings and Statements. Edited and with prefatory notes by George Breitman. New York: Grove Press, 1965.

Malo, David. *Letters*. In the Archives of the State of Hawaii, Honolulu.

"On the Decrease of Population in the Hawaiian Islands." Translated by L. Andrews. Honolulu: *The Hawaiian Spectator,* Vol. II, No. 2, April, 1839.

Malone, Dumas, and Rauch, Basil. *Empire for Liberty*. New York: Appleton-Century-Crofts, 1960.

Mannix, Daniel P. *Black Cargoes*. New York: Viking Press, 1962.

Mears, E. G. *Resident Orientals on the American Pacific Coast: Their Legal and Economic Status*. Chicago: University of Chicago Press, 1928.

Meier, August. *Negro Thought in America, 1880–1915: Racial Ideologies in the Age of Booker T. Washington*. Ann Arbor: University of Michigan Press, 1966.

Merriam, George S. *The Negro and the Nation*. New York: Henry Holt & Co., 1906.

Miller, Stuart Creighton. *The Unwelcome Immigrant: The American Image of the Chinese, 1785–1882*. Berkeley and Los Angeles: University of California Press, 1969.

Millis, H. A. *Japanese Problem in the United States*. New York: Macmillan Company, 1915.

Mills, C. Wright; Senior, Clarence; and Goldsen, Rose Kohn. *The Puerto Rican Journey*. Reissue. New York: Russell and Russell, 1967.

Miyamoto, Kazuo. *Hawaii, End of the Rainbow*. Bridgeway Press, 1964.

Moorehead, Alan. *The Fatal Impact: An Account of the Invasion of the South Pacific, 1767–1840*. New York: Harper & Row, 1966.

Morley, Charles, trans. "Sienkiewicz on Chinese in California." *California Historical Society Quarterly*, Vol. 34, 1955.

Morison, Samuel Eliot. *Oxford History of the American People*. New York: Oxford University Press, 1965.

Murphy, Thomas D. *Ambassadors in Arms*. Honolulu: University of Hawaii Press, 1954.

Myrdal, Gunnar. *An American Dilemma: The Negro Problem and Modern Democracy*. New York and London: Harper & Bros., 1944.

Nichi Bei Times, San Francisco.

Nichols, Charles H. "Slave Narratives." *Negro History Bulletin*, March, 1952.

Nolen, Claude H. *Negro's Image in the South*. Lexington, Ky.: University of Kentucky Press, 1967.

O'Gorman, Edmundo. *The Invention of America*. Bloomington, Ind.: Indiana University Press, 1961.

Okubo, Mine, *Citizen* 13660. New York: AMS Press, Inc., 1966.

Okumura, Takie, and Okumura, Umetaro. "Hawaii's American-Japanese Problem, Report of the Campaign, 1921–1927." [No citation of publisher or date.]

Olmsted, Frederick Law. *The Cotton Kingdom: A Traveller's Observations on Cotton and Slavery in the American Slave States*. New York: Alfred A. Knopf, 1953.

A Journey in the Seaboard Slave States. New York: Dix & Edwards, 1856.

Osofsky, Gilbert. *The Burden of Race: A Documentary History of Negro-White Relations in America*. New York: Harper & Row, 1967.

Ozawa, Takao v. United States, 260 U.S. 178 (1922).

Paredes, Américo. *With His Pistol in His Hand*. Austin: University of Texas Press, 1958.

Parton, James. *The Life of Andrew Jackson*. New York: Mason Bros., 1860.

People v. George W. Hall, 4 Cal. 399 (1854).

Petersen, William. "Success Story, Japanese-American Style." *The New York Times Magazine*, January 9, 1966.

Petrullo, Vincenzo. *Puerto Rican Paradox*. Philadelphia: University of Pennsylvania Press, 1947.

Phillips, Ulrich B. *American Negro Slavery*. Baton Rouge: Louisiana State University Press, 1918.

Pier, Arthur S. *American Apostles to the Philippines*. Boston: The Beacon Press, 1950.

Pitt, Leonard. *The Decline of the Californios*. Berkeley: University of California Press, 1966.

Polanco, Vicente Géigel. *El Despertar de un Pueblo*. San Juan,

Puerto Rico: Biblioteca de Autores Puertorriqueños, 1942.

Porter, Dorothy B. "Sarah Parker Remond, Abolitionist and Physician." *Journal of Negro History,* Vol. XX, No. 3, July, 1935.

Pratt, Julius W. *Expansionists of 1898.* Baltimore: The Johns Hopkins Press, 1936.

Quarles, Benjamin. *The Negro in the Civil War.* Boston: Little, Brown & Co., 1953.

The Negro in the American Revolution. Chapel Hill: University of North Carolina Press, 1961.

Negro in the Making of America. New York: Macmillan Co., 1964.

Rand, Christopher. *The Puerto Ricans.* New York: Oxford University Press, 1958.

Reid, Whitelaw. *Problems of Expansion.* New York: The Century Co., 1900.

Richardson, Lewis C. *Puerto Rico: Caribbean Crossroads.* New York: U.S. Camera Publishing Corp., 1947.

Robinson, Alfred. *Life in California During a Residence of Several Years in that Territory.* San Francisco: W. Doxey Co., 1891.

Rogers, Joel Augustus. *Sex and Race.* New York: Rogers Pub. Co., 1941–44.

Romanell, Patrick. *Making of the Mexican Mind.* Lincoln: University of Nebraska Press, 1952.

Roosevelt, Theodore. *Presidential Messages and State Papers.* New York: Review of Reviews Company, 1910.

Ross, Arthur M., and Hill, Herbert, eds. *Employment, Race and Poverty.* Harcourt, Brace & World, 1967.

Rowan, Helen. "A Minority Nobody Knows." *The Atlantic Monthly,* June, 1967.

Royce, Josiah. *California, A Study of American Character.* New York: Alfred A. Knopf & Co., 1948.

Samora, Julian, *La Raza: Forgotten Americans.* Notre Dame, Ind.: University of Notre Dame Press, 1966.

Saxton, Alexander Plaisted. *The Indispensable Enemy: A Study of the Anti-Chinese Movement in California.* Unpublished Ph.D. thesis, University of California, Berkeley: 1967.

Sayre, J. G. "More Chinese Atrocities." *The Nation,* August 10, 1927.

Scheer, Robert, ed. *Eldridge Cleaver: Post-Prison Writings and Speeches.* New York: Random House, 1969.

Schlesinger, Arthur M. *The Rise of Modern America.* New York: Macmillan Co., 1951.

The Age of Jackson. Boston: Little, Brown & Co., 1945.

Senior, Clarence. *The Puerto Ricans: Strangers—Then Neighbors.* Chicago: Quadrangle Books, Inc., 1961.

Seward, George F. *Chinese Immigration in Its Social and Economic Aspects.* New York: Charles Scribner's Sons, 1881.

Sexton, Patricia Cayo. *Spanish Harlem*. New York: Harper & Row, 1965.

Simpson, G. E., and Yinger, J. M. *Racial and Cultural Minorities*. New York: Harper & Row, 1953.

Smith, Bradford. *Americans from Japan*. Philadelphia & New York: J. B. Lippincott, 1948.

Smith, Robert F. *The United States and Cuba*. New York: Bookman Associates, 1960.

Smith, William Henry. *A Political History of Slavery*. New York: G. P. Putnam's Sons, 1903.

Smyth, Albert Henry, ed. *The Works of Benjamin Franklin*. New York: Macmillan Co., 1905.

Smyth, George B. "Causes of anti-Foreign Feeling in China." *The Crisis in China*. New York: The North American Review, 1900.

Social Process in Hawaii. Published jointly by the Romanzo Adams Social Research Laboratory and the Sociology Club of Hawaii. Honolulu.

Soyeda, J., and Kamiya, T. *A Survey of the Japanese Question in California*. San Francisco: 1913.

Sparks, Jared, ed. *The Works of Benjamin Franklin*. Boston: Hilliard, Gray & Co., 1836.

Spears, John Randolph. *The American Slave Trade*. New York: Charles Scribner's Sons, 1900.

Stampp, Kenneth M. *The Peculiar Institution: Slavery in the Antebellum South*. New York: Vintage Books, 1956.

The Causes of the Civil War. Edited by Kenneth M. Stampp. Englewood, N.J.: Prentice-Hall, Inc., 1959.

The Era of Reconstruction, 1865–1877. New York: Alfred A. Knopf Co., 1965.

Steiner, Stan. *The New Indians*. New York: Harper & Row, 1968.

Storey, Moorfield, and Lichauco, Marcial P. *The Conquest of the Philippines by the United States 1898–1925*. New York: G. P. Putnam's Sons, 1926.

Sullivan, Josephine. *A History of C. Brewer & Co., Ltd.: One Hundred Years in the Hawaiian Islands, 1826–1926*. Boston: 1926.

Sung, B. L. *The Mountain of Gold: The Story of the Chinese in America*. New York: The Macmillan Co., 1967.

Sun Yat-sen et al., eds. *Sources of Chinese Tradition*. New York: Columbia University Press, 1960.

Sydnor, Charles S. *Slavery in Mississippi*. Gloucester, Mass.: P. Smith, 1965.

Taylor, George E. *The Philippines and the United States: Problems of Partnership*. Published for the Council on Foreign Relations. New York: Frederick A. Praeger Co., 1964.

Tebbel, John, and Jennison, Keith. *The American Indian Wars*. New York: Harper & Row, 1960.

ten Broek, Jacobus; Barnhart, Edward N.; and Matson, Floyd.

Prejudice, War and the Constitution. Berkeley and Los Angeles: University of California Press, 1954.

Thomas, Dorothy Swaine; Kikuchi, Charles; and Sakoda, James. *The Salvage.* Berkeley and Los Angeles: University of California Press, 1952.

Thomas, Dorothy Swaine, and Nishimoto, Richard S. *The Spoilage.* Berkeley and Los Angeles: University of California Press, 1946.

Thomas, Piri. *Down These Mean Streets.* New York: Alfred A. Knopf, 1967.

Trumbull, Henry. *History of the Indian Wars.* Boston: George Clark Co., 1841.

Tuck, Ruth. *Not With the Fist.* New York: Harcourt, Brace, 1946.

Tugwell, Rexford Guy. *The Stricken Land: The Story of Puerto Rico.* Garden City, N.Y.: Doubleday & Co., Inc., 1947.

United States Army, Western Defense Command and Fourth Army. *Final Report: Japanese Evacuation from the West Coast.* Washington, D.C.: Government Printing Office, 1943.

U.S., Congress. *American State Papers.* Class V. Vol. VI. Washington. Gales and Seaton, 1832–61.

U.S., Congress. *Hearings of the Select Committee Investigating National Defense Migration.* San Francisco, Feb. 21–22, 1942. 77th Cong., 2nd sess., part 29.

U.S., Congress, House. *Hearings before Subcommittee No. 5 of the Committee on the Judiciary.* 83rd Cong., 2nd sess., 1954.

U.S., Congress, House. *House Executive Documents.* 48th Cong., 1st sess., 1883–84, Vol. II.

U.S., Congress, House. *Depredations on the Frontiers of Texas: House Executive Documents.* 42nd Cong., 3rd sess., 1872–73, Vol. VII.

U.S., Congress, House. *Difficulties on Southwestern Frontier: House Executive Documents.* 36th Cong., 1st sess., 1859–60, Vol. VIII, No. 52.

U.S., Congress, House. *Troubles on Texas Frontier: House Executive Documents.* 36th Cong., 1st sess., 1859–60, Vol. XII, No. 81.

U.S., Congress, House. *Texas Frontier Troubles: House of Representatives Reports.* 44th Cong., 1st sess., 1876–77, Vol. II, No. 343.

U.S., Congress, Senate. *Report of the Joint Special Committee to Investigate Chinese Immigration: Senate Document No. 689.* 44th Cong., 2nd sess., February 27, 1877.

U.S., Congress. *Senate Report No. 1664.* 89th Cong., 2nd sess.

U.S., Department of the Interior, Annual Reports of the Commissioner of Indian Affairs.

United States Federal Writers Project. "Unionization of Filipinos in California Agriculture." Bancroft Library, University of California, Berkeley.

Vasconcelos, José. *Aspects of Mexican Civilization.* Chicago: University of Chicago Press, 1926.
Mexican Ulysses. Translated and abridged by W. R. Crawford. Bloomington, Ind.: Indiana University Press, 1963.
Vivas, José Luis. *Historia de Puerto Rico.* New York: Las Americas Publishing Co., 1960.
Vogel, Virgil J. *The Indian in American History.* Chicago: Integrated Education Associates, 1968.
Walker, David. *David Walker's Appeal to the Colored Citizens of the World, 1829–30.* Published for the American Institute for Marxist Studies. New York: Humanities Press, 1965.
Waskow, Arthur I. *From Race Riot to Sit-in.* Garden City, N.Y.: Doubleday & Co., 1966.
Webb, Walter Prescott. *The Texas Rangers.* Boston: Houghton Mifflin & Co., 1935.
Weinberg, Alfred Katz. *Manifest Destiny: A Study of Nationalist Expansion in American History.* Baltimore: Johns Hopkins Press, 1935.
Wheeler, Col. Homer W. *Buffalo Days.* New York & Chicago: A. L. Burt, Publishers, 1923.
White, Mary Frances. "Wewoka and the Seminoles." *Journal of the Daughters of the American Revolution,* February, 1967.
White, Owen P. *Them Was the Days.* New York: Minton, Balch & Co., 1925.
White, Trumbull. *Puerto Rico and Its People.* New York: Frederick A. Stokes Co., 1938.
Whitfield, Theodore M. *Slavery Agitation in Virginia.* Baltimore: Johns Hopkins Press, 1930.
Williams, Eric. *Capitalism and Slavery.* London: Andre Deutsch Co., 1914.
Williams, Robert F. *Negroes with Guns.* Marc Schleifer, ed. New York: Marzani and Munsell, 1962.
Williams, William A. *The Contours of American History.* New York: World Publishing Co., 1961.
Wish, Harvey. *Slavery in the South.* New York: Farrar, Straus, 1964.
Witherbee, Sidney A., compiler and ed. *Spanish-American War Songs.* Detriot: Sidney A. Witherbee, pub., 1989.
Wolff, Leon. *Little Brown Brother.* Garden City, N.Y.: Doubleday and Co., Inc., 1961.
Woodman, Lyman L. *Cortina, Rogue of the Rio Grande.* San Antonio: The Naylor Co., 1950.
Woodson, Carter G. *History of the Negro Church.* Washington, D.C.: The Associated Publishers, 1945.
Woodson, Carter G. *The Negro in Our History.* Washington, D.C.: Associated Publishers, 1966.

Woodward, C. Vann. *Origins of the New South*. Baton Rouge: Louisiana State University Press, 1951.
Young, John P. "The Support of the Anti-Oriental Movement," *Annals of the Academy of Political and Social Science*. Vol. XXIV, No. 2, Sept., 1909.
Zilversmit, Arthur. *The First Emancipation*. Chicago: University of Chicago Press, 1967.

INDEX

About the Authors

Paul Jacobs is a writer and television commentator whose books and articles of social criticism have been published in America and abroad. Saul Landau, who collaborated with Paul Jacobs in writing *The New Radicals,* is also a film maker whose movie *Fidel* has been widely praised. Eve Pell is a writer whose previous work has appeared in a number of magazines. All three live in San Francisco.